Clashing Views
on Controversial
Legal Issues

5th edition

Clashing Views
on Controversial
Legal Issues

5th edition

Edited, Selected, and with Introductions by

M. Ethan Katsh
University of Massachusetts - Amherst

The Dushkin Publishing Group, Inc.

To Beverly

Taking Sides ® is a registered trademark of
The Dushkin Publishing Group, Inc.

Library of Congress Catalog Card Number:
92–71143

Manufactured in the United States of America

Fifth Edition, First Printing
ISBN: 1–56134–118–5

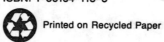 Printed on Recycled Paper

PREFACE

> The study of law should be introduced as part of a liberal education, to
> train and enrich the mind. . . . I am convinced that, like history,
> economics, and metaphysics—and perhaps even to a greater degree
> than these—the law could be advantageously studied with a view to the
> general development of the mind.
>
> —Justice Louis D. Brandeis

The general study of law in colleges, universities, and even high schools has
grown rapidly during the last 10 years. Accompanying this development has
been the publication of new curriculum materials that go beyond the
analysis of legal cases and doctrines that make up much of professional law
study in law schools. This book is part of the effort to view and study law as
an institution that continuously interacts with other social institutions. Law
should be examined from an interdisciplinary perspective and be accessible
to all students.

This book focuses on a series of controversial issues involving law and the
legal system. It is, I believe, an appropriate starting point for law study since
controversy and conflict are inherent in law. Law is based on an adversary
approach to conflict resolution, in which two advocates representing opposing sides are pitted against each other. Judicial decisions often contain both
majority and dissenting opinions, which reveal some of the arguments that
went on in the judges' chambers. Perhaps most relevant to a discussion of
the place of controversy in the legal system is the First Amendment
guarantee of freedom of speech and press, which presumes that we all
benefit by a vigorous debate of important issues.

Since many of the issues in *Taking Sides* are often in the news, you probably
already have opinions on them. What you should remember, however, is
that there is usually more to learn about any given issue, and the topics
discussed here are best approached with an open mind. You should not be
surprised if your views change as you read the selections.

Changes to this edition This fifth edition represents a considerable
revision. There are six completely new issues: *Is the Legal System Damaging the
American Economy?* (Issue 1); *Is "Hate Speech" Fully Protected by the Constitution?* (Issue 5); *Do Prayers at Public School Graduation Ceremonies Violate the
Constitution?* (Issue 6); *Should Homosexuality Bar a Parent from Being Awarded
Custody of a Child?* (Issue 11); *Should "Battered Wife Syndrome" Be Barred as a
Defense in a Murder Case?* (Issue 14); and *Does Caller ID Invade Privacy?* (Issue
16). For one issue, *Is Abortion Protected by the Constitution?* (Issue 7), I have
retained the issue but have replaced both the YES and NO readings and
revised the issue introduction and postscript to bring the debate up to date.

i

Supplements An *Instructor's Manual with Test Questions* (multiple-choice and essay) is available through the publisher for the instructor using *Taking Sides* in the classroom. And a general guidebook, which discusses methods and techniques for integrating the pro-contra approach into any classroom setting, is also available.

Acknowledgments I received helpful comments and suggestions from the many users of *Taking Sides* across the United States and Canada. Their suggestions have markedly enhanced the quality of this edition of the book and are reflected in the six totally new issues and the updated selection.

Special thanks go to those who responded with specific suggestions for the fifth edition:

Ron Berger
University of Wisconsin–
  Whitewater

Bernard H. Cochran
Meredith College

Murray Comarow
American University

Susan Adair Dwyer-Shick
Pacific Lutheran University

Phillip Finney
Southeast Missouri State
  University

David B. Fletcher
Wheaton College

Kate Greene
University of Southern
  Mississippi

M. Harry Lease, Jr.
University of Minnesota
  at Duluth

J. Ralph Lindren
Lehigh University

Patricia Loveless
University of Delaware

Robert J. McCormack
Trenton State College

Lansing Pollock
SUNY College at Buffalo

Thomas W. Ramsbey
Rhode Island College

Alan Reitman
Rutgers–The State University

Jack E. Rossotti
American University

George Schedler
Southern Illinois University at
  Carbondale

Randy Siefkin
Modesto Junior College

C. T. Sistare
Muhlenberg College

Otis H. Stephens
University of Tennessee

Susan R. Takata
University of Wisconsin–Parkside

Susan Thomas
Oakland University

Loren C. Wingblade
Jackson Community College

William J. Zanardi
St. Edwards University

A note on case citations Throughout this book you will see references to judicial opinions. The judge's opinion or decision refers to the written statement of reasons the judge provides when making an interpretation of law or deciding a case. These opinions are printed and distributed in books called *reporters*, which can be found in law libraries and many university libraries. There are separate reporters for federal and state cases. When you see a reference to a case such as *Brown v. Board of Education*, 347 U.S. 483 (1954), it means that the case with that name can be found in volume 347 of the United States Reports on page 483 and that the case was decided in 1954. When you see a legal citation with a series of numbers and words, the first number is always the volume number and the last number is the page number.

M. Ethan Katsh
University of Massachusetts, Amherst

CONTENTS IN BRIEF

CONTENTS

Attorney Peter Huber claims that litigation and liability laws deter innovation
and advances in quality and discourage improvements in product safety.
Journalist Kenneth Jost contests claims that the American legal system hurts
economic competitiveness, and he asserts that such arguments are based on
flawed evidence.

Professor of law Harry I. Subin examines the ethical responsibilities of
criminal defense lawyers and argues that greater responsibility should be
placed on lawyers not to pervert the truth to help their clients. Attorney John
B. Mitchell disputes the contention that the goal of the criminal justice
process is to seek the truth and argues that it is essential that there be
independent defense attorneys to provide protection against government
oppression.

Professor of philosophy Kenneth Kipnis makes the case that justice cannot be traded on the open market and that plea bargaining often subverts the cause of justice. District Attorney Nick Schweitzer finds that plea bargaining is fair, useful, desirable, necessary, and practical.

Supreme Court justice Anthony Kennedy believes that drug tests of Customs Service officials are reasonable under the Fourth Amendment of the Constitution even when there is no probable cause or individualized suspicion. Justice Antonin Scalia, in dissent, argues that the Customs Service rules were not justified, serve no reasonable purpose, and are unnecessary invasions of privacy.

Supreme Court justice Antonin Scalia finds that the St. Paul ordinance punishing "hate speech" cannot be constitutional because it regulates speech depending on the subject the speech addresses. Justice John Paul Stevens concurs that this particular ordinance is not constitutional, but he argues that it is perhaps simply overbroad.

Supreme Court justice Thurgood Marshall points to past discrimination and argues that we must find a way to compensate for the years of disadvantage. Justice Potter Stewart contends that the law and the Constitution must not discriminate on the basis of race, for whatever reason.

Supreme Court chief justice William H. Rehnquist recognizes that a competent individual may refuse medical treatment but believes a showing of clear and convincing proof of the individual's wishes is required before allowing the termination of feeding to an incompetent person. Justice William J. Brennan, Jr., argues that the Court is erecting too high a standard for allowing an individual's wishes to be followed and that Nancy Cruzen did indeed wish to have her feeding discontinued.

Judge Hewitt P. Tomlin, Jr., argues that an award of child custody to a homosexual parent cannot be in the best interests of the child. Justice Melvin P. Antell refuses to allow one parent's homosexuality to be a deciding factor in the custody decision of the court.

Law professor Jack Greenberg argues that capital punishment should be banned because it is applied erratically and in a racially and regionally biased manner. Distinguished scholar Ernest van den Haag responds that the death penalty is moral and just and should be employed against those who commit murder.

Former U.S. Court of Appeals judge Malcolm Richard Wilkey raises objections to the exclusionary rule on the grounds that it may suppress evidence and allow the guilty to go free. Professor of law Yale Kamisar argues that the exclusionary rule is necessary to prevent abuses by police and to protect citizens' rights.

Justice Burley B. Mitchell, Jr., is unwilling to recognize "battered wife syndrome" as meeting the standards of immediacy and necessity needed for a self-defense claim in a homicide case. Justice Harry C. Martin, dissenting in the same case, believes that, given the actions of the husband, the wife's behavior can be viewed in such a way as to meet the standards of self-defense.

Law student Mark Udulutch examines the gun control problem and asserts that gun control is necessary and that effective and enforceable federal regulations are feasible. Professor of sociology James D. Wright concludes, after examining how guns are used, that banning guns would not be beneficial.

Attorney Janlori Goldman believes that regulation of Caller ID is needed to protect privacy and to prevent misuse of the technology that reveals the telephone number of callers. Professor Arthur R. Miller evaluates the rights of callers and those being called and concludes that the privacy rights of the latter are deserving of more protection, which Caller ID provides.

Editor Jonathan Rowe examines the insanity defense as it is now administered and finds that it is most likely to be used by white middle- or upper-class defendants and that its application is unfair and leads to unjust results. Professor of law Richard Bonnie argues that the abolition of the insanity defense would be immoral and leaves no alternative for those who are not responsible for their actions.

INTRODUCTION

The Role of Law

M. Ethan Katsh

Two hundred years ago, Edmund Burke, the influential British statesman and orator, commented that "in no other country perhaps in the world, is the law so general a study as it is in the United States." Today, in this country, general knowledge about law is at a disappointing level. One study conducted several years ago concluded that "the general public's knowledge of and direct experience with courts is low."[1] Three out of four persons surveyed admitted that they knew either very little or nothing at all about state and local courts. More than half believed that the burden of proving innocence in a criminal trial is on the accused, and 72 percent thought that every decision made by a state could be reviewed by the Supreme Court. In a 1990 study, 59 percent could not name at least one current justice of the Supreme Court.

One purpose of this volume is to provide information about some specific and important legal issues. In your local newspaper today, there is probably at least one story concerning an issue in this book. The quality of your life will be directly affected by how many of these issues are resolved. But gun control (Issue 15), the insanity defense (Issue 17), drug use testing (Issue 4), abortion (Issue 7), legal ethics (Issue 2), and other issues in this book are often the subject of superficial, misleading, or inaccurate statements. *Taking Sides* is designed to encourage you to become involved in the public debate on these issues and to raise the level of the discussion on them.

The issues that are debated in this book represent some of the most important challenges our society faces. How they are dealt with will influence what kind of society we will have in the future. While it is important to look at and study them separately, it is equally necessary to think about their relationship to each other and about the fact that there is a tool called "law," which is being called upon to solve a series of difficult conflicts. The study of discrete legal issues should enable you to gain insight into some broad theoretical questions about law. This introduction, therefore, will focus on several basic characteristics of law and the legal process that you should keep in mind as you read this book.

THE NATURE OF LAW

The eminent legal anthropologist E. Adamson Hoebel once noted that the search for a definition of law is as difficult as the search for the Holy Grail.

Law is certainly complicated, and trying to define it precisely can be frustrating. What follows, therefore, is not a definition of law but a framework or perspective for looking at and understanding law.

Law as a Body of Rules
One of the common incorrect assumptions about law is that it is merely a body of rules, invoked by those who need them, and then applied by a judge. Under this view, the judge is essentially a machine whose task is simply to find and apply the right rule to the dispute in question. This perspective makes the mistake of equating law with the rules of law. It is sometimes even assumed that there exists somewhere in the libraries of lawyers and judges one book with all the rules or laws in it, which can be consulted to answer legal questions. As may already be apparent, such a book could not exist. Rules alone do not supply the solutions to many legal problems. The late Supreme Court justice William O. Douglas once wrote, "The law is not a series of calculating machines where definitions and answers come tumbling out when the right levers are pushed." As you read the debates about the issues in this book, you will see that much more goes into a legal argument than the recitation of rules.

Law as a Process
A more meaningful way of thinking about law is to look at it as a process or system, keeping in mind that legal rules are one of the elements in the process. This approach requires a considerably broader vision of law: to think not only of the written rules, but also of the judges, the lawyers, the police, and all the other people in the system. It requires an even further consideration of all the things that influence these people, such as their values and economic status.

"Law," one legal commentator has stated, "is very like an iceberg; only one-tenth of its substance appears above the social surface in the explicit form of documents, institutions, and professions, while the nine-tenths of its substance that supports its visible fragment leads a sub-aquatic existence, living in the habits, attitudes, emotions and aspirations of men."[2]

In reading the discussions of controversial issues in this book, try to identify what forces are influencing the content of the rules and the position of the writers. Three of the most important influences on the nature of law are economics, moral values, and public opinion.

Law and Economics
Laws that talk about equality, such as the Fourteenth Amendment, which guarantees that no state shall "deny to any person . . . equal protection of the laws," suggest that economic status is irrelevant in the making and application of the law. As Anatole France, the nineteenth-century French satirist, once wrote, however, "The law, in its majestic equality, forbids the rich as well as the poor to sleep under bridges, to beg in streets, and to steal

bread." Sometimes the purpose and effect of the law cannot be determined merely from the words of the law.

Marxist critics of law in capitalistic societies assert that poverty results from the manipulation of the law by the wealthy and powerful. It is possible to look at several issues in this book and make some tentative judgments about the influence of economic power on law. For example, what role does economics play in the debate over drug use testing (Issue 4)? Is drug abuse a public health problem or an economic problem, in that it costs companies billions of dollars each year? In considering whether or not pornography should be protected (Issue 8), is the controversy purely over morality and values, or is it related to the enormous growth of the pornographic videotape industry? Plea bargaining (Issue 3), which mostly affects poor persons who cannot afford bail, also involves the question of whether or not the law is responsible for or perpetuates poverty and economic classes.

Law and Values

The relationship between law and values has been a frequent theme of legal writers and a frequent source of debate. Clearly, there is in most societies some relationship between law and morality. One writer has summarized the relationship as follows:

1. *There is a moral order in society.* Out of the many different and often conflicting values of the individuals and institutions that make up society may emerge a dominant moral position, a "core" of the moral order. The position of this core is dynamic, and as it changes, the moral order of society moves in the direction of that change.

2. *There is a moral content to the law.* The moral content of law also changes over time, and as it changes, the law moves in the direction of that change.

3. *The moral content of the law and moral order in society are seldom identical.*

4. *A natural and necessary affinity exists between the two "bodies" of law and moral order.*

5. *When there is a gap between the moral order of society and the law, some movement to close the gap is likely.* The law will move closer to the moral order of society, or the moral order will move closer to the law, or each will move toward the other. The likelihood of the movement to close the gap between law and moral order depends upon the size of the gap between the two bodies and the perceived significance of the subject matter concerning which the gap exists.[3]

Law and morality will not be identical in a pluralistic society, but there will also be attempts by dominant groups to insert their views of what is right into the legal code. The First Amendment prohibition against establishment of religion and the guarantee of freedom of religion are designed to protect those whose beliefs are different. Yet there have also been many historical examples of legal restrictions or limitations being imposed on minorities or of laws being ineffective because of the resistance of powerful groups. Prayers in the public schools, for example, which have been forbidden since the early 1960s, are still said in a few local communities.

Of the topics in this book, the insertion of morality into legal discussions has occurred most frequently in the abortion and capital punishment debates (Issues 7 and 12). It is probably fair to say that these issues remain high on the agenda of public debate because they involve strongly held values and beliefs. The nature of the debates is also colored by strong feelings that are held by the parties. Although empirical evidence about public health and abortion or about deterrence and capital punishment does exist, the debates are generally more emotional than objective.

Public Opinion and the Law

It is often claimed that the judicial process is insulated from public pressures. Judges are elected or appointed for long terms or for life, and the theory is that they will, therefore, be less subject to the force of public opinion. As a result, the law should be uniformly applied in different places, regardless of the nature of the community. It is fair to say the judicial process is less responsive to public sentiment than is the political process, but that is not really saying much. What is important is that the legal process is not totally immune from public pressure. The force of public opinion is not applied directly through lobbying, but it would be naive to think that the force of what large numbers of people believe and desire never gets reflected in what happens in court. The most obvious examples are trials in which individuals are tried as much for their dissident beliefs as for their actions. Less obvious is the fact that the outcomes of cases may be determined in some measure by popular will. Judicial complicity in slavery or the internment of Japanese Americans during World War II are blatant examples of this.

Many of the issues selected for this volume are controversial because a large group is opposed to some practice sanctioned by the courts. Does this mean that the judges have taken a courageous stand and ignored public opinion? Not necessarily. Only in a few of the issues have courts adopted an uncompromising position. In most of the other issues, the trend of court decisions reflects a middle-of-the-road approach that could be interpreted as trying to satisfy everyone but those at the extremes. For example, in capital punishment (Issue 12), the original decision declaring the death penalty statutes unconstitutional was followed by the passing of new state laws, which were then upheld and which have led to a growing number of executions. Similarly, in affirmative action (Issue 9), the *Bakke* decision, while generally approving of affirmative action, was actually won by Bakke and led to the abolition of all such programs that contained rigid quotas.

ASSESSING INFLUENCES ON THE LAW

This summary of what can influence legal decisions is not meant to suggest that judges consciously ask what the public desires when interpretations of law are made. Rather, as members of society and as individuals who read newspapers and magazines and form opinions on political issues, there are subtle forces at work on judges that may not be obvious in any particular opinion but that can be discerned in a line of cases over a period of time. This may be explicitly denied by judges, such as in the statement by Justice Blackmun in the abortion case that "Our task, of course, is to resolve the issue by constitutional measurement, free of emotion and predilection." When you read the opinion, however, you should ask yourself whether or not Blackmun succeeds in being totally objective in his interpretation of law and history.

Do these external and internal influences corrupt the system, create injustice, inject bias and discrimination, and pervert the law? Or, do these influences enable judges to be flexible, to treat individual circumstances, and to fulfill the spirit of the law? Both of these ends are possible and do occur. What is important to realize is that there are so many points in the legal system where discretion is employed that it is hopeless to think that we could be governed by rules alone. "A government of laws, not men," aside from the sexism of the language, is not a realistic possibility, and it is not an alternative that many would find satisfying either.

On the other hand, it is also fair to say that the law, in striving to get the public to trust in it, must persuade citizens that it is more than the whim of those who are in power. While it cannot be denied that the law may be used in self-serving ways, there are also mechanisms at work that are designed to limit abuses of discretionary power. One quality of law that is relevant to this problem is that the legal process is fundamentally a conservative institution, which is, by nature, resistant to radical change. Lawyers are trained to give primary consideration in legal arguments to precedent, previous cases involving similar facts. As attention is focused on how the present case is similar to or different from past cases, some pressure is exerted on new decisions to be consistent with old ones and on the law to be stable. Thus, the way in which a legal argument is constructed tends to reduce the influence of currently popular psychological, sociological, philosophical, or anthropological theories. Prior decisions will reflect ideologies, economic considerations, and ethical values that were influential when these decisions were made and, if no great change has occurred in the interim, the law will tend to preserve the status quo, both perpetuating old injustices and protecting traditional freedoms.

LEGAL PROCEDURE

The law's great concern with the procedure of decision-making is one of its more basic and important characteristics. Any discussion of the law that did not note the importance of procedure would be inadequate. Legal standards are often phrased not in terms of results but in terms of procedure. For example, it is not unlawful to convict the innocent if the right procedures are used (and it is unlawful to convict the guilty if the wrong procedures are followed). The law feels that it cannot guarantee that the right result will always be reached and that only the guilty will be caught, so it minimizes the risk of reaching the wrong result or convicting the innocent by specifying procedural steps to be followed. Lawyers, more than most people, are satisfied if the right procedures are followed even if there is something disturbing about the outcome. Law, therefore, has virtually eliminated the word *justice* from its vocabulary and has substituted the phrase *due process*, meaning that the proper procedures, such as right to counsel, right to a public trial, and right to cross-examine witnesses, have been followed. This concern with method is one of the pillars upon which law is based. It is one of the characteristics of law that distinguishes it from nonlegal methods of dispute resolution, where the atmosphere will be more informal and there may be no set procedures. It is a trait of the law that is illustrated in Issue 2 (*Should Lawyers Be Prohibited from Presenting a False Case?*).

CONCLUSION

There is an often-told anecdote about a client who walks into a lawyer's office and asks the receptionist if the firm has a one-armed lawyer. The receptionist asks why in the world anyone would have such a preference. The client responds that he has already visited several lawyers to discuss his problem but could not get a definite answer from any of them. Their stock reply to his question of whether or not he would win his case began "on the one hand this could happen and on the other hand. . . ."

You may feel similarly frustrated as you examine the issues in this book. The subjects are not simple or amenable to simple solutions. The legal approach to problem solving is usually methodical and often slow. We frequently become frustrated with this process and, in fact, it may be an inappropriate way to deal with some problems. For the issues in this book, however, an approach that pays careful attention to the many different aspects of these topics will be the most rewarding. Many of the readings provide historical, economic, and sociological data as well as information about law. The issues examined in *Taking Sides* involve basic cultural institutions such as religion, schools, and the family as well as basic cultural values such as privacy, individualism, and equality. While the law takes a narrow approach to problems, reading these issues should broaden your outlook on the problems discussed and, perhaps, encourage you to do further reading on those topics that are of particular interest to you.

NOTES

1. Yankelovich, Skelly, and White, Inc., *The Public Image of Courts* (1978).
2. Iredell Jenkins, *Social Order and the Limits of Law* (Princeton University Press, 1980), p. xi.
3. Wardle, "The Gap Between Law and Moral Order: An Examination of the Legitimacy of the Supreme Court Abortion Decisions," *Brigham Young University Law Review* (1980), pp. 811–835.

PART 1

The Operation of Legal Institutions

New York Stock Exchange

According to much of what appears in the mass media, the public is increasingly disenchanted with many of the institutions that are part of the legal process. Critics complain about the proliferation of needless lawsuits, about lawyers and their tactics, and about courts that seem too lenient in their sentencing of serious criminals.

In this section we examine issues that involve our legal institutions, and the picture that emerges from these debates will reveal realities with which you may not be familiar.

Is the Legal System Damaging the American Economy?

Should Lawyers Be Prohibited from Presenting a False Case?

Should Plea Bargaining Be Abolished?

ISSUE 1

Is the Legal System Damaging the American Economy?

YES: Peter Huber, from Statement Before the Subcommittee on the Consumer, Committee on Commerce, Science, and Transportation, U.S. Senate (April 5, 1990)

NO: Kenneth Jost, from "Tampering With Evidence: The Liability and Competitiveness Myth," *ABA Journal* (April 1992)

ISSUE SUMMARY

YES: Attorney Peter Huber claims that litigation and liability laws deter innovation and advances in quality and discourage improvements in product safety.
NO: Journalist Kenneth Jost contests claims that the American legal system hurts economic competitiveness, and he asserts that such arguments are based on flawed evidence.

> Scarcely any political question arises in the United States that is not resolved, sooner or later, into a judicial question.
>
> —Alexis de Toqueville

In August 1991, at the annual meeting of the American Bar Association, Vice President Dan Quayle charged that the legal system and the legal profession were damaging the ability of the United States to compete in the world economy. "Our system of civil justice," he argued, "is, at times, a self-inflicted competitive disadvantage."

Vice President Quayle was, at the time, the chairperson of the President's Committee on Competitiveness. Reform of the legal profession seemed to be one of the means the Committee assumed would invigorate business. Quayle asked, "Does America really need 70 percent of the world's lawyers? Is it healthy for our economy to have 18 million new lawsuits coursing through the system annually?"

Lawyers and lawsuits, it has been argued recently, hurt the U.S. economy because manufacturers are reluctant to introduce new products because they might be sued. This particularly affects the drug and high-tech industries, whose products might cause unforeseen side effects for users. The following article, by Peter Huber, expands on the argument made by the vice president and argues that fear of being sued has been a deterrent to industry to take chances and be innovative. In response, Kenneth Jost, a journalist, argues that there really is no valid evidence to suggest that creative businesspeople should fear litigation.

What could be bad about going to court to settle a dispute? Judge Learned Hand once wrote, "I must say that, as a litigant, I should dread a lawsuit beyond almost anything else short of sickness and death." Historian Jerold Auerbach has stated that "root canal work seems mild by comparison." This suggests, quite accurately, that the process of suing, regardless of the outcome, involves some pain. Frequently, in a lawsuit, the only winners are the lawyers, since the process itself generally heightens tension, promotes hostility, and makes the parties more angry at each other than they were initially.

As important as the consequences for individuals are the societal implications. Lawsuits should be a last resort, something done when all other attempts to settle the problem have failed. If litigation has become "too much," then one explanation is that other institutions that have been relied upon in the past are no longer working in the ways they once were. Large numbers of lawsuits involving families may imply that the family as an institution is weaker than it once was. If one found large numbers of lawsuits involving schools or religious institutions, one could make a similar argument about the deterioration of those institutions. Conflict exists in all societies, but it is desirable to have many different mechanisms and devices for resolving the conflict. If there has been rapid growth in the use of law, therefore, it could suggest that these other institutions, which may be more desirable forums for resolving the conflict, and which may involve less cost, both economic and emotional, are no longer functioning as they once did.

Does all this mean that lawsuits being brought by injured parties are frivolous? Should we continue to expect compensation from persons or institutions that cause us injury? These questions are at the heart of the following debate.

YES

Peter Huber

STATEMENT OF PETER HUBER

MOVING BACKWARD

The theory that many lawyers and many state courts came to accept in the 1960s, 1970s, and much of the 1980s, was that if we sue more people more often we will enhance safety and spur innovation and technological progress. Concern about potential liability, the argument runs, will encourage the best and the brightest of our scientists and engineers, physicians and pharmacologists to develop new products, processes, and procedures that will make life safer and generally improve the public welfare.

Today, some twenty years after this theory first gained prominence, it is becoming quite apparent that the theory is wrong. Or at the very least, the theory is not working as promised under the liability rules that U.S. courts have fashioned to implement it. As liability has advanced, our most innovative capital and talent have retreated. Entire sectors of industry, of enterprise, and of innovation have actually shut down. And no business has proved more unsafe—in legal terms—than the business of enhancing consumer safety.

Let's start with a look at the record in just a few of the industries that have been targeted most aggressively and successfully by liability lawyers in the past 10 or 20 years.

No one should expect that Merrell-Dow pharmaceuticals will soon be developing a new anti-nausea drug for pregnant women; I can report with some assurance that it will not be. And this notwithstanding the fact the company *won* time and time again when the perils of Benedectin came to be litigated in court. It won the verdicts, but still incurred colossal losses in legal fees, in the endless vexation of interminable litigation, and in reams of adverse publicity that no large company can possibly afford. As the bitter joke among company lawyers has it, if you're pregnant and suffering from debilitating morning sickness, go see your lawyer. Your doctor has nothing left to prescribe.

From U.S. Senate. Committee on Commerce, Science, and Transportation. Subcommittee on the Consumer. *Product Liability Reform Act.* Hearing, April 5, 1990. Washington, DC: Government Printing Office, 1990. (S.Hrg. 101–743.) Some notes omitted.

In the early 1960s, the United States led the world in contraceptive research and marketing. Today, the smart money is out of the business. U.S. research and development expenditures in this area peaked in 1972, and have plummeted 90 percent since. Steroidal oral contraceptives in this country underwent their last significant change in 1976, and the last truly new contraceptive entity was introduced in 1968. Europe already has access to at least two later-generation oral contraceptives, and a variety of other options completely unavailable in the U.S. There is no shortage of demand for a better, safer contraceptive. But thanks to proliferating lawsuits and skyrocketing liability costs, no real profit beckons anybody who is in the contraceptive or reproductive health industry today.

The virtual demise of the U.S. vaccine industry tells a similar story. The United States used to have at least eight large centers of private capital and R&D in vaccines. Today we are down to two. The public health consequences of this cannot be quantified, but they are surely incalculably large. Scientists associated with the government, educational institutions, or private foundations, are working furiously to develop an AIDS vaccine. But what large company will have the resources, the manufacturing capabilities—and most important of all, the insurance and the will—to mass market such a product if it is ever developed. I expect that this Committee, some years hence, will probably find itself debating legislation identical to the Swine Flu bill of 1976, whereby the federal government assumes liability for such a product because no one else is willing to.

The pharmaceutical industry's problems are relatively well known. The liability system's adverse impact on innovation, however, extends far beyond pharmaceuticals, to a number of industries where the United States once held a technological lead.

I happen to be a private pilot, so I'm familiar with the light aircraft industry. I'm well aware that the Senate is considering a separate bill for the aviation industry—a bill that I commend to your attention—but the problems of this industry, though you address them in separate legislation—are symptomatic of problems in many other high-tech engineering sectors of the economy. As rising liability costs imposed a 50 percent surcharge on new-model light aircraft, companies like Piper, Beech and Cessna virtually abandoned the low end of the market. Some have recently crept back at the margins—though without liability insurance, relying on scorched earth litigation tactics to try to keep the trial bar at bay. It is far from clear, as of this writing, whether those tactics will succeed.

The disappearance of new small planes has done nothing to improve the safety of light aircraft. Quite the opposite! People—like me—still fly in small planes, because there are plenty of them around. They just happen to be 10 or 20 years old. Small planes last forever because pilots, for fairly obvious reasons, are quite scrupulous about checking the oil and such. So the planes survive, but the technology is decades out of date. Some will brush this aside, as a problem for only a few eccentrics who insist on flying their own planes. But if you look at the history of aviation technology in this country, innovation—the development and testing of new engines, new airfoils, canards, and control surfaces, new fuselage materials—has generally come from the small, private sector and then trickled upward. The United States has long enjoyed a technological and competitive advantage in aviation. Now we have cut this industry off at its roots.

Similar problems beset other manufacturers of complex engineering systems. Companies that make escalators and elevators, machine tools, industrial robots, and other types of heavy industrial machinery all face similar liability pressures. And when those companies retreat or abandon certain lines of business altogether, the effects on safety can be equally regressive. The products are long lived, and if new technologies are not developed and deployed, the old ones will be nursed along years after they should have been replaced. This is as bad for consumers as it is for the companies that could have provided the replacements.

Other examples are not difficult to find. Asbestos is usually pointed to as one of the great success stories of the modern liability system. After all, some forms of asbestos, used in some conditions, can be very dangerous, as many grievously injured people can attest. But very few people know the latest chapter in the asbestos story. Asbestos is still widely used in this country for such things as brake linings and brake gaskets, for the very simple reason that you need a product with its unique thermal and other physical properties for these applications. There is no good substitute available.

Correction: There probably *is* a good substitute, but the company that developed it dares not bring it to market. The substitute is calcium sodium metaphosphate, developed by Monsanto a few years ago. By all appearances, the product is safer than asbestos, and could be an ideal substitute in many applications. It is biodegradable, so if the fibers do lodge in the lungs, they break up and are metabo-lized. But Monsanto has pulled the plug on the product, and for good reason. Any lawyer in the country who has studied the liability scene would have had to advise the same. You would have to verge on the lunatic to think of marketing any product that would be distributed through the same channels as asbestos, that might come to be mixed up with asbestos-containing substitutes, and that thus might all-to-easily be swept up in the conflagration of asbestos litigation. Even as we speak, asbestos lawyers in this country are coming into billions of dollars of new capital from successful asbestos lawsuits. They are looking for new places to invest their money. The obvious new targets will be asbestos substitutes on the scene, which even if much safer than asbestos are unlikely to be completely risk free.

Yet another major chemical company—I have talked with the executives in question, but they prefer to remain unnamed—recently developed a composite concrete material to be used in bridges. The product marks, by the company's best internal estimates, a significant improvement in both price and performance over existing materials. The company halted development of the product a couple of years ago, however, after watching another chemical company become mired in litigation over a concrete additive widely used in buildings in the 1960s. The decision was based purely on liability considerations. If you sell this new bridge product across the country, and get thousands of municipalities and contractors to use it, and then one bridge goes down, the ensuing litigation could mean the end of your company. It is far safer, from the legal perspective, to stick with what is already ubiquitous and familiar, so well entrenched and commonplace that it ranks with butter, as familiar, standard, and therefore impossible to sue.

One must recognize that these are not just a few isolated examples that can be addressed by a few industry-specific fixes. Other products that could have been on the market today but for the unpredictable specter of open-ended liability include a non-chemical pesticide replacement, a portable kidney dialysis machine, and a chemical process that speeds up decomposition of hazardous wastes, to mention just a few. . . . One of the most disturbing features about this is that so many of these products have marked in the past—or promise, for the future—important *advances* in quality or safety. It is ironic that among products abandoned by sporting goods companies, many of them were protective or safety equipment. Rather than assuming unrealistic and speculative responsibilities as guarantors of absolute safety, many of these manufacturers decided to abandon the markets altogether.

The conclusion is now beyond dispute: Businesses react to the actual or perceived threat of liability by withdrawing products, halting research, and altogether avoiding new product lines. Plant closings or business failures have been attributed directly to U.S. product liability laws for the manufacturers of textile machinery, medical devices, and gymnastic equipment. The chilling effects of liability extend far beyond companies that are actually sued; through the insurance system, these effects propagate across entire industries and categories of enterprise. Several studies have referred to the disparate impact of product liability laws on small businesses, which have far less capacity to absorb extraordinary increases in liability insurance premiums or open-ended legal expenses from defending against groundless litigation.

Even academic institutions have been adversely affected. Many universities, often the source of new product development and technological advances, license new products to small businesses that need the advantages a particularly innovative product might bring. But, due to concerns that large, well-financed universities might be targets for product liability suits involving these new products, universities are reluctant to continue this licensing scheme.

CHANGING RULES

What exactly has gone wrong? Why have the consequences of expanded liability in U.S. courts been so very different from what many jurists and legal academics expected when liability rules were rewritten from the 1960s to the 1980s? Various legal changes, though often well intentioned, had consequences that were simply not anticipated or properly thought out. As has happened elsewhere, grand social experiments sometimes end up backfiring to the utter amazement and consternation of party theoreticians.

To begin with, the new rules of strict liability invented by U.S. courts in the 1960s and 1970s instruct juries to assess the actual design of a new product—not the conduct of those who create and market the product. The good faith, reasonable care, and conscientious training of the designers or the assembly-line workers is irrelevant. Technology itself stands in the dock. The U.S. stands alone in the world in imposing such standards of liability.

This seemingly modest change in legal doctrine has tilted the entire liability system against innovation. Jurors can make reasonably sensible, intuitive judgments about other individuals, even professionals. But they are not experts in engineering, pharmacology, or aerodynamics.

Consider how a typical liability lawsuit proceeds in a U.S. court today. After an accident, jurors are given a few days, occasionally a few weeks, to evaluate the design of a mass-vaccination program, a power plant, a military aircraft, an escalator, or a lathe. Sympathy for the victim, while quite understandable, does not improve the technical analysis. If the only way to help out some unfortunate claimant is to find a design defect, then that is what many juries will find. Moreover, human nature is predisposed to accepting the old and familiar risk, while rejecting the novel and exotic. Cigarette makers win, whereas pioneers of vaccines or medical devices are in constant peril. One result—and here I speak from my own experience—is that consulting engineers are pressed to favor older design options in their specifications, fearing that new ones will carry greater risk. Not physical risk—newer is, more often than not, safer than older—but rather *legal* risk.

At the same time, U.S. courts have become exceedingly particular about safety warnings. Up to a point, one would want nothing less—but only up to a point. As the law in various states stands today, it will not suffice to warn of a risk of death; the seller must warn specifically of the risk of stroke or serum sickness or acute encephalopathy. It will not suffice to warn the prescribing doctor of a drug's hazards; the drug company must somehow also get the information to the patient too. Grossly obvious risks must be flagged, but so must some risks that arise only from the most bizarre forms of consumer abuse. The only way to learn how to meet such demands is through long perseverance in the market and the courts. The warnings provided with oral contraceptives have been honed for thirty years, to the point where they occupy pages of densely detailed text, with substantial parts developed, one at a time, in the aftermath of adverse liability verdicts. No equivalent detail can be provided for a truly new IUD, because the risks are much less familiar—even if their general nature is known and even if the IUD is demonstrably safer, overall, than the pill it could replace.

The U.S. law's attitude toward safety improvements made after an accident has also changed. At one time, courts used to bar a plaintiff from offering any evidence of such conduct—the redesign or recall of a product, a post-sale or post-accident change in a process, or the addition of a new safety system. Safety improvements must be encouraged, the logic ran, and so should never be used to condemn past shortcomings. But in the 1960s, this rule too came under direct attack. Evidence of subsequent remedial measures was first admitted to impeach witnesses, then to prove that the defendant controlled the premises in question, then to show that conditions had changed since the time of the accident or that changes in design were feasible. The exceptions nibbled away at the rule until some courts were so emboldened, they swept the tattered remains aside entirely.

Changes in U.S. rules on when suits may be filed have had a second effect that is particularly hostile to the commercialization of new products. Suits can now be filed decades after the car gear box, herbicide, or strip-mining machine was designed or used. Defects in technology, like negligence in human conduct, depend critically on the context of time and place. The best-designed cars of 1950 were clearly deficient by 1980 standards, as were the best medical procedures, industrial chemicals, pesticides, or home appliances. When the sun never sets on the possibility of litigation, each improvement in method, material, or design can establish a new standard against which all of your earlier undertakings, no matter of what vintage, may then be judged. Finding a way to do better today immediately invites an indictment of what you did less well yesterday, or twenty years ago. Mature firms that sell long-lived products therefore have good reason to hesitate before commercializing a significant new improvement; doing so may very well promote successful litigation against the company's older vaccine, small plane, escalator, or lathe, still in use in the market.

There has also been a sharp rise in demands for—and awards of—punitive damages in U.S. courts. Many factors go into such awards, and some of the awards are undoubtedly justified by egregious misconduct. But here too, abandoning familiar and established technology may—for legal purposes—be the riskiest course of all. Many of the breakthrough punitive awards were assessed in the early 1970s against manufacturers of small cars, when such vehicles (and their attendant risks) were still novelties on the U.S. market. By contrast, it can hardly be termed "reckless" or "outrageous misconduct" (the usual triggers for punitive damages) to do what the great mass of society has done for decades. This may help to explain why U.S. tobacco companies have yet to be assessed any punitive damages, and indeed have so far lost only one verdict for compensatory damages.

Most generally, one animating principal of modern tort law is that products should come wrapped in a special-purpose insurance contract, to help spread the costs of accidents. But when can such wrapping be found at a reasonable price? The availability of insurance depends largely on an accumulation of accident experience. That is something that established technologies always have and truly innovative ones never do. Insurance is easiest to find when a good has been used by many people for many years, so that the frolics and caprices of tort liability have been as far as possible washed out and the statistics of experience speak for themselves. Innovation necessarily starts without an established market, and so is often condemned to start without insurance as well. For the prudent businessperson, a start without insurance is often worse than no start at all.

Orphan drugs reveal some of these problems in particularly tragic circumstances. Only a few hundred American children suffer from cystinosis, a fatal kidney disease. About 2,000 adults suffer from Charcot-Marie-Tooth disease, a rare nerve disorder (unrelated to teeth) that severely impairs motor function. About 1,000 suffer from leprosy and experience an extremely painful allergic reaction on their skin. A tiny number suffer from a rare but incapacitating disease characterized by uncontrollable twitching of the eye muscles.[1] There are some 5,000 other orphan diseases that shorten lives or bring agonizing disability to tiny groups. Therapies are available or under development for some 500 of them.[2] But insurance is often all but impossible to obtain. Chemie Grunenthal, for example, a West German company that once supplied thalidomide to American leprosy victims, announced in 1986 that it planned to abandon the U.S. market to avoid the risk of liability that might arise if, for example the drug was used in excess or fell into the wrong hands.[3] Until recently, another West German chemical company supplied Americans with botulinum, a paralytic poison that is just right for controlling the eye-twitching disease, but the company cut off supplies in 1986 for similar reasons.[4] Orphan drugs are condemned, in a sense, to be perennial newcomers to the commercial world and are therefore forever uninsurable under the modern rules. Business realities take care of the rest.

In these and other diverse, often subtle ways, U.S. product liability laws decrease innovative product development because innovative products, by definition, create unknown liability risks.[5] Manufacturers cannot protect against these risks with insurance, because insurance often is not available for innovative products.[6] Because insurers cannot accurately determine the probability of the risks from the innovative products they are asked to insure, they refuse to provide insurance.[7] Few manufacturers have the financial reserves needed to go forward with a product that poses unknown liability risks without the safety net of liability insurance.[8]

COMPETITIVE IMPLICATIONS

Liability rules in the U.S. have grave implications not only for American consumers, who lose domestic products, but also for American producers, who lose international markets. While U.S. high technology is caught in the grip of tort liability, other countries around the world are free to pursue innovation and competitive advantage.

Made in America often means you can sue in America. A U.S. firm selling an American-made drug, car, chemical factory, or aircraft to India is forced today to sell expensive accident insurance along with it; a German firm competing for the same sale is not. Of course, the Indian consumer will get something extra along with the American product—the right to sue in U.S. courts if an accident should occur. But how much is it worth to him? The tort-mandated accident insurance that is even a bad deal for the American bank janitor (because it is priced to compensate the lost earnings of the bank presidents too) is a horrendous deal for the impoverished Indian farmer.

The American competitive position is disadvantaged even within the U.S. market. Manufacturers remain liable for their products as long as they are in use. When an established U.S. company goes shopping every year to renew its insurance policy, it is therefore likely to be paying in part for its commercial history. More recent business arrivals on our shores do not carry the excess insurance baggage of their own past. In industries as diverse as light aircraft, truck wheel rims, machine tools, sporting goods, and industrial machinery—all long-lived products—U.S. tort law has given foreign manufacturers an important competitive edge, not just in overseas markets but in the United States as well.

Simple diseconomies of scale also play their part. American companies have their commercial base in the United States, and thus shoulder U.S. liability costs on all their startup development and production. Foreign competitors can build up a large base of operations without this element of overhead—which tends to be especially large with young and innovative technology—and then move into the U.S. market at the margin, when the product is mature enough to make exact warnings possible and insurance affordable.

Finally, many foreign companies can effectively limit their total liability on U.S. operations by the cold-blooded expedient of keeping only limited assets in this country. No American concern can get away with such a strategy.

These factors almost certainly are a significant part of the reason why foreign manufacturers have completely taken over the markets for hockey equipment, trampolines and other gymnastic equipment; and the markets for certain vaccines and contraceptive devices.

GETTING BACK TO YES

With the help of our courts, we have become the world's greatest experts at saying no. A just-say-no philosophy of government is useful for some problems, in some circumstances. But for most of the more subtle choices we face in life, one must also have the legal power to say yes—selectively, of course, but emphatically nonetheless. Without an effective legal system that lets people make binding positive choices, we all end up living in a spare world, devoid of many goods and services that would provide social benefits far in excess of their social costs.

What has eroded, under the pressure of turbulent liability, is our ability, individual (through contract) or collective (through such agencies as the FDA) to say yes. The pregnant mother debilitated by morning sickness may desperately want relief. The FDA may approve Bendectin, and continue to approve it to the present day. But scattered juries, perhaps even a single run-away jury sitting in Washington D.C., well intentioned no

doubt but utterly incapable of assessing the drugs' nationwide costs and benefits, can effectively override the preferences of millions of individual consumers and the approval of a federal regulatory agency. One cannot run a national railroad, or an international pharmaceutical business when safety choices are so dispersed, so uncoordinated, and so unpredictable, that any random panel of twelve stout citizens, unguided by any national norms at all, can promulgate standards for the nation.

If the only goal of U.S. product liability laws is to change business behavior, product liability laws are surely fulfilling their objective: without doubt, they have profoundly influenced corporate behavior from the highest echelons of management to the worker on the plant floor. But what we want is not just change, but change for the better, and that is not what we have been getting. Time and again, however, the actual effect of product liability laws has been to modify corporate behavior that never was unreasonable; that, in fact, was beneficial to society.[9] . . .

Let me close by acknowledging that liability reform is a tough political issue to tackle. The opponents of reform—who are also the principal beneficiaries of legal business as usual—have a great deal at stake. Many members of the plaintiffs' bar, so adept at styling themselves as great defenders and protectors of the common citizen, are in fact people of truly enormous wealth and influence. Many of them, indeed, are both wealthier and politically more influential than the captains of industry—often the small business man and woman—who they claim to be policing.

The most important victims of our current system, those numbered among workers and consumers, are much harder to identify. We can't easily point to a patient who would have been cured by a drug that was never developed, or a worker who would have been hired by an industry that was never born.

Liability reform is, and should be viewed, as a consumer issue. But it requires either ignorance or disingenuousness to maintain that whatever is good for producers is therefore bad for consumers, that an unlimited right to play litigation roulette is an unqualified consumer benefit. Unless the government is to supply everything to everyone—an approach to things in some disrepute these days—consumers need producers as much as producers need consumers. Balanced liability standards, that preserve the right to sue within reasonable bounds that accommodate the demands of national production and international competition, are better not only for those who wish to sell, but also for those who need to buy.

NOTES

1. P. Boffey, "Loss of Drug Relegates Many to Blindness Again," *New York Times*, 14 October 1986, p. C1.

2. N. R. Kleinfield, " 'Orphan' Drugs: Caught in Limbo," *New York Times*, 20 July 1986, Section F, pp. 1, 27.

3. *Id.*

4. *Id.*

5. *See* Marley, "Delayed Decisions Often Result in Lost Opportunities," Marketing News, at 16, May 8, 1987.

6. Priest, *The Current Insurance Crisis and Modern Tort Law*, 96 Yale L.J. 1521, 1527 (1987).

7. *Id.* at 1544–1545.

8. *Id.*

9. *See, e.g.,* Huber, *Liability, The Legal Revolution and Its Consequences*, ch. 10 (1988); Project on Civil Justice Reform, Manhattan Institute for Policy Research, *Comparative Risk*, at 1–2 (June 13, 1987); Research and Policy Committee, Committee for Economic Development, *Who Should Be Liable? A Guide to Policy for Dealing with Risk*, at ch. 5 (1989).

NO

Kenneth Jost

TAMPERING WITH EVIDENCE: THE LIABILITY AND COMPETITIVENESS MYTH

Americans anxious about the United States' precarious position in the world economy were given a new but familiar target to blame last summer: the legal system. From the nation's second highest office, Americans were told that "unrestrained litigation" was exacting a "terrible toll" on the U.S. economy: costing U.S. consumers up to $300 billion, deterring U.S. manufacturers from product innovation, and hampering their ability to compete with foreign companies.

"A self-inflicted competitive disadvantage" was how Vice President Dan Quayle described it. The message struck a responsive chord in people naturally distrustful of lawyers and accustomed to hearing of daffy lawsuits and extravagant jury awards and settlements.

It also provided new impetus for a bill being pushed in Congress by a business and insurance industry coalition to change the rules for trying damage suits involving product-related injuries.

The message is fundamentally false—the product of dubious anecdotes, questionable research, concocted statistics, factual and legal misstatements, and willful disregard of contradictory evidence.

It exaggerates the extent and cost of litigation for consumers and manufacturers alike. It gives phony credibility to unscientific cost estimates, like the $300 billion figure, manufactured by business groups and their supporters. And it ignores the benefits in product safety that have resulted in part from lawsuits—and the resulting publicity—attacking dangerous or unsafe products ranging from chemicals to contraceptives to cars and airplanes.

The product liability reform lobby's own evidence does not support many of the broad assertions being made in this latest argument in a decade-long drive to limit damages paid to plaintiffs in product-related tort suits. Critics call it a propaganda campaign and chafe at its seeming invulnerability to factual refutation.

From Kenneth Jost, "Tampering With Evidence: The Liability and Competitiveness Myth," *ABA Journal* (April 1992). Copyright © 1992 by Kenneth Jost. Reprinted by permission.

• **Myth No. One: "The Avalanche of Claims."** The best evidence contradicts the notion of an out-of-control litigation system. The most comprehensive studies—by experts sympathetic to the tort reform cause—indicate that, except for the special case of asbestos litigation, product suits have declined sharply—by 40 percent—over the past five years.

The vast majority of product-related claims are either dropped or settled before trial for relatively small amounts, the studies show. . . .

• **Myth No. Two: "The Liability Tax."** The evidence does not show that legal and liability costs are major competitive factors for most industries or a major disincentive to product innovation. A 1987 study by the Conference Board, a New York–based business research group, indicated that liability costs amount to less than 1 percent of total costs for more than two-thirds of the companies surveyed. The General Accounting Office, an arm of Congress, made a similar finding two years later.

A new study by a pro-tort reform economist, W. Kip Viscusi of Duke University, does suggest that large liability costs can sometimes deter product innovation. But he found that occurring in only a handful of industries. For most industries, Viscusi's study said, liability costs actually serve as an incentive to innovation—the very argument advanced by plaintiffs' attorneys and the consumer, health and safety groups that support the existing system.

• **Myth No. Three: "The Unlevel Playing Field."** The evidence also suggests that the supposed competitive advantages enjoyed by foreign manufacturers because of legal differences between the United States and their own countries are being exaggerated.

Foreign manufacturers selling products in the United States generally face the same product liability rules that American firms do. Japanese and German auto manufacturers, for example, are frequent defendants in product liability suits in U.S. courts.

"In form, there's a kind of level playing field," says Gary Schwartz, a professor at UCLA School of Law who has studied U.S., European and Japanese tort systems. Schwartz says American plaintiffs may face some practical problems in pursuing suits against foreign concerns, but that difference creates no more than a "moderate advantage" for the foreign competitor against the U.S. firm.

THE EVIDENCE FOR THAT VIEW, WHICH FEW people have read closely, does not do well under cross-examination. Several of the "safe" products said to have been driven from the market had been found to be dangerous—not just by plaintiffs' lawyers and consumer groups but by government agencies, courts or insurers as well.

As for the Huber-Litan book ["The Liability Maze," a collection of papers that examine the liability system's impact on product safety and innovation, edited by Peter Huber and Robert Litan], the various papers describe more positive effects on safety than the tort reformers acknowledged and found no adverse impact on innovation in one of the four manufacturing sectors studied: chemicals. And the most damning evidence on innovation came from papers on automobiles, pharmaceuticals and general-aviation aircraft, each written by someone with long-standing financial ties to the industry he examined.

When the Senate Commerce Committee approved S. 640, the current product liability bill, 13–7 last fall, two dissenting members—Democrats Ernest F. Hollings of South Carolina and Al Gore of Tennessee—dissected some of the evidence on innovation. Using information provided by Consumers Union lobbyist Lipsen, the senators said "legitimate questions" had been raised about the safety of several products cited in the business lobby's testimony.

The senators noted, for example, that the EPA had reviewed Monsanto's own studies of its abandoned asbestos substitute in 1986 and concluded that the testing "offers reasonable support for the conclusion that calcium sodium metaphosphate fibers can cause cancer."

According to the agency memo, animal tests showed that the calcium phosphate fibers "induced low but essentially equal incidences" of cancer as asbestos fibers did. Monsanto officials responded by challenging the EPA's conclusion and repeating that fear of litigation was the only reason for dropping the product.

The senators said other products had been pulled from the market after lawsuits or regulatory actions challenged their safety.

• The Copper 7 IUD manufactured by G. D. Searle Co., for example, had been found to carry a high risk of causing serious infection or infertility when used by women who had not previously had children.

• An anesthesia gas machine manufactured by Puritan-Bennett had been recalled by the Food and Drug Administration because of a faulty valve blamed for four deaths due to overdoses of anesthesia.

• American Motors' CJ-5 and CJ-7 Jeeps had been described as dangerously susceptible to rollover after investigations by the Federal Trade Commission and the private Insurance Institute for Highway Safety.

The arguments advanced in "The Liability Maze" are harder to dissect, but the book's proof of anti-innovation impacts depends largely on conjecture, extrapolation, and disregard of other factors affecting product decisions and research.

Automobile expert Murray MacKay of the University of Birmingham in England, for example, says U.S. carmakers have been slower to make safety improvements than their European counterparts. He blames product liability without ever mentioning what many other experts list as the major factor: Detroit's steadfast belief until recently that safety does not sell cars.

In their preface, Huber and Litan blame product liability for drying up U.S. research on contraceptives, but fail to mention other important disincentives for U.S. firms, including the political spillover from the abortion debate and the lack of government funding for contraception-related research.

And Robert Martin, a lawyer for Beech Aircraft in Wichita, Kan., blames the general-aviation aircraft manufacturers' woes on rising liability costs while sliding over the industry's other problems—chiefly, the difficulty of selling new private planes in an economic slump, while planes manufactured in earlier periods are still airworthy.

Duke economist Viscusi provides the book's most comprehensive study about liability and innovation. He and his colleague, Michael Moore, correlated industry-by-industry insurance costs with new patents in each industry—one way of measuring product innovation.

"For most levels of liability costs," they concluded, "a higher liability burden fosters additional product-related research. However, once those costs become sufficiently large, the effect of product liability is counterproductive, since it dampens innovation."

Viscusi found that counterproductive effect only in one of the four industries covered in the book—general-aviation aircraft—and, since then, in two other small manufacturing sectors: composition goods installation (for example, asbestos) and miscellaneous chemicals (battery acid, jet fuels, firecrackers and so forth). For most industries—including such attractive product-liability targets as automobiles, pharmaceuticals and the bulk of the chemical industry—Viscusi concludes that the costs of product liability "provide safety incentive effects that more than offset the product withdrawal effects."

IN THE FACE OF THIS EVIDENCE, THE PRODuct liability reform lobby repeats a litany of statistics and anecdotes that wither under close scrutiny. The vice president's Council on Competitiveness, for example, quotes a 1984 study "commissioned by the Department of Commerce" that found U.S. firms "often" have product liability insurance costs 20 to 50 times higher than foreign firms.

The study, it turns out, was based on just five machine-tool manufacturing industries and was directed by a lobbyist for a group of trade associations pushing product liability legislation.

To show the impact of product liability on business innovation, the Competitiveness Council cited a second study conducted by the Conference Board in 1988. Without mentioning the earlier, less alarmist Conference Board survey, the council said this study showed that product liability concerns had caused 47 percent of U.S. manufacturers to withdraw

products from the market, 25 percent to discontinue forms of product research, and 15 percent to lay off workers.

The study, however, was statistically flawed—based on 500 responses from some 4,000 business executives who received a mailed questionnaire. Statisticians call that "a self-selecting sample" and warn that the results are virtually certain to be biased.

"The flaws in such a study," says Theodore Eisenberg, a Cornell University law professor who has conducted statistical studies of litigation for eight years, "are so substantial and so obvious that no self-respecting legislature should act on its results."

The anecdotal evidence fares no better. One oft-quoted "statistic" says that the price of a ladder includes a "liability tax" that has been variously described over the years as 30 percent, 20 percent, 15 percent, or, most recently, "15 to 25 percent."

Dan Brady, executive director of the Chicago-based American Ladder Institute, says he got the last figure from a telephone survey last summer of company executives who gave him undocumented estimates of their legal and liability costs. The executives were asked to count any cost remotely related to legal or liability issues—even the salaries for telephone receptionists who field consumer complaints. Brady says he has no figures for ladder manufacturers' payouts in product safety cases.

As an example of the products that have been kept off the market because of groundless liability concerns, Quayle last year cited a supposedly safe substitute for asbestos that Monsanto Co. developed but dropped for fear of being subjected to asbestos-like product liability suits. The Environmental Protection Agency, however, citing laboratory tests, believes the product—a calcium phosphate fiber—may be a cancer-causing agent as dangerous as asbestos.

Despite the demonstrated flaws in its evidence, the product liability reform lobby's major points have gained wide acceptance—to the frustration of its opponents. "If consumer groups tried to push an issue with as little supporting data as the manufacturers have, we'd be summarily told to leave," says Linda Lipsen, legislative counsel for Consumers Union, which publishes *Consumer Reports* magazine.

One reason appears to be the intense feelings on the issue on both sides. "It approaches a theological debate," says Brookings Institution lawyer-economist Robert Litan, co-editor of an influential book examining product liability's effects on safety and innovation. "With raw emotions out there, it's hard to find people in the middle. The debate is dominated by people at the extremes."

THESE STRONG EMOTIONS CAN BE TRACED to judicial decisions beginning in the 1960s that expanded manufacturers' legal responsibility for injuries that consumers or workers suffered while using their products. A negligence standard, requiring plaintiffs to prove the manufacturer was "at fault," was supplanted in some cases by doctrines of strict liability—liability without fault.

The doctrine was first articulated in a 1963 ruling by the influential California Supreme Court Justice Roger Traynor in a suit brought by a home woodworker injured when a piece of wood flew out of a power-driven lathe. Traynor's decision upholding a $65,000 verdict against the manufacturer broadly declared that manufacturers are strictly liable for injuries

resulting from a defect that made the product "unsafe for its intended use."

The defenders of strict liability view it as a natural evolution of common law, breaking down artificial legal barriers to ensure compensation for people injured through no fault of their own. Critics denounce it as social engineering that imposed an economic penalty on manufacturers solely because of their ability to pay, and that devalued personal responsibility and contract principles in the marketplace.

To these critics, the expansion of the doctrine in the '60s and '70s amounted to a legal revolution. Strict liability, they said, was extended willy-nilly to all kinds of product-related suits, forcing manufacturers to pay for injuries from ostensibly defective products, even if plaintiffs had recklessly misused the product and even if the product could not have been made safer at the time.

The defenders of expanding product liability—and some more detached observers—say the revolution was far less sweeping than critics pictured. Strict liability took hold in cases of manufacturing defects. But in the most numerous cases where plaintiffs claimed that the product had an inherently unsafe design defect or that the manufacturer had failed to warn buyers of risks from using the product, strict liability was applied only with balancing tests that amounted, more or less, to old-fashioned negligence.

Rarefied debates about legal doctrine mattered less to business groups and the general public, however, than dollars and cents. With hard numbers about civil cases difficult to come by, the public's view of the legal trend was shaped by recurring headlines about whopping six- and seven-figure verdicts or even larger damage claims in suits that, on the surface, seemed to range from trivial to absurd.

By the end of the '70s, a large segment of the public was inclined to think the legal system had gone too far. Building on that sentiment, business and insurance groups turned to Washington for help. They began lobbying Congress for federal legislation to ease the rules for product-related suits not just in federal courts, but in the 50 state-court systems as well.

Initially, they argued that national manufacturers needed uniform rules to govern product-related suits—sliding over the fact that the uniform standards proposed were generally less stringent than the rules in effect in most states.

Then, the "insurance crisis" of the mid-1980s lent greater urgency to the drive as premiums soared and insurance dried up. But the crisis passed with the bills still languishing, and supporters needed a new theme to get the issue moving again.

AS THE U.S. ECONOMY SLUMPED AT THE end of the '80s, the product liability reform lobby could not have struck a more powerful theme than competitiveness. And the message found a strong and effective voice in Peter Huber, an MIT-trained engineer-turned-lawyer who used his double-barreled expertise to blast away at the liability system with full force.

In his 1988 book, "Liability: The Legal Revolution and its Consequences," Huber recited horror story after horror story of litigation run amok. Writing under the sponsorship of a conservative think-tank, the Manhattan Institute, Huber assailed the broadened theories of liability with an absolutist zeal made palatable by his erudite wit.

Many of the stories were familiar—like the mega-suits against the morning-sickness drug Bendectin and the chemical defoliant Agent Orange—but no one before had gathered them so comprehensively in a book aimed at the general public.

Huber's special contribution, though, was to catalogue adverse effects on innovation in some of the industries most often targeted by product-related suits, like automobiles, chemicals, pharmaceuticals and general-aviation aircraft.

Bendectin, he said, had been driven off the market by baseless suits, and pregnant women would be getting no new drug to substitute. Research into contraceptives had been all but halted by fear of suits like those that drove the Dalkon Shield and the CU-7 IUD from the market.

Litigation had similarly scared drug companies away from research on new vaccines. And the assembly lines for small general-aviation aircraft were all but idle after manufacturers-paid claims in crash cases had soared from $24 million in 1977 to $210 million in 1985.

Innovation and competitiveness, secondary themes in earlier congressional hearings, now became the leitmotif. When the Senate Commerce Committee returned to the product liability bill in 1990, a chorus of witnesses took up the theme. At their head was former Commerce Secretary Robert Mosbacher, who said the product liability system was undermining competitiveness by raising prices, forcing discontinuation of existing products, and discouraging research and development of new products.

Huber testified, too, providing the senators with an appendix of 17 instances where, he said, manufacturers had dropped or abandoned products,

Calculating the "Liability Tax"

No one knows exactly how much the liability system costs the U.S. economy, but the $300 billion estimate cited by the President's Council on Competitiveness is about as genuine as a $3 bill.

Here's how tort reform advocate Peter Huber arrived at the figure in his book, "Liability: The Legal Revolution and Its Consequences."

Take the $80 billion figure cited as the total cost of all insurance in the United States—individual, private and governmental. Then, borrowing from a 1987 study by the American Medical Association about doctors, assume that indirect costs—"the tremendous effort, inconvenience and sacrifice" to avoid liability—amount to $3.50 for every $1 in direct costs.

"If similar multipliers operate in other areas," Huber writes, the total "liability tax" on the U.S. economy "may amount" to $300 billion.

Mark Hager, a tort law expert at American University, Washington College of Law, calls the projection "a huge exaggeration." Writing in the *Stanford Law Review,* he says Huber has misread an AMA study that was done at the height of the medical malpractice crisis and that cannot be generalized to other sectors of the economy.

In an interview, Huber says the AMA study was "biased, no doubt," and then adopts an agnostic stance toward his own calculation. "Nobody knows what the indirect cost is," he says. "What I said was that if the same multipliers operate in other areas, it's $300 billion. If they don't, it's not."

—K. J.

raised prices or shut down because of liability costs.

Later that summer, innovation was again a primary focus as Huber and Robert Litan presided over a Brookings Institution–sponsored conference exploring the impacts of the product liability system on U.S. industry. Litan, a Democrat who had worked on regulatory issues in the Carter administration and authored a civil justice delay-reduction plan passed by Congress in 1990, calls himself "a cautious tort reformer."

He asked Huber to help find experts to write contrasting papers on the liability system's effects on safety and innovation in selected industries. The conference it-self drew limited attention. But when the papers were published last spring as a 514-page book, "The Liability Maze," critics of the product liability system embraced the findings as proof positive that liability was having devastating impacts on product innovation, and doing little to protect health and safety besides.

Despite his sophisticated studies, economist Viscusi contributes to the exaggerated myths surrounding the issue. Aircraft manufacturers, for example, say that liability costs now amount to $100,000 of the price of a newly manufactured plane. In his new book, "Reforming Product Liability," Viscusi describes that figure as "misleadingly high," because the liability cost is "the cost of *all* planes ever produced and the number of planes currently produced is low."

Nonetheless, Viscusi repeated the figure without qualification in his testimony to the Senate Small Business Committee in November.

Legal misstatements abound in the debate, too. Huber strongly argues that when manufacturers discover product defects, they hesitate to make safety improvements because plaintiffs can use evidence of post-accident repairs to make their case.

But, as Georgetown University Law Center Professor Joseph Page points out in a critical review of Huber's book, the old doctrine excluding such evidence is still "alive and well" in many jurisdictions.

When contradictory evidence can no longer be denied, reformers simply ignore it. Punitive damage awards, for example, are a major complaint of business groups. But several studies—by the GAO, the Rand Corp. in California, and, most recently, the plaintiffs bar-funded Roscoe Pound Foundation—show that punitive damage awards are rare: just 355 over a 25-year period.

And punitive damages are usually in line with the plaintiff's compensatory damages and likely to be reduced or set aside on appeal when out of line. Huber's response: "The point is punitive damages cause tremendous amounts of economic harm when they do happen."

THE CONCLUSION IS INESCAPABLE: THE competitiveness theme is a defective product manufactured by business groups to reduce costs for product-related injuries without really reforming the legal system. The bill in Congress helps defendants—by raising the burden of proof for punitive damages, for example—without any provisions to reduce litigation costs for both sides or make compensation more certain in valid claims.

Yet recent studies by the American Law Institute and Rand Corp. researcher Deborah Hensler—both sympathetic to tort reform—conclude that the product liability system leaves many plaintiffs uncompensated or undercompensated.

As the ALI report said, "Deserving victims with legitimate claims continue to face high barriers to obtaining tort redress."

Even-handed product liability reform might benefit consumers and manufacturers alike, but the polarized debate makes compromise unlikely. When Quayle proposed discovery reform, for example, the corporate bar was quick to criticize it, fearing plaintiffs would gain access too easily to corporate files.

The idea of setting fixed awards for "pain and suffering" damages—suggested by the Brookings Institution's Litan and others—is unlikely to materialize because business groups would insist on levels too low to make the plan acceptable to plaintiffs or consumer groups. And neither side has much to gain by attacking what economist Viscusi has identified as the single greatest factor in rising insurance and liability costs: the soaring price of health care, privately financed in the United States but paid for by national health systems in other countries.

The tort reformers' arguments also deflect attention from the real problems undermining U.S. competitiveness. When Chrysler President Lee Iacocca listed the U.S. automobile industry's problems while visiting Japan with President Bush in January, he made no mention of product liability. But with the product liability system as a scapegoat, businesses can avoid hard questions about their own shortfalls in investment, marketing, research and worker training.

Legal reforms may be needed, but they will not matter much in solving those problems. The best thing business can do for U.S. competitiveness is get its own house in order. "That's "Job One" for American business—and the global marketplace will not be forgiving if U.S. industry fails to get on with it.

POSTSCRIPT

Is the Legal System Damaging the American Economy?

In the first edition of his best-selling book, *Megatrends: Ten New Directions Transforming Our Lives* (Warner, 1982), John Naisbitt argued that modern communications technologies make possible relationships and interactions between persons and institutions that could not exist in earlier times. He wrote that "an industrial society pits man against fabricated nature. In an information society—for the first time in civilization—the game is interacting with other people. This increases personal transactions geometrically; that is, all forms of interactive communication: telephone calls, checks written, memos, messages, letters, and more. This is one basic reason why we are bound to be a litigious-intensive society." The impressive capabilities of the electronic media undoubtedly do provide new opportunities for conflict to occur. Will we, however, also be likely to rely on litigation, rather than on some nontraditional technique, such as mediation or arbitration, as the principal means for resolving these conflicts? Naisbitt's conclusion that our society will become "litigious-intensive" assumes that courts will be used the same way in the future as they are today, and it does not take into account changes that may occur in our attitudes toward law and in the manner in which law and courts are employed.

Claims that litigation, particularly tort litigation, is damaging competitiveness are discussed more fully in P. Huber, *Liability* (Basic Books, 1988); P. Huber and R. Litan, *The Liability Maze* (Brookings Institution, 1991); and National Legal Center for the Public Interest, *Pernicious Ideas and Costly Consequences: The Intellectual Roots of the Tort Crisis* (1990). The most recent critique of many of the statistics about the legal profession used by Huber and others can be found in M. Galanter, "Pick a Number, Any Number," *The American Lawyer* (April 1992). Further reading on the litigation explosion may be found in Hurst, "The Functions of Courts in the United States, 1950–1980," 15 *Law and Society Review*, pp. 400–471 (1980); Friedman, "The Six Million Dollar Man: Litigation and Rights Consciousness in Modern America," 39 *Maryland Law Review*, pp. 661–667 (1980); Curran, *The Legal Needs of the Public* (American Bar Association, 1977); Clark, "Adjudication to Administration: A Statistical Analysis of Federal District Courts in the Twentieth Century," 55 *Southern California Law Review* 65 (1981); Saks, "In Search of the 'Lawsuit Crisis,' " 14 *Law, Medicine and Health Care* 77 (1987); Bunch and Hardy, "A Re-Examination of Litigation Trends in the United States," *Journal of Dispute Resolution* 87 (1986); and Catenacci, "Hyperlexis or Hyperbole: Subdividing the Landscape of Disputes and Defusing the Litigation Explosion," 8 *Review of Litigation* 297 (1989).

ISSUE 2

Should Lawyers Be Prohibited from Presenting a False Case?

YES: Harry I. Subin, from "The Criminal Lawyer's 'Different Mission': Reflections on the 'Right' to Present a False Case," *Georgetown Journal of Legal Ethics* (vol. 1, 1987)

NO: John B. Mitchell, from "Reasonable Doubts Are Where You Find Them: A Response to Professor Subin's Position on the Criminal Lawyer's 'Different Mission,' " *Georgetown Journal of Legal Ethics* (vol. 1, 1987)

ISSUE SUMMARY

YES: Professor of law Harry I. Subin examines the ethical responsibilities of criminal defense lawyers and argues that greater responsibility should be placed on lawyers not to pervert the truth to help their clients.
NO: Attorney John B. Mitchell disputes the contention that the goal of the criminal justice process is to seek the truth and argues that it is essential that there be independent defense attorneys to provide protection against government oppression.

In 1732, Georgia was founded as a colony that was to have no lawyers. This was done with the goal of having a "happy, flourishing colony . . . free from that pest and scourge of mankind called lawyers." While there are no serious efforts to abolish the legal profession today, public opinion surveys reveal that lawyers still are not held in the highest esteem. The public today may feel a little more positive about lawyers than did citizens of colonial America, and large numbers of students aspire to become lawyers, but hostility and criticism of what lawyers are and what they do are still common.

Part of the reason for the public's ambivalent attitude about lawyers concerns the adversary system and the lawyer's role in it. The adversary system requires that the lawyer's main responsibility be to the client. Except in rare instances, the lawyer is not to consider whether the client's cause is right or wrong and is not to allow societal or public needs to affect the manner in which the client is represented. The adversary system assumes that someone other than the client's lawyer is responsible for determining truth and guaranteeing justice.

The code of ethics of the legal profession instructs lawyers not to lie. However, it is permissible to mislead opponents—indeed, to do anything short of lying, if done to benefit the client. We have a system of "legal ethics" because some things lawyers are obligated to do for their clients would violate traditional standards of ethical behavior. As one legal scholar has written, "Where the attorney-client relationship exists, it is often appropriate and many times even obligatory for the attorney to do things that, all other things being equal, an ordinary person need not, and should not, do" (Richard W. Wasserstrom, "Lawyers as Professionals: Some Moral Issues," 5 *Human Rights* 1 [1975]).

In a highly publicized case that occurred a few years ago, two criminal defense lawyers learned from their client that, in addition to the crimes he was charged with, the client had murdered two girls who were missing. The lawyers discovered where the bodies were but refused to provide the parents of the missing children with any of this information. There was a public outcry when it was later discovered what the lawyers had done, but their position was generally felt to be consistent with standards of legal ethics.

Why do we have a legal system that allows truth to be concealed? Is a diminished concern with truth necessary in order to preserve the status and security of the individual? What should be the limits as to how one-sided legal representation should be? Would it be desirable to require lawyers to be more concerned with truth, so that they would be prohibited from putting forward positions they know are false? In the following articles, Harry I. Subin and John B. Mitchell debate whether or not increasing the attorney's "truth" function would be both desirable and feasible. As you read the articles, determine whether Subin's suggestion is a dangerous first step toward a more powerful state and less protection for the individual or whether it would increase public respect toward the legal system and the legal profession with little cost.

At the heart of the adversary system's attention to the relationship between client and counsel is the belief that there is something more important than discovering truth in every case. Finding the guilty and punishing them is not the sole goal of the criminal justice process. We rely on the criminal process, particularly trials, to remind us that our liberty depends on placing restrictions on the power of the state. The argument on behalf of the adversary model is that increasing the power of the state to find truth in one case may hurt all of us in the future. As you read the following articles, it will be difficult not to be troubled by the lawyer's dilemma; you may wonder if there is any acceptable middle ground when state power and individual rights clash.

YES

Harry I. Subin

THE CRIMINAL LAWYER'S "DIFFERENT MISSION": REFLECTIONS ON THE "RIGHT" TO PRESENT A FALSE CASE

I. THE INQUIRY

Should the criminal lawyer be permitted to represent a client by putting forward a defense the lawyer knows is false? . . .

Presenting a "false defense," as used here, means attempting to convince the judge or jury that facts established by the state and known to the attorney to be true are not true, or that facts known to the attorney to be false are true. While this can be done by criminal means—e.g., perjury, introduction of forged documents, and the like—I exclude these acts from the definition of false defense used here. I am not concerned with them because such blatant criminal acts are relatively uninteresting ethically, and both the courts and bar have rejected their use.[1]

My concern, instead, is with the presently legal means for the attorney to reach favorable verdict even if it is completely at odds with the facts. The permissible techniques include: (1) cross-examination of truthful government witnesses to undermine their testimony or their credibility; (2) direct presentation of testimony, not itself false, but used to discredit the truthful evidence adduced by the government, or to accredit a false theory; and (3) argument to the jury based on any of these acts. One looks in vain in ethical codes or case law for a definition of "perjury" or "false evidence" that includes these acts, although they are also inconsistent with the goal of assuring a truthful verdict.

To the extent that these techniques of legal truth-subversion have been addressed at all, most authorities have approved them. The American Bar Association's *Standards for Criminal Justice*,[2] for example, advises the criminal defense attorney that it is proper to destroy a truthful government witness when essential to provide the defendant with a defense, and that failure to

From Harry I. Subin, "The Criminal Lawyer's 'Different Mission': Reflections on the 'Right' to Present a False Case," *Georgetown Journal of Legal Ethics*, vol. 1 (1987), pp. 125–138, 141–153. Copyright © 1987 by *Georgetown Journal of Legal Ethics*. Reprinted by permission. Some notes omitted.

do so would violate the lawyer's duty under the *Model Code of Professional Responsibility* to represent the client zealously.[3] The *Standards for Criminal Justice* cite as authority for this proposition an opinion by Justice White in *United States v. Wade*,[4] which, in the most emphatic form, is to the same effect. In *Wade*, the Court held that in order to assure the reliability of the pretrial line-up, the right to counsel must be extended to the defendant compelled to participate in one.[5] Justice White warned that the presence of counsel would not necessarily assure that the identification procedure would be more accurate than if the police were left to conduct it themselves. The passage dealing with this issue, which includes the phrase that inspired the title of this piece, is worth repeating at length:

> Law enforcement officers have the obligation to convict the guilty and to make sure they do not convict the innocent. They must be dedicated to making the criminal trial a procedure for the ascertainment of the true facts surrounding the commission of the crime. To this extent, our so-called adversary system is not adversary at all; nor should it be. But defense counsel has no comparable obligation to ascertain or present the truth. Our system assigns him a different mission. He must be and is interested in preventing the conviction of the innocent, but . . . we also insist that he defend his client whether he is innocent or guilty. The State has the obligation to present evidence. Defense counsel need present nothing, even if he knows what the truth is. He need not furnish any witnesses to the police, or reveal any confidences of his client, or furnish any other information to help the prosecution's case. If he can confuse a witness, even a truthful one,

or make him appear at a disadvantage, unsure or indecisive, that will be his normal course. Our interest in not convicting the innocent permits counsel to put the State to its proof, to put the State's case in the worst possible light, regardless of what he thinks or knows to be the truth. Undoubtedly there are some limits which defense counsel must observe but more often than not, defense counsel will cross-examine a prosecution witness, and impeach him if he can, even if he thinks the witness is telling the truth, just as he will attempt to destroy a witness who he thinks is lying. In this respect, as part of our modified adversary system and as part of the duty imposed on the most honorable defense counsel, we countenance or require conduct which in many instances has little, if any, relation to the search for truth.[6]

. . . The article begins with a description of a case I handled some years ago, one that I believe is a good illustration of the false defense problem. I next address the threshold question of the attorney's knowledge. It has been argued that the attorney cannot "know" what the truth is, and therefore is free to present any available defense theory. I attempt to demonstrate that the attorney can, in fact, know the truth, and I propose a process to determine when the truth is known.

I then analyze the arguments that have been advanced in support of the "different mission" theory: that the defense attorney, even if he or she knows the truth, remains free to disregard it in presenting a defense. I argue that neither the right to a defense nor the needs of the adversary system justify the presentation of a false defense. Finally, I describe a new standard that explicitly prohibits the defense attorney from asserting a false defense. I conclude with some thoughts as to why this rule would produce a generally more just system.

II. TRUTH SUBVERSION IN ACTION: THE PROBLEM ILLUSTRATED

A. The Accusation

About fifteen years ago I represented a man charged with rape and robbery. The victim's account was as follows: Returning from work in the early morning hours, she was accosted by a man who pointed a gun at her and took a watch from her wrist. He told her to go with him to a nearby lot, where he ordered her to lie down on the ground and disrobe. When she complained that the ground was hurting her, he took her to his apartment, located across the street. During the next hour there, he had intercourse with her. Ultimately, he said that they had to leave to avoid being discovered by the woman with whom he lived.[7] The complainant responded that since he had gotten what he wanted, he should give her back her watch. He said that he would.

As the two left the apartment, he said he was going to get a car. Before leaving the building, however, he went to the apartment next door, leaving her to wait in the hallway. When asked why she waited, she said that she was still hoping for the return of her watch, which was a valued gift, apparently from her boyfriend.

She never did get the watch. When they left the building, the man told her to wait on the street while he got the car. At that point she went to a nearby police precinct and reported the incident. She gave a full description of the assailant that matched my client. She also accu-

rately described the inside of his apartment. Later, in response to a note left at his apartment by the police, my client came to the precinct, and the complainant identified him. My client was released at that time but was arrested soon thereafter at his apartment, where a gun was found.[8] No watch was recovered.

My client was formally charged, at which point I entered the case. At our initial interview and those that followed it, he insisted that he had nothing whatever to do with the crime and he had never seen the woman before.[9] He stated that he had been in several places during the night in question: visiting his aunt earlier in the evening, then traveling to a bar in New Jersey, where he was during the critical hours. He gave the name of a man there who would corroborate this. He said that he arrived home early the next morning and met a friend. He stated that he had no idea how this woman had come to know things about him such as what the apartment looked like, that he lived with a woman, and that he was a musician, or how she could identify him. He said that he had no reason to rape anyone, since he already had a woman, and that in any event he was recovering from surgery for an old gun shot wound and could not engage in intercourse. He said he would not be so stupid as to bring a woman he had robbed and was going to rape into his own apartment.

I felt that there was some strength to these arguments, and that there were questionable aspects to the complainant's story. In particular, it seemed strange that a man intending rape would be as solicitous of the victim's comfort as the woman said her assailant was at the playground. It also seemed that a person who had just been raped would flee when she had the chance to, and in any case would not be primarily concerned with the return of her watch. On balance, however, I suspected that my client was not telling me the truth. I thought the complaining witness could not possibly have known what she knew about him and his apartment, if she had not had any contact with him. True, someone else could have posed as him, and used his apartment. My client, however, could suggest no one who could have done so.[10] Moreover, that hypothesis did not explain the complainant's accurate description of him to the police. Although the identification procedure used by the police, a one person "show up," was suggestive,[11] the woman had ample opportunity to observe her assailant during the extended incident. I could not believe that the complainant had selected my client randomly to accuse falsely of rape. By both her and my client's admission, the two had not had any previous association.

That my client was probably lying to me had two possible explanations. First, he might have been lying because he was guilty and did not see any particular advantage to himself in admitting it to me. It is embarrassing to admit that one has committed a crime, particularly one of this nature. Moreover, my client might well have feared to tell me the truth. He might have believed that I would tell others what he said, or, at the very least, that I might not be enthusiastic about representing him.

He also might have lied not because he was guilty of the offense, but because he thought the concocted story was the best one under the circumstances. The sexual encounter may have taken place voluntarily, but the woman complained to the police because she was angry at my client for refusing to return the valued wrist watch, perhaps not stolen, but left, in my client's apartment. My client may not have been able to admit this, because he had other needs that took precedence over the particular legal one that brought him to me. For example, the client might have felt compelled to deny any involvement in the incident because to admit to having had a sexual encounter might have jeopardized his relationship with the woman with whom he lived. Likewise, he might have decided to "play lawyer," and put forward what he believed to be his best defense. Not understanding the heavy burden of proof on the state in criminal cases, he might have thought that any version of the facts that showed that he had contact with the woman would be fatal because it would simply be a case of her word against his.

I discussed all of these matters with the client on several occasions. Judging him a man of intelligence, with no signs of mental abnormality, I became convinced that he understood both the seriousness of his situation, and that his exculpation did not depend upon maintaining his initial story. In ensuring that he did understand that, in fact, I came close enough to suggesting the "right" answers to make me a little nervous about the line between subornation of perjury and careful witness preparation, known in the trade as "horseshedding."[12] In the end, however, he held to his original account.

B. The Investigation
At this point the case was in equipoise for me. I had my suspicions about both the complainant's and the client's version of what had occurred, and I supposed a jury would as well. That problem was theirs, however, not mine. All I had to do

was present my client's version of what occurred in the best way that I could.

Or was that all that was required? Committed to the adversarial spirit reflected in Justice White's observations about my role, I decided that it was not. The "different mission" took me beyond the task of presenting my client's position in a legally correct and persuasive manner, to trying to untrack the state's case in any lawful way that occurred to me, regardless of the facts.

With that mission in mind, I concluded that it would be too risky to have the defendant simply take the stand and tell his story, even if it were true. Unless we could create an iron-clad alibi, which seemed unlikely given the strength of the complainant's identification, I thought it was much safer to attack the complainant's story, even if it were true. I felt, however, that since my client had persisted in his original story I was obligated to investigate the alibi defense, although I was fairly certain that I would not use it. My students and I therefore interviewed everyone he mentioned, traveled and timed the route he said he had followed, and attempted to find witnesses who may have seen someone else at the apartment. We discovered nothing helpful. The witness my client identified as being at the bar in New Jersey could not corroborate the client's presence there. The times the client gave were consistent with his presence at the place of the crime when the victim claimed it took place. The client's aunt verified that he had been with her, but much earlier in the evening.

Because the alibi defense was apparently hopeless, I returned to the original strategy of attempting to undermine the complainant's version of the facts. I demanded a preliminary hearing, in which the complainant would have to testify under oath to the events in question. Her version was precisely as I have described it, and she told it in an objective manner that, far from seeming contrived, convinced me that she was telling the truth. She seemed a person who, if not at home with the meanness of the streets, was resigned to it. To me that explained why she was able to react in what I perceived to be a nonstereotypical manner to the ugly events in which she had been involved.

I explained to my client that we had failed to corroborate his alibi, and that the complainant appeared to be a credible witness. I said that in my view the jury would not believe the alibi, and that if we could not obtain any other information, it might be appropriate to think about a guilty plea, which would at least limit his exposure to punishment. The case, then in the middle of the aimless drift towards resolution that typifies New York's criminal justice system, was left at that.

Some time later, however, my client called me and told me that he had new evidence; his aunt, he said, would testify that he had been with her at the time in question. I was incredulous. I reminded him that at no time during our earlier conversations had he indicated what was plainly a crucial piece of information, despite my not too subtle explanation of an alibi defense. I told him that when the aunt was initially interviewed with great care on this point, she stated that he was not with her at the time of the crime. Ultimately, I told him that I thought he was lying, and that in my view even if the jury heard the aunt's testimony, they would not believe it.

Whether it was during that session or later that the client admitted his guilt I do not recall. I do recall wondering whether, now that I knew the truth, that should make a difference in the way in which the case was handled. I certainly wished that I did not know it and began to understand, psychologically if not ethically, lawyers who do not want to know their clients' stories.[13]

I did not pause very long to ponder the problem, however, because I concluded that knowing the truth in fact did not make a difference to my defense strategy, other than to put me on notice as to when I might be suborning perjury. Because the mission of the defense attorney was to defeat the prosecution's case, what I knew actually happened was not important otherwise. What did matter was whether a version of the "facts" could be presented that would make a jury doubt the client's guilt.

Viewed in this way, my problem was not that my client's story was false, but that it was not credible, and could not be made to appear so by legal means. To win, we would therefore have to come up with a better theory than the alibi, avoiding perjury in the process. Thus, the defense would have to be made out without the client testifying, since it would be a crime for him to assert a fabricated exculpatory theory under oath.[14] This was not a serious problem, however, because it would not only be possible to prevail without the defendant's testimony, but it would probably be easier to do so. Not everyone is capable of lying successfully on the witness stand, and I did not have the sense that my client would be very good at it.

There were two possible defenses that could be fabricated. The first was mistaken identity. We could argue that the opportunity of the victim to observe the defendant at the time of the original encounter was limited, since it had occurred on a dark street. The woman could be made out to have been in great emotional distress during the incident.[15] Expert testimony would have to be adduced to show the hazards of eyewitness identification.[16] We could demonstrate that an unreliable identification procedure had been used at the precinct.[17] On the other hand, given that the complainant had spent considerable time with the assailant and had led the police back to the defendant's apartment, it seemed doubtful that the mistaken identification ploy would be successful.

The second alternative, consent, was clearly preferable. It would negate the charge of rape and undermine the robbery case.[18] To prevail, all we would have to do would be to raise a reasonable doubt as to whether he had compelled the woman to have sex with him. The doubt would be based on the scenario that the woman and the defendant met, and she voluntarily returned to his apartment. Her watch, the subject of the alleged robbery, was either left there by mistake or, perhaps better, was never there at all.

The consent defense could be made out entirely through cross-examination of the complainant, coupled with the argument to the jury about her lack of credibility on the issue of force. I could emphasize the parts of her story that sounded the most curious, such as the defendant's solicitude in taking his victim back to his apartment, and her waiting for her watch when she could have gone immediately to the nearby precinct that she went to later. I could point to her inability to identify the gun she claimed was used (although it was the one actually used), that the allegedly stolen watch was never found, there was no sign of physical violence, and no one heard screaming or any other signs of a struggle. I could also argue as my client had that even if he were reckless enough to rob and rape a woman across the street from his apartment, he would not be so foolish as to bring the victim there. I considered investigating the complainant's background, to take advantage of the right, unencumbered at the time, to impeach her on the basis of her prior unchastity.[19] I did not pursue this, however, because to me this device, although lawful, was fundamentally wrong. No doubt in that respect I lacked zeal, perhaps punishably so.

Even without assassinating this woman's character, however, I could argue that this was simply a case of a casual tryst that went awry. The defendant would not have to prove whether the complainant made the false charge to account for her whereabouts that evening, or to explain what happened to her missing watch. If the jury had reason to doubt the complainant's charges it would be bound to acquit the defendant.

How all of this would have played out at trial cannot be known. Predictably, the case dragged on so long that the prosecutor was forced to offer the unrefusable plea of possession of a gun.[20] As I look back, however, I wonder how I could justify doing what I was planning to do had the case been tried. I was prepared to stand before the jury posing as an officer of the court in search of the truth, while trying to fool the jurors into believing a wholly fabricated story, i.e., that the woman had consented, when in fact she had been forced at gunpoint to have sex with the defendant. I was also prepared to demand an acquittal because the state had not met its burden of proof when, if it had not, it would have been because I made the truth look like a lie. If there is any redeeming social value in permitting an attorney to do such things, I frankly cannot discern it. . . .

III. CAN LAWYERS "KNOW" THE TRUTH?

A. "The Adversary System" Excuse[21]
A principle argument in favor of the propriety of asserting a "false" defense is that there is, for the lawyer, no such thing. The "truth," insofar as it is relevant to the lawyer, is what the trier of the fact determines it to be.[22] The role of the lawyer in the adversary system is not to interpose his or her own belief about what the facts are.[23] Instead, the truth will emerge through a dialectical process, in which the vigorous advocacy of thesis and antithesis will equip the neutral arbiter to synthesize the data and reach a conclusion. . . .

. . . Suppose, for example, that I had interviewed the neighbor into whose apartment the defendant had gone following the rape—and who was unknown to the police. Suppose that he had told me that at the time of the incident he heard screams, and the sound of a struggle, and that my client had made incriminating remarks to him about what had occurred. It may be that there are reasons of policy that permit me to conceal these facts from the prosecution. It is ludicrous to assert, however, that because I can conceal them I do not know them. It is also ludicrous to suggest that if in addition I use my advocacy skills—and rights—to advance the thesis that there were no witnesses to the crime, I have engaged in a truth finding process.[24]

The argument that the attorney cannot know the truth until a court decides it fails. Either it is sophistry, designed to simplify the moral life of the attorney,[25] or it rests on a confusion between "factual truth" and "legal truth." The former relates to historical fact. The latter relates to the principle that a fact cannot be acted upon by the legal system until it is proven in accordance with legal rules. Plainly one can know the factual truth, for example, that one's client forced a woman to have sex with him, without or before knowing the legal truth that he is punishable for the crime of rape. The question is not whether an attorney can know the truth, but what standards should be applied in determining what the truth is. . . .

IV. DOES THE TRUTH MATTER? APPRAISING THE DIFFERENT MISSION

We confront at last the "Different Mission" argument we set out initially to examine. It is that the defense attorney has a broader function than protecting the innocent against wrongful conviction. Equally important is the task of protecting the factually guilty individual against overreaching by the state. The defense attorney may well be able to know the truth, but can be indifferent to it because it is the state's case, not the client's with which he or she is concerned. Professor Freedman puts it this way:

> The point . . . is not that the lawyer cannot know the truth, or that the lawyer refuses to recognize the truth, but rather that the lawyer is told: "You, personally, may very well know the truth, but your personal knowledge is irrelevant. In your capacity as an advocate (and, if you will, as an officer of the court) you are forbidden to act upon your personal knowledge of the truth,

as you might want to do as a private person, because the adversary system could not function properly if lawyers did so."

The adversary system must function because it is our basic protection against governmental overreaching. The danger of such overreaching is so great, moreover, that we must allow the defense attorney broad latitude in disrupting that case, even by presenting a spurious defense.

Two principal arguments have been advanced to explain why the needs of the adversary system permit the attorney to assert a defense not founded upon the truth. The first is that a false defense may have to be asserted to protect the defendant's right in a particular case right to have a defense at all. The second argument is that it may be necessary to subvert the truth in a particular case as a way of demonstrating the supremacy of the autonomous individual in the face of the powerful forces of organized society.

A. Subverting the Truth to Protect the Defendant's Right to a Defense

The most commonly offered justification for a right to undermine a truthful case is that if there were no such right, the guilty defendant would effectively be deprived of a defense. All defendants, it is asserted, are entitled to have the state prove the case against them, whether they are factually innocent or guilty. If the spurious defense were not allowed it would be impossible to represent persons who had confessed their guilt to their lawyers, or who, in accordance with rules of the sort I advanced in the last section, were "found" guilty by them. The trial, if there were one at all, would not be an occasion to test the government's case, but a kind of elaborate plea of guilty. I believe that this argument fails for two reasons: first, because it proves too much, and second, because it is based on an erroneous assumption as to what the defendant's rights are.

If it were true that a false defense must be allowed to assure that the guilty defendant has a defense, it would seem to follow that presently established constraints on the defense attorney representing the guilty person, let alone an innocent person against whom the state had incriminating evidence, should be removed. An exception to the criminal laws prohibiting the deliberate introduction of false evidence would have to be adopted. Some have argued that a criminal defendant has a right to commit perjury, and that the defense attorney has a concomitant duty not to interfere with such testimony, or for that matter with even more extraordinary means of prevailing at trial.

The notion of a right to commit perjury, however, has been forcefully rejected by the courts[26] and by the organized bar, albeit less forcefully.[27] I suggest, however, that it cannot logically be rejected by those who espouse the Different Mission theory in defense of subverting the truth. If the right to mount a defense is paramount, and if the only conceivable defense which the guilty defendant can mount involves the defendant, or his or her witnesses committing perjury, and the defense attorney arguing that that perjury is true, then it follows that the restraints of the penal law should not be conceded to be applicable.[28] . . .

The extravagant notion of the right to put on a defense is the second fallacy in the argument supporting a right to assert a false defense. Again, a moment's reflection on prevailing penal law limitations on advocacy will demonstrate that the defendant is not entitled to gain an acquittal by any available means.[29] Unless we abandon completely the notion that verdicts should be based upon the truth, we must accept the fact that there may simply be no version of the facts favorable to the defense worthy of assertion in a court. In such cases, the role of the defense attorney should be limited to assuring that the state adduces sufficient legally competent evidence to sustain its burden of proof. . . .

Subverting the Truth to Preserve Individual Autonomy Against Encroachment by the State

The second prong of the "different mission" theory is that the truth must be sacrificed in individual cases as a kind of symbolic act designed to reaffirm our belief in the supremacy of the individual. This theory in turn is argued in several different ways.

1. The false defense may be necessary to preserve the individual's access to the legal system.

This argument is based on the proposition that because the legal system is so complex, meaningful access requires representation by an attorney. An attorney cannot perform his or her function unless the client provides the facts. The client will not do that if the facts will be used against the client, as, in this context, by not providing an available false defense. Thus it is necessary to permit the attorney to conceal harmful information obtained from the client and to act as if it did not exist.

As I have argued elsewhere, the importance of confidentiality to the performance of the lawyer's role has been greatly overstated. Even conceding its value, it does not seem to me that permitting the attorney to achieve the client's ends by subverting the truth advances the cause of individual autonomy. The legitimate concern of those who advance the autonomy argument is that the government must be prevented from interfering wrongfully or unnecessarily with individual freedom, not that there should be no interference with individual liberty at all. Here we are positing that the government has behaved reasonably, and the lawyer knows it. In my view, permitting such a case to be undermined by false evidence glorifies winning, but has very little to do with assuring justice.[30]

2. A false defense may be necessary to preserve the rigorous process by which guilt is determined.

Those taking this view see the criminal process not as a truth-seeking one, but a "screening system" designed to assure the utmost certainty before the criminal sanction is imposed. Only by permitting the defense attorney to use all of the tools which we have described here can we be certain that the prosecution will be put to its proof in all cases. The argument seems to be that if the prosecutor knows that the defense attorney will attempt to demolish the government's case, the prosecutor will in a sense be kept on his or her toes, and will seek the strongest evidence possible.[31]

This position is difficult to understand. In the situation under discussion here the prosecution has presented the strongest case possible, i.e., the truthful testimony of the victim of a crime. In any case, it is one thing to attack a weak government case by pointing out its weakness. It is another to attack a strong government case by confusing the jury with falsehoods. Finally, as a proponent

of this "screening theory" concedes, there may be a danger that if the prosecutor sees that the truth alone is inadequate, he or she may be inspired to embellish it. That, of course, is not likely to make the screening mechanism work better.

For others, the desirability of prevailing against the state seems to be seen not as a means to assure that the prosecution will strive for high standards of proof, but as a positive good in its own right. The goal, as Professor Schwartz has put it, is to prevent the "behemoth" state from becoming a "juggernaut."[32] Schwartz states that "[c]ross-examination to give the impression that [witnesses] are telling falsehoods may be justified as a way of keeping the state from overreaching,"[33] but we are not told what precise danger this will avert, or how it will do so. I cannot discern these, either, unless one takes the view that the exercise of a particular state power is inherently wrong, justifying resistance by any means. Otherwise, it would seem sufficient to insure that the defendant had a right to make a good faith challenge to the state's allegations.

V. ACCOMPLISHING THE DEFENSE ATTORNEY'S DIFFERENT MISSION—MORALLY

I propose a system in which the defense attorney would operate not with the right to assert defenses known to be untrue, but under the following rule:

It shall be improper for an attorney who knows beyond a reasonable doubt the truth of a fact established in the state's case to attempt to refute that fact through the introduction of evidence, impeachment of evidence, or argument.

In the face of this rule, the attorney who knew there were no facts to contest would be limited to the "monitoring" role. Assuming that a defendant in my client's situation wanted to assert his right to contest the evidence against him, the attorney would work to assure that all of the elements of the crime were proven beyond a reasonable doubt, on the basis of competent and admissible evidence. This would include enforcing the defendant's rights to have privileged or illegally obtained evidence excluded: The goal sought here is not the elimination of all rules that result in the suppression of truth, but only those not supported by sound policy. It would also be appropriate for the attorney to argue to the jury that the available evidence is not sufficient to sustain the burden of proof. It would not, however, be proper for the attorney to use any of the presently available devices to refute testimony known to be truthful. I wish to make clear, however, that this rule would not prevent the attorney from challenging *inaccurate* testimony, even though the attorney knew that the defendant was guilty. Again, the truth-seeking goal is not applicable when a valid policy reason exists for ignoring it. Forcing the state to prove its case is such a reason.[34]

Applying these principles to my rape case, I would engage fully in the process of testing the admissibility of the state's evidence, moving to suppress testimony concerning the suggestive "show-up" identification at the precinct, and the gun found in the defendant's apartment after a warrantless search, should the state attempt to offer either piece of evidence. At the trial, I would be present to assure that the complainant testified in accordance with the rules of evidence.

Assuming that she testified at trial as she had at the preliminary hearing, however, I would not cross-examine her, because I would have no good faith basis for impeaching either her testimony or her character, since I "knew" that she was providing an accurate account of what had occurred.[35] Nor would I put on a defense case. I would limit my representation at that stage to putting forth the strongest argument I could that the facts presented by the state did not sustain its burden. In these ways, the defendant would receive the services of an attorney in subjecting the state's case to the final stage of the screening process provided by the system to insure against unjust convictions. That, however, would be all that the defense attorney could do. . . .

VI. CONCLUSION

. . . If this proposal seems radical, consider that it is essentially an adaptation of what today is the principal function of the defense attorney in every criminal justice system of significance in this nation. That function is not to create defenses out of whole cloth to present to juries, but to guide the defendant through a process that will usually end in a guilty plea. It will so end, at least when competent counsel are involved, very frequently because the defense attorney has concluded after thorough analysis that there is no answer to the state's case. If that role can be played in out of court resolution of the matter there seems to be no reason why it cannot be played in court, when the defendant insists upon his right to a trial. The important point is that the right to a trial does not embody the right to present to the tribunal any evidence at all, no matter how fictitious it is.

NOTES

1. *Nix v. Whiteside*, 106 S. Ct. 988 (1986) (criminal defendant not denied effective assistance of counsel when attorney refused to allow him to present perjured testimony); . . .

2. Standard 4-7.6 (2d ed. 1980 & Supp. 1986). The ABA apparently has had a complete reversal in its view of this matter. *See* ABA STANDARDS RELATING TO THE ADMINISTRATION OF CRIMINAL JUSTICE, Compilation, at 132 (1974). Standard 4-7.6 states that the lawyer "should not misuse the power of cross-examination or impeachment by employing it to discredit or undermine a witness if he knows the witness is testifying truthfully."

3. MODEL CODE DR 7-101(A)(1) and EC 7-1. DR 7-102 appears on its face to be to the contrary, prohibiting lawyers from, *inter alia*, conducting a defense merely to harass another (subd. (1)); knowingly using false evidence (subd. (3)); making a false statement of fact (subd. (5)); creating or preserving false evidence (subd. (6)); or assisting the client in fraudulent conduct (subd. (7)). None of the noncriminal acts with which this article is concerned, however, have, to the author's knowledge, been cited by the bar as coming within the proscription of DR 7-102.

A similar conclusion can be reached with respect to the *Model Rules*. Rule 3.3 is an adaptation of DR 7-102, *see* rule 3.3, model code comparison. Rule 3.1 suggests that the drafters approved of the precise conduct under discussion here, at least for criminal lawyers. The rule prohibits assertion or controversion of an issue at trial unless there is a reasonable basis for doing so, except in criminal cases. The criminal case exception is based upon the drafter's conclusion, mistaken in my view, that the constitutional requirement that the state shoulder the burden of proof requires that the defense attorney be permitted to "put the prosecution to its proof even if there is no 'reasonable basis' for the defense." MODEL RULES Rule 3.1 model code comparison.

4. 388 U.S. 218, 250 (1967) (White, J., joined by Harlan and Stewart, J.J., dissenting in part and concurring in part).

5. *Id.* at 236–37.

6. *Id.* at 256–58 (footnotes omitted).

7. She also said that he told her that he was a musician. The significance of this remark will appear shortly.

8. The woman was not able to make a positive identification of the gun as the weapon used in the incident.

9. A student working on the case with me photographed the complainant on the street. My client stated that he could not identify her.

10. The woman had indicated that her assailant opened the door with a key. There was no evidence of a forced entry.

11. *Cf. Stovall v. Denno*, 338 U.S. 293 (1967) (identification in which murder suspect shown alone to and positively identified by bedridden, hospitalized victim not unnecessarily suggestive and therefore did not deny defendant due process).

12. The dilemma faced by the lawyer is whether, in explaining to the client the legal implications of conduct, he or she is shaping the client's version of the facts. The issue was put dramatically in R. TRAVER, ANATOMY OF A MURDER (1958), in which the attorney explained the facts needed to establish an insanity defense to an apparently normal person accused of murder. *Id.* at 44–47. Whether I was quite as blatant I frankly cannot remember, but it is clear that I did more than simply listen to what the client said. I explained how one would make out an alibi defense, and I made sure that he understood both that consent was a defense to rape, and that corroboration was necessary to support a rape conviction.

13. *See* Mitchell, *The Ethics of the Criminal Defense Attorney—New Answers to Old Questions*, 32 STAN L. REV. 293 n. 12 (1980) (author properly analogizes lawyer's preference not to know of the client's guilt to the doctrine of "conscious avoidance," which constitutes "knowledge" under criminal law).

14. The notion that the defendant in a criminal case has a right to commit perjury was finally put to rest in *Nix v. Whiteside*, 106 S. Ct. 988 (1986) (criminal defendant not denied effective assistance of counsel when attorney refused to allow him to present perjured testimony).

15. This would be one of those safe areas in cross-examination, where the witness was damned no matter what she answered. If she testified that she was distressed, it would make my point that she was making an unreliable identification; if she testified that she was calm, no one would believe her. Perhaps this is why cross-examination has been touted as "beyond any doubt the greatest legal engine ever invented for the discovery of truth." 5 J. WIGMORE, EVIDENCE § 1367 (J. Chadbourn rev. ed. 1974). Another commentator makes similar claims for his art, and while he acknowledges in passing that witnesses might tell the truth, he at no point suggests what the cross-examiner should do when faced with such a situation. F. WELLMAN, THE ART OF CROSS-EXAMINATION 7 (4th ed. 1936). The cross-examiner's world, rather, seems to be divided into two types of witnesses: those whose testimony is harmless and those whose testimony must be destroyed on pain of abandoning "all hope for a jury verdict." *Id.* at 9.

16. On the dangers of misidentification, *see, e.g.*, *United States v. Wade*, 388 U.S. 218 (1967). The use of experts to explain the misidentification problem to the jury is well established. *See generally* E. LOFTUS, EYEWITNESS TESTIMONY 191–203 (1979) (discussing ways expert testimony on eye witness testimony can be used and problems arising from its use).

17. *See Watkins v. Sowders*, 499 U.S. 341 (1981) (identification problems properly attacked during cross-examination at trial; no per se rule compelling judicial determination outside presence of jury concerning admissibility of identification evidence).

18. Consent is a defense to a charge of rape. *E.g.*, N.Y. PENAL LAW § 130.05 (McKinney 1975 & Supp. 1987). While consent is not a defense to a robbery charge, N.Y. PENAL LAW § 160.00–15 (McKinney 1975 & Supp. 1987), if the complainant could be made out to be a liar about the rape, there was a good chance that the jury would not believe her about the stolen watch either.

19. When this case arose it was common practice to impeach the complainant in rape cases by eliciting details of her prior sexual activities. Subsequently the rules of evidence were amended to require a specific showing of relevance to the facts of the case. N.Y. CRIM. PROC. LAW § 60.42 (McKinney 1981 & Supp. 1987).

20. The client, who had spent time in jail awaiting trial, was not given an additional prison sentence.

21. The phrase is the title of David Luban's essay, *The Adversary System Excuse*, in THE GOOD LAWYER: LAWYERS' ROLES AND LAWYERS' ETHICS 83 (D. Luban ed. 1983).

22. *See* M. FRANKEL, PARTISAN JUSTICE, *supra* note 43, at 24. Judge Frankel, who is critical of this theory, quotes the famous answer of Samuel Johnson to the question how he can represent a bad cause: "Sir, you do not know it to be good or bad till the judge determines it." *Id.* (quoting J. BOSWELL, THE LIFE OF SAMUEL JOHNSON 366 (1925)).

23. MODEL CODE DR 7-106©(4) provides in part that a lawyer shall not "[a]ssert his personal opinion as to the justness of a cause, as to the credibility of a witness . . . or as to the guilt or innocence of an accused. . . ."

24. My "proof" that there were no witnesses to the crime would come in the form of an "accrediting" cross-examination of the complainant and/or a police officer who testified. I could inquire of both concerning whether they saw or otherwise became aware of the presence of any witnesses, and then argue to the jury that their negative answers established that there were none.

25. As all lawyers who are honest with themselves know, occasions arise when doubts about a client turn into suspicion and then moral certainty that a client is lying. Although his professional role may require a lawyer to take a detached attitude of unbelief, the law of lawyering does not permit a lawyer to escape all accountability by suspending his intelligence and common sense. A lawyer may try to persuade himself that he is not absolutely sure whether his client is committing perjury. . . . But all authorities agree . . . that there comes a point when only brute rationalization, moral irresponsibility, and pure sophistry can support the contention that the lawyer does not "know" what the situation is.

G. HAZARD & W. HODES, THE LAW OF LAWYERING: A HANDBOOK ON THE MODEL RULES OF PROFESSIONAL CONDUCT 343 (1985) (citing M. FREEDMAN, *supra* note 6, at 52–55, 71–76 (1975)).

26. *Nix v. Whiteside*, 106 S. Ct. 988 (1986) (criminal defendant not denied effective assistance of counsel when attorney refused to permit him to present perjured testimony).

27. The *Model Code* prohibits the knowing introduction of perjured testimony or false evidence. MODEL CODE DR 7-102(A)(4). The *Model Code* essentially eliminates, however, the duty of the attorney to disclose the client's attempt to commit these crimes, by prohibiting such disclosure if it would reveal a protected privileged communication. MODEL CODE DR 7-102(B)(1). The *Model Rules*, however, prohibit the introduction of false testimony, and appear to modify the restriction on disclosure of client misconduct in this area. The *Model Rules* require the attorney to disclose to the court that false evidence has been introduced. MODEL RULES Rule 3.3. The disclosure requirement ends, however, if the criminal conduct of the client is not discovered until after the proceeding has ended.

28. For example, if in my rape case there were incontrovertible evidence that force had been used on the complainant, the consent defense would have been impossible. I would then have had to revert to the mistaken identification defense. Given the strength of the complainant's identification testimony, the defendant's or his aunt's perjurious testimony might have been necessary to provide a defense at all.

29. In addition to the laws against perjury, there are laws, for example, against tampering with witnesses, 18 U.S.C. § § 1512–14 (1982 & Supp. 1985) and bribery, 18 U.S.C. § 201 (1982).

30. It is ironic that some who have supported the right to put on a false defense do so as part of the argument that defending the guilty teaches a lesson to the defendant, especially the indigent defendant, that the system is fair. . . . Again, the problem is the failure to distinguish between the

right to a defense and the right to a false defense. Commenting on the criminal justice system in general, Jonathan Casper has observed that it "not only fails to teach [defendants] moral lessons, but reinforces the idea that the system has no moral content." Casper, *Did You Have A Lawyer When You Went to Court? No, I Had A Public Defender,* 1 YALE REV. L. & SOC. ACTION 4, 9 (1971). The same could very well be said of a method of representation in which the defendant sees the lawyer, an official of the system, attempting to win by engaging in conduct similar to that which may have brought the defendant to court.

31. The cross-examination of the "truthful" witness is justified . . . [because] [w]eaknesses in the witness' testimony brought out on cross-examination will make the prosecution understand the range in "quality" of evidence for subsequent cases so that in the future he or she will recognize and seek the best evidence possible.

Mitchell, *supra* note 34, at 312 n.67.

32. Schwartz, *The Zeal of the Civil Advocate,* 1983 AM. B. FOUND. RES. J. 543, 554.

33. *Id.*

34. My colleague Stephen Gillers, for whose thoughtful criticism of my view I am indebted, called my attention to this illustrative case, ruled on by the Michigan State Bar Committee on Professional and Judicial Ethics:

A defendant is charged with armed robbery. The victim testifies that the defendant robbed him at 1:00 p.m. The defendant has confessed to his lawyer. In fact, the robbery took place at 1:30 p.m. The victim is in error about the time. The defendant has a solid and truthful alibi witness who will testify that the defendant was with the witness at 1:00 p.m.

The question presented was whether the defense could call the alibi witness. The Bar Committee answered affirmatively. Michigan State Bar Committee of Professional and Judicial Ethics Op. CI-1164, Jan. 23, 1987, *reported in* 3 LAWYER'S MANUAL ON PROFESSIONAL CONDUCT (ABA/BNA) No. 3, at 44 (March 4, 1987). I would agree. The state's proof of the time of the crime was incorrect, and therefore subject to impeachment. I would not, however, permit the defense to offer evidence that the crime occurred at 1:00 p.m. if the victim correctly testified that it occurred at 1:30 p.m.

35. I recently made an informal presentation of this position to a group of my colleagues, who beseiged me with hypotheticals, the most provocative of which were these: (A) A witness not wearing her glasses, identifies my client as having been at a certain place. If my client were in fact at that place, could I cross-examine the witness on the grounds that she was not wearing her glasses? The answer is yes: The witness' ability to perceive affects the quality of the state's proof, and the fact that she happened to be correct is irrelevant. (B) In the same situation, except here I knew that the witness was wearing her glasses. Could I cross-examine the witness in an effort to show that she was not? The answer is no: The state had adduced reliable evidence, and that is all that it was required to do.

I was also asked whether I would apply the same truth based rule and refuse, in the situation described in (B), to impeach the witness if I knew that my client were innocent. My first response was something of a dodge: If I knew that, it was difficult for me to see why I would have to impeach this witness. Ultimately (albeit tentatively) I would conclude that it was too dangerous to adopt the notion that even these ends justified subverting the truth, and I would not cross-examine on that point.

NO

John B. Mitchell

REASONABLE DOUBTS ARE WHERE YOU FIND THEM: A RESPONSE TO PROFESSOR SUBIN'S POSITION ON THE CRIMINAL LAWYER'S "DIFFERENT MISSION"

I. INTRODUCTION

In *A Criminal Lawyer's "Different Mission": Reflections on the "Right" to Present a False Case*,[1] Professor Harry I. Subin attempts to draw what he considers to be the line between attorney as advocate, and attorney as officer of the court. Specifically, he "attempts to define the limits on the methods a lawyer should be willing to use when his client's goals are inconsistent with truth."[2] This is no peripheral theme in professional responsibility. Quite the contrary, Professor Subin has chosen a difficult issue which touches upon the very nature of our criminal justice system, the role of the attorney in that system, the relationship of the individual to the state, and the Constitution. Further, Professor Subin takes a tough and controversial stand on this issue and, although I disagree with him, I respect his position. . . .

II. PROFESSOR SUBIN'S ASSUMPTIONS

Professor Subin rests his entire analysis on two basic premises: (1) the principle goal of the criminal justice system is "truth"; and (2) it is contrary to the goal of "truth" to permit a criminal defense attorney to put on a "false defense." In Subin's terms, a false defense is an attempt to "convince the judge or jury that facts established by the state and known to the attorney to be true are not true, or that the facts known to the attorney to be false are true." Such a defense is put on by: " . . . (1) cross-examination of truthful government witnesses to undermine their testimony or their credibility; (2) direct presentation of testimony, not in itself false, but used to discredit the

From John B. Mitchell, "Reasonable Doubts Are Where You Find Them: A Response to Professor Subin's Position on the Criminal Lawyer's 'Different Mission,' " *Georgetown Journal of Legal Ethics*, vol. 1 (1987), pp. 339–361. Copyright © 1987 by John B. Mitchell. Reprinted by permission. Some notes omitted.

truthful evidence adduced by the government, or to accredit a false theory; and, (3) argument to the jury based on any of these acts." I take exception to both of these premises, as set out below.[3]

The Principal Concern of the Criminal Justice System Is Not "Truth"

The idea that the focus of the criminal justice system is not "truth" may initially sound shocking. I have valued truth throughout my life and do not condone lying in our legal system. But the job of our criminal justice system is simply other than determining "truth." . . .

A system focused on truth would first collect all information relevant to the inquiry. In our system, the defendant is generally the best source of information in the dispute, but he is not available unless he so chooses. The police may not question him. He may not be called to the stand with his own lawyer beside him and with a judge controlling questioning under the rules of evidence. The prosecutor may not even comment to the jury about the defendant's failure to testify, even though fair inferences may be drawn from the refusal to respond to serious accusations.

A system focused on truth would have the factfinder look at all the information and then decide what it believed had occurred. In our system, the inquiry is dramatically skewed against finding guilt. "Beyond a reasonable doubt" expresses the deep cultural value that "it is better to let ten guilty men go than convict one innocent man." It is a system where, after rendering a verdict of not guilty, jurors routinely approach defense counsel and say, "I thought your guy was guilty, but that prosecutor did not prove it to me beyond a reasonable

doubt." What I have just described is not a "truth system" in any sense in which one could reasonably understand that term.[4] Truth may play a role, but it is not a dominant role; there is something else afoot.[5] The criminal defense attorney does not have a "different mission";[6] the system itself has a "different mission." . . .

Put directly, the criminal justice system protects the individual from the police power of the executive branch of government. Between the individual citizen and the enormous governmental power residing in the executive stands a panel of that individual's peers—a jury. Through them, the executive must pass. Only if it proves its case "beyond a reasonable doubt," thereby establishing legal guilt, may the executive then legitimately intrude into the individual citizen's life. Thus, "factual" guilt or innocence, or what Professor Subin would call "truth," is not the principle issue in the system. Our concern is with the legitimate use of the prosecutor's power as embodied in the concept of "legal guilt." . . .

B. A Defense Attorney Acting in a Manner Meeting with Subin's Disapproval Is Not Putting on a "False Defense"

When placed in the "reasonable doubt" context, Professor Subin's implicit distinction between "true" and "false" defenses misportrays both how a defense attorney may actually function in a case, and the very nature of evidence in that case. His categories are too imprecise to capture the subtle middle ground of a pure reasonable doubt defense, in which counsel presents the jury with alternative possibilities that counsel knows are false, without asserting the truth of those alternatives.

For example, imagine I am defending a young woman accused of shoplifting a star one places on top of Christmas trees. I interview the store manager and find that he stopped my client when he saw her walk straight through the store, star in hand, and out the door. When he stopped her and asked why she had taken the star without paying, she made no reply and burst into tears. He was then about to take her inside to the security office when an employee called out, "There's a fire!" The manager rushed inside and dealt with a small blaze in the camera section. Five minutes later he came out to find my client sitting where he had left her. He then took her back to the security room and asked if she would be willing to empty her pockets so that he could see if she had taken anything else. Without a word, she complied. She had a few items not belonging to the store and a ten-dollar bill. The star was priced at $1.79.

In an interview with my client, she admitted trying to steal the star: "It was so pretty, and would have looked so nice on the tree. I would have bought it, but I also wanted to make a special Christmas dinner for Mama and didn't have enough money to do both. I've been saving for that dinner and I know it will make her so happy. But that star. . . . I could just see the look in Mama's eyes if she saw that lovely thing on our tree."

At trial, the manager tells the same story he told me, except he *leaves out* the part about her waiting during the fire and having a ten-dollar bill. If I bring out these two facts on cross-examination and argue for an acquittal based upon my client "accidentally" walking out of the store with the star, surely Professor Subin will accuse me of raising a "false defense." I have brought out testimony,

not itself false, to accredit a false theory and have argued to the jury based on this act. But I am not really arguing a false theory in Professor Subin's sense.

My defense is not that the defendant accidentally walked out, but rather that the prosecution cannot prove the element of intent to permanently deprive beyond a reasonable doubt. Through this theory, I am raising "doubt" in the prosecution's case, and therefore questioning the legitimacy of the government's lawsuit for control over the defendant. In my effort to carry out this legal theory, I will *not assert* that facts known by me to be true are false or those known to be false are true. As a defense attorney, I do not have to prove what *in fact* happened. That is an advantage in the process I would not willingly give up. Under our constitutional system, I do not need to try to convince the factfinder about the truth of any factual propositions. I need only try to convince the factfinder that the prosecution has not met its burden. Again, I will not argue that particular facts are true or false. Thus, in this case I will not claim that my client walked out of the store with innocent intent (a fact which I know is false); rather, I will argue:

The prosecution claims my client stole an ornament for a Christmas tree. The prosecution further claims that when my client walked out of that store she intended to keep it without paying. Now, maybe she did. None of us were there. On the other hand, she had $10.00 in her pocket, which was plenty of money with which to pay for the ornament without the risk of getting caught stealing. Also, she didn't try to conceal what she was doing. She walked right out of the store holding it in her hand. Most of us have come close to innocently doing the same thing. So, maybe she didn't. But then she cried the minute she was stopped. She might have been feeling guilty. So, maybe she did. On the other hand, she might just have been scared when she realized what had happened. After all, she didn't run away when she was left alone even though she knew the manager was going to be occupied with the fire inside. So, maybe she didn't. The point is that, looking at all the evidence, you're left with "maybe she intended to steal, maybe she didn't." But, you knew that before the first witness was even sworn. The prosecution has the burden, and he simply can't carry any burden let alone "beyond a reasonable doubt" with a maybe she did, maybe she didn't case. . . .

Is this a "false defense" for Professor Subin? Admittedly, I am trying to raise a doubt by persuading the jury to appreciate "possibilities" other than my client's guilt. Perhaps Professor Subin would say it is "false" because I know the possibilities are untrue. But if that is so, Professor Subin will have taken a leap from defining "false defense" as the assertion that true things are false and false things are true, for I am doing neither of those things here. The fact that one cannot know how Subin would reach this "pure" reasonable doubt case only reinforces my initial statement that Professor Subin's categories are imprecise.

Another perspective from which to look at the function of a defense attorney involves understanding that function in the context of the nature of evidence at trial. Professor Subin speaks of facts and the impropriety of trying to make "true facts" look false and "false facts" look true. But in a trial there are no such things as facts. There is only information, lack of information, and chains of inferences therefrom. In the courtroom there

will be no crime, no store, no young girl with a star in her hand. All there will be is a collection of witnesses who are strangers to the jury, giving information which may include physical evidence and documents. For example, most people would acknowledge the existence of eyewitness identifications; however, in an evidentiary sense they do not exist. Rather, a particular person with particular perceptual abilities and motives and biases will recount an observation made under particular circumstances and utter particular words on the witness stand (e.g., "That's the man"). From this mass of information, the prosecution will argue, in story form, in favor of the inference that the defendant is their man (e.g., "The victim was on her way home, when . . ."). The defense will not then argue that the defendant is the wrong man in a *factual sense*, but instead will attack the persuasiveness of the criminal inference and resulting story (e.g., "The sun was in the witness' eyes; she was on drugs").

In our shoplifting example, the prosecution will elicit that the defendant burst into tears when stopped by the manager. From this information will run a chain of inferences: defendant burst into tears, people without a guilty conscience would explain their innocence, not cry; defendant has a guilty conscience; her guilty conscience is likely motivated by having committed a theft. Conversely, if the defense brings out that the manager was shaking a lead pipe in his hand when he stopped the defendant, defense counsel is *not asserting* that defendant did not have a guilty conscience when stopped. Counsel is merely *weakening* the persuasiveness of the prosecution's inference by raising the "possibility" that she was crying not from guilt, but from fear. By raising such "possibilities," the defense is making arguments against the ability of the prosecution's inferences to meet their burden of "beyond a reasonable doubt." The defense is not arguing what are true or false facts (i.e., that the tears were from fear as opposed to guilt). Whatever Professor Subin cares to call it, this commentary on the prosecution's case, complete with raising possibilities which weaken the persuasiveness of central inferences in that case, is in no ethical sense a "false case." "False case" is plainly a misnomer. In a system where factual guilt is not at issue, Professor Subin's "falsehoods" are, in fact, "reasonable doubts."

C. Even If Criminal Defense Attorneys Do Raise a "False Defense," the Role of the Defense Attorney in the Criminal Justice System Permits Such a Defense

Professor Subin does not seek to eliminate all impediments to truth, just those based upon sound policy. In failing to appreciate fully the institutional role of the defense attorney, he glosses over a major countervailing policy: even if the attorney is putting forth what Subin would term "false defense," this defense is the side effect, not the goal or function of the defense attorney's role in the criminal justice system.

Subin apparently believes that the principal position he must overcome from his opponents who seek leeway with the "truth" is that such leeway is necessary to protect the adversary system, and the adversary system, in turn, is necessary to protect the factually guilty from "overreaching by the state."[7] My position, however, does not rest on these ideas. Though the adversary system serves to protect the factually guilty from state overreaching, my position is principally based upon the criminal justice system—a system with rationales different from the general adversary system, including the protection of the factually innocent.[8]

Our criminal justice system is more appropriately defined as a screening system than as a truth-seeking one.[9] The ultimate objective of this screening system is to determine who are the proper subjects of criminal sanction. The process goes on continually. Someone notices a window which looks pried open or a suspicious-looking stranger. Neighbor talks to neighbor, and information filters to the police. The police comb the streets gathering information, focusing upon those whose behavior warrants special attention. Those selected by the police for special attention are then placed in the hands of prosecutors, courts, and juries who constantly sift through this "residue" to make final determinations about who is to be subjected to criminal sanction.

The criminal justice system is itself composed of a series of "screens," of which trial is but one. These screens help keep innocents out of the process and, at the same time, limit the intrusion of the state into people's lives. Each of these screens functions to protect the values of human dignity and autonomy, while enforcing our criminal laws. Further, to ensure that the intrusion of the state into the individual's life will be halted at the soonest possible juncture, our system provides a separate screen at each of the several stages of the criminal process. At any screen, the individual may be taken out of the criminal process and returned to society with as little disruption as possible.

By pushing hard in every case (whether the client is factually guilty or not) and thereby raising "reasonable doubts" in the prosecution's case whenever possible, the defense attorney helps "make the screens work" and thus protects the interests of the factually innocent.[10]. . .

III. PROFESSOR SUBIN'S APPROACH

. . . My analysis in this section will focus upon Professor Subin's basic approach to "defin[ing] the limits on the methods a lawyer should be willing to use when his or her client's goals are inconsistent with the truth"; i.e., distinguishing between the role of what Subin calls a "monitor" and the more familiar role of "advocate." . . .

To illustrate, imagine I am representing a defendant accused of robbery. I have seen the victim at a preliminary hearing, and based upon the circumstances of the identification and my overall impression of the witness, I am certain that he is truthful and accurate. My client has confessed his factual guilt. And therefore I "know" (in Professor Subin's sense) beyond a reasonable doubt that my client has been accurately identified.

In his direct examination, the victim states, "The defendant had this big, silvery automatic pistol right up near my face the whole time he was asking for money." In accordance with Professor Subin's view that defense counsel can "persuade the jury that there are legitimate reasons to doubt the state's evidence," may I raise the general vagaries of eyewitness identification?

All of us have had some stranger come up to us, call us by an unfamiliar name, and indicate they thought we were someone they knew. We have been with a friend who points to someone a few tables over exclaiming, "Isn't she an exact double of Sue Smith? Could be her twin," and we think to ourselves that other than the hair color, there is no resemblance at all.

Perhaps Subin would say I cannot make the misidentification argument. He might argue that the "legitimacy" of reasons to doubt the state's evidence is not to be judged from the perspective of a reasonable juror hearing the prosecution's evidence but from my subjective knowledge. Since I "know" that there was no difficulty with the identification, I cannot put forward a "legitimate" reason to doubt. If this is Professor Subin's meaning, I, as monitor, am left with the following closing argument: "Ladies and gentlemen, thank you for your attention to this case. Remember, the prosecution must prove each element beyond a reasonable doubt. Thank you." The Constitution aside (and in my view this would be putting the Constitution aside), it is hard to imagine this is Subin's intended result.

"Legitimate reason" to doubt must refer to a reasonable juror's perception of the state's evidence, not to the defense attorney's private knowledge. Bringing out reasonable doubts in the state's evidence concerning the identification therefore must be legitimate, and yet this would seem to raise a "false defense" (i.e., mistaken identification). Presumably, Subin would permit this defense because of a greater policy than "truth," i.e., the right to have the state prove guilt beyond a reasonable doubt. If this is permissible in Subin's view, it is difficult to understand why it would not be permissible to call an expert on eyewitness identification to testify.

In the hypothetical case described above, I should also be permitted to bring specific evidence about the gun into my closing argument because it offers a "legitimate" reason to doubt the accuracy of the identification (e.g., "The eyewitness was not someone sitting calmly in a restaurant looking at someone else a few tables away. Here, the eyewitness had a gun in his face.") Of course, if I can bring the gun into my closing, I presumably can do it in a manner I believe most effective; for I don't believe Professor Subin's position is that you are permitted to do it, but not very well:

> And did he notice that gun? Was he staring at that big . . . silvery . . . automatic? Wouldn't you? Not knowing if this assailant was going to beat or kill you. Wouldn't your mind turn inward? Inward to that gun, to calming your fear of death, to not provoking this spectre who could end your life in a moment? Would you be thinking "Let me see. His eyes are hazel . . . I want to get a good look at him so I can identify him later"? Would you want to do anything to make that person with a big . . . silvery . . . automatic gun in your face think you could identify him? . . .

What then is Subin really saying? Subin could not mean by his reference to the "state's evidence" that I can use evidence of the gun to raise a reasonable doubt in aid of the "false defense" of misidentification if the information is elicited on *the state's direct examination*, but that I am not permitted to bring out the information through cross-examination or defense witnesses. He could not mean that information I thus actively elicit is not "legitimate" for raising doubts. Yet, the only mechanisms he lists

for putting on a "false defense" are defense cross-examination, defense witnesses, and arguments therefrom. If this distinction between information elicited by the prosecution and that elicited by the defense is really what he intends to divine the legitimate from the illegitimate, it is a strange structure upon which to rest a principle of ethical guidance, especially given the nature of the trial process. As a practical matter, this structure would allow conviction or acquittal to rest on such fortuitous circumstances as whether, when asked on direct examination if he saw a weapon in the hands of the robber, the witness in our hypothetical answered:

— "Yes."
— "Yes. Pointing at me."
— "Yes. Pointing at my face."
— "Yes. A big, silvery, automatic pointing at my face."

Much of cross-examination emphasizes points elicited in the direct examination (e.g., "Now, this gun was pointing at you?") and expands upon helpful points made during the direct (e.g., "You said on direct the gun was pointing at you. Where exactly was it pointing?"). If Professor Subin would not let me aid the "false defense" of mistaken identification by this type of cross-examination, then my client's chances for acquittal will vary with which of these responses happens to flow from the witness' mouth during direct examination on the day of trial.

Statements, however, do not just, "flow from" witnesses' mouths on direct examination. Witnesses are often coached regarding their testimony. That reality is at the core of my next point. If the content of the prosecution's direct examination limits the range of my ethical behavior, then my adversary controls my client's fate by deciding what to ask in the direct examination (e.g., "When I ask you in your direct examination about the gun, be certain you *do not* mention that it was directly pointed at you, and especially *do not* say it was pointed at your face."). Is this prosecutorial manipulation, in conjunction with the serendipity of answers proffered on the prosecution's direct examination, the basis for Professor Subin's ethical standards for criminal defense? If not, and if I may fully cross-examine in support of my "false defense" of misidentification, then it is difficult to see Professor Subin's point.

It is possible Subin was thinking about a situation where a defense attorney argues that the crime did not occur at all. For example, assume that when asked by the prosecution where he was going with a wallet full of money, the robbery victim's testimony is that he was going to get his wife a gift because she was angry at him for wasting his paycheck gambling the previous week. In closing, the defense argues an alternative explanation for the information the prosecution has presented, one based on the possibility that the victim had created the entire robbery story to cover up further gambling losses. While this would be a "false defense," there appears no real difference between a "false defense" that seeks acquittal by raising doubts that the defendant committed the crime (questioning identification evidence), which Professor Subin would seem to sanction, and one which raises doubts, as in this example, that the crime occurred at all. The former more closely tracks the prosecution's theory that there *was* a robbery, but this is a distinction of no apparent significance. In both examples, the defense counsel takes information in the

case and arranges it differently than the prosecution to present alternative "possibilities" which resonate with reasonable doubts. Both are equally "false" in Subin's sense. Once Subin allows the defense attorney to argue reasonable doubts in support of a "false" defense, the line between the permissible and the impermissible is blurred and is definable only in terms of the false dichotomy between evidence brought in by the prosecution and evidence elicited by the defense.

Another indication that Subin would not adhere to the "stark" definition of lawyer as monitor is that he would allow the defense to demonstrate the inaccuracy of information that may be harmful to its case. Imagine that the robbery victim in my hypothetical testifies that Bloogan's Department Store, directly across the street from where the nighttime robbery occurred, had all of its lights on at the time of the robbery. In fact, I find out in investigation that Bloogan's was closed for remodeling that evening. Subin would undoubtedly allow me to bring this out. What, after all, would a "truth" theory be if I were not permitted to confront "lies" and "misperceptions." If Professor Subin permits me to bring out this "inaccuracy" on cross-examination and/or through other witnesses, he must also allow me to use it in closing or my initial access to this information would be meaningless. In closing, my only real use for this information would be in support of my "false defense" of mistaken identification. The line between advocate and monitor is again blurred.

Another example of the unworkability of his distinction between advocate and monitor is reflected in the defense lawyer's use of inaccurate information brought out in the prosecution's case that is helpful to the defense. The victim of the robbery now testifies that the robbery took place at 10 p.m. My client has a strong alibi for 10 p.m. I "know," however, that the robbery actually took place at 10:30 p.m. May I put on my alibi in support of my "false defense," raising doubts that my client was the robber? Subin would say yes. In a similar set of circumstances Subin stated: "The state's proof of the time of the crime was incorrect, and therefore subject to impeachment." This, however, is not "impeachment." The probative value of the information is not being questioned. Quite the contrary, the incorrect information is being embraced as true. A prosecution witness has simply made a "mistake" and Professor Subin allows the defense attorney to take advantage of it, furthering a "false defense." Without some analysis tied to the rationales for the advocate-monitor distinction in the first place, the distinction seems to depend on ad hoc judgments. . . .

A. A Reevaluation of a Monitor's Role in Subin's Rape Case

To summarize, our monitor may bring in information and draw inferences which support "false defense" if the information or inferences fall within any one of six categories: (1) quality, (2) reliability, (3) mistakes in the prosecution's case, (4) adequacy, (5) inaccuracy, or (6) legitimate reasons to doubt. These broad, imprecise categories are not very confining for a profession which makes its living developing plausible positions for filing things into categories. It is instructive focusing on Subin's principal example, the rape case in which he "knows" his client is factually guilty, with these categories in mind.

In that case, two principal pieces of information emerged which were potentially helpful for the defense: 1) the victim stated that the defendant took her to his apartment; and 2) the victim was left alone for a time in a hallway after the rape but did not try to flee. Professor Subin recognized the significance of these and other miscellaneous pieces of information for the defense:

> I could emphasize the parts of her story that sounded the most curious, such as the defendant's solicitude in taking his victim back to his apartment, and her waiting for her watch when she could have gone immediately to the nearby precinct that she went to later. I could point to her inability to identify the gun she claimed was used (although it was the one actually used), that the allegedly stolen watch was never found, that there was no sign of physical violence, and no one heard screaming or any other signs of a struggle. I could also argue as my client had that even if he were reckless enough to rob and rape a woman across the street from his apartment, he would not be so foolish as to bring the victim there.

However, Subin is unclear as to what he would have done with this information. He claims he would have had no right to raise the "false defense" of consent. He would not have cross-examined the victim or put on defense witnesses. Instead, Subin would "limit my representation at that stage to putting forth the strongest argument I could that the facts presented by the state did not sustain its burden." Assuming sufficient information was elicited on the victim's direct examination to make the two helpful points above, what "strong argument" would defense counsel Subin make? Without using any of the information helpful to the defense, his argument could not have been other than: "Thank you, the prosecution has the burden."

Imagine instead he had taken the information and argued as follows:

> This just doesn't make sense. If he took her to his apartment, he'd have to know he'd be identified within hours. There's no evidence he blindfolded her or in any other way made an effort to conceal the identity and location of the apartment. And here she'd just been raped at gunpoint by a man who, for all she knew, might now kill her, and she was alone in the hallway, neighbors around, a staircase 10 feet away leading to the outside and safety. Yet her testimony is she just sat there and waited for the defendant. None of this makes sense, and the prosecution cannot carry its burden if the story it is presenting does not make sense.

Would this have been a "false defense" for Professor Subin? The argument raises "legitimate" doubts. The fact that the prosecution's underlying story does not make sense goes to the quality, reliability, and adequacy of the prosecution's case. Maybe the line would have been crossed if as defense counsel he had added:

> Who knows from this evidence what really happened? Maybe she consented and then felt guilty—afraid to acknowledge the truth to herself and her boyfriend. Who knows? All we know is that the story does not make sense.

Does even mentioning the possibility of consent really cross Subin's line between the ethical and unethical? One major shortcoming in Subin's presentation is his failure to illustrate what a monitor in this rape case *may* do. He tells us what he would do, but does not show us what his "monitor's" closing argument would really look like.

Subin has left us in a quandary. The "stark" definition of monitor may have been at odds with the nature of the criminal justice system and the Constitution, but at least it was consistent with an unmitigated desire for truth. This current wavering line between advocates and monitors, based as it is on permissible versus impermissible information and inferences, is somewhat more in step with the Constitution and the justice system, but hopelessly vague and uncertain.

B. Bigger Problems: Constitutional Concerns and Jeopardizing an Independent Defense Bar

If Professor Subin's approach is more than a statement of his own private ethics, the vagueness and uncertainty of the line which divides the advocate from the monitor presents a serious problem. First, constitutional concerns additional to those already expressed may arise. Criminal defense representation touches significant interests: 1) protection of the individual from the state; 2) the freedom of the defendant in a nation which values liberty; and 3) significant constitutional rights (fourth, fifth, sixth, eighth, and fourteenth amendments). It is within these areas that the impreciseness in Professor Subin's categories comes to the fore. To the extent defense attorneys are guided by ethical rules which are vague about what conduct is proper, the representation of the clients is hampered. Counsel, uncertain as to appropriate behavior, may fall into a "conflict" between pushing the client's interests as far as is legitimate and protecting himself against charges of unethical conduct. Attorneys' decisions may then tend to fall on the self-protective side, raising constitutional concerns regarding zealous representation.

Second, if Subin's approach were enforced as a rule of professional conduct, the independent defense bar would be seriously jeopardized. Professor Subin may or may not be correct that the public and the bar have a low view of the criminal defense bar. Nonetheless, the independence of that bar has provided all citizens with significant protection against government oppression.[11] With Professor Subin's approach, however, if an acquittal were gained by a defense attorney who was a thorn in the government's side, the prosecutor's office might be tempted to file an ethical complaint stating that defense counsel should have known he put on a "false defense." Subin's position now becomes a weapon of repression in the hands of the government. Even if vindication follows upon a disciplinary hearing, time, expense, and public humiliation might ensue. This will deliver a powerful message to defense attorneys. Don't risk fighting, plead your clients guilty.

IV. CONCLUSION

Discussions of "monitors," "advocates," and "false defenses," while interesting, are premature. If the legal profession is ever to develop meaningful guidelines for criminal and civil attorneys, the focus must be on certain basic premises. Specifically, we must consider: What is the relationship between our criminal and civil systems, and what is the implication of that relationship for those practicing in the two systems? Is the criminal justice system primarily a truth system? Is it primarily a screening system intended as a check on governmental power? It seems to me that here is where we must begin.

NOTES

1. Subin, *The Criminal Lawyer's "Different Mission": Reflections on the "Right" to Present a False Case*, 1 Geo. J. Legal Ethics 125 (1987).
2. Subin, *supra* note 1, at 125.
3. For a very well-thought out recent discussion which generally takes the position that the defense attorney's knowledge of the client's guilt should have no bearing upon that attorney's representation, *see* Kaplan, *Defending Guilty People*, 7 U. Bridgeport L. Rev. 223 (1986).
4. Mitchell, *supra* note 3, at 300–01.
5. For an interesting discussion of various justifications for the truth-dysfunctional nature of the criminal trial which implicitly leads one to conclude that Professor Subin's quest for factual truth is the least of what is going on, *see* Goodpaster, *On the Theory of American Adversary Criminal Trials*, 78 J. Crim. L. & Criminology 118 (1987).
6. Subin, *supra* note 1, at 127–29, 143. As the title presages, Professor Subin makes this concept of a "different mission" the metaphorical focus of his article.
7. Subin, *supra* note 1, at 143.
8. For a defense of the lawyer's position as an "amoral" actor on behalf of a client which does not rely on the adversary system rationale, *see* Pepper, *The Lawyer's Amoral Ethical Role: A Defense, A Problem, and Some Possibilities*, A.B.A. Research J. 613 (1986).
9. Mitchell, *supra* note 3, at 299–302.
10. *Id.* at 302–21.
11. They did after all defend strikers in the early labor movement, were present during the McCarthy hearings and the Smith Act prosecutions and defended those voicing objections to the government's policies in Vietnam. Most of us take comfort in thinking they will be there in the future. *Cf.* Babcock, *Defending the Guilty*, 32 Clev. St. L. Rev. 175 (1983–84) (discussing reasons to defend a person one knows is guilty).

POSTSCRIPT

Should Lawyers Be Prohibited from Presenting a False Case?

During the last 30 years, the legal profession has experienced unprecedented change. The most frequently publicized development of this period has been the great increase in the size of the profession. The United States now has more than 750,000 lawyers, more than double the number in 1970.

In addition to larger numbers of lawyers, recent years have seen the following significant changes take place: (1) A decline in the number of lawyers practicing independently or in firms and an increase in the number of lawyers employed by corporations and institutions. As a result, "a profession that was 85 percent self-employed in 1948 and about 60 percent self-employed in 1980 soon may be more than half employees." (2) Elimination of some anti-competitive practices previously enjoyed by the profession, such as minimum fee schedules and restrictions on advertising. (3) An increase in the size of law firms. The largest firms now have hundreds of lawyers with offices in many states. (4) Increasing heterogeneity of the legal profession. Due to the recent growth of the bar, members of the profession are younger, with more women and minorities. There are more fields of specialization and types of practice.

Clearly, the legal profession is not as stable as it once was. The work that lawyers do and where and how they do it is changing. This may have an impact on the ethical standards of lawyers. One of the characteristics of a "profession" is that it sets its own standards. But what happens when, because of changes in the makeup of the profession, it becomes harder to do this? What happens when there is less and less agreement in the profession about what the standards should be? What happens when there are increasing challenges from outside the profession to the traditional standards?

For further insight into the role and nature of the legal profession and of legal ethics, see Elliston and van Schaick, *Legal Ethics: An Annotated Bibliography and Research Guide* (Fred Rothman, 1984); R. Abel, *American Lawyers* (Oxford University Press, 1989); M. S. Larson, *The Rise of Professionalism: A Sociological Analysis* (University of California Press, 1977); Hazard and Rhode, eds., *The Legal Profession: Responsibility and Regulation*, 2d ed. (The Foundation Press, 1988); and Babcock, "Defending the Guilty," 32 *Cleveland State Law Review* 175 (1983). *Bates v. State Bar of Arizona*, 97 S. Ct. 2691 (1977) permitted lawyers to advertise. Recent cases involving the ethical practices of lawyers are *Shapero v. Kentucky Bar Association*, 108 S. Ct. 1916 (1988), allowing lawyers to use mailing lists to advertise their services to potential clients, and *Nix v. Whiteside*, 106 S. Ct. 988 (1986), which held that it is not a violation of the right to counsel for an attorney to threaten to resign if the client insists on lying while testifying.

ISSUE 3

Should Plea Bargaining Be Abolished?

YES: Kenneth Kipnis, from "Criminal Justice and the Negotiated Plea," *Ethics* (vol. 86, 1976)

NO: Nick Schweitzer, from "Plea Bargaining: A Prosecutor's View," *Wisconsin Bar Bulletin* (October 1988)

ISSUE SUMMARY

YES: Professor of philosophy Kenneth Kipnis makes the case that justice cannot be traded on the open market and that plea bargaining often subverts the cause of justice.
NO: District Attorney Nick Schweitzer finds that plea bargaining is fair, useful, desirable, necessary, and practical.

One of the most common myths fostered by television programs about lawyers concerns the place of the trial in the American legal system. The television lawyer, who is invariably a criminal trial lawyer, defends an innocent individual and, at a particularly dramatic point in the trial, achieves vindication for the client. If you visit a courthouse, you may be able to find a trial being held that resembles what you have seen on television. The lawyer may be less dramatic, the judge less dour, and the defendant less appealing, but the main elements of the television version of justice, such as cross-examination of witnesses, opening and closing arguments, and, perhaps, a jury verdict, will be present. What is important to understand, however, is that of the cases processed by the criminal justice system, only a handful are disposed of in this manner. Instead, as many as 90 percent of the cases are resolved through plea bargaining.

Plea bargaining is a method of avoiding trials by securing guilty pleas from defendants. It occurs primarily because trials are expensive and time consuming. In plea bargaining, the defendant agrees to plead guilty in exchange for an agreement by the prosecutor to reduce the charges or recommend a lenient sentence. The defendant essentially has a choice between going to trial and possibly being found guilty on a more serious charge or pleading guilty now and suffering less severe consequences.

This is a difficult choice for any defendant, and at the center of the debate over the legitimacy of plea bargaining is the question of whether or not the defendant, in these circumstances, is making a voluntary choice. In the following articles, Kenneth Kipnis argues that there is too much coercion involved for the choice to be considered voluntary, that the process is inherently unjust, and that innocent individuals may be coerced into pleading guilty. District attorney Nick Schweitzer believes that the system is not at fault and that if the standard legal procedures are followed, plea bargaining is not only indispensable but also just and desirable.

Plea bargaining has been upheld by the Supreme Court, but only when the Court was persuaded that the plea was made voluntarily. Yet it is rare for a convicted defendant to make a successful challenge to the voluntariness of a guilty plea because the defendant must admit in open court, prior to making the plea, that it is being made voluntarily. In every courtroom in which plea bargaining occurs, the judge asks the defendant the following questions:

1. Do you understand the charges against you and the maximum penalties authorized by law?
2. Are you, in fact, guilty of the charge you are pleading guilty to?
3. Are you pleading guilty voluntarily?
4. Do you understand that you have the right to a trial by jury and that you are waiving that right?

The judge will not accept a plea unless the defendant answers yes to all of these questions. For a plea of guilty to be challenged later, therefore, the defendant must persuade a higher court that he was coerced into lying when he was asked these questions.

Another important issue in the controversy over plea bargaining is the fact that plea bargaining is mainly a poor person's problem. The reason for this is that the greatest incentive to plead guilty exists for those persons who are in jail awaiting trial and cannot afford bail. Their choice is to plead guilty now and get out of jail immediately, or at some definite future date, or to insist on a trial, stay in jail until the trial occurs, and risk a long sentence if convicted. As you read the following articles, you should consider how important this factor is in making a decision about whether or not plea bargaining should be abolished.

YES

Kenneth Kipnis

CRIMINAL JUSTICE AND THE NEGOTIATED PLEA

In recent years it has become apparent to many that, in practice, the criminal justice system in the United States does not operate as we thought it did. The conviction secured through jury trial, so familiar in countless novels, films, and television programs, is beginning to be seen as the aberration it has become. What has replaced the jury's verdict is the negotiated plea. In these "plea bargains" the defendant agrees to plead guilty in exchange for discretionary consideration on the part of the state. Generally, this consideration amounts to some kind of assurance of a minimal sentence. The well-publicized convictions of Spiro Agnew and Clifford Irving were secured through such plea bargains. In 1974 in New York City, 80 percent of all felony cases were settled as misdemeanors through plea bargains.[1] Only 2 percent of all felony arrests resulted in a trial.[2] It is at present a commonplace that plea bargaining could not be eliminated without substantial alterations in our criminal justice system.

Plea bargaining involves negotiations between the defendant (through an attorney in the standard case) and the prosecutor as to the conditions under which the defendant will enter a guilty plea.[3] Both sides have bargaining power in these negotiations. The prosecutor is ordinarily burdened with cases and does not have the wherewithal to bring more than a fraction of them to trial. Often there is not sufficient evidence to ensure a jury's conviction. Most important, the prosecutor is typically under administrative and political pressure to dispose of cases and to secure convictions as efficiently as possible. If the defendant exercises the constitutional right to a jury trial, the prosecutor must decide whether to drop the charges entirely or to expend scare resources to bring the case to trial. Since neither prospect is attractive, prosecutors typically exercise their broad discretion to induce defendants to waive trial and to plead guilty.

From the defendant's point of view, such prosecutorial discretion has two aspects; it darkens the prospect of going to trial as it brightens the prospect of pleading guilty. Before negotiating, a prosecutor may improve his bargain-

From Kenneth Kipnis, "Criminal Justice and the Negotiated Plea," *Ethics*, vol. 86 (1976). Copyright © 1976 by the University of Chicago. Reprinted by permission of the University of Chicago Press as publisher.

ing position by "overcharging" defendants[4] or by developing a reputation for severity in the sentences he recommends to judges. Such steps greatly increase the punishment that the defendant must expect if convicted at trial. On the other hand, the state may offer to reduce or to drop some charges, or to recommend leniency to the judge if the defendant agrees to plead guilty. These steps minimize the punishment that will result from a guilty plea. Though the exercise of prosecutorial discretion to secure pleas of guilty may differ somewhat in certain jurisdictions and in particular cases, the broad outlines are as described.

Of course a defendant can always reject any offer of concessions and challenge the state to prove its case. A skilled defense attorney can do much to force the prosecutor to expend resources in bringing a case to trial.[5] But the trial route is rarely taken by defendants. Apart from prosecutorial pressure, other factors may contribute to a defendant's willingness to plead guilty: feelings of guilt which may or may not be connected with the charged crime; the discomforts of the pretrial lockup as against the comparatively better facilities of a penitentiary; the costs of going to trial as against the often cheaper option of consenting to a plea; a willingness or unwillingness to lie; and the delays which are almost always present in awaiting trial, delays which the defendant may sit out in jail in a kind of preconviction imprisonment which may not be credited to a postconviction sentence. It is not surprising that the right to a trial by jury is rarely exercised.

If one examines the statistics published annually by the Administrative Office of the U.S. Courts,[6] one can appreciate both the size of the concessions gained by agreeing to plead guilty and (what is the same thing) the size of the additional burdens imposed upon those convicted without so agreeing. According to the 1970 report, among all convicted defendants, those pleading guilty at arraignment received average sentences of probation and/or under one year of imprisonment. Those going to a jury trial received average sentences of three to four years in prison.[7] If one looks just at those convicted of Marijuana Tax Act violations with no prior record, one finds that those pleading guilty at arraignment received average sentences of probation and/or six months or less of imprisonment while those going to trial received average sentences more than eight times as severe: four to five years in prison.[8] Among all Marijuana Tax Act convictions, defendants pleading guilty at the outset had a 76 percent chance of being let off without imprisonment, while those who had gone to trial had only an 11 percent chance.[9] These last two sets of figures do not reflect advantages gained by charge reduction, nor do they reflect advantages gained by electing a bench trial as opposed to a jury trial. What these figures do suggest is that the sentences given to convicted defendants who have exercised their constitutional right to trial are many times as severe as the sentences given to those who do not. In *United States v. Wiley*[10] Chief Judge Campbell laid to rest any tendency to conjecture that these discrepancies in sentences might have explanations not involving plea bargains.

. . . I believe, and it is generally accepted by trial judges throughout the United States, that it is entirely proper and logical to grant some defendants some degree of leniency in exchange for a plea of guilty. If then, a trial judge grants leniency in exchange for a plea of guilty, it follows, as the reverse side of the same coin, that he must necessarily forego leniency, generally speaking, where the defendant stands trial and is found guilty.

. . . I might make general reference to a "standing policy" not to consider probation where a defendant stands trial even though I do not in fact strictly adhere to such a policy.

No deliberative body ever decided that we would have a system in which the disposition of criminal cases is typically the result of negotiations between the prosecutor and the defendant's attorney on the conditions under which the defendant would waive trial and plead guilty to a mutually acceptable charge. No legislature ever voted to adopt a procedure in which defendants who are convicted after trial typically receive sentences far greater than those received by defendants charged with similar offenses but pleading guilty. The practice of plea bargaining has evolved in the unregulated interstices of our criminal justice system. Its development has not gone unnoticed. There is now a substantial literature on the legality and propriety of plea bargaining.[11] But though philosophers do not often treat issues arising in the area of criminal procedure, there are problems here that cry for our attention. In the preceding pages I have been concerned to sketch the institution of plea bargaining. In what follows I will raise some serious questions about it that should concern us. I will first discuss generally the intrinsic fairness of plea bargains and then, in the final section, I will examine critically the place of such bargains in the criminal justice system.

I

As one goes through the literature on plea bargaining one gets the impression that market forces are at work in this unlikely context. The terms "bargain" and "negotiation" suggest this. One can see the law of supply and demand operating in that, other things being equal, if there are too many defendants who want to go to trial, prosecutors will have to concede more in order to get the guilty pleas that they need to clear their case load. And if the number of prosecutors and courts goes up, prosecutors will be able to concede less. Against this background it is not surprising to find one commentator noting:[12] "In some places a 'going rate' is established under which a given charge will automatically be broken down to a given lesser offense with the recommendation of a given lesser sentence." Prosecutors, like retailers before them, have begun to appreciate the efficiency of the fixed-price approach.

The plea bargain in the economy of criminal justice has many of the important features of the contract in commercial transactions. In both institutions offers are made and accepted, entitlements are given up and obtained, and the notion of an exchange, ideally a fair one, is presented to both parties. Indeed one detects something of the color of consumer protection law in a few of the decisions on plea bargaining. In *Baily v. MacDougal*[13] the court held that "a guilty plea cannot be accepted unless the defendant understands its consequences." And in *Santo Bello v. New York*[14] the court secured a defendant's entitlement to a prosecutorial concession when a second prosecutor replaced the one who had made the promise. Rule 11 of the Federal Rules of Criminal Procedure requires that "if a plea agreement has been reached by the parties which contemplates entry of a plea of guilty or nolo contendere in the expectation that a specific sentence will be imposed or that other charges before the court will be dismissed, the court shall require the disclosure of the agreement in open court at the time the plea is offered." These procedures all have analogues in contract law. Though plea bargains may not be seen as contracts by the parties, agreements like them are the stuff of contract case law. While I will not argue that plea bargains are contracts (or even that they should be treated as such), I do think it proper to look to contract law for help in evaluating the justice of such agreements.

The law of contracts serves to give legal effect to certain bargain-promises. In particular, it specifies conditions that must be satisfied by bargain-promises before the law will recognize and enforce them as contracts. As an example, we could look at that part of the law of contracts which treats duress. Where one party wrongfully compels another to consent to the terms of an agreement the resulting bargain has no legal effect. Dan B. Dobbs, a commentator on the law in this area, describes the elements of duress as follows: "The defendant's act must be wrongful in some attenuated sense; it must operate coercively upon the will of the plaintiff, judged subjectively, and the plaintiff must have no adequate remedy to avoid the coercion except to give in. . . . The earlier requirement that the coercion must have been the kind that would coerce a reasonable man, or even a brave one, is now generally dispensed with, and it is enough if it in fact coerced a spineless plaintiff."[15] Coercion is not the same as fraud, nor is

it confined to cases in which a defendant is physically compelled to assent. In Dobb's words: "The victim of duress knows the facts but is forced by hard choices to act against his will." The paradigm case of duress is the agreement made at gunpoint. Facing a mortal threat, one readily agrees to hand over the cash. But despite such consent, the rules of duress work to void the effects of such agreements. There is no legal obligation to hand over the cash and, having given it over, entitlement to the money is not lost. The gunman has no legal right to retain possession even if he adheres to his end of the bargain and scraps his murderous plans.

Judges have long been required to see to it that guilty pleas are entered voluntarily. And one would expect that, if duress is present in the plea-bargaining situation, then, just as the handing over of cash to the gunman is void of legal effect (as far as entitlement to the money is concerned), so no legal consequences should flow from the plea of guilty which is the product of duress. However, Rule 11 of the Federal Rules of Criminal Procedure requires the court to insure that a plea of guilty (or nolo contendere) is voluntary by "addressing the defendant personally in open court, determining that the plea is voluntary and not the result of force or promises *apart from a plea agreement*" (emphasis added). In two important cases (*North Carolina v. Alford* and *Brady v. United States*)[16] defendants agreed to plead guilty in order to avoid probable death sentences. Both accepted very long prison sentences. In both cases the Supreme Court decided that guilty pleas so entered were voluntary (through Brennan, Douglas, and Marshall dissented). In his dissent in *Alford*, Brennan writes: " . . . the facts set out in the majority opinion demonstrate that Alford was 'so gripped by fear of the death penalty' that his decision to plead guilty was not voluntary but was the 'product of duress as much so as choice reflecting physical constraint.' " In footnote 2 of the *Alford* opinion, the Court sets out the defendant's testimony given at the time of the entry of his plea of guilty before the trial court. That testimony deserves examination: "I pleaded guilty on second degree murder because they said there is too much evidence, but I ain't shot no man, but I take the fault for the other man. We never had an argument in our life and I just pleaded guilty because they said if I didn't they would gas me for it, and that is all." The rule to be followed in such cases is set out in *Brady*: "A plea of guilty entered by one fully aware of the direct consequences, including the actual value of any commitments made to him by the court, prosecutor or his own counsel, must stand unless induced by threats (or promises to discontinue improper harassment), misrepresentation (including unfilled or unfillable promises), or perhaps by promises that are by their very nature improper as having no proper relationship to the prosecutor's business (e.g. bribes)." Case law and the Federal Rules both hold that the standard exercise of prosecutorial discretion in order to secure a plea of guilty cannot be used to prove that such a plea is involuntary. Even where the defendant enters a guilty plea in order to avert his death at the hands of the state, as in *Alford*, the Court has not seen involuntariness. Nevertheless, it may be true that some guilty pleas are involuntary in virtue of prosecutorial inducement considered proper by the Supreme Court.

Regarding the elements of duress, let us compare the gunman situation with an example of plea bargaining in order to examine the voluntariness of the latter. Albert W. Alschuler, author of one of the most thorough studies of plea bargaining, describes an actual case:

> San Francisco defense attorney Benjamin M. Davis recently represented a man charged with kidnapping and forcible rape. The defendant was innocent, Davis says, and after investigating the case Davis was confident of an acquittal. The prosecutor, who seems to have shared the defense attorney's opinion on this point, offered to permit a guilty plea to simple battery. Conviction on this charge would not have led to a greater sentence than thirty days' imprisonment, and there was every likelihood that the defendant would be granted probation. When Davis informed his client of this offer, he emphasized that conviction at trial seemed highly improbable. The defendant's reply was simple: "I can't take the chance."[17]

Both the gunman and the prosecutor require persons to make hard choices between a very certain smaller imposition and an uncertain greater imposition. In the gunman situation I must choose between the very certain loss of my money and the difficult-to-assess probability that my assailant is willing and able to kill me if I resist. As a defendant I am forced to choose between a very certain smaller punishment and a substantially greater punishment with a difficult-to-assess probability. As the size of the certain smaller imposition comes down and as the magnitude and probability of the larger imposition increases, it becomes more and more reasonable to choose the former. This is what seems to be occurring in Alschuler's example: "Davis reports that he is uncomfortable when he permits innocent defendants to plead guilty; but in this case it would have been playing God to stand in the defendant's way. The attorney's assessment of the outcome at trial can always be wrong, and it is hard to tell a defendant that 'professional ethics' require a course that may ruin his life." Davis's client must decide whether to accept a very certain, very minor punishment or to chance a ruined life. Of course the gunman's victim can try to overpower his assailant and the defendant can attempt to clear himself at trial. But the same considerations that will drive reasonable people to give in to the gunman compel one to accept the prosecutor's offer. Applying the second and third elements of duress, one can see that, like the gunman's act, the acts of the prosecutor can "operate coercively upon the will of the plaintiff, judged subjectively," and both the gunman's victim and the defendant may "have no adequate remedy to avoid the coercion except to give in." In both cases reasonable persons might well conclude (after considering the gunman's lethal weapon or the gas chamber) "I can't take the chance." A spineless person would not need to deliberate.

That prosecutors could exercise such duress apparently seemed plain to the authors of the *Restatement of Contracts*.[18] Their summarization of the law of contracts, adopted in 1932 by the American Law Institute, contained the following: "A threat of criminal prosecution . . . ordinarily is a threat of imprisonment and also . . . a threat of bringing disgrace upon the accused. Threats of this sort may be of such compelling force that acts done under their influence are coerced, and the better foundation there is for the prosecution, the greater is the coercion." While it is always true that even in the most desperate circum-

stances persons are free to reject the terms offered and risk the consequences, as Morris Raphael Cohen put it: "such choice is surely the very opposite of what men value as freedom."[19]

Indeed if one had to choose between being in the position of Davis's client and facing a fair-minded gunman, I think that it would be reasonable to prefer the latter. While the law permits one to recover money upon adverting to the forced choice of the gunman, it does not permit one to retract a guilty plea upon adverting to the forced choice of the prosecutor. This is the impact of *Brady* and Rule 11.

Note that the duress is not eliminated by providing defendants with counsel. While a good attorney may get better concessions and may help in the evaluation of options, in the end the defendant will still have to decide whether to settle for the smaller penalty or to risk a much heavier sentence. One does not eliminate the injustice in the gunman situation by providing victims with better advice.

Nor does it help matters to insure that promises of prosecutorial concessions are kept. The gunman who violates his part of the bargain—murdering his victims after they give over their money—has compounded his wrongdoing. Reputations for righteousness are not established by honoring such bargains.

Nor is it legitimate to distinguish the prosecutor from the gunman by saying that, while the gunman is threatening harm unless you hand over the cash, the prosecutor is merely promising benefits if you enter a guilty plea. For, in the proper context, threats and promises may be intertranslatable. Brandishing his pistol, the holdup man may promise to leave me unharmed if I hand over the cash. Similarly, the prosecutor may threaten to "throw the book" at me if I do not plead guilty to a lesser charge. In the proper context, one may be compelled to act by either form of words.

One might argue that not all "hard choices" are examples of duress. A doctor could offer to sell vital treatment for a large sum. After the patient has been cured it will hardly do for her to claim that she has been the victim of duress. The doctor may have forced the patient to choose between a certain financial loss and the risk of death. But surely doctors are not like gunmen.

Two important points need to be made in response to this objection. First, the doctor is not, one assumes, responsible for the diseased condition of the patient. The patient would be facing death even if she had never met the doctor. But this is not true in the case of the gunman, where both impositions are his work. And in this respect the prosecutor offering a plea bargain in a criminal case is like the gunman rather than like the doctor. For the state forces a choice between adverse consequences that it imposes. And, of course, one cannot say that in the defendant's wrongdoing he has brought his dreadful dilemma upon himself. To do so would be to ignore the good reasons there are for the presumption of innocence in dispositive criminal proceedings.

Second, our laws do not prohibit doctors from applying their healing skills to maximize their own wealth. They are free to contract to perform services in return for a fee. But our laws do severely restrict the state in its prosecution of criminal defendants. Those who framed our constitution were well aware of the great potential for abuse that the criminal law affords. Much of the constitution (especially the Bill of Rights) checks the activity of the state in this area. In particular, the Fifth Amendment provides that no person "shall be compelled in any criminal case to be a witness against himself." If I am right in judging that defendants like Alford and Davis's client do not act freely in pleading guilty to the facts of their cases, that the forced choice of the prosecutor may be as coercive as the forced choice of the gunman, that a defendant may be compelled to speak against himself (or herself) by a prosecutor's discretion inducing him to plead guilty, then, given the apparent constitutional prohibition of such compulsion, the prosecutor acts wrongfully in compelling such pleas. And in this manner it may be that the last element of duress, wrongfulness, can be established. But it is not my purpose here to establish the unconstitutionality of plea bargaining, for it is not necessary to reach unconstitutionality to grasp the wrongfulness of that institution. One need only reflect upon what justice amounts to in our system of criminal law. This is the task I will take up in the final section of this paper.

II

Not too long ago plea bargaining was an officially prohibited practice. Court procedures were followed to ensure that no concessions had been given to defendants in exchange for guilty pleas. But gradually it became widely known that these procedures had become charades of perjury, shysterism, and bad faith involving judges, prosecutors, defense attorneys and defendants. This was scandalous. But rather than cleaning up the practice in order to square it with the rules, the rules were changed in order to bring them in line with the practice.

There was a time when it apparently seemed plain that the old rules were the right rules. One finds in the *Restatement of Contracts:*[20] " . . . even if the accused is guilty and the process valid, so that as against the State the imprisonment is lawful, it is a wrongful means of inducing the accused to enter into a transaction. To overcome the will of another for the prosecutor's advantage is *an abuse of the criminal law which was made for another purpose*" (emphasis added). The authors of the *Restatement* do not tell us what they were thinking when they spoke of the purpose of the criminal law. Nonetheless it is instructive to conjecture and to inquire along the lines suggested by the *Restatement*.

Without going deeply into detail, I believe that it can be asserted without controversy that the liberal-democratic approach to criminal justice—and in particular the American criminal justice system—is an institutionalization of two principles. The first principle refers to the intrinsic point of systems of criminal justice.

A. Those (and only those) individuals who are clearly guilty of certain serious specified wrongdoings deserve an officially administered punishment which is proportional to their wrongdoing.

In the United States it is possible to see this principle underlying the activities of legislators specifying and grading wrongdoings which are serious enough to warrant criminalization and, further, determining the punishment appropriate to each offense; the activities of policemen and prosecutors bringing to trial those who are suspected of having committed such wrongdoings; the activities of jurors determining if defendants are guilty beyond a reasonable doubt; the

activities of defense attorneys insuring that relevant facts in the defendant's favor are brought out at trial; the activities of judges seeing to it that proceedings are fair and that those who are convicted receive the punishment they deserve; and the activities of probation officers, parole officers, and prison personnel executing the sentences of the courts. All of these people play a part in bringing the guilty to justice.

But in liberal-democratic societies not everything is done to accomplish this end. A second principle makes reference to the limits placed upon the power of the state to identify and punish the guilty.

B. Certain basic liberties shall not be violated in bringing the guilty to justice.

This second principle can be seen to underlie the constellation of the constitutional checks on the activities of virtually every person playing a role in the administration of the criminal justice system.

Each of these principles is related to a distinctive type of injustice that can occur in the context of criminal law. An injustice can occur in the outcome of the criminal justice procedure. That is, an innocent defendant may be convicted and punished, or a guilty defendant may be acquitted or, if convicted, he or she may receive more or less punishment than is deserved. Because these injustices occur in the meting out of punishment to defendants who are being processed by the system, we can refer to them as internal injustices. They are violations of the first principle. On the other hand, there is a type of injustice which occurs when basic liberties are violated in the operation of the criminal justice system. It may be true that Star Chamber proceedings, torture, hostages, bills of attainder, dragnet arrests, unchecked searches, *ex post facto* laws, unlimited invasions of privacy, and an arsenal of other measures could be employed to bring more of the guilty to justice. But these steps lead to a dystopia where our most terrifying nightmares can come true. However we limit the activity of the criminal justice system in the interest of basic liberty, that limit can be overstepped. We can call such infringements upon basic liberties external injustices. They are violations of the second principle. If, for example, what I have suggested in the previous section is correct, then plea bargaining can bring about an external injustice with respect to a basic liberty secured by the Fifth Amendment. The remainder of this section will be concerned with internal injustice or violations of the first principle.

It is necessary to draw a further distinction between aberrational and systemic injustice. It may very well be that in the best criminal justice system that we are capable of devising human limitations will result in some aberrational injustice. Judges, jurors, lawyers, and legislators with the best of intentions may make errors in judgment that result in mistakes in the administration of punishment. But despite the knowledge that an unknown percentage of all dispositions of criminal cases are, to some extent, miscarriages of justice, it may still be reasonable to believe that a certain system of criminal justice is well calculated to avoid such results within the limits referred to by the second principle.[21] We can refer to these incorrect outcomes of a sound system of criminal justice as instances of aberrational injustice. In contrast, instances of systemic injustice are those that result from structural flaws in the criminal justice system itself. Here incorrect outcomes in the operations of the system are not the result of human error. Rather, the system itself is not well calculated to avoid injustice. What would be instances of aberrational injustice in a sound system are not aberrations in an unsound system: they are a standard result.

This distinction has an analogy in the area of quality control. Two vials of antibiotic may be equally contaminated. But depending upon the process used to produce each, the contamination may be aberrational or systemic. The first sample may come from a factory where every conceivable step is taken to insure that such contamination will not take place. The second vial may come from a company which uses a cheap manufacturing process offering no protection against contamination. There is an element of tragedy if death results when all possible precautions have been taken: there just are limits to human capability at our present level of understanding. But where vital precautions are dropped in the name of expediency, the contamination that results is much more serious if only because we knew it would take place and we knew what could be done to prevent it. While we have every reason to believe that the first sample is pure, we have no reason to believe that the second sample is uncontaminated. Indeed, one cannot call the latter contamination accidental as one can in the first case. It would be more correct to call it an accident if contamination did not take place in the total absence of precaution.

Likewise, systematic injustice in the context of criminal law is a much more serious matter than aberrational injustice. It should not be forgotten that the criminal sanction is the most severe imposition that the state can visit upon one of its citizens. While it is possible to tolerate occasional error in a sound system, systematic carelessness in the administration of punishment is negligence of the highest order.

With this framework in mind, let us look at a particular instance of plea bargaining recently described by a legal aid defense attorney.[22] Ted Alston has been charged with armed robbery. Let us assume that persons who have committed armed robbery (in the way Alston is accused of having committed it) deserve five to seven years of prison. Alston's attorney sets out the options for him: "I told Alston it was possible, perhaps even probable, that if he went to trial he would be convicted and get a prison term of perhaps five to seven years. On the other hand, if he agreed to plead guilty to a low-grade felony, he would get a probationary sentence and not go to prison. The choice was his." Let us assume that Alston accepts the terms of the bargain and pleads guilty to a lesser offense. If Alston did commit the armed robbery, there is a violation of the first principle in that he receives far less punishment than he deserves. On the other hand, if Alston did not commit the armed robbery, there is still a violation of the first principle in that he is both convicted of and punished for a crime that he did not commit, a crime that no one seriously believes to be his distinctive wrongdoing. It is of course possible that while Alston did not commit the armed robbery, he did commit the lesser offense. But though justice would be done here, it would be an accident. Such a serendipitous result is a certain sign that what we have here is systemic injustice.

If we assume that legislatures approximate the correct range of punishment for each offense, that judges fairly sentence those who are convicted by juries, and that prosecutors reasonably charge defendants, then, barring accidents, justice will *never* be the outcome of the plea-bargaining procedure: the defendant who "cops a plea" will never receive the punishment which is deserved. Of course legislatures can set punishments too high, judges can oversentence those who are convicted by juries, and prosecutors can overcharge defendants. In these cases the guilty can receive the punishment they deserve through plea bargaining. But in these cases we compensate for one injustice by introducing others that unfairly jeopardize the innocent and those that demand trials.

In contrast to plea bargaining, the disposition of criminal cases by jury trial seems well calculated to avoid internal injustices even if these may sometimes occur. Where participants take their responsibilities seriously we have good reason to believe that the outcome is just, even when this may not be so. In contrast, with plea bargaining we have no reason to believe that the outcome is just even when it is.

I think that the appeal that plea bargaining has is rooted in our attitude toward bargains in general. Where both parties are satisfied with the terms of an agreement, it is improper to interfere. Generally speaking, prosecutors and defendants are pleased with the advantages they gain by negotiating a plea. And courts, which gain as well, are reluctant to vacate negotiated pleas where only "proper" inducements have been applied and where promises have been understood and kept. Such judicial neutrality may be commendable where entitlements are being exchanged. But the criminal justice system is not such a context. Rather it is one in which persons are justly given, not what they have bargained for, but what they deserve, irrespective of their bargaining position.

To appreciate this, let us consider another context in which desert plays a familiar role; the assignment of grades in an academic setting. Imagine a "grade bargain" negotiated between a grade-conscious student and a harried instructor. A term paper has been submitted and, after glancing at the first page, the instructor says that if he were to read the paper carefully, applying his usually rigid standards, he would probably decide to give the paper a grade of D. But if the student were to waive his right to a careful reading and conscientious critique, the instructor would agree to a grade of B. The grade-point average being more important to him than either education or justice in grading, the student happily accepts the B, and the instructor enjoys a reduced workload.

One strains to imagine legislators and administrators commending the practice of grade bargaining because it permits more students to be processed by fewer instructors. Teachers can be freed from the burden of having to read and to criticize every paper. One struggles to envision academicians arguing for grade bargaining in the way that jurists have defended plea bargaining, suggesting that a quick assignment of a grade is a more effective influence on the behavior of students, urging that grade bargaining is necessary to the efficient functioning of the schools. There can be no doubt that students who have negotiated a grade are more likely to accept and to understand the verdict of the instructor. Moreover, in recognition of a student's help to the school (by waiving both the reading and the critique), it is proper for the instructor to be lenient. Finally, a quickly assigned grade enables the guidance personnel and the registrar to respond rapidly and appropriately to the student's situation.

What makes all of this laughable is what makes plea bargaining outrageous. For grades, like punishments, should be deserved. Justice in retribution, like justice in grading, does not require that the end result be acceptable to the parties. To reason that because the parties are satisfied the bargain should stand is to be seriously confused. For bargains are out of place in contexts where persons are to receive what they deserve. And the American courtroom, like the American classroom, should be such a context.

In this section, until now I have been attempting to show that plea bargaining is not well calculated to insure that those guilty of wrongdoing will receive the punishment they deserve. But a further point needs to be made. While the conviction of the innocent would be a problem in any system we might devise, it appears to be a greater problem under plea bargaining. With the jury system the guilt of the defendant must be established in an adversary proceeding and it must be established beyond a reasonable doubt to each of the twelve jurors. This is very staunch protection against an aberrational conviction. But under plea bargaining the foundation for conviction need only include a factual basis for the plea (in the opinion of the judge) and the guilty plea itself. Considering the coercive nature of the circumstances surrounding the plea, it would be a mistake to attach much reliability to it. Indeed, as we have seen in *Alford*, guilty pleas are acceptable even when accompanied by a denial of guilt. And in a study of 724 defendants who had pleaded guilty, only

13.1 percent admitted guilt to an interviewer, while 51.6 percent asserted their innocence.[23] This leaves only the factual basis for the plea to serve as the foundation for conviction. Now it is one thing to show a judge that there are facts which support a plea of guilty and quite another to prove to twelve jurors in an adversary proceeding guilt beyond a reasonable doubt. Plea bargaining substantially erodes the standards for guilt and it is reasonable to assume that the sloppier we are in establishing guilt, the more likely it is that innocent persons will be convicted. So apart from having no reason whatever to believe that the guilty are receiving the punishment they deserve, we have far less reason to believe that the convicted are guilty in the first place than we would after a trial.

In its coercion of criminal defendants, in its abandonment of desert as the measure of punishment, and in its relaxation of the standards for conviction, plea bargaining falls short of the justice we expect of our legal system. I have no doubt that substantial changes will have to be made if the institution of plea bargaining is to be obliterated or even removed from its central position in the criminal justice system. No doubt we need more courts and more prosecutors. Perhaps ways can be found to streamline the jury trial procedure without sacrificing its virtues.[24] Certainly it would help to decriminalize the host of victimless crimes—drunkenness and other drug offenses, illicit sex, gambling and so on—in order to free resources for dealing with more serious wrongdoings. And perhaps crime itself can be reduced if we begin to attack seriously those social and economic injustices that have for too long sent their victims to our prisons in disproportionate numbers. In any case, if we are to

expect our citizenry to respect the law, we must take care to insure that our legal institutions are worthy of that respect. I have tried to show that plea bargaining is not worthy, that we must seek a better way. Bargain justice does not become us.

NOTES

1. Marcia Chambers, "80% of City Felony Cases Settled by Plea Bargaining," *New York Times* (February 11, 1975), p. 1.

2. Tom Goldstein, "Backlog of Felonies Rose Sharply Here Despite Court Drive," *New York Times* (February 12, 1975), p. 1.

3. Often the judge will play an important role in these discussions, being called upon, for example, to indicate a willingness to go along with a bargain involving a reduction in sentence. A crowded calendar will make the bench an interested party.

4. In California, for example, armed robbers are technically guilty of kidnapping if they point a gun at their victim and tell him to back up. Thus, beyond the charge of armed robbery, they may face a charge of kidnapping which will be dropped upon entry of a guilty plea (see Albert W. Alschuler, "The Prosecutor's Role in Plea Bargaining," *University of Chicago Law Review* 36 (Fall 1968): 88).

5. Arthur Rosett, "The Negotiated Guilty Plea," *Annals of the American Academy of Political and Social Science* 374 (November 1967): 72.

6. Administrative Office of the United States Courts, *Federal Offenders in the United States District Courts* (Washington, D.C. 1970).

7. Ibid., pp. 57, 59.

8. Ibid., pp. 57, 65.

9. Ibid., p. 60.

10. 184 F. Supp. 679 (N.D. Ill. 1960).

11. Some of the most significant treatments of plea bargaining are Alschuler; Arnold Enker, "Perspectives on Plea Bargaining," in *Task Force Report: The Courts*, by the President's Commission on Law Enforcement and Administration of Justice (Washington, D.C., 1967), p. 108; "The Unconstitutionality of Plea Bargaining," *Harvard Law Review* 83 (April 1970); 1387; Donald J. Newman, *Conviction: The Determination of Guilt or Innocence without Trial* (Boston, 1966); Abraham S. Blumberg, *Criminal Justice* (Chicago, 1967); National Advisory Commission on Criminal Justice Standards and Goals, *Task Force Report: The Courts* (Washington, D.C., 1973): American Bar Association Project on Minimum Standards for Criminal Justice, *Standards Relating to Pleas of Guilty, Approved Draft* (New York, 1968).

12. Rosett, p. 71.

13. 392 F.2d 155 (1968).

14. 404 U.S. 257 (1971).

15. Dan B. Dobbs, *Handbook on the Law of Remedies* (Saint Paul, 1973), p. 658.

16. 400 U.S. 25 (1970) and 397 U.S. 742 (1970), respectively.

17. Alschuler, p. 61.

18. American Law Institute, *Restatement of Contracts* (Saint Paul, 1933), p. 652.

19. Morris Raphael Cohen, "The Basis of Contract," in *Law and the Social Order* (New York, 1933), p. 86.

20. American Law Institute, p. 652.

21. My discussion here owes much to John Rawls's treatment of "imperfect procedural justice" in his *A Theory of Justice* (Cambridge, 1971), pp. 85–86.

22. Robert Hermann, "The Case of the Jamaican Accent," *New York Times Magazine* (December 1, 1974), p. 93 (© The New York Times Company).

23. Blumberg, p. 91.

24. John Langbein has suggested that we look to the German legal system to see how this might be done. See his "Controlling Prosecutorial Discretion in Germany," *University of Chicago Law Review* 41 (Spring 1974): 439.

NO

Nick Schweitzer

PLEA BARGAINING:
A PROSECUTOR'S VIEW

More than nine out of every ten cases I handle are disposed of by plea bargaining. And, to the best of my knowledge, except for Marco Polo-like reports from exotic foreign jurisdictions like Alaska and New Orleans, that ratio holds true for all prosecutors. Yet, despite the pervasiveness of the practice, plea bargaining often is criticized as improper—a conspiracy to emasculate the criminal justice system.

Plea bargaining is a useful, nay vital, tool. It is a response to a court system that never could accord the luxury of a trial to every criminal charge and civil suit brought before it. It is a practical way to dispose of matters that do not require the full solemnity of legal procedure. Plea bargaining in criminal cases is the equivalent of negotiation and mediation in civil cases. While the latter are praised and encouraged, the former is frequently condemned. Why?

At one level, academicians and other legal thinkers disapprove of prosecutors' unbridled discretion as not fitting into an orderly scheme. But, I see the criticism more often arising out of dissatisfaction with a particular case and expanding to the generalization that plea bargaining is bad. I find two basic reasons for such criticism. The first is that a particular plea-bargain genuinely may be "bad," which means that an offender is offered either a charge reduction or a sentence concession, or both, which is unmerited by the offender and unjustified by any necessity. Experience shows that such "bad" plea-bargains do occur in a small number of cases—generally for expedience, as explained later. The second source of criticism is much more common. This is where an interested party is dissatisfied with the outcome, finding it wholly inadequate to salve his or her injured feelings. I find that this is as likely to occur with a "good" plea-bargain, which is reasoned, conscientious and practical, as it is with a "bad" one.

The reason, I believe, lies in the differing expectations held by experienced criminal attorneys and the general public. Experienced attorneys know the inherent constraints and time-honored practices of our criminal justice

From Nick Schweitzer, "Plea Bargaining: A Prosecutor's View," *Wisconsin Bar Bulletin* (October 1988). Reprinted by permission of *Wisconsin Bar Bulletin*, the official publication of the State Bar of Wisconsin.

system, which imposed practical limits on the punishment of an offender even if she or he were convicted at trial. However, if the case happens to be disposed of by a negotiated plea, critics may ascribe all their frustrations and disappointments to the plea-bargain.

LOOKING AHEAD TO SENTENCING

Strange as it sounds, and despite all the criticism, an essential aspect of plea bargaining is the need to be fair. Plea negotiations, like the sentencing discretion of judges, reflect the need to individualize justice. Only the most naive person would think that a single determinate sentence awaits the end of any particular prosecution. For any given defendant, on any given charge, there is a range of penalties. Most criminal statutes carry a maximum penalty, and some a minimum penalty. However, all Wisconsin statutes, except that for first-degree murder, permit a range. In addition, sentencing options may include community service and probation as well as conditions on probation such as counseling, restitution, jail time and alcohol and drug treatment. Except in certain categories of cases for which sentencing guidelines have been set,[1] sentencing is a human decision. At some stage, some person must decide what sentence will deter future acts by this offender and by other potential offenders without being unduly harsh and at the same time sufficiently assuage the victim.

The sentencing decision is not the function of a trial. A trial is held to determine facts and the essential facts are truly at issue in only a small fraction of criminal cases. The majority of people charged with crimes are guilty and know

it, but before they plead guilty or no contest, they want to know what punishment they face. Often, the only argument is over one or more mitigating factors that do not rise to the level of legal defenses, so a trial in most criminal cases would be a waste of time. Sentencing is the bottom line for most defendants. If they can live with the sentence, most defendants are happy to save the court system and themselves the trouble of a trial. Generally, a bargain can be struck when the advantage to the defendant of an acceptable, known, sentence meets the advantage to the prosecutor of concluding the case for what it realistically is worth.

THE PROSECUTOR'S ROLE

The responsibility for sentencing ultimately lies with a judge. However, no judge has the time to check into the details of every felony, misdemeanor and ordinance that comes before the court. Court calendars being what they are, most judges want a recommendation from someone who already has taken the time to investigate the offense, the situation of any victims and the background of the defendant. A judge can accomplish this by ordering the local probation office to conduct a presentence investigation, but resources limit this option to only the more serious cases.

The prosecution and defense attorneys are in a position to review the offense, check the defendant's record and character, contact any victims and recommend an appropriate sentence. The prosecuting attorney knows the details of the offense and the defendant's prior record. The defense attorney knows the defendant and any mitigating factors. In most routine cases, these two lawyers are in the best position early on to discuss the merits of the case and are best able to find the time to negotiate before trial. If these two sides can reach agreement, the judge's decision can reasonably be reduced to review and ratification.

Another important reason for negotiation to take place at this level is the prosecutor's exclusive discretion to reduce or amend charges. A charge may be totally dismissed only with the court's approval.[2] However, the judge has no mandate to amend or reduce a charge. The discretion to amend charges is vested in the prosecutor to cover those rare cases where the wrong charge is issued.[3] This authority turns out to be even more useful in the frequent cases where some penalty is inappropriate. As an example, cooperative first offenders usually are offered some alternative, such as a county ordinance, that allows them to avoid a criminal record. This discretion to amend adds a second dimension to plea negotiations; the parties can consider not only the range of penalties associated with the original charge, but also the ranges associated with all related charges.

There are other reasons for a prosecutor to make concessions in return for a guilty or no contest plea. More often than not, a prosecutor will dismiss or read in one or more offenses for a defendant facing multiple charges. Usually, the prosecutor still will insist on a sentence consistent with the total number of offenses, but there is a general belief that reducing the number of convictions on the defendant's record will induce the defendant not to tie up the court system by trying all the cases. There also are cases in which the prosecutor faces some

obstacle to conviction, other than the defendant's innocence, such as an unavailable witness or a witness who would be compromised or traumatized by having to testify. In such cases, any conviction, even on a reduced charge, generally is seen as better than a dismissal, an acquittal or a Pyrrhic conviction. Then, there are the infrequent cases in which a concession is necessary to secure a defendant's testimony against a co-defendant in an unrelated case. Plea bargaining also can be used to expedite cases that would drag on for months or years. A prosecutor may agree to a charge or sentence concession in return for a speedy disposition that benefits a victim or quickly takes an offender out of circulation.

THE QUALITY OF THE BARGAIN

For all the above reasons, cases will continue to be settled at the trial attorneys' level. The real issue is the quality of the decisions made. Plea bargaining is a tool and its mark largely depends on the skill and care of the crafter. If the product is flawed, the fault lies less with the tool than with the user. The quality of the plea-bargain depends on the values, interests and abilities of the attorneys. If both sides are interested in finding a "just" sentence, the result is as likely to be "good" as that made by a conscientious judge. But if one or both sides are mainly interested in expedience, primarily want to "win" or have priorities unrelated to the merits of the defendant and the case, then the bargain may well be "bad." Unfortunately, it is true that prosecutors and defense attorneys make some "bad" plea-bargains. It also is true that judges can make sentencing decisions that are injudicious. Since the majority of cases are disposed of by negotiated plea, the opportunity for a "bad" decision by prosecutors is that much greater.

Two weaknesses exist in the plea bargaining process. First, it can become routine and thereby an end rather than a means. As stated earlier, very few cases crossing a prosecutor's desk deserve a trial. The majority of cases do settle and prosecutors develop a strong work habit of managing their caseload that way. As a result, a holdout case may be seen as a nuisance, causing plea bargaining to deteriorate into coercion, concession and compromise without regard for the merits of the case. The indiscriminate use of plea bargaining to clear court calendars justly has been condemned. But under pressure, a prosecutor's definition of a "reasonable" plea-bargain has an unfortunate tendency to expand.

Second, plea bargaining does not encourage participation by the victim. The criminal justice system historically has treated victims cavalierly. It is only with the recent development of victim/witness programs that victims' involvement is being encouraged.

Most victims want to have a voice in the outcome of a case, but this very seldom happens when cases are plea-bargained. Victims generally are left out because negotiations often are informal and unscheduled and talking to victims can be time-consuming and painful, as a victim's viewpoint often is very different from that of an experienced criminal attorney. Victims have difficulty accepting the concept of "what a case is worth" in criminal justice terms and understanding the realistic limitations on punishment. The prosecutor risks becoming the focus of the victim's anger, disappointment and abuse.

SUGGESTIONS

There are no standards or checks imposed on plea bargaining by statute or case law. In fact, courts strictly have avoided involvement in the process.[4] Whether to subject plea-bargaining to some degree of quality control is a policy decision balancing discretion and accountability. However, I offer a few suggestions to district attorneys and judges.

First, have set guidelines as have some D.A. offices. Well-understood policies for reductions and sentencing recommendations can limit very effectively the possibilities for poor judgment. Guidelines could be developed statewide, similar to the sentencing guidelines for judges, which set standard dispositions yet allow departure from the standards for good reason.

Second, plea-bargains could be reduced to writing and reviewed within the D.A.'s office before final agreement. Although this would add a step or two to the process, it would go a long way toward establishing uniformity, avoiding bad decisions and, if part of the policy, assuring that victims' views are considered.

Finally, any judge who is concerned about the quality of the plea-bargains brought before the court could develop questions for accepting a plea bargain, similar to those for the taking of a guilty plea. This allows the judge to play a more active role, or at least to signal that certain aspects of plea bargaining are open to scrutiny, without taking part in the actual negotiations. One question might ask the attorneys for justification of any reduction or sentencing recommendation. Another might ask whether a victim was involved and, if so, whether the victim has been consulted.

CONCLUSION

Despite my reservations about the potential and occasional weaknesses of plea bargaining, I defend the practice as a practical solution to some of the needs and pressures of today's criminal justice system. Plea bargaining is a vital part of the complex system of powers and responsibilities that has evolved in our efforts to make justice as equal, fair and efficient as resources permit. Without it, other parts of the system would have to absorb increased stress. Specifically, if we wanted judges to make all the decisions (even assuming that their decisions would uniformly be better), we would need more judges, more courtrooms, more jurors and more trials. This is not because defendants want trials but largely because most defendants will "plead in" only if they know ahead of time what sentence is likely to be imposed. Plea bargaining is essential until society decides to allocate sufficient resources to these ends. When exercised with a due regard to the case, the victim and the defendant, plea-bargains can result in outcomes as "just" as any available in our current system.

NOTES

1. State of Wisconsin Sentencing Commission, "Wisconsin Sentencing Guidelines Manual," (1985).

2. *State v. Kenyon*, 85 Wis. 2d 36, 270 N.W.2d 160 (1978).

3. Wis. Stat. § 971.29.

4. *See In the Matter of the Amendment of Rules of Civil & Criminal Procedure: Sections 971.07 & 971.08, Stats.*, 128 Wis. 2d 422, 383 N.W.2d 496 (1986); *State v. Erickson*, 53 Wis. 2d 474, 192 N.W.2d 872 (1972); *Rahhal v. State*, 52 Wis. 2d 144, 187 N.W.2d 800 (1971); *State v. Wolfe*, 46 Wis. 2d 478, 175 N.W.2d 216 (1970).

POSTSCRIPT

Should Plea Bargaining Be Abolished?

Plea bargaining, former Supreme Court chief justice Warren E. Burger has stated, "is an essential component of the administration of criminal justice." What is more debatable is another statement by Burger that "properly administered, it is to be encouraged." We do not know how many innocent persons have pleaded guilty in order to avoid a trial. On the other hand, abolitionists have difficulty describing what a workable replacement for plea bargaining would be like.

Interesting experiments to reform or abolish plea bargaining have taken place in Texas, as seen in Weninger, "The Abolition of Plea Bargaining: A Case Study of El Paso County, Texas," 35 *UCLA Law Review* 265 (1987), and Callan, "An Experiment in Justice Without Plea Negotiation," 13 *Law and Society Review*, pp. 327–347 (1979); Alaska, as seen in Rubinstein and White, "Plea Bargaining: Can Alaska Live Without It?" *Judicature* (December–January, 1979); and Arizona, as seen in Berger, "The Case Against Plea Bargaining," *ABA Journal*, p. 621 (1976). These and other alternatives to the plea bargaining system are examined in Alschuler, "Implementing the Criminal Defendant's Right to Trial: Alternatives to the Plea Bargaining System," 50 *University of Chicago Law Review* 931 (1983); Cohen and Doob, "Public Attitudes to Plea Bargaining," 32 *Criminal Law Quarterly* 85 (1989); "The Victim's Veto: A Way to Increase Victim Impact on Criminal Case Dispositions," 77 *California Law Review* 417 (1989); Fine, "Plea Bargaining: An Unnecessary Evil," 70 *Marquette Law Review* 615 (1987); Schulhofer, "Is Plea Bargaining Inevitable?" *Harvard Law Review* 1037 (1984); and Note, "Constitutional Alternatives to Plea Bargaining: A New Waive," 132 *University of Pennsylvania Law Review* 327 (1984).

Plea bargaining has been the subject of a considerable number of Supreme Court cases. Among the most noteworthy are *Boykin v. Alabama*, 395 U.S. 238 (1969); *Brady v. U.S.*, 397 U.S. 742 (1970); *North Carolina v. Alford*, 400 U.S. 25 (1970); *Santobello v. New York*, 404 U.S. 257 (1971); and *Bordenkircher v. Hayes*, 434 U.S. 357 (1978). Each of these cases describes the plight of a particular defendant, but probably the most vivid account of the plea bargaining process is a journalist's description. See Mills, "I Have Nothing To Do With Justice," *Life* (March 12, 1971), reprinted in Bonsignore et al., *Before the Law: An Introduction to the Legal Process* (Houghton Mifflin, 1979).

PART 2

Law and Social Values

In any democratic society, the laws must reflect some consensus concerning the values of that society. Some of these values are clearly and easily determined. Laws against murder and theft, for example, command respect and acceptance and reflect widely held values.

In an increasingly complex, diverse, and technologically advanced society, however, questions of how best to protect individual rights of minorities and those with unpopular views inspire intense emotional debate, as evidenced by the issues in this section.

Is Drug Use Testing Permitted Under the Fourth Amendment?

Is "Hate Speech" Fully Protected by the Constitution?

Do Prayers at Public School Graduation Ceremonies Violate the Constitution?

Is Abortion Protected by the Constitution?

Should Pornography Be Protected by the First Amendment?

Is Affirmative Action Constitutional?

Can States Restrict the Right to Die?

Should Homosexuality Bar a Parent from Being Awarded Custody of a Child?

ISSUE 4

Is Drug Use Testing Permitted Under the Fourth Amendment?

YES: Anthony Kennedy, from Majority Opinion, *National Treasury Employees Union v. William Von Raab,* U.S. Supreme Court (1989)

NO: Antonin Scalia, from Dissenting Opinion, *National Treasury Employees Union v. William Von Raab,* U.S. Supreme Court (1989)

ISSUE SUMMARY

YES: U.S. Supreme Court justice Anthony Kennedy believes that drug tests of Customs Service officials are reasonable under the Fourth Amendment even when there is no probable cause or individualized suspicion.
NO: Justice Antonin Scalia, in dissent, argues that the Customs Service rules are not justified, serve no reasonable purpose, and are unnecessary invasions of privacy.

Assume that you have recently completed your education and have applied for a job at a local public high school. You submitted a written application and have been invited for an interview. When you appear at school department headquarters, the receptionist tells you that prior to the interview you will have to provide a urine sample, which will be tested for the presence of drugs. If the test shows traces of certain drugs, your application for employment will be denied. What would be your response to such a request? Would you take the test? Do you have any objections or concerns about such tests? Do you think such practices should be allowed?

As public concern about drug abuse in this country has grown, drug use testing has become increasingly common. More than a quarter of all *Fortune* 500 companies test employees for drug use. Professional and college athletes are tested. The Department of Defense began mandatory urinalysis for members of the armed forces in 1982, and it claims that drug use in the military has been cut in half as a result. Yet, critics argue, drug tests are often inaccurate and administered improperly, innocent people are hurt, privacy is invaded unduly, and testing programs are often a substitute for long-range solutions involving education or treatment.

In trying to develop a legal response to expanded proposals for drug use testing, consider the circumstances that courts might find significant in the hypothetical example above.

1. *Private or public institution* The case described above involves a government agency as employer. The Constitution provides more protection to citizens from governmental invasions of privacy than from similar acts by private employers. Even if the Fourth Amendment, which protects against unreasonable searches and seizures, were held to bar drug use testing by the government, private employers might still be allowed to conduct such tests. Unless privacy or civil rights laws are found to be applicable, legislation, either by states or by Congress, would probably be necessary to regulate private drug testing.

2. *Test reliability* Urine tests give false positive results between 5 and 20 percent of the time. In addition, some over-the-counter drugs and even some foods have been known to trigger positive readings. If you had a cold the day of your interview and took a Contac or Sudafed pill that morning, your test might suggest the presence of amphetamines. Thus, urine tests will identify all illegal users but will also direct suspicion on some innocent persons. More expensive follow-up tests can be used to separate the legal from the illegal drug users, but sometimes action is taken merely on the basis of the first urine screen. Should this be permitted? How much suspicion of drug use should be required before some action is taken?

3. *Privacy* In thinking about the drug testing process, you might be concerned with two different privacy issues. The most obvious is the intrusiveness of the testing procedure itself. In addition, however, drug use testing raises the question of whether or not employers have a legitimate interest in the off-the-job activities of employees. A positive reading by the most commonly used urine tests will not reveal when the drug was used. Drug traces may remain in the urine for days or weeks. Thus, the employer often is not testing for drugs that were consumed on the job or are affecting job performance. Should it be lawful for employers to concern themselves with the off-hours activities of employees, even if they are illegal?

Drug use testing is becoming increasingly common. Many, if not most, individuals can live their lives without being fingerprinted or experiencing a lie detector test, but drug use testing is something that is becoming more difficult to avoid. It is a condition of employment in much of the private sector and in a variety of public sector occupations. It is a test that is of value only if given periodically and without notice. In the following opinion by Justice Anthony Kennedy, a majority of the Supreme Court finds that nothing in the Constitution bars such testing programs. In a very vigorous response, Justice Antonin Scalia, one of the most conservative members of the current Supreme Court, accuses the majority of needlessly invading privacy and weakening the Fourth Amendment.

YES

Anthony Kennedy

MAJORITY OPINION

NATIONAL TREASURY EMPLOYEES UNION v WILLIAM VON RAAB,
Commissioner, United States Customs Service

Justice Kennedy delivered the opinion of the Court.

We granted certiorari to decide whether it violates the Fourth Amendment for the United States Customs Service to require a urinalysis test from employees who seek transfer or promotion to certain positions.

I
A

The United States Customs Service, a bureau of the Department of the Treasury, is the federal agency responsible for processing persons, carriers, cargo, and mail into the United States, collecting revenue from imports, and enforcing customs and related laws. An important responsibility of the Service is the interdiction and seizure of contraband, including illegal drugs. In 1987 alone, Customs agents seized drugs with a retail value of nearly 9 billion dollars. In the routine discharge of their duties, many Customs employees have direct contact with those who traffic in drugs for profit. Drug import operations, often directed by sophisticated criminal syndicates, may be effected by violence or its threat. As a necessary response, many Customs operatives carry and use firearms in connection with their official duties.

In December 1985, respondent, the Commissioner of Customs, established a Drug Screening Task Force to explore the possibility of implementing a drug screening program within the Service. After extensive research and consultation with experts in the field, the Task Force concluded "that drug screening through urinalysis is technologically reliable, valid and accurate." Citing this conclusion, the Commissioner announced his intention to require drug tests of employees who applied for, or occupied, certain positions

From *National Treasury Employees Union et al. v. William Von Raab*, 109 S.Ct. 1384, 103 L.Ed. 2d 685 (1989). Some notes and case citations omitted.

within the Service. The Commissioner stated his belief that "Customs is largely drug-free," but noted also that "unfortunately no segment of society is immune from the threat of illegal drug use." Drug interdiction has become the agency's primary enforcement mission, and the Commissioner stressed that "there is no room in the Customs Service for those who break the laws prohibiting the possession and use of illegal drugs."

In May 1986, the Commissioner announced implementation of the drug-testing program. Drug tests were made a condition of placement or employment for positions that meet one or more of three criteria. The first is direct involvement in drug interdiction or enforcement of related laws, an activity the Commissioner deemed fraught with obvious dangers to the mission of the agency and the lives of customs agents. The second criterion is a requirement that the incumbent carry firearms, as the Commissioner concluded that "[p]ublic safety demands that employees who carry deadly arms and are prepared to make instant life or death decisions be drug free." The third criterion is a requirement for the incumbent to handle "classified" material, which the Commissioner determined might fall into the hands of smugglers if accessible to employees who, by reason of their own illegal drug use, are susceptible to bribery or blackmail.

After an employee qualifies for a position covered by the Customs testing program, the Service advises him by letter that his final selection is contingent upon successful completion of drug screening. An independent contractor contacts the employee to fix the time and place for collecting the sample. On reporting for the test, the employee must produce photographic identification and remove any outer garments, such as a coat or a jacket, and personal belongings. The employee may produce the sample behind a partition, or in the privacy of a bathroom stall if he so chooses. To ensure against adulteration of the specimen, or substitution of a sample from another person, a monitor of the same sex as the employee remains close at hand to listen for the normal sounds of urination. Dye is added to the toilet water to prevent the employee from using the water to adulterate the sample.

Upon receiving the specimen, the monitor inspects it to ensure its proper temperature and color, places a tamper-proof custody seal over the container, and affixes an identification label indicating the date and the individual's specimen number. The employee signs a chain-of-custody form, which is initialed by the monitor, and the urine sample is placed in a plastic bag, sealed, and submitted to a laboratory.[1]

The laboratory tests the sample for the presence of marijuana, cocaine, opiates, amphetamines, and phencyclidine. Two tests are used. An initial screening test uses the enzyme-multiplied-immunoassay technique (EMIT). Any specimen that is identified as positive on this initial test must then be confirmed using gas chromatography/mass spectrometry (GC/MS). Confirmed positive results are reported to a "Medical Review Officer," "[a] licensed physician . . . who has knowledge of substance abuse disorders and has appropriate medical training to interpret and evaluate the individual's positive test result together with his or her medical history and any other relevant biomedical information." HHS Reg § 1.2, 53 Fed Reg 11980 (1988); HHS Reg § 2.4(g), id., at 11983. After verifying the positive result, the Medical Review Officer transmits it to the agency.

Customs employees who test positive for drugs and who can offer no satisfactory explanation are subject to dismissal from the Service. Test results may not, however, be turned over to any other agency, including criminal prosecutors, without the employee's written consent.

B

Petitioners, a union of federal employees and a union official, commenced this suit in the United States District Court for the Eastern District of Louisiana on behalf of current Customs Service employees who seek covered positions. Petitioners alleged that the Custom Service drug-testing program violated, inter alia, the Fourth Amendment. The District Court agreed. 649 F Supp. 380 (1986). The court acknowledged "the legitimate governmental interest in a drug-free work place and work force," but concluded that "the drug testing plan constitutes an overly intrusive policy of searches and seizures without probable cause or reasonable suspicion, in violation of legitimate expectations of privacy." Id., at 387. The court enjoined the drug testing program, and ordered the Customs Service not to require drug tests of any applicants for covered positions.

A divided panel of the United States Court of Appeals for the Fifth Circuit vacated the injunction. 816 F2d 170 (1987). The court agreed with petitioners that the drug screening program, by requiring an employee to produce a urine sample for chemical testing, effects a search within the meaning of the Fourth Amendment. The court held further that the searches required by the Commissioner's directive are reasonable under the Fourth Amendment. It first noted that the "[t]he Service has attempted to minimize the intrusiveness of the search" by not requiring visual observation of the act of urination and by affording notice to the employee that he will be tested. Id., at 177. The court also considered it significant that the program limits discretion in determining which employees are to be tested, ibid., and noted that the tests are an aspect of the employment relationship. Id., at 178.

The court further found that the Government has a strong interest in detecting drug use among employees who meet the criteria of the Customs program. It reasoned that drug use by covered employees casts substantial doubt on their ability to discharge their duties honestly and vigorously, undermining public confidence in the integrity of the Service and concomitantly impairing the Service's efforts to enforce the drug laws. Illicit drug users, the court found, are susceptible to bribery and blackmail, may be tempted to divert for their own use portions of any drug shipments they interdict, and may, if required to carry firearms, "endanger the safety of their fellow agents, as well as their own, when their performance is impaired by drug use." Ibid. "Considering the nature and responsibilities of the jobs for which applicants are being considered at Customs and the limited scope of the search," the court stated, "the exaction of consent as a condition of assignment to the new job is not unreasonable." Id., at 179.

The dissenting judge concluded that the Customs program is not an effective method for achieving the Service's goals. He argued principally that an employee "given a five day notification of a test date need only abstain from drug use to prevent being identified as a user." Id., at 184. He noted also that persons already employed in sensitive positions are not subject to the test. Ibid. Because he did not believe the Customs program can achieve its purposes, the dissenting judge found it unreasonable under the Fourth Amendment.

We granted certiorari. 485 US _____, 99 L Ed 2d 232, 108 S Ct 1072 (1988). We now affirm so much of the judgment of the court of appeals as upheld the testing of employees directly involved in drug interdiction or required to carry firearms. We vacate the judgment to the extent it upheld the testing of applicants for positions requiring the incumbent to handle classified materials, and remand for further proceedings.

II

In *Skinner v Railway Labor Executives' Assn.*, ante, at _____, 103 L Ed 2d 639, 109 S Ct _____, decided today, we hold that federal regulations requiring employees of private railroads to produce urine samples for chemical testing implicate the Fourth Amendment, as those tests invade reasonable expectations of privacy. Our earlier cases have settled that the Fourth Amendment protects individuals from unreasonable searches conducted by the government, even when the Government acts as an employer, and, in view of our holding in Railway Labor Executives that urine tests are searches, it follows that the Customs Service's drug testing program must meet the reasonableness requirement of the Fourth Amendment.

While we have often emphasized, and reiterate today, that a search must be supported, as a general matter, by a warrant issued upon probable cause, our decision in Railway Labor Executives reaffirms the longstanding principle that neither a warrant nor probable cause, nor, indeed, any measure of individualized suspicion, is an indispensable component of reasonableness in every circumstance. As we note in Railway Labor Executives, our cases establish that where a Fourth Amendment intrusion serves special governmental needs, beyond the normal need for law enforcement, it is necessary to balance the individual's privacy expectations against the Government's interests to determine whether it is impractical to require a warrant or some level of individualized suspicion in the particular context.

It is clear that the Customs Service's drug testing program is not designed to serve the ordinary needs of law enforcement. Test results may not be used in a criminal prosecution of the employee without the employee's consent. The purposes of the program are to deter drug use among those eligible for promotion to sensitive positions within the Service and to prevent the promotion of drug users to those positions. These substantial interests, no less than the Government's concern for safe rail transportation at issue in Railway Labor Executives, present a special need that may justify departure from the ordinary warrant and probable cause requirements. . . .

B

Even where it is reasonable to dispense with the warrant requirement in the particular circumstances, a search ordinarily must be based on probable cause. Our cases teach, however, that the probable-cause standard " 'is peculiarly related to criminal investigations.' " In particular, the traditional probable-cause standard may be unhelpful in analyzing the reasonableness of routine administrative functions, especially where the Government seeks to *prevent* the development of hazardous conditions or to detect violations that rarely generate articulable grounds for searching any particular place or person. Cf. *Camara v Municipal Court*, 387 US, at 535–536, 18 L Ed 2d 930, 87 S Ct 1727 (noting that building code inspections, unlike searches conducted pursuant to a criminal investigation, are designed "to prevent even the unintentional development of conditions which are hazardous to public health and safety"); *United States v Martinez-Fuerte*, 428 US, at 557, 49 L Ed 2d 1116, 96 S Ct 3074 (noting that requiring particularized suspicion before routine stops on major highways near the Mexican border "would be impractical because the flow of traffic tends to be too heavy to allow the particularized study of a given car that would enable it to be identified as a possible carrier of illegal aliens"). Our precedents have settled that, in certain limited circumstances, the Government's need to discover such latent or hidden conditions, or to prevent their development, is sufficiently compelling to justify the intrusion on privacy entailed by conducting such searches without any measure of individualized suspicion. We think the Government's need to conduct the suspicionless searches required by the Customs program outweighs the privacy interests of employees engaged directly in drug interdiction, and of those who otherwise are required to carry firearms.

The Customs Service is our Nation's first line of defense against one of the greatest problems affecting the health and welfare of our population. We have adverted before to "the veritable national crisis in law enforcement caused by smuggling of illicit narcotics." *United States v Montoya de Hernandez*, 473 US 531, 538, 87 L Ed 2d 381, 105 S Ct 3304 (1985).

See also *Florida v Royer*, 460 US 491, 513, 75 L Ed 2d 229, 103 S Ct 1319 (Blackmun, J., dissenting). Our cases also reflect the traffickers' seemingly inexhaustible repertoire of deceptive practices and elaborate schemes for importing narcotics. e.g., *United States v Montoya de Hernandez*, supra, at 538–539, 87 L Ed 2d 381, 105 S Ct 3304; *United States v Ramsey*, 431 US 606, 608–609, 52 L Ed 2d 617, 97 S Ct 1972 (1977). The record in this case confirms that, through the adroit selection of source locations, smuggling routes, and increasingly elaborate methods of concealment, drug traffickers have managed to bring into this country increasingly large quantities of illegal drugs. The record also indicates, and it is well known, that drug smugglers do not hesitate to use violence to protect their lucrative trade and avoid apprehension.

Many of the Service's employees are often exposed to this criminal element and to the controlled substances they seek to smuggle into the country. The physical safety of these employees may be threatened, and many may be tempted not only by bribes from the traffickers with whom they deal, but also by their own access to vast sources of valuable contraband seized and controlled by the Service. The Commissioner indicated below that "Customs [o]fficers have been shot, stabbed, run over, dragged by automobiles, and assaulted with blunt objects while performing their duties." At least nine officers have died in the line of duty since 1974. He also noted that Customs officers have been the targets of bribery by drug smugglers on numerous occasions, and several have been removed from the Service for accepting bribes and other integrity violations. Id., at 114. See also Customs USA, Fiscal Year 1987, at 31 (reporting internal investigations that resulted in the arrest of 24 employees and 54 civilians); Customs USA, Fiscal Year 1986, p 32 (reporting that 334 criminal and serious integrity investigations were conducted during the fiscal year, resulting in the arrest of 37 employees and 17 civilians); Customs USA, Fiscal Year 1985, at 32 (reporting that 284 criminal and serious integrity investigations were conducted during the 1985 fiscal year, resulting in the arrest of 15 employees and 51 civilians).

It is readily apparent that the Government has a compelling interest in ensuring that front-line interdiction personnel are physically fit, and have unimpeachable integrity and judgment. Indeed, the Government's interest here is at least as important as its interest in searching travelers entering the country. We have long held that travelers seeking to enter the country may be stopped and required to submit to a routine search without probable cause, or even founded suspicion, "because of national self protection reasonably requiring one entering the country to identify himself as entitled to come in, and his belongings as effects which may be lawfully brought in." Carroll v United States, 267 US 132, 154, 69 L Ed 543, 45 S Ct 280, 39 ALR 790 (1985). This national interest in self protection could be irreparably damaged if those charged with safeguarding it were, because of their own drug use, unsympathetic to their mission of interdicting narcotics. A drug user's indifference to the Service's basic mission or, even worse, his active complicity with the malefactors, can facilitate importation of sizable drug shipments or block apprehension of dangerous criminals. The public interest demands effective measures to bar drug users from positions directly involving the interdiction of illegal drugs.

The public interest likewise demands effective measures to prevent the promotion of drug users to positions that require the incumbent to carry a firearm, even if the incumbent is not engaged directly in the interdiction of drugs. Customs employees who may use deadly force plainly "discharge duties fraught with such risks of injury to others that even a momentary lapse of attention can have disastrous consequences." Railway Labor Executives, ante at 103 L Ed 2d 639. We agree with the Government that the public should not bear the risk that employees who may suffer from impaired perception and judgment will be promoted to positions where they may need to employ deadly force. Indeed, ensuring against the creation of this dangerous risk will itself further Fourth Amendment values, as the use of deadly force may violate the Fourth Amendment in certain circumstances. See Tennessee v Garner, 471 US 1, 7–12, 85 L Ed 2d 1, 105 S Ct 1694 (1985).

Against these valid public interests we must weigh the interference with individual liberty that results from requiring these classes of employees to undergo a urine test. The interference with individual privacy that results from the collection of a urine sample for subsequent chemical analysis could be substantial in some circumstances. We have recognized, however, that the "operational realities of the workplace" may render entirely reasonable certain work-related intrusions by supervisors and co-workers that might be viewed as unreasonable in other contexts. While these operational realities will rarely affect an employee's expectations of privacy with respect to searches of his person, or of personal effects that the employee may bring to the workplace, it is plain that certain forms of public employment may diminish privacy expectations even with respect to such personal searches. Employees of the United States Mint, for example, should expect to be subject to certain routine personal searches when they leave the workplace every day. Similarly, those who join our military or intelligence services may not only be required to give what in other contexts might be viewed as extraordinary assurances of trustworthiness and probity, but also may expect intrusive inquiries into their physical fitness for those special positions. Cf. *Snepp v United States*, 444 US 507, 509, n 3, 62 L Ed 2d 704, 100 S Ct 763 (1980); *Parker v Levy*, 417 US 733, 758, 41 L Ed 2d 439, 94 S Ct 2547 (1974); *Committee for GI Rights v Callaway*, 171 US App DC 73, 84, 518 F 2d 466, 477 (1975).

We think Customs employees who are directly involved in the interdiction of illegal drugs or who are required to carry firearms in the line of duty likewise have a diminished expectation of privacy in respect to the intrusions occasioned by a urine test. Unlike most private citizens or government employees in general, employees involved in drug interdiction reasonably should expect effective inquiry into their fitness and probity. Much the same is true of employees who are required to carry firearms. Because successful performance of their duties depends uniquely on their judgment and dexterity, these employees cannot reasonably expect to keep from the Service personal information that bears directly on their fitness. While reasonable tests designed to elicit this information doubtless infringe some privacy expectations, we do not believe these expectations outweigh the Government's compelling interests in safety and in the integrity of our borders.[2]

Without disparaging the importance of the governmental interests that support the suspicionless searches of these employees, petitioners nevertheless contend that the Service's drug testing program is unreasonable in two particulars. First, petitioners argue that the program is unjustified because it is not based on a belief that testing will reveal any drug use by covered employees. In pressing this argument, petitioners point out that the Service's testing scheme was not implemented in response to any perceived drug problem among Customs employees, and that the program actually has not led to the discovery of a significant number of drug users. Counsel for petitioners informed us at oral argument that no more than 5 employees out of 3,600 have tested positive for drugs. Second, petitioners contend that the Service's scheme is not a "sufficiently productive mechanism to justify [its] intrusion upon Fourth Amendment interests," *Delaware v Prouse*, 440 US, at 648, 658–659, 59 L Ed 2d 660, 99 S Ct 1391, because illegal drug users can avoid detection with ease by temporary abstinence or by surreptitious adulteration of their urine specimens. These contentions are unpersuasive.

Petitioners' first contention evinces an unduly narrow view of the context in which the Service's testing program was implemented. Petitioners do not dispute, nor can there be doubt, that drug abuse is one of the most serious problems confronting our society today. There is little reason to believe that American workplaces are immune from this pervasive social problem, as is amply illustrated by our decision in Railway Labor Executives. See also *Masino v United States*, 589 F2d 1048, 1050 (Ct Cl 1978) (describing marijuana use by two Customs Inspectors). Detecting drug impairment on the part of employees can be a difficult task, especially where, as here, it is not feasible to subject employees and their work-product to the kind of day-to-day scrutiny that is the norm in more traditional office environments. Indeed, the almost unique mission of the Service gives the Government a compelling interest in ensuring that many of these covered employees do not use drugs even off-duty, for such use creates risks of bribery and blackmail against which the Government is entitled to guard. In light of the extraordinary safety and national security hazards that would attend the promotion of drug users to positions that require the carrying of firearms or the interdiction of controlled substances, the Service's policy of deterring drug users from seeking such promotions cannot be deemed unreasonable.

The mere circumstance that all but a few of the employees tested are entirely innocent of wrongdoing does not impugn the program's validity. The same is likely to be true of householders who are required to submit to suspicionless housing code inspections, see *Camara v Municipal Court*, 387 US 523, 18 L Ed 2d 930, 87 S Ct 1727 (1967), and of motorists who are stopped at the checkpoints we approved in *United States v Martinez-Fuerte*, 428 US 543, 49 L Ed 2d 1116, 96 S Ct 3074 (1976). The Service's program is designed to prevent the promotion of drug users to sensitive positions as much as it is designed to detect those employees who use drugs. Where, as here, the possible harm against which the Government seeks to guard is substantial, the need to prevent its occurrence furnishes an ample justification for reasonable searches calculated to advance the Government's goal.[3]

We think petitioners' second argument—that the Service's testing program is ineffective because employees may attempt to deceive the test by a brief abstention before the test date, or by adulterating their urine specimens—overstates the case. As the Court of Appeals noted, addicts may be unable to abstain even for a limited period of time, or may be unaware of the "fade-away effect" of certain drugs. 816 F2d, at 180. More importantly, the avoidance techniques suggested by petitioners are fraught with uncertainty and risks for those employees who venture to attempt them. A particular employee's pattern of elimination for a given drug cannot be predicted with perfect accuracy, and, in any event, this information is not likely to be known or available to the employee. Petitioners' own expert indicated below that the time it takes for particular drugs to become undetectable in urine can vary widely depending on the individual, and may extend for as long as 22 days. Thus, contrary to petitioners' suggestion, no employee reasonably can expect to deceive the test by the simple expedient of abstaining after the test date is assigned. Nor can he expect attempts at adulteration to succeed, in view of the precautions taken by the sample collector to ensure the integrity of the sample. In all the circumstances, we are persuaded that the program bears a close and substantial relation to the Service's goal of deterring drug users from seeking promotion to sensitive positions.

In sum, we believe the Government has demonstrated that its compelling interests in safeguarding our borders and the public safety outweigh the privacy expectations of employees who seek to be promoted to positions that directly involve the interdiction of illegal drugs or that require the incumbent to carry a firearm. We hold that the testing of these employees is reasonable under the Fourth Amendment.

C

We are unable, on the present record, to assess the reasonableness of the Government's testing program insofar as it covers employees who are required "to handle classified material." We readily agree that the Government has a compelling interest in protecting truly sensitive information from those who, "under compulsion of circumstances or for other reasons, . . . might compromise [such] information." *Department of the Navy v Egan*, 98 L Ed 2d 918, 108 S Ct 818 (1988). See also *United States v Robel*, 389 US 258, 267, 19 L Ed 2d 508, 88 S Ct 419 (1967) ("We have recognized that, while the Constitution protects against invasions of individual rights, it does not withdraw from the Government the power to safeguard its vital interests . . . The Government can deny access to its secrets to those who would use such information to harm the Nation"). We also agree that employees who seek promotions to positions where they would handle sensitive information can be required to submit to a urine test under the Service's screening program, especially if the positions covered under this category require background investigations, medical examinations, or other intrusions that may be expected to diminish their expectations of privacy in respect of a urinalysis test. Cf. Department of the *Navy v Egan*, supra, at 98 L Ed 2d 918, 108 S Ct 818 (noting that the Executive branch generally subjects those desiring a security clearance to "a background investigation that varies according to the degree of adverse effect the applicant could have on the national security").

It is not clear, however, whether the category defined by the Service's testing directive encompasses only those Customs employees likely to gain access to sensitive information. Employees who are tested under the Service's scheme include those holding such diverse positions as "Accountant," "Accounting Technician," "Animal Caretaker," "Attorney (All)," "Baggage Clerk," "Co-op Student (All)," "Electric Equipment Repairer," "Mail Clerk/Assistant," and "Messenger." We assume these positions were selected for coverage under the Service's testing program by reason of the incumbent's access to "classified" information, as it is not clear that they would fall under either of the two categories we have already considered. Yet it is not evident that those occupying these positions are likely to gain access to sensitive information, and this apparent discrepancy raises in our minds the question whether the Service has defined this category of employees more broadly than necessary to meet the purposes of the Commissioner's directive.

We cannot resolve this ambiguity on the basis of the record before us, and we think it is appropriate to remand the case to the court of appeals for such proceedings as may be necessary to clarify the scope of this category of employees subject to testing. Upon remand the court of appeals should examine the criteria used by the Service in determining what materials are classified and in deciding whom to test under this rubric. In assessing the reasonableness of requiring tests of these employees, the court should also consider pertinent information bearing upon the employees' privacy expectations, as well as the supervision to which these employees are already subject.

III

Where the Government requires its employees to produce urine samples to be analyzed for evidence of illegal drug use, the collection and subsequent chemical analysis of such samples are searches that must meet the reasonableness requirement of the Fourth Amendment. Because the testing program adopted by the Customs Service is not designed to serve the ordinary needs of law enforcement, we have balanced the public interest in the Service's testing program against the privacy concerns implicated by the tests, without reference to our usual presumption in favor of the procedures specified in the Warrant Clause, to assess whether the tests required by Customs are reasonable.

We hold that the suspicionless testing of employees who apply for promotion to positions directly involving the interdiction of illegal drugs, or to positions which require the incumbent to carry a firearm, is reasonable. The Government's compelling interests in preventing the promotion of drug users to positions where they might endanger the integrity of our Nation's borders or the life of the citizenry outweigh the privacy interests of those who seek promotion to these positions, who enjoy a diminished expectation of privacy by virtue of the special, and obvious, physical and ethical demands of those positions. We do not decide whether testing those who apply for promc   ositions where they would ha   formation is reasonab   inadequ

The i
for th
and

remanded for further proceedings consistent with this opinion.
It is so ordered.

NOTES

1. After this case was decided by the Court of Appeals, 816 F2d 170 (CA5 1987), the United States Department of Health and Human Services, in accordance with recently enacted legislation, Pub L 100-71, § 503, 101 Stat 468–471, promulgated regulations (hereinafter HHS Regulations or HHS Reg) governing certain federal employee drug testing programs. 53 Fed Reg 11979 (1988). To the extent the HHS Regulations add to, or depart from, the procedures adopted as part of a federal drug screening program covered by Pub L 100-71, the HHS Regulations control. Pub L 100-71, § 503(b)(2)(B), 101 Stat. 470. Both parties agree that the Customs Service's drug testing program must conform to the HHS Regulations. See Brief for Petitioners 6, n 8; Brief for Respondents 4–5, and n 4. We therefore consider the HHS Regulations to the extent they supplement or displace the Commissioner's original directive. See *California Bankers Assn. v Shultz,* 416 US 21, 53, 39 L Ed 2d 812, 94 S Ct 1494 (1974); *Thorpe v Housing Authority,* 393 US 268, 281–282, 21 L Ed 2d 474, 89 S Ct 518, 49 Ohio Ops 2d 374 (1969).

One respect in which the original Customs directive differs from the now-prevailing regime concerns the extent to which the employee may be required to disclose personal medical information. Under the Service's original plan, each tested employee was asked to disclose, at the time the urine sample was collected, any medications taken within the last 30 days, and to explain any circumstances under which he may have been in legitimate contact with illegal substances within the last 30 days. Failure to provide this information at this time could result in the agency not considering the effect of medications or other licit contacts with drugs on a positive test result. Under the HHS Regulations, an employee need not provide information concerning medications when he produces the sample for testing. He may instead present such information only after he is notified that his specimen tested positive for illicit drugs, at which time the Medical Review Officer reviews all records made available by the employee to determine whether the positive indication could have been caused   lawful use of drugs. See HHS Reg § 2.7, 53   5–11986 (1988).

               dures prescribed by the Customs
               e collection and analysis of the
               ples do not carry the grave poten-

tial for "arbitrary and oppressive interference with the privacy and personal security of individuals." *United States v Martinez-Fuerte*, 428 US 543, 554, 49 L Ed 2d 1116, 96 S Ct 3074 (1976), that the Fourth Amendment was designed to prevent. Indeed, these procedures significantly minimize the program's intrusion on privacy interests. Only employees who have been tentatively accepted for promotion or transfer to one of the three categories of covered positions are tested, and applicants know at the outset that a drug test is a requirement of those positions. Employees are also notified in advance of the scheduled sample collection, thus reducing to a minimum any "unsettling show of authority," *Delaware v Prouse*, 440 US 648, 657, 59 L Ed 2d 660, 99 S Ct 1391 (1979), that may be associated with unexpected intrusions on privacy. Cf. *United States v Martinez-Fuerte*, supra, at 559, 49 L Ed 2d 1116, 96 S Ct 3074 (noting that the intrusion on privacy occasioned by routine highway checkpoints is minimized by the fact that motorists "are not taken by surprise as they know, or may obtain knowledge of, the location of the checkpoints and will not be stopped elsewhere"); *Wyman v James*, 400 US 309, 320–321, 27 L Ed 2d 408, 91 S Ct 381 (1971) (providing a welfare recipient with advance notice that she would be visited by a welfare caseworker minimized the intrusion on privacy occasioned by the visit). There is no direct observation of the act of urination, as the employee may provide a specimen in the privacy of a stall.

Further, urine samples may be examined only for the specified drugs. The use of samples to test for any other substances is prohibited. See HHS Reg § 2.1(c), 53 Fed Reg 11980 (1988). And, as the court of appeals noted, the combination of EMIT and GC/MS tests required by the Service is highly accurate, assuming proper storage, handling, and measurement techniques. 816 F2d, at 181. Finally, an employee need not disclose personal medical information to the Government unless his test result is positive, and even then any such information is reported to a licensed physician. Taken together, these procedures significantly minimize the intrusiveness of the Service's drug screening program.

3. The point is well illustrated also by the Federal Government's practice of requiring the search of all passengers seeking to board commercial airliners, as well as the search of their carry-on luggage, without any basis for suspecting any particular passenger of an untoward motive. Applying our precedents dealing with administrative searches, see, e.g., *Camara v Municipal Court*, the lower courts that have considered the question have consistently concluded that such searches are reasonable under the Fourth Amendment. As Judge Friendly explained in a leading case upholding such searches:

"When the risk is the jeopardy to hundreds of human lives and millions of dollars of property inherent in the pirating or blowing up of a large airplane, that danger *alone* meets the test of reasonableness, so long as the search is conducted in good faith for the purpose of preventing hijacking or like damage and with reasonable scope and the passenger has been given advance notice of his liability to such a search so that he can avoid it by choosing not to travel by air." *United States v Edwards*, 498 F2d 496, 500 (CA2 1974) (emphasis in original). See also *United States v Skipwith*, 482 F2d 1272, 1275–1276 (CA5 1973); *United States v Davis*, 482 F2d 893, 907–912 (CA9 1973).

It is true, as counsel for petitioners pointed out at oral argument, that these air piracy precautions were adopted in response to an observable national and international hijacking crisis. Tr of Oral Arg 13. Yet we would not suppose that, if the validity of these searches be conceded, the Government would be precluded from conducting them absent a demonstration of danger as to any particular airport or airline. It is sufficient that the Government have a compelling interest in preventing an otherwise pervasive societal problem from spreading to the particular context.

Nor would we think, in view of the obvious deterrent purpose of these searches, that the validity of the government's airport screening program necessarily turns on whether significant numbers of putative air pirates are actually discovered by the searches conducted under the program. In the 15 years the program has been in effect, more than 9.5 *billion* persons have been screened, and over 10 *billion* pieces of luggage have been inspected. See Federal Aviation Administration, Semiannual Report to Congress on the Effectiveness of The Civil Aviation Program (Nov. 1988) (Exhibit 6). By far the overwhelming majority of those persons who have been searched, like Customs employees who have been tested under the Service's drug screening scheme, have proved entirely innocent—only 42,000 firearms have been detected during the same period. Ibid. When the Government's interest lies in deterring highly hazardous conduct, a low incidence of such conduct, far from impugning the validity of the scheme for implementing this interest, is more logically viewed as a hallmark of success. See *Bell v Wolfish*, 441 US 520, 559, 60 L Ed 2d 447, 99 S Ct 1861 (1979).

NO

Antonin Scalia

DISSENTING OPINION OF
ANTONIN SCALIA

Justice Scalia, with whom Justice Stevens joins, dissenting.

The issue in this case is not whether Customs Service employees can constitutionally be denied promotion, or even dismissed, for a single instance of unlawful drug use, at home or at work. They assuredly can. The issue here is what steps can constitutionally be taken to *detect* such drug use. The Government asserts it can demand that employees perform "an excretory function traditionally shielded by great privacy," *Skinner v Railway Labor Executives' Assn.*, ante, at 103 L Ed 2d 6539, while "a monitor of the same sex . . . remains close at hand to listen for the normal sounds," ante, at 103 L Ed 2d 699, and that the excretion thus produced be turned over to the Government for chemical analysis. The Court agrees that this constitutes a search for purposes of the Fourth Amendment—and I think it obvious that it is a type of search particularly destructive of privacy and offensive to personal dignity.

Until today this Court had upheld a bodily search separate from arrest and without individualized suspicion of wrongdoing only with respect to prison inmates, relying upon the uniquely dangerous nature of that environment. See *Bell v Wolfish*, 441 US 520, 558–560, 60 L Ed 2d 447, 99 S Ct 1861 (1979). Today, in *Skinner*, we allow a less intrusive bodily search of railroad employees involved in train accidents. I joined the Court's opinion there because the demonstrated frequency of drug and alcohol use by the targeted class of employees, and the demonstrated connection between such use and grave harm, rendered the search a reasonable means of protecting society. I decline to join the Court's opinion in the present case because neither frequency of use nor connection to harm is demonstrated or even likely. In my view the Customs Service rules are a kind of immolation of privacy and human dignity in symbolic opposition to drug use.

The Fourth Amendment protects the "right of the people to be secure in their persons, houses, papers, and effects, against unreasonable searches and seizures." While there are some absolutes in Fourth Amendment law, as

From *National Treasury Employees Union et al. v. William Von Raab*, 109 S.Ct. 1384, 103 L.Ed. 2d 685 (1989). Some case citations omitted.

soon as those have been left behind and the question comes down to whether a particular search has been "reasonable," the answer depends largely upon the social necessity that prompts the search. Thus, in upholding the administrative search of a student's purse in a school, we began with the observation (documented by an agency report to Congress) that "[m]aintaining order in the classroom has never been easy, but in recent years, school disorder has often taken particularly ugly forms: drug use and violent crime in the schools have become major social problems." *New Jersey v T. L. O.*, 469 US 325, 339, 83 L Ed 2d 720, 105 S Ct 733 (1985). When we approved fixed checkpoints near the Mexican border to stop and search cars for illegal aliens, we observed at the outset that "the Immigration and Naturalization Service now suggests there may be as many as 10 or 12 million aliens illegally in the country," and that "[i]nterdicting the flow of illegal entrants from Mexico poses formidable law enforcement problems." *United States v Martinez-Fuerte*, 428 US 543, 551–552, 49 L Ed 2d 1116, 96 S Ct 3074 (1976). And the substantive analysis of our opinion today in *Skinner* begins, "[t]he problem of alcohol use on American railroads is as old as the industry itself," and goes on to cite statistics concerning that problem and the accidents it causes, including a 1979 study finding that "23% of the operating personnel were 'problem drinkers' " *Skinner*, ante, at 103 L Ed 2d 639.

The Court's opinion in the present case, however, will be searched in vain for real evidence of a real problem that will be solved by urine testing of Customs Service employees. Instead, there are assurances that "[t]he Customs Service is our Nation's first line of defense against one of the greatest problems affecting the health and welfare of our population," ante, at 103 L Ed 2d 704; that "[m]any of the Service's employees are often exposed to [drug smugglers] and to the controlled substances they seek to smuggle into the country," ante, at 103 L Ed 2d 704; that "Customs officers have been the targets of bribery by drug smugglers on numerous occasions, and several have been removed from the Service for accepting bribes and other integrity violations," ibid.; that "the Government has a compelling interest in ensuring that front-line interdiction personnel are physically fit, and have unimpeachable integrity and judgment," ibid.; that the "national interest in self protection could be irreparably damaged if those charged with safeguarding it were, because of their own drug use, unsympathetic to their mission of interdicting narcotics," ante, at 103 L Ed 2d 705; and that "the public should not bear the risk that employees who may suffer from impaired perception and judgment will be promoted to positions where they may need to employ deadly force," ibid. To paraphrase Churchill, all this contains much that is obviously true, and much that is relevant; unfortunately, what is obviously true is not relevant, and what is relevant is not obviously true. The only pertinent points, it seems to me, are supported by nothing but speculation, and not very plausible speculation at that. It is not apparent to me that a Customs Service employee who uses drugs is significantly more likely to be bribed by a drug smuggler, any more than a Customs Service employee who wears diamonds is significantly more likely to be bribed by a diamond smuggler—unless, perhaps, the addiction to drugs is so severe, and requires so much money to maintain, that it would be detectable even without benefit of a urine test. Nor is it apparent to me that Customs officers who use drugs will be appreciably less "sympathetic" to their drug-interdiction mission, any more than police officers who exceed the speed limit in their private cars are appreciably less sympathetic to their mission of enforcing the traffic laws. (The only difference is that the Customs officer's individual efforts, if they are irreplaceable, can theoretically affect the availability of his own drug supply—a prospect so remote as to be an absurd basis of motivation.) Nor, finally, is it apparent to me that urine tests will be even marginally more effective in preventing gun-carrying agents from risking "impaired perception and judgment" than is their current knowledge that, if impaired, they may be shot dead in unequal combat with unimpaired smugglers—unless, again, their addiction is so severe that no urine test is needed for detection.

What is absent in the Government's justifications—notably absent, revealingly absent, and as far as I am concerned dispositively absent—is the recitation of *even a single instance* in which any of the speculated horribles actually occurred: an instance, that is, in which the cause of bribe-taking, or of poor aim, or of unsympathetic law enforcement, or of compromise of classified information, was drug use. Although the Court points out that several employees have in the past been removed from the Service for accepting bribes and other integrity violations, and that at least nine officers have died in the line of duty since 1974, ante, at 103 L Ed 2d 704, there is no indication whatever that these incidents were related to drug use by Service employees. Perhaps concrete evidence of the severity of a problem is unnecessary when it is so well known that courts can almost take judicial notice of it; but that is surely not the case here. The Commissioner of Customs himself has stated that he "believe[s] that Customs is largely drug-free," that "[t]he extent of illegal drug use by Customs employees was not the reason for establishing this program," and that he "hope[s] and expect[s] to receive reports of very few positive findings through drug screening." App 10, 15. The test results have fulfilled those hopes and expectations. According to the Service's counsel, out of 3,600 employees tested, no more than 5 tested positive for drugs. See ante, at 103 L Ed 2d 707.

The Court's response to this lack of evidence is that "[t]here is little reason to believe that American workplaces are immune from [the] pervasive social problem" of drug abuse. Ante, at 103 L Ed 2d 707. Perhaps such a generalization would suffice if the workplace at issue could produce such catastrophic social harm that no risk whatever is tolerable—the secured areas of a nuclear power plant, for example, see *Rushton v Nebraska Public Power District*, 844 F2d 562 (CA8 1988). But if such a generalization suffices to justify demeaning bodily searches, without particularized suspicion, to guard against the bribing or blackmailing of a law enforcement agent, or the careless use of a firearm, then the Fourth Amendment has become frail protection indeed. In *Skinner, Bell, T. L. O.,* and *Martinez-Fuerte*, we took pains to establish the existence of special need for the search or seizure—a need based not upon the existence of a "pervasive social problem" combined with speculation as to the effect of that problem in the field at issue, but rather upon well known or well demonstrated evils *in that field*, with well known or well demonstrated consequences. In *Skinner,* for example, we pointed to a long history of alcohol abuse in the railroad industry, and noted that in an 8-year period 45 train accidents and incidents had occurred because of alcohol- and drug-impaired railroad employees, killing 34 people, injuring 66, and causing more than $28 million in property damage. Ante, at 103 L Ed 2d 639. In the present case, by contrast, not only is the Customs Service thought to be "largely drug-free," but the connection between whatever drug use may exist and serious social harm is entirely speculative. Except for the fact that the search of a person is much more intrusive than the stop of a car, the present case resembles *Delaware v Prouse,* 440 US 648, 59 L Ed 2d 660, 99 S Ct 1391 (1979), where we held that the Fourth Amendment prohibited random stops to check drivers' licenses and motor vehicle registration. The contribution of this practice to highway safety, we concluded, was "marginal at best" since the number of licensed drivers that must be stopped in order too find one unlicensed one "will be large indeed." Id., at 660, 59 L Ed 2d 660, 99 S Ct 1391.

Today's decision would be wrong, but at least of more limited effect, if its approval of drug testing were confined to that category of employees assigned specifically to drug interdiction duties. Relatively few public employees fit that description. But in extending approval of drug testing to that category consisting of employees who carry firearms, the Court exposes vast numbers of public employees to this needless indignity. Logically, of course, if those who carry guns can be treated in this fashion, so can all others whose work, if performed under the influence of drugs, may en-

danger others—automobile drivers, operators of other potentially dangerous equipment, construction workers, school crossing guards. A similarly broad scope attaches to the Court's approval of drug testing for those with access to "sensitive information."[1] Since this category is not limited to Service employees with drug interdiction duties, nor to "sensitive information" specifically relating to drug traffic, today's holding apparently approves drug testing for all federal employees with security clearances—or, indeed, for all federal employees with valuable confidential information to impart. Since drug use is not a particular problem in the Customs Service, employees throughout the government are no less likely to violate the public trust by taking bribes to feed their drug habit, or by yielding to blackmail. Moreover, there is no reason why this super-protection against harms arising from drug use must be limited to public employees; a law requiring similar testing of private citizens who use dangerous instruments such as guns or cars, or who have access to classified information would also be constitutional.

There is only one apparent basis that sets the testing at issue here apart from all these other situations—but it is not a basis upon which the Court is willing to rely. I do not believe for a minute that the driving force behind these drug-testing rules was any of the feeble justifications put forward by counsel here and accepted by the Court. The only plausible explanation, in my view, is what the Commissioner himself offered in the concluding sentence of his memorandum to Customs Service employees announcing the program: "Implementation of the drug screening program would set an important example in our country's struggle with this most serious threat to our national health and security." App 12. Or as respondent's brief to this Court asserted: "if a law enforcement agency and its employees do not take the law seriously, neither will the public on which the agency's effectiveness depends." Brief for United States 36. What better way to show that the Government is serious about its "war on drugs" than to subject its employees on the front line of that war to this invasion of their privacy and affront to their dignity? To be sure, there is only a slight chance that it will prevent some serious public harm resulting from Service employee drug use, but it will show to the world that the Service is "clean," and—most important of all—will demonstrate the determination of the Government to eliminate this scourge of our society! I think it obvious that this justification is unacceptable; that the impairment of individual liberties cannot be the means of making a point; that symbolism, even symbolism for so worthy a cause as the abolition of unlawful drugs, cannot validate an otherwise unreasonable search.

There is irony in the Government's citation, in support of its position, of Justice Brandeis's statement in *Olmstead v United States*, 277 US 438, 485, 72 L Ed 944, 48 S Ct 564, 66 ALR 376 (1928) that "[f]or good or for ill, [our Government] teaches the whole people by its example." Brief for the United States 36. Brandeis was there *dissenting* from the Court's admission of evidence obtained through an unlawful Government wiretap. He was not praising the Government's example of vigor and enthusiasm in combating crime, but condemning its example that "the end justified the means," 277 US, at 485, 72 L Ed 944, 48 S Ct 564, 66 ALR 376. An even more apt

quotation from that famous Brandeis dissent would have been the following:

"[I]t is . . . immaterial that the intrusion was in aid of law enforcement. Experience should teach us to be most on our guard to protect liberty when the Government's purposes are beneficent. Men born to freedom are naturally alert to repel invasion of their liberty by evil-minded rulers. The greatest dangers to liberty lurk in insidious encroachment by men of zeal, well-meaning but without understanding." Id., at 479, 72 L Ed 944, 48 S Ct 564, 66 ALR 376.

Those who lose because of the lack of understanding that begot the present exercise in symbolism are not just the Customs Service employees, whose dignity is thus offended, but all of us—who suffer a coarsening of our national manners that ultimately give the Fourth Amendment its content, and who become subject to the administration of federal officials whose respect for our privacy can hardly be greater than the small respect they have been taught to have for their own.

NOTES

1. The Court apparently approves application of the urine tests to personnel receiving access to "sensitive information." Ante, at 103 L Ed 2d 710. Since, however, it is unsure whether "classified material" is "sensitive information," it remands with instructions that the court of appeals "examine the criteria used by the Service in determining what materials are classified and in deciding whom to test under this rubric." Ante, at 103 L Ed 2d 710. I am not sure what these instructions mean. Surely the person who classifies information *always* considers it "sensitive" in some sense—and the Court does not indicate what particular sort of sensitivity is crucial. Moreover, it seems to me most unlikely that "the criteria used by the Service in determining what materials are classified" are any different from those prescribed by the President in his Executive Order on the subject, see Exec Order No. 12356, 3 CFR 166 (1982 Comp)—and if there is a

difference it is probably unlawful, see § 5.4(b)(2), id., at 177. In any case, whatever idiosyncratic standards for classification the Customs Service might have would seem to be irrelevant, inasmuch as the rule at issue here is not limited to material classified *by the Customs Service*, but includes (and may well apply principally to) material classified elsewhere in the Government—for example, in the Federal Bureau of Investigation, the Drug Enforcement Administration or the State Department—and conveyed to the Service. See App 24-25.

POSTSCRIPT

Is Drug Use Testing Permitted Under the Fourth Amendment?

The pressure to pursue drug testing programs is political, economic, and technological. Drug abuse has surfaced a principal domestic concern of voters. Economically, government studies claim that drug abuse costs employers between $30 and $40 billion in property damage, quality control, absenteeism, employee theft, and increased insurance costs. Widely divergent estimates of narcotics traffic range from $27 to $110 billion. In addition, technologies for drug testing that are cheaper and more revealing but seem less intrusive are being developed. Would the objection to drug testing be as strong if the test consisted of cutting and analyzing one or two hairs rather than obtaining a urine specimen? The new technologies that will become available for testing and the new technologies that already exist for communicating private information guarantee that there will be a growing amount of litigation during the next few years.

The number of cases involving the legality of drug use testing is proliferating. In addition to customs officials, courts have allowed such tests for jockeys, *Shoemaker v. Handel*, 795 F.2d 1136 (1986); prison employees, *McDonell v. Hunter*, 809 F.2d 1302 (1987); and school bus drivers, *Division 241 Amalgamated Transit Union v. Sucsy*, 538 F.2d 1264 (1976). However, testing has not been allowed for firefighters, *Capua v. City of Plainfield*, 643 F. Supp. 1507 (1986). For a state court case that ruled that teachers may not be tested without particularized suspicion, see *Patchogue-Medford Congress of Teachers v. Board of Education*, 70 N.Y.2d 57, 517 N.Y.S.2d 456, 510 N.E.2d 325 (1987). A landmark case that allowed forcibly obtained blood tests in drunk driving cases was *Schmerber v. California*, 86 S. Ct. 1826 (1966).

Recent analyses of drug use testing can be found in "Alternative Challenges to Drug Testing of Government Employees: Options After *Von Raab* and *Skinner*," 58 *George Washington Law Review* 148 (1989); "Testing for Drug Use in the American Workplace: A Symposium," 11 *Nova Law Review* 291 (1987); Morrow, "Drug Testing in the Workplace: Issues for the Arbitrator," 4 *Journal of Dispute Resolution* 273 (1989); Leeson, "The Drug Testing of College Athletes," 16 *Journal of College and University Law* 325 (1989); Adams, "Random Drug Testing of Government Employees: A Constitutional Procedure," 54 *University of Chicago Law Review* 1335 (1987); and Kamisar, "The Fourth Amendment in an Age of Drug and AIDS Testing," *The New York Times Magazine* (September 13, 1987). J. M. Chaiken and M. R. Chaiken, in *Varieties of Criminal Behavior* (Rand, 1982), studied the history of drug abuse among career criminals.

ISSUE 5

Is "Hate Speech" Fully Protected by the Constitution?

YES: Antonin Scalia, from Majority Opinion, *R. A. V. v. City of St. Paul, Minnesota,* U.S. Supreme Court (1992)

NO: John Paul Stevens, from Concurring Opinion, *R. A. V. v. City of St. Paul, Minnesota,* U.S. Supreme Court (1992)

ISSUE SUMMARY

YES: Supreme Court justice Antonin Scalia finds that the St. Paul ordinance punishing "hate speech" cannot be constitutional because it regulates speech depending on the subject the speech addresses.
NO: Justice John Paul Stevens concurs that this particular ordinance is not constitutional, but he argues that it is perhaps simply overbroad.

> There are certain well-defined and narrowly limited classes of speech, the prevention and punishment of which have never been thought to raise any Constitutional problem. These include the lewd and obscene, the profane, the libelous, and the insulting or "fighting" words—those which by their very utterance inflict injury or tend to incite an immediate breach of the peace. It has been well observed that such utterances are no essential part of any exposition of ideas, and are of such slight social value as a step to truth that any benefit that may be derived from them is clearly outweighed by the social interest in order and morality.
>
> —*Chaplinsky v. New Hampshire*

Six hundred and seventy-two hate crimes were recorded in Los Angeles County in 1991, an increase of 27 percent over the previous year. Four hundred and thirty-two of them occurred in the city of Los Angeles, a 58 percent increase over the 273 reported the previous year. The Anti-Defamation League (ADL) of B'nai B'rith reports 1,879 anti-Semitic incidents in the United States in 1991, up 11 percent from 1990 and the highest number in the 13 years the league has kept track. Klanwatch, a project of the Southern Poverty Law Center in Montgomery, Alabama, reported a record number of white supremacist groups—346—actively operating in 1991 and a doubling of reported incidents of cross burnings, from 50 in 1990 to 101 in 1991.

We do not live in particularly tranquil, quiet, or harmonious times. Even on college campuses, controversies over courses of study or "political correctness" seem to have a more strident tone than they used to. In 1990 Congress enacted the "Hate Crimes Statistics Act," which requires the FBI to compile data tracking the frequency of hate crimes. And cities and universities have dealt with situations where speech is racist or sexist or denigrating and offensive to someone or some group by enacting regulations that punish such speech.

Typical of hate speech codes at universities is the excerpt below, which was enacted at the University of Wisconsin and then declared unconstitutional by a court.

The university may discipline a student in nonacademic matters in the following situations:

(2)(a) For racist or discriminatory comments, epithets or other expressive behavior directed at an individual or on separate occasions at different individuals, or for physical conduct, if such comments, epithets or other expressive behavior or physical conduct intentionally:

1. Demean the race, sex, religion, color, creed, disability, sexual orientation, national origin, ancestry or age of the individual or individuals and

2. Create an intimidating, hostile or demeaning environment for education, university-related work, or other university-authorized activity.

Current First Amendment law allows regulation over a very limited class of expressions, among them obscenity, fighting words, and libel. Advocates of hate speech codes argue that hate speech causes deep and permanent injury, that words can at times injure as much as sticks and stones. Opponents argue that the best antidote for hate speech is not to punish speech, but to produce more speech. As Benno Schmidt, former president of Yale University, has stated, "It is precisely societies that are diverse, pluralistic, and contentious that most urgently need freedom of speech." In addition, opponents claim that it is not really possible to distinguish the worst hate speech from that which is moderately disagreeable and offensive.

Are there other avenues for institutions to confront racism, sexism, anti-Semitism and homophobia? Would hate speech codes lead us down the slippery slope toward uniformity of thought? Or is the dehumanization that occurs with such speech too harmful to tolerate? The following opinions constitute a fairly strong warning to state and local governmental bodies and institutions to be extremely careful in trying to restrict speech. The majority opinion, by Justice Antonin Scalia, indicates that it is unlikely that any hate speech codes could be found to be constitutional in the future. The concurring opinion, by Justice John Paul Stevens, agrees with the result in this particular case; however, he suggests that a more narrowly drawn code might be approved.

YES

Antonin Scalia

MAJORITY OPINION

R. A. V. v. ST. PAUL

JUSTICE SCALIA delivered the opinion of the Court.

In the predawn hours of June 21, 1990, petitioner and several other teenagers allegedly assembled a crudely-made cross by taping together broken chair legs. They then allegedly burned the cross inside the fenced yard of a black family that lived across the street from the house where petitioner was staying. Although this conduct could have been punished under any of a number of laws, one of the two provisions under which respondent city of St. Paul chose to charge petitioner (then a juvenile) was the St. Paul Bias-Motivated Crime Ordinance, St. Paul, Minn. Legis. Code Sec. 292.02 (1990), which provides:

> "Whoever places on public or private property a symbol, object, appellation, characterization or graffiti, including, but not limited to, a burning cross or Nazi swastika, which one knows or has reasonable grounds to know arouses anger, alarm or resentment in others on the basis of race, color, creed, religion or gender commits disorderly conduct and shall be guilty of a misdemeanor." . . .

I

In construing the St. Paul ordinance, we are bound by the construction given to it by the Minnesota court. *Posadas de Puerto Rico Associates v. Tourism Co. of Puerto Rico*, 478 U.S. 328, 339 (1986); *New York v. Ferber*, 458 U.S. 747, 769, n. 24 (1982); *Terminiello v. Chicago*, 337 U.S. 1, 4 (1949). Accordingly, we accept the Minnesota Supreme Court's authoritative statement that the ordinance reaches only those expressions that constitute "fighting words" within the meaning of *Chaplinsky*. 464 N. W. 2d, at 510–511. Petitioner and his *amici* urge us to modify the scope of the Chaplinsky formulation, thereby invalidating the ordinance as "substantially overbroad," *Broadrick v. Oklahoma*, 413 U.S.

From *R. A. V. v. City of St. Paul, Minnesota*, 60 L.W. 4667 (1992). Notes and some case citations omitted.

601, 610 (1973). We find it unnecessary to consider this issue. Assuming, *arguendo*, that all of the expression reached by the ordinance is proscribable under the "fighting words" doctrine, we nonetheless conclude that the ordinance is facially unconstitutional in that it prohibits otherwise permitted speech solely on the basis of the subjects the speech addresses.

The First Amendment generally prevents government from proscribing speech, or even expressive conduct, because of disapproval of the ideas expressed. Content-based regulations are presumptively invalid. From 1791 to the present, however, our society, like other free but civilized societies, has permitted restrictions upon the content of speech in a few limited areas, which are "of such slight social value as a step to truth that any benefit that may be derived from them is clearly outweighed by the social interest in order and morality." *Chaplinsky, supra,* at 572. We have recognized that "the freedom of speech" referred to by the First Amendment does not include a freedom to disregard these traditional limitations. See, e.g., *Roth v. United States*, 354 U.S. 476 (1957) (obscenity); *Beauharnais v. Illinois*, 343 U.S. 250 (1952) (defamation); *Chaplinsky v. New Hampshire, supra,* ("fighting words"); see generally *Simon & Schuster, supra,* at _____ (KENNEDY, J., concurring in judgment) (slip op., at 4). Our decisions since the 1960's have narrowed the scope of the traditional categorical exceptions for defamation, see *New York Times Co. v. Sullivan*, 376 U.S. 254 (1964); *Gertz v. Robert Welch, Inc.*, 418 U.S. 323 (1974); see generally *Milkovich v. Lorain Journal Co.*, 497 U.S. 1, 13–17 (1990), and for obscenity, see *Miller v. California*, 413 U.S. 15 (1973), but a limited categorical approach has remained an important part of our First Amendment jurisprudence.

We have sometimes said that these categories of expression are "not within the area of constitutionally protected speech," or that the "protection of the First Amendment does not extend" to them. Such statements must be taken in context, however, and are no more literally true than is the occasionally repeated shorthand characterizing obscenity "as not being speech at all," Sunstein, Pornography and the First Amendment, 1986 Duke L. J. 589, 615, n. 146. What they mean is that these areas of speech can, consistently with the First Amendment, be regulated *because of their constitutionally proscribable content* (obscenity, defamation, etc.)—not that they are categories of speech entirely invisible to the Constitution, so that they may be made the vehicles for content discrimination unrelated to their distinctively proscribable content. Thus, the government may proscribe libel; but it may not make the further content discrimination of proscribing only libel critical of the government. We recently acknowledged this distinction in *Ferber*, 458 U.S., at 763, where, in upholding New York's child pornography law, we expressly recognized that there was no "question here of censoring a particular literary theme. . . ."

Our cases surely do not establish the proposition that the First Amendment imposes no obstacle whatsoever to regulation of particular instances of such proscribable expression, so that the government "may regulate [them] freely," *post*, at 4 (WHITE, J., concurring in judgment). That would mean that a city council could enact an ordinance prohibiting only those legally obscene works that contain criticism of the city government or, indeed, that do not include endorsement of the city government. Such a simplistic, all-or-nothing-at-all approach to First Amendment protection is at odds with common sense and with our jurisprudence as well. It is not true that "fighting words" have at most a "de minimis" expressive content, *ibid.*, or that their content is *in all respects* "worthless and undeserving of constitutional protection"; sometimes they are quite expressive indeed. We have not said that they constitute "*no* part of the expression of ideas," but only that they constitute "no *essential* part of any exposition of ideas." *Chaplinsky*, 315 U.S., at 572 (emphasis added).

The proposition that a particular instance of speech can be proscribable on the basis of one feature (e.g., obscenity) but not on the basis of another (e.g., opposition to the city government) is commonplace, and has found application in many contexts. We have long held, for example, that nonverbal expressive activity can be banned because of the action it entails, but not because of the ideas it expresses—so that burning a flag in violation of an ordinance against outdoor fires could be punishable, whereas burning a flag in violation of an ordinance against dishonoring the flag is not. See *Johnson*, 491 U.S., at 406–407. Similarly, we have upheld reasonable "time, place, or manner" restrictions, but only if they are "justified without reference to the content of the regulated speech." *Ward v. Rock Against Racism*, 491 U.S. 781, 791 (1989); see also *Clark v. Community for Creative Non-Violence*, 468 U.S. 288, 298 (1984) (noting that the O'Brien test differs little from the standard applied to time, place, or manner restrictions). And just as the power to proscribe particular speech on the basis of a noncontent element (e.g., noise) does not entail the power to proscribe the same speech on the basis of a content element; so also, the power to proscribe it on the basis of *one* content element (e.g., obscenity) does not entail the power to proscribe it on the basis of *other* content elements.

In other words, the exclusion of "fighting words" from the scope of the First Amendment simply means that, for purposes of that Amendment, the unprotected features of the words are, despite their verbal character, essentially a "nonspeech" element of communication. Fighting words are thus analogous to a noisy sound truck: Each is, as Justice Frankfurter recognized, a "mode of speech," *Niemotko v. Maryland*, 340 U.S. 268, 282 (1951) (Frankfurter, J., concurring in result); both can be used to convey an idea; but neither has, in and of itself, a claim upon the First Amendment. As with the sound truck, however, so also with fighting words: The government may not regulate use based on hostility—or favoritism—towards the underlying message expressed. Compare *Frisby v. Schultz*, 487 U.S. 474 (1988) (upholding, against facial challenge, a content-neutral ban on targeted residential picketing) with *Carey v. Brown*, 447 U.S. 455 (1980) (invalidating a ban on residential picketing that exempted labor picketing). . . .

When the basis for the content discrimination consists entirely of the very reason the entire class of speech at issue is proscribable, no significant danger of idea or viewpoint discrimination exists. Such a reason, having been adjudged neutral enough to support exclusion of the entire class of speech from First Amendment protection, is also neutral enough to form the basis of distinction within the class. To illustrate: A State might choose to prohibit only that obscenity which is the most patently offensive *in its prurience*—i.e., that which involves the most lascivious displays of sexual activity. But it may not prohibit, for example, only that obscenity which includes offensive *political* messages. And the Federal Government can criminalize only those threats of violence that are directed against the President, see 18 U.S.C. sec. 871—since the reasons why threats of violence are outside the First Amendment (protecting individuals from the fear of violence, from the disruption that fear engenders, and from the possibility that the threatened violence will occur) have special force when applied to the person of the President. See *Watts v. United States*, 394 U.S. 705, 707 (1969) (upholding the facial validity of § 871 because of the "overwhelmin[g] interest in protecting the safety of [the] Chief Executive and in allowing him to perform his duties without interference from threats of physical violence"). But the Federal Government may not criminalize only those threats against the President that mention his policy on aid to inner cities. And to take a final example (one mentioned by Justice Stevens, *post*, at 6–7), a State may choose to regulate price advertising in one industry but not in others, because the risk of fraud (one of the characteristics of commercial speech that justifies depriving it of full First Amendment protection, see *Virginia Pharmacy Bd. v. Virginia Citizens Consumer Council, Inc.*, 425 U.S. 748, 771–772 (1976)) is in its view greater there. But a State may not prohibit only that commercial advertising that depicts men in a demeaning fashion.

Another valid basis for according differential treatment to even a content-defined subclass of proscribable speech is that the subclass happens to be associated with particular "secondary effects"

of the speech, so that the regulation is "justified without reference to the content of the . . . speech," *Renton v. Playtime Theatres, Inc.*, 475 U.S. 41, 48 (1986). A State could, for example, permit all obscene live performances except those involving minors. Moreover, since words can in some circumstances violate laws directed not against speech but against conduct (a law against treason, for example, is violated by telling the enemy the nation's defense secrets), a particular content-based subcategory of a proscribable class of speech can be swept up incidentally within the reach of a statute directed at conduct rather than speech. Thus, for example, sexually derogatory "fighting words," among other words, may produce a violation of Title VII's general prohibition against sexual discrimination in employment practices, 42 U.S.C. § 2000e-2; 29 CFR § 1604.11 (1991). See also 18 U.S.C. § 242; 42 U.S.C. § 1981, 1982. Where the government does not target conduct on the basis of its expressive content, acts are not shielded from regulation merely because they express a discriminatory idea or philosophy.

These bases for distinction refute the proposition that the selectivity of the restriction is "even arguably 'conditioned upon the sovereign's agreement with what a speaker may intend to say.' " *Metromedia, Inc. v. San Diego*, 453 U.S. 490, 555 (1981) (STEVENS, J., dissenting in part) (citation omitted). There may be other such bases as well. Indeed, to validate such selectivity (where totally proscribable speech is at issue) it may not even be necessary to identify any particular "neutral" basis, so long as the nature of the content discrimination is such that there is no realistic possibility that official suppression of ideas is afoot. (We cannot think of any First Amendment interest that would stand in the way of a State's prohibiting only those obscene motion pictures with blue-eyed actresses.) Save for that limitation, the regulation of "fighting words," like the regulation of noisy speech, may address some offensive instances and leave other, equally offensive, instances alone.

II

Applying these principles to the St. Paul ordinance, we conclude that, even as narrowly construed by the Minnesota Supreme Court, the ordinance is facially unconstitutional. Although the phrase in the ordinance, "arouses anger, alarm or resentment in others," has been limited by the Minnesota Supreme Court's construction to reach only those symbols or displays that amount to "fighting words," the remaining, unmodified terms make clear that the ordinance applies only to "fighting words" that insult, or provoke violence, "on the basis of race, color, creed, religion or gender." Displays containing abusive invective, no matter how vicious or severe, are permissible unless they are addressed to one of the specified disfavored topics. Those who wish to use "fighting words" in connection with other ideas—to express hostility, for example, on the basis of political affiliation, union membership, or homosexuality—are not covered. The First Amendment does not permit St. Paul to impose special prohibitions on those speakers who express views on disfavored subjects.

In its practical operation, moreover, the ordinance goes even beyond mere content discrimination, to actual viewpoint discrimination. Displays containing some words—odious racial epithets, for example—would be prohibited to proponents of all views. But "fighting words" that do not themselves invoke race, color, creed, religion, or gender—aspersions upon a person's mother, for example—would seemingly be usable *ad libitum* in the placards of those arguing *in favor* of racial, color, etc., tolerance and equality, but could not be used by that speaker's opponents. One could hold up a sign saying, for example, that all "anti-Catholic bigots" are misbegotten; but not that all "papists" are, for that would insult and provoke violence "on the basis of religion." St. Paul has no such authority to license one side of a debate to fight freestyle, while requiring the other to follow Marquis of Queensbury Rules.

What we have here, it must be emphasized, is not a prohibition of fighting words that are directed at certain persons or groups (which would be *facially* valid if it met the requirements of the Equal Protection Clause); but rather, a prohibition of fighting words that contain (as the Minnesota Supreme Court repeatedly emphasized) messages of "bias-motivated" hatred and in particular, as applied to this case, messages "based on virulent notions of racial supremacy." 464 N. W. 2d, at 508, 511. One must wholeheartedly agree with the Minnesota Supreme Court that "[i]t is the responsibility, even the obligation, of diverse communities to confront such notions in whatever form they appear," *ibid.*, but the manner of that confrontation cannot consist of selective limitations upon speech. St. Paul's brief asserts that a general "fighting words" law would not meet the city's needs because only a content-specific measure can communicate to minority groups that the "group hatred" aspect of such speech "is not condoned by the majority." Brief for Respondent 25. The point of the First Amendment is that majority preferences must be expressed in some fashion other than silencing speech on the basis of its content.

Despite the fact that the Minnesota Supreme Court and St. Paul acknowledge that the ordinance is directed at expression of group hatred, Justice Stevens suggests that this "fundamentally misreads" the ordinance. It is directed, he claims, not to speech of a particular content, but to particular "injur[ies]" that are "qualitatively different" from other injuries. This is word-play. What makes the anger, fear, sense of dishonor, etc. produced by violation of this ordinance distinct from the anger, fear, sense of dishonor, etc. produced by other fighting words is nothing other than the fact that it is caused by a distinctive idea, conveyed by a distinctive message. The First Amendment cannot be evaded that easily. It is obvious that the symbols which will arouse "anger, alarm or resentment in others on the basis of race, color, creed, religion or gender" are those symbols that communicate a message of hostility based on one of these characteristics. St. Paul concedes in its brief that the ordinance applies only to "racial, religious, or gender-specific symbols" such as "a burning cross, Nazi swastika or other instrumentality of like import." Brief for Respondent 8. Indeed, St. Paul argued in the Juvenile Court that "[t]he burning of a cross does express a message and it is, in fact, the content of that message which the St. Paul Ordinance attempts to legislate." Memorandum from the Ramsey County Attorney to the Honorable Charles A. Flinn, Jr., dated July 13, 1990, in *In re Welfare of R. A. V.*, No. 89-D-1231 (Ramsey Cty. Juvenile Ct.), p. 1, reprinted in App. to Brief for Petitioner C-1.

The content-based discrimination reflected in the St. Paul ordinance comes within neither any of the specific exceptions to the First Amendment prohibition we discussed earlier, nor within a more general exception for content discrimination that does not threaten censorship of ideas. It assuredly does not fall within the exception for content discrimination based on the very reasons why the particular class of speech at issue (here, fighting words) is proscribable. As explained earlier, the reason why fighting words are categorically excluded from the protection of the First Amendment is not that their content communicates any particular idea, but that their content embodies a particularly intolerable (and socially unnecessary) *mode* of expressing *whatever* idea the speaker wishes to convey. St. Paul has not singled out an especially offensive mode of expression—it has not, for example, selected for prohibition only those fighting words that communicate ideas in a threatening (as opposed to a merely obnoxious) manner. Rather, it has proscribed fighting words of whatever manner that communicate messages of racial, gender, or religious intolerance. Selectivity of this sort creates the possibility that the city is seeking to handicap the expression of particular ideas. That possibility would alone be enough to render the ordinance presumptively invalid, but St. Paul's comments and concessions in this case elevate the possibility to a certainty.

St. Paul argues that the ordinance comes within another of the specific exceptions we mentioned, the one that allows content discrimination aimed only at the "secondary effects" of the speech. According to St. Paul, the ordinance is intended, "not to impact on [sic] the right of free expression of the accused," but rather to "protect against the victimization of a person or persons who are particularly vulnerable because of their membership in a group that historically has been discriminated against." Brief for Respondent 28. Even assuming that an ordinance that completely proscribes, rather than merely regulates, a specified category of speech can ever be considered to be directed only to the secondary effects of such speech, it is clear that the St. Paul ordinance is not directed to secondary effects within the meaning of *Renton.* As we said in *Boos v. Barry,* 485 U.S. 312 (1988), "listeners' reactions to speech are not the type of 'secondary effects' we referred to in *Renton.*" *Id.,* at 321. "The emotive impact of speech on its audience is not a 'secondary effect.' "

It hardly needs discussion that the ordinance does not fall within some more general exception permitting *all* selectivity that for any reason is beyond the suspicion of official suppression of ideas. The statements of St. Paul in this very case afford ample basis for, if not full confirmation of, that suspicion.

Finally, St. Paul and its *amici* defend the conclusion of the Minnesota Supreme Court that, even if the ordinance regulates expression based on hostility towards its protected ideological content, this discrimination is nonetheless justified because it is narrowly tailored to serve compelling state interests. Specifically, they assert that the ordinance helps to ensure the basic human rights of members of groups that have historically been subjected to discrimination, including the right of such group members to live in peace where they wish. We do not doubt that these interests are compelling, and that the ordinance can be said to promote them. But the "danger of censorship" presented by a facially content-based statute requires that that weapon be employed only where it is

"*necessary* to serve the asserted [compelling] interest," (emphasis added). The existence of adequate content-neutral alternatives thus "undercut[s] significantly" any defense of such a statute, casting considerable doubt on the government's protestations that "the asserted justification is in fact an accurate description of the purpose and effect of the law." The dispositive question in this case, therefore, is whether content discrimination is reasonably necessary to achieve St. Paul's compelling interests; it plainly is not. An ordinance not limited to the favored topics, for example, would have precisely the same beneficial effect. In fact the only interest distinctively served by the content limitation is that of displaying the city council's special hostility towards the particular biases thus singled out. That is precisely what the First Amendment forbids. The politicians of St. Paul are entitled to express that hostility—but not through the means of imposing unique limitations upon speakers who (however benightedly) disagree.

Let there be no mistake about our belief that burning a cross in someone's front yard is reprehensible. But St. Paul has sufficient means at its disposal to prevent such behavior without adding the First Amendment to the fire.

The judgment of the Minnesota Supreme Court is reversed, and the case is remanded for proceedings not inconsistent with this opinion.

It is so ordered.

NO

John Paul Stevens

OPINION OF JOHN PAUL STEVENS

Concurring opinion by Justice Stevens:
  Conduct that creates special risks or causes special harms may be prohibited by special rules. Lighting a fire near an ammunition dump or a gasoline storage tank is especially dangerous; such behavior may be punished more severely than burning trash in a vacant lot. Threatening someone because of her race or religious beliefs may cause particularly severe trauma or touch off a riot, and threatening a high public official may cause substantial social disruption; such threats may be punished more severely than threats against someone based on, say, his support of a particular athletic team. There are legitimate, reasonable, and neutral justifications for such special rules.
  This case involves the constitutionality of one such ordinance. Because the regulated conduct has some communicative content—a message of racial, religious or gender hostility—the ordinance raises two quite different First Amendment questions. Is the ordinance "overbroad" because it prohibits too much speech? If not, is it "underbroad" because it does not prohibit enough speech? . . .

I

Fifty years ago, the Court articulated a categorical approach to First Amendment jurisprudence.

> "There are certain well-defined and narrowly limited classes of speech, the prevention and punishment of which have never been thought to raise any Constitutional problem. . . . It has been well observed that such utterances are no essential part of any exposition of ideas, and are of such slight social value as a step to truth that any benefit that may be derived from them is clearly outweighed by the social interest in order and morality." *Chaplinsky v. New Hampshire*, 315 U.S. 568, 571-572 (1942).

We have, as Justice White observes, often described such categories of expression as "not within the area of constitutionally protected speech." *Roth v. United States*, 354 U.S. 476, 483 (1957).

From *R. A. V. v. City of St. Paul, Minnesota*, 60 L.W. 4678 (1992). Some notes and case citations omitted.

The Court today revises this categorical approach. It is not, the Court rules, that certain "categories" of expression are "unprotected," but rather that certain "elements" of expression are wholly "proscribable." To the Court, an expressive act, like a chemical compound, consists of more than one element. Although the act may be regulated because it contains a proscribable element, it may not be regulated on the basis of another (nonproscribable) element it also contains. Thus, obscene antigovernment speech may be regulated because it is obscene, but not because it is antigovernment. It is this revision of the categorical approach that allows the Court to assume that the St. Paul ordinance proscribes *only* fighting words, while at the same time concluding that the ordinance is invalid because it imposes a content-based regulation on expressive activity.

As an initial matter, the Court's revision of the categorical approach seems to me something of an adventure in a doctrinal wonderland, for the concept of "obscene antigovernment" speech is fantastical. The category of the obscene is very narrow; to be obscene, expression must be found by the trier of fact to "appea[l] to the prurient interest, . . . depic[t] or describ[e], in a patently offensive way, sexual conduct, [and] taken as a whole, *lac[k] serious literary, artistic, political or scientific value.*" *Miller v. California*, 413 U.S. 15, 24 (1973) (emphasis added). "Obscene antigovernment" speech, then, is a contradiction in terms: If expression is antigovernment, it does not "lac[k] serious . . . political . . . value" and cannot be obscene.

The Court attempts to bolster its argument by likening its novel analysis to that applied to restrictions on the time, place, or manner of expression or on expressive conduct. It is true that loud speech in favor of the Republican Party can be regulated because it is loud, but not because it is pro-Republican; and it is true that the public burning of the American flag can be regulated because it involves public burning and not because it involves the flag. But these analogies are inapposite. In each of these examples, the two elements (e.g., loudness and pro-Republican orientation) can coexist; in the case of "obscene antigovernment" speech, however, the presence of one element ("obscenity") by definition means the absence of the other. To my mind, it is unwise and unsound to craft a new doctrine based on such highly speculative hypotheticals.

I am, however, even more troubled by the second step of the Court's analysis—namely, its conclusion that the St. Paul ordinance is an unconstitutional content-based regulation of speech. Drawing on broadly worded *dicta*, the Court establishes a near-absolute ban on content-based regulations of expression and holds that the First Amendment prohibits the regulation of fighting words by subject matter. Thus, while the Court rejects the "all-or-nothing-at-all" nature of the categorical approach, it promptly embraces an absolutism of its own: within a particular "proscribable" category of expression, the Court holds, a government must either proscribe *all* speech or no speech at all. This aspect of the Court's ruling fundamentally misunderstands the role and constitutional status of content-based regulations on speech, conflicts with the very nature of First Amendment jurisprudence, and disrupts well-settled principles of First Amendment law.

Although the Court has, on occasion, declared that content-based regulations of speech are "never permitted," *Police*

Dept. of Chicago v. Mosley, 408 U.S. 92, 99 (1972), such claims are overstated. Indeed, in *Mosley* itself, the Court indicated that Chicago's selective proscription of nonlabor picketing was not *per se* unconstitutional, but rather could be upheld if the City demonstrated that nonlabor picketing was "clearly more disruptive than [labor] picketing." *Id.*, at 100. Contrary to the broad *dicta* in *Mosley* and elsewhere, our decisions demonstrate that content-based distinctions, far from being presumptively invalid, are an inevitable and indispensable aspect of a coherent understanding of the First Amendment.

This is true at every level of First Amendment law. In broadest terms, our entire First Amendment jurisprudence creates a regime based on the content of speech. The scope of the First Amendment is determined by the content of expressive activity: Although the First Amendment broadly protects "speech," it does not protect the right to "fix prices, breach contracts, make false warranties, place bets with bookies, threaten, [or] extort." Schauer, Categories and the First Amendment: A Play in Three Acts, 34 Vand. L. Rev. 265, 270 (1981). Whether an agreement among competitors is a violation of the Sherman Act or protected activity under the *Noerr-Pennington* doctrine hinges upon the content of the agreement. Similarly, "the line between permissible advocacy and impermissible incitation to crime or violence depends, not merely on the setting in which the speech occurs, but also on exactly what the speaker had to say." *Young v. American Mini Theatres, Inc.*, 427 U.S. 50, 66 (1976) (plurality opinion).

Likewise, whether speech falls within one of the categories of "unprotected" or "proscribable" expression is determined, in part, by its content. Whether a mag-azine is obscene, a gesture a fighting word, or a photograph child pornography is determined, in part, by its content. Even within categories of protected expression, the First Amendment status of speech is fixed by its content. *New York Times Co. v. Sullivan*, 376 U.S. 254 (1964), and *Dun & Bradstreet, Inc. v. Greenmoss Builders, Inc.*, 472 U.S. 749 (1985), establish that the level of protection given to speech depends upon its subject matter: speech about public officials or matters of public concern receives greater protection than speech about other topics. It can, therefore, scarcely be said that the regulation of expressive activity cannot be predicated on its content: much of our First Amendment jurisprudence is premised on the assumption that content makes a difference.

Consistent with this general premise, we have frequently upheld content-based regulations of speech. For example, in *Young v. American Mini Theatres*, the Court upheld zoning ordinances that regulated movie theaters based on the content of the films shown. In *FCC v. Pacifica Foundation*, 438 U.S. 726 (1978) (plurality opinion), we upheld a restriction on the broadcast of *specific* indecent words. In *Lehman v. City of Shaker Heights*, 418 U.S. 298 (1974) (plurality opinion), we upheld a city law that permitted commercial advertising, but prohibited political advertising, on city buses. In *Broadrick v. Oklahoma*, 413 U.S. 601 (1973), we upheld a state law that restricted the speech of state employees, but only as concerned partisan political matters. We have long recognized the power of the Federal Trade Commission to regulate misleading advertising and labeling, and the National Labor Relations Board's power to regulate an employer's election-related speech on the basis of its content. It is also beyond question that the Government may choose to limit advertisements for cigarettes, see 15 U.S.C. § 1331–1340, but not for cigars; choose to regulate airline advertising, but not bus advertising; or choose to monitor solicitation by lawyers, see *Ohralik v. Ohio State Bar Assn.*, 436 U.S. 447 (1978), but not by doctors.

All of these cases involved the selective regulation of speech based on content—precisely the sort of regulation the Court invalidates today. Such selective regulations are unavoidably content based, but they are not, in my opinion, "presumptively invalid." As these many decisions and examples demonstrate, the prohibition on content-based regulations is not nearly as total as the *Mosley* dictum suggests.

Disregarding this vast body of case law, the Court today goes beyond even the overstatement in *Mosley* and applies the prohibition on content-based regulation to speech that the Court had until today considered wholly "unprotected" by the First Amendment—namely, fighting words. This new absolutism in the prohibition of content-based regulations severely contorts the fabric of settled First Amendment law.

Our First Amendment decisions have created a rough hierarchy in the constitutional protection of speech. Core political speech occupies the highest, most protected position; commercial speech and nonobscene, sexually explicit speech are regarded as a sort of second-class expression; obscenity and fighting words receive the least protection of all. Assuming that the Court is correct that this last class of speech is not wholly "unprotected," it certainly does not follow that fighting words and obscenity receive the *same* sort of protection afforded core political speech. Yet in ruling that proscribable speech cannot be regulated based on subject matter, the Court does just that. Perversely, this gives fighting words *greater* protection than is afforded commercial speech. If Congress can prohibit false advertising directed at airline passengers without also prohibiting false advertising directed at bus passengers and if a city can prohibit political advertisements in its buses while allowing other advertisements, it is ironic to hold that a city cannot regulate fighting words based on "race, color, creed, religion or gender" while leaving unregulated fighting words based on "union membership or homosexuality." The Court today turns First Amendment law on its head: Communication that was once entirely unprotected (and that still can be wholly proscribed) is now entitled to greater protection than commercial speech—and possibly greater protection than core political speech.

Perhaps because the Court recognizes these perversities, it quickly offers some ad hoc limitations on its newly extended prohibition on content-based regulations. First, the Court states that a content-based regulation is valid "[w]hen the content discrimination is based upon the very reason the entire class of speech . . . is proscribable." In a pivotal passage, the Court writes

"the Federal Government can criminalize only those physical threats that are directed against the President, see 18 U.S.C. § 871—since the reasons why threats of violence are outside the First Amendment (protecting individuals from the fear of violence, from the disruption that fear engenders, and from the possibility that the threatened violence will occur) have special force when applied to the . . . President."

As I understand this opaque passage, Congress may choose from the set of unprotected speech (all threats) to proscribe only a subset (threats against the President) because those threats are particularly likely to cause "fear of violence," "disruption," and actual "violence."

Precisely this same reasoning, however, compels the conclusion that St. Paul's ordinance is constitutional. Just as Congress may determine that threats against the President entail more severe consequences than other threats, so St. Paul's City Council may determine that threats based on the target's race, religion, or gender cause more severe harm to both the target and to society than other threats. This latter judgment—that harms caused by racial, religious, and gender-based invective are qualitatively different from that caused by other fighting words—seems to me eminently reasonable and realistic.

Next, the Court recognizes that a State may regulate advertising in one industry but not another because "the risk of fraud (one of the characteristics that justifies depriving [commercial speech] of full First Amendment protection . . .)" in the regulated industry is "greater" than in other industries. Again, the same reasoning demonstrates the constitutionality of St. Paul's ordinance. "[O]ne of the characteristics that justifies" the constitutional status of fighting words is that such words "by their very utterance inflict injury or tend to incite an immediate breach of the peace." *Chaplinsky,* 315 U.S., at 572. Certainly a legislature that may determine that the risk of fraud is greater in the legal trade than in the medical trade may determine that the risk of injury or breach of peace created by race-based threats is greater than that created by other threats. . . .

In sum, the central premise of the Court's ruling—that "[c]ontent-based regulations are presumptively invalid"—has simplistic appeal, but lacks support in our First Amendment jurisprudence. To make matters worse, the Court today extends this overstated claim to reach categories of hitherto unprotected speech and, in doing so, wreaks havoc in an area of settled law. Finally, although the Court recognizes exceptions to its new principle, those exceptions undermine its very conclusion that the St. Paul ordinance is unconstitutional. Stated directly, the majority's position cannot withstand scrutiny. . . .

III

As the foregoing suggests, I disagree with both the Court's and part of Justice White's analysis of the constitutionality [of the] St. Paul ordinance. Unlike the Court, I do not believe that all content-based regulations are equally infirm and presumptively invalid; unlike Justice White, I do not believe that fighting words are wholly unprotected by the First Amendment. To the contrary, I believe our decisions establish a more complex and subtle analysis, one that considers the content and context of the regulated speech, and the nature and scope of the restriction on speech. Applying this analysis and assuming *arguendo* (as the Court does) that the St. Paul ordinance is *not* overbroad, I conclude that such a selective, subject-matter regulation on proscribable speech is constitutional.

Not all content-based regulations are alike; our decisions clearly recognize that some content-based restrictions raise more constitutional questions than others. Although the Court's analysis of content-based regulations cannot be reduced to a simple formula, we have considered a number of factors in determining the validity of such regulations.

First, as suggested above, the scope of protection provided expressive activity depends in part upon its content and character. We have long recognized that when government regulates political speech or "the expression of editorial opinion on matters of public importance," *FCC v. League of Women Voters of California*, 468 U.S. 364, 375–376 (1984), "First Amendment protectio[n] is 'at its zenith.' " *Meyer v. Grant*, 486 U.S. 414, 425 (1988). In comparison, we have recognized that "commercial speech receives a limited form of First Amendment protection," *Posadas de Puerto Rico Associates v. Tourism Co. of Puerto Rico*, 478 U.S. 328, 340 (1986), and that "society's interest in protecting [sexually explicit films] is of a wholly different, and lesser magnitude than [its] interest in untrammeled political debate." *Young v. American Mini Theatres*, 427 U.S., at 70; see also *FCC v. Pacifica Foundation*, 438 U.S. 726 (1978). The character of expressive activity also weighs in our consideration of its constitutional status. As we have frequently noted, "the government generally has a freer hand in restricting expressive conduct than it has in restricting the written or spoken word." *Texas v. Johnson*, 491 U.S. 397, 406 (1989); see also *United States v. O'Brien*, 391 U.S. 367 (1968).

The protection afforded expression turns as well on the context of the regulated speech. We have noted, for example, that "[a]ny assessment of the precise scope of employer expression, of course, must be made in the context of its labor relations setting . . . [and] must take into account the economic dependence of the employees on their employers." *NLRB v.*

Gissel Packing Co., 395 U.S., at 617. Similarly, the distinctive character of a university environment or a secondary school environment, see *Hazelwood School Dist. v. Kuhlmeier*, 484 U.S. 260 (1988), influences our First Amendment analysis. The same is true of the presence of a " 'captive audience, [one] there as a matter of necessity, not of choice.' " *Lehman v. City of Shaker Heights*, 418 U.S., at 302 (citation omitted). Perhaps the most familiar embodiment of the relevance of context is our "fora" jurisprudence, differentiating the levels of protection afforded speech in different locations.

The nature of a contested restriction of speech also informs our evaluation of its constitutionality. Thus, for example, "[a]ny system of prior restraints of expression comes to this Court bearing a heavy presumption against its constitutional validity." *Bantam Books, Inc. v. Sullivan*, 372 U.S. 58, 70 (1963). More particularly to the matter of content-based regulations, we have implicitly distinguished between restrictions on expression based on *subject matter* and restrictions based on *viewpoint*, indicating that the latter are particularly pernicious. "If there is a bedrock principle underlying the First Amendment, it is that the Government may not prohibit the expression of an idea simply because society finds the idea itself offensive or disagreeable." *Texas v. Johnson*, 491 U.S., at 414. "Viewpoint discrimination is censorship in its purest form," *Perry Education Assn. v. Perry Local Educators' Assn.*, 460 U.S. 37, 62 (1983) (Brennan, J., dissenting), and requires particular scrutiny, in part because such regulation often indicates a legislative effort to skew public debate on an issue. See, e.g., *Schacht v. United States*, 398 U.S. 58, 63 (1970). "Especially where . . . the legislature's suppression of speech suggests an attempt to give one side of a debatable public question an advantage in expressing its views to the people, the First Amendment is plainly offended." *First National Bank of Boston v. Bellotti*, 435 U.S. 765, 785–786 (1978). Thus, although a regulation that on its face regulates speech by subject matter may in some instances effectively suppress particular viewpoints, in general, viewpoint-based restrictions on expression require greater scrutiny than subject-matter based restrictions.

Finally, in considering the validity of content-based regulations we have also looked more broadly at the scope of the restrictions. For example, in *Young v. American Mini Theatres*, 427 U.S., at 71, we found significant the fact that "what [was] ultimately at stake [was] nothing more than a limitation on the place where adult films may be exhibited." Similarly, in *FCC v. Pacifica Foundation*, the Court emphasized two dimensions of the limited scope of the FCC ruling. First, the ruling concerned only broadcast material which presents particular problems because it "confronts the citizen . . . in the privacy of the home"; second, the ruling was not a complete ban on the use of selected offensive words, but rather merely a limitation on the times such speech could be broadcast. 438 U.S., at 748–750.

All of these factors play some role in our evaluation of content-based regulations on expression. Such a multi-faceted analysis cannot be conflated into two dimensions. Whatever the allure of absolute doctrines, it is just too simple to declare expression "protected" or "unprotected" or to proclaim a regulation "content-based" or "content-neutral."

In applying this analysis to the St. Paul ordinance, I assume *arguendo*—as the Court does—that the ordinance regulates

only fighting words and therefore is *not* overbroad. Looking to the content and character of the regulated activity, two things are clear. First, by hypothesis the ordinance bars only low-value speech, namely, fighting words. By definition such expression constitutes "no essential part of any exposition of ideas, and [is] of such slight social value as a step to truth that any benefit that may be derived from [it] is clearly outweighed by the social interest in order and morality." *Chaplinsky*, 315 U.S., at 572. Second, the ordinance regulates "expressive conduct [rather] than . . . the written or spoken word." *Texas v. Johnson*, 491 U.S., at 406.

Looking to the context of the regulated activity, it is again significant that the statute (by hypothesis) regulates *only* fighting words. Whether words are fighting words is determined in part by their context. Fighting words are not words that merely cause offense; fighting words must be directed at individuals so as to "by their very utterance inflict injury." By hypothesis, then, the St. Paul ordinance restricts speech in confrontational and potentially violent situations. The case at hand is illustrative. The cross-burning in this case—directed as it was to a single African-American family trapped in their home—was nothing more than a crude form of physical intimidation. That this cross-burning sends a message of racial hostility does not automatically endow it with complete constitutional protection.

Significantly, the St. Paul ordinance regulates speech not on the basis of its subject matter or the viewpoint expressed, but rather on the basis of the *harm* the speech causes. In this regard, the Court fundamentally misreads the St. Paul ordinance. The Court describes the St. Paul ordinance as regulating expression "addressed to one of [several] specified disfavored *topics*," as policing "disfavored *subjects*," and as "prohibit-[ing] . . . speech solely on the basis of the *subjects* the speech addresses" (emphasis supplied). Contrary to the Court's suggestion, the ordinance regulates only a subcategory of expression that causes *injuries based* on race, color, creed, religion or gender," not a subcategory that involves discussions that concern those characteristics.[1] The ordinance, as construed by the Court, criminalizes expression that "one knows . . . [by its very utterance inflicts injury on] others on the basis of race, color, creed, religion or gender." In this regard, the ordinance resembles the child pornography law at issue in *Ferber*, which in effect singled out child pornography because those publications caused far greater harms than pornography involving adults.

Moreover, even if the St. Paul ordinance did regulate fighting words based on its subject matter, such a regulation would, in my opinion, be constitutional. As noted above, subject-matter based regulations on commercial speech are widespread and largely unproblematic. As we have long recognized, subject-matter regulations generally do not raise the same concerns of government censorship and the distortion of public discourse presented by viewpoint regulations. Thus, in upholding subject-matter regulations we have carefully noted that viewpoint-based discrimination was not implicated. . . . Indeed, some subject-matter restrictions are a functional necessity in contemporary governance: "The First Amendment does not require States to regulate for problems that do not exist."

Contrary to the suggestion of the majority, the St. Paul ordinance does *not*

regulate expression based on viewpoint The Court contends that the ordinance requires proponents of racial intolerance to "follow the Marquis of Queensbury Rules" while allowing advocates of racial tolerance to "fight freestyle." The law does no such thing.

The Court writes:

"One could hold up a sign saying, for example, that all 'anti-Catholic bigots' are misbegotten; but not that all 'papists' are, for that would insult and provoke violence 'on the basis of religion.' "

This may be true, but it hardly proves the Court's point. The Court's reasoning is asymmetrical. The response to a sign saying that "all [religious] bigots are misbegotten" is a sign saying that "all advocates of religious tolerance are misbegotten." Assuming such signs could be fighting words (which seems to me extremely unlikely), neither sign would be banned by the ordinance for the attacks were not "based on . . . religion" but rather on one's beliefs about tolerance. Conversely (and again assuming such signs are fighting words), just as the ordinance would prohibit a Muslim from hoisting a sign claiming that all Catholics were misbegotten, so the ordinance would bar a Catholic from hoisting a similar sign attacking Muslims.

The St. Paul ordinance is evenhanded. In a battle between advocates of tolerance and advocates of intolerance, the ordinance does not prevent either side from hurling fighting words at the other on the basis of their conflicting ideas, but it does bar *both* sides from hurling such words on the basis of the target's "race, color, creed, religion or gender." To extend the Court's pugilistic metaphor, the St. Paul ordinance simply bans punches "below the belt"—*by either party*. It does not, therefore, favor one side of any debate.

Finally, it is noteworthy that the St. Paul ordinance is, as construed by the Court today, quite narrow. The St. Paul ordinance does not ban all "hate speech," nor does it ban, say, all cross-burnings or all swastika displays. Rather it only bans a subcategory of the already narrow category of fighting words. Such a limited ordinance leaves open and protected a vast range of expression on the subjects of racial, religious, and gender equality. As construed by the Court today, the ordinance certainly does not " 'raise the specter that the Government may effectively drive certain ideas or viewpoints from the marketplace.' " Petitioner is free to burn a cross to announce a rally or to express his views about racial supremacy, he may do so on private property or public land, at day or at night, so long as the burning is not so threatening and so directed at an individual as to "by its very [execution] inflict injury." Such a limited proscription scarcely offends the First Amendment.

In sum, the St. Paul ordinance (as construed by the Court) regulates expressive activity that is wholly proscribable and does so not on the basis of viewpoint, but rather in recognition of the different harms caused by such activity. Taken together, these several considerations persuade me that the St. Paul ordinance is not an unconstitutional content-based regulation of speech. Thus, were the ordinance not overbroad, I would vote to uphold it.

NOTE

1. The Court contends that this distinction is "wordplay," reasoning that "[w]hat makes [the harms caused by race-based threats] distinct from [the harms] produced by other fighting words is . . . the fact that [the former are] caused by a *distinctive idea*" (emphasis added). In this way, the Court concludes that regulating speech based on the injury it causes is no different from regulating speech based on its subject matter. This analysis fundamentally miscomprehends the role of "race, color, creed, religion [and] gender" in contemporary American society. One need look no further than the recent social unrest in the Nation's cities to see that race-based threats may cause more harm to society and to individuals than other threats. Just as the statute prohibiting threats against the President is justifiable because of the place of the President in our social and political order, so a statute prohibiting race-based threats is justifiable because of the place of race in our social and political order. Although it is regrettable that race occupies such a place and is so incendiary an issue, until the Nation matures beyond that condition, laws such as St. Paul's ordinance will remain reasonable and justifiable.

POSTSCRIPT

Is "Hate Speech" Fully Protected by the Constitution?

Law professor Rodney Smolla has inquired, "Should an open culture tolerate speech designed to spread intolerance? This may be the hardest free speech question of all, because an open culture is largely built on the ethos of tolerance." Smolla's question becomes even more significant because the principal arena where hate speech codes have been put into place has been college campuses, arguably the institution in our society that is most tolerant of deviant speech.

When the Supreme Court in 1989 ruled that state laws to punish flag burning were unconstitutional, the outcry was fairly brief. Many disagreed with the decision, but instances of flag burning are not very numerous. Racist speech, sexist speech, homophobic speech, and anti-Semitic speech, however, touch many on a daily basis. Hundreds of college campuses had hate speech codes in place at the time of the *R. A. V.* decision, and most of these codes, if not all of them, will have to be reconsidered in light of it.

The Supreme Court decision in *R. A. V.* was not all that surprising, given the breadth of the St. Paul statute. Judges have more experience with First Amendment theory than do campus administrators or politicians. They are more likely to have a clearer historical perspective, and they are certainly removed from the pressures facing those who have enacted such codes. The traditional answer of the courts to disturbing speech has been that the antidote is more speech and counterprotests that will educate the public and not simply punish those who have caused anger and hurt. Whether this is an appropriate response to hate speech, which degrades and injures and which seems to be on the increase, will, in spite of the opinions you have just read, continue to challenge us.

Recent readings discussing hate speech include R. Smolla, *Free Speech in an Open Society* (Alfred A. Knopf, 1992); L. Bollinger, *The Tolerant Society* (Oxford University Press, 1986); Matsuda, "Public Response to Racist Speech: Considering the Victim's Story," 87 *Michigan Law Review* 2320 (1989); and Minow, "Speaking and Writing Against Hate," 11 *Cardozo Law Review* 1393 (1990). A famous case involving a plan by a Nazi group to march in the largely Jewish community of Skokie, Illinois, is recounted in D. Downs, *Nazis in Skokie* (University of Notre Dame Press, 1985), and in *Skokie v. National Socialist Party of America*, 373 N.E.2d 21 (1978) and *Collin v. Smith*, 578 F.2d 1197 (7th Cir. 1978). The case declaring flag burning constitutionally protected is *Texas v. Johnson*, 109 S. Ct. 2533 (1989). The University of Wisconsin code was declared unconstitutional in *UWM Post v. Regents*, 774 F. Supp. 1163 (1991). Also see the Hate Crime Statistics Act, 28 U.S.C.S. § 534. The impact of computers and electronic communication on the First Amendment is discussed in E. Katsh, *The Electronic Media and the Transformation of Law* (Oxford University Press, 1989).

ISSUE 6

Do Prayers at Public School Graduation Ceremonies Violate the Constitution?

YES: Anthony Kennedy, from Majority Opinion, *Robert E. Lee et al. v. Daniel Weisman et al.*, U.S. Supreme Court (1992)

NO: Antonin Scalia, from Dissenting Opinion, *Robert E. Lee et al. v. Daniel Weisman et al.*, U.S. Supreme Court (1992)

ISSUE SUMMARY

YES: Supreme Court justice Anthony Kennedy finds that prayers offered at a middle school's graduation ceremonies were coercive and violated the Constitution's Establishment Clause.
NO: Justice Antonin Scalia finds neither coercion nor government involvement to a degree warranting invalidation of the practices in question.

> An Easter egg hunt on the White House lawn.
>
> Christmas as a national holiday.
>
> Prayers opening legislative sessions of state legislatures.

If you were a judge and these practices were being challenged as unconstitutional, how would you rule?

The First Amendment to the Constitution states that "Congress shall make no law respecting an establishment of religion, or prohibiting the free exercise thereof." Interpreting these words and applying them in particular cases has been exceedingly difficult for the courts. What, for example, does "respecting an establishment of religion" mean? Is any governmental involvement or support for religion, direct or indirect, small or great, barred by this phrase?

While the courts have struggled to keep church and state separate, they have also recognized that it would be impossible to have an absolute prohibition on the celebration of religious values and holidays. Cases continue to be brought, therefore, challenging the courts to determine how the words of the Constitution and the standards of prior cases should be applied to the facts of the new case.

The clearest and most well known of the establishment of religion cases are the school prayer decisions. In 1963, in *School District of Abington Township*,

Pennsylvania v. Schempp, 374 U.S. 203, the Supreme Court ruled that it was unconstitutional to require students to open the school day by reading biblical passages and reciting the Lord's Prayer. A year earlier, in *Engel v. Vitale*, 370 U.S. 421 (1962), the Supreme Court had ruled that recitation of the New York Regent's Prayer was unconstitutional. This prayer read, "Almighty God, we acknowledge our dependence upon Thee, and we beg thy blessings upon us, our parents, our teachers, and our country."

The Supreme Court has attempted to make its decisions in this area appear less subjective by considering the following three questions:

1. Does the statute have a secular legislative purpose?
2. Does its principal effect advance or inhibit religion?
3. Does the statute foster an excessive governmental entanglement with religion?

Using this standard, the courts have upheld some questionable practices, such as blue laws (regulating work, commerce, and amusements on Sundays) and the loaning of secular textbooks to parochial schools. But they have struck down other statutes, such as the Kentucky law that required posting the Ten Commandments in the classroom (see *Stone v. Graham*, 101 S. Ct. 192, 1980). More generally, the Court has upheld prayers at the beginning of a legislative session, the existence of after-school religious clubs, and tuition tax credits for parochial schools. Yet, using the same test, it has held unconstitutional a statute requiring a moment of silence in public schools, remedial programs for parochial schools, and a law requiring the teaching of "creation science" whenever evolution was taught.

The many cases involving religion that have been considered by the Supreme Court in the past 25 years indicate that the task of defining precisely what role religion should have in government-sponsored activities is extraordinarily difficult. Religion has not been banned from public life. "In God We Trust" appears on our coins, prayers are said at presidential inaugurations, Christmas is a national holiday, the lighting of the national Christmas tree at the White House is treated as a newsworthy event, and tax exemptions are given to religious institutions. It is probably still accurate, as a Supreme Court justice once wrote, that "we are a religious people whose institutions presuppose a Supreme Being." It is also true, however, that many religious activities may not be sponsored by the government.

The following readings concern whether or not prayers may be said in connection with public schools. The case involved a prayer said at a middle school graduation ceremony and led to very different conclusions by the majority and dissenting justices about how much governmental involvement in religion is permissible and whether or not listening to a prayer at such a ceremony is in any way coercive.

YES

Anthony Kennedy

MAJORITY OPINION

LEE *v.* WEISMAN

JUSTICE KENNEDY delivered the opinion of the Court.

School principals in the public school system of the city of Providence, Rhode Island, are permitted to invite members of the clergy to offer invocation and benediction prayers as part of the formal graduation ceremonies for middle schools and for high schools. The question before us is whether including clerical members who offer prayers as part of the official school graduation ceremony is consistent with the Religion Clauses of the First Amendment, provisions the Fourteenth Amendment makes applicable with full force to the States and their school districts.

I

A

Deborah Weisman graduated from Nathan Bishop Middle School, a public school in Providence, at a formal ceremony in June 1989. She was about 14 years old. For many years it has been the policy of the Providence School Committee and the Superintendent of Schools to permit principals to invite members of the clergy to give invocations and benedictions at middle school and high school graduations. Many, but not all, of the principals elected to include prayers as part of the graduation ceremonies. Acting for himself and his daughter, Deborah's father, Daniel Weisman, objected to any prayers at Deborah's middle school graduation, but to no avail. The school principal, petitioner Robert E. Lee, invited a rabbi to deliver prayers at the graduation exercises for Deborah's class. Rabbi Leslie Gutterman, of the Temple Beth El in Providence, accepted.

It has been the custom of Providence school officials to provide invited clergy with a pamphlet entitled "Guidelines for Civic Occasions," prepared

From *Robert E. Lee et al. v. Daniel Weisman et al.*, 60 L.W. 4723 (1992). Some case citations omitted.

by the National Conference of Christians and Jews. The Guidelines recommend that public prayers at nonsectarian civic ceremonies be composed with "inclusiveness and sensitivity," though they acknowledge that "[p]rayer of any kind may be inappropriate on some civic occasions." The principal gave Rabbi Gutterman the pamphlet before the graduation and advised him the invocation and benediction should be nonsectarian.

Rabbi Gutterman's prayers were as follows:

"INVOCATION

"God of the Free, Hope of the Brave:
"For the legacy of America where diversity is celebrated and the rights of minorities are protected, we thank You. May these young men and women grow up to enrich it.

"For the liberty of America, we thank You. May these new graduates grow up to guard it.

"For the political process of America in which all its citizens may participate, for its court system where all may seek justice, we thank You. May those we honor this morning always turn to it in trust.

"For the destiny of America, we thank You. May the graduates of Nathan Bishop Middle School so live that they might help to share it.

"May our aspirations for our country and for these young people, who are our hope for the future, be richly fulfilled.

AMEN"

"BENEDICTION

"O God, we are grateful to You for having endowed us with the capacity for learning which we have celebrated on this joyous commencement.

"Happy families give thanks for seeing their children achieve an important milestone. Send Your blessings upon the teachers and administrators who helped prepare them.

"The graduates now need strength and guidance for the future, help them to understand that we are not complete with academic knowledge alone. We must each strive to fulfill what You require of us all: To do justly, to love mercy, to walk humbly.

"We give thanks to You, Lord, for keeping us alive, sustaining us and allowing us to reach this special, happy occasion.

AMEN"

The record in this case is sparse in many respects, and we are unfamiliar with any fixed custom or practice at middle school graduations, referred to by the school district as "promotional exercises." We are not so constrained with reference to high schools, however. High school graduations are such an integral part of American cultural life that we can with confidence describe their customary features, confirmed by aspects of the record and by the parties' representations at oral argument. In the Providence school system, most high school graduation ceremonies are conducted away from the school, while most middle school ceremonies are held on school premises. Classical High School, which Deborah now attends, has conducted its graduation ceremonies on school premises. The parties stipulate that attendance at graduation ceremonies is voluntary. The graduating students enter as a group in a processional, subject to the direction of teachers and school officials, and sit together, apart from their families. We assume the clergy's participation in any high school graduation exercise would be about what it was at Deborah's middle school ceremony. There the students stood for the Pledge of Allegiance and remained standing during the Rabbi's prayers. Even on the assumption that there was a respectful moment of silence both before and after the prayers, the Rabbi's two presentations must not have extended much beyond a minute each, if that. We do not know whether he remained on stage during the whole ceremony, or whether the students received individual diplomas on stage, or if he helped to congratulate them.

The school board (and the United States, which supports it as *amicus curiae*) argued that these short prayers and others like them at graduation exercises are of profound meaning to many students and parents throughout this country who consider that due respect and acknowledgement for divine guidance and for the deepest spiritual aspirations of our people ought to be expressed at an event as important in life as a graduation. We assume this to be so in addressing the difficult case now before us, for the significance of the prayers lies also at the heart of Daniel and Deborah Weisman's case.

B

Deborah's graduation was held on the premises of Nathan Bishop Middle School on June 29, 1989. Four days before the ceremony, Daniel Weisman, in his individual capacity as a Providence taxpayer and as next friend of Deborah, sought a temporary restraining order in the United States District Court for the District of Rhode Island to prohibit school officials from including an invocation or benediction in the graduation ceremony. The court denied the motion for lack of adequate time to consider it. Deborah and her family attended the graduation, where the prayers were re-

cited. In July 1989, Daniel Weisman filed an amended complaint seeking a permanent injunction barring petitioners, various officials of the Providence public schools, from inviting the clergy to deliver invocations and benedictions at future graduations. We find it unnecessary to address Daniel Weisman's taxpayer standing, for a live and justiciable controversy is before us. Deborah Weisman is enrolled as a student at Classical High School in Providence and from the record it appears likely, if not certain, that an invocation and benediction will be conducted at her high school graduation.

. . . The District Court held that petitioners' practice of including invocations and benedictions in public school graduations violated the Establishment Clause of the First Amendment, and it enjoined petitioners from continuing the practice. 728 F. Supp. 68 (RI 1990). The court applied the three-part Establishment Clause test set forth in *Lemon v. Kurtzman*, 403 U.S. 602 (1971). Under that test as described in our past cases, to satisfy the Establishment Clause a governmental practice must (1) reflect a clearly secular purpose; (2) have a primary effect that neither advances nor inhibits religion; and (3) avoid excessive government entanglement with religion. *Committee for Public Education & Religious Liberty v. Nyquist*, 413 U.S. 756, 773 (1973). The District Court held that petitioners' actions violated the second part of the test, and so did not address either the first or the third. The court decided, based on its reading of our precedents, that the effects test of *Lemon* is violated whenever government action "creates an identification of the state with a religion, or with religion in general," 728 F. Supp., at 71, or when "the effect of the governmental action is to endorse one religion over another, or to endorse religion in general." *Id.*, at 72. The court determined that the practice of including invocations and benedictions, even so-called nonsectarian ones, in public school graduations creates an identification of governmental power with religious practice, endorses religion, and violates the Establishment Clause. In so holding the court expressed the determination not to follow *Stein v. Plainwell Community Schools*, 822 F.2d 1406 (1987), in which the Court of Appeals for the Sixth Circuit, relying on our decision in *Marsh v. Chambers*, 463 U.S. 783 (1983), held that benedictions and invocations at public school graduations are not always unconstitutional. In *Marsh* we upheld the constitutionality of the Nebraska State Legislature's practice of opening each of its sessions with a prayer offered by a chaplain paid out of public funds. The District Court in this case disagreed with the Sixth Circuit's reasoning because it believed that *Marsh* was a narrow decision, "limited to the unique situation of legislative prayer," and did not have any relevance to school prayer cases. 728 F. Supp., at 74.

On appeal, the United States Court of Appeals for the First Circuit affirmed. The majority opinion by Judge Torruella adopted the opinion of the District Court. 908 F.2d 1090 (1990). Judge Bownes joined the majority, but wrote a separate concurring opinion in which he decided that the practices challenged here violated all three parts of the *Lemon* test. Judge Bownes went on to agree with the District Court that *Marsh* had no application to school prayer cases and that the *Stein* decision was flawed. He concluded by suggesting that under Establishment Clause rules no prayer, even one excluding any mention of the Deity, could be offered at a public school graduation

ceremony. 908 F.2d, at 1090–1097. Judge Campbell dissented, on the basis of *Marsh* and *Stein*. He reasoned that if the prayers delivered were nonsectarian, and if school officials ensured that persons representing a variety of beliefs and ethical systems were invited to present invocations and benedictions, there was no violation of the Establishment Clause. 908 F.2d, at 1099. We granted certiorari and now affirm.

II

These dominant facts mark and control the confines of our decision: State officials direct the performance of a formal religious exercise at promotional and graduation ceremonies for secondary schools. Even for those students who object to the religious exercise, their attendance and participation in the state-sponsored religious activity are in a fair and real sense obligatory, though the school district does not require attendance as a condition for receipt of the diploma.

This case does not require us to revisit the difficult questions dividing us in recent cases, questions of the definition and full scope of the principles governing the extent of permitted accommodation by the State for the religious beliefs and practices of many of its citizens. See *Allegheny County v. Greater Pittsburgh ACLU*, 492 U.S. 573 (1989); *Wallace v. Jaffree*, 472 U.S. 38 (1985); *Lynch v. Donnelly*, 465 U.S. 668 (1984). For without reference to those principles in other contexts, the controlling precedents as they relate to prayer and religious exercise in primary and secondary public schools compel the holding here that the policy of the city of Providence is an unconstitutional one. We can decide the case without reconsidering the general constitutional framework by which public schools' efforts to accommodate religion are measured. Thus we do not accept the invitation of petitioners and *amicus* the United States to reconsider our decision in *Lemon v. Kurtzman, supra.* The government involvement with religious activity in this case is pervasive, to the point of creating a state-sponsored and state-directed religious exercise in a public school. Conducting this formal religious observance conflicts with settled rules pertaining to prayer exercises for students, and that suffices to determine the question before us.

The principle that government may accommodate the free exercise of religion does not supersede the fundamental limitations imposed by the Establishment Clause. It is beyond dispute that, at a minimum, the Constitution guarantees that government may not coerce anyone to support or participate in religion or its exercise, or otherwise act in a way which "establishes a [state] religion or religious faith, or tends to do so." *Lynch, supra,* at 678; see also *Allegheny County, supra,* at 591 quoting *Everson v. Board of Education of Ewing,* 330 U.S. 1, 15–16 (1947). The State's involvement in the school prayers challenged today violates these central principles.

That involvement is as troubling as it is undenied. A school official, the principal, decided that an invocation and a benediction should be given; this is a choice attributable to the State, and from a constitutional perspective it is as if a state statute decreed that the prayers must occur. The principal chose the religious participant, here a rabbi, and that choice is also attributable to the State. The reason for the choice of a rabbi is not disclosed by the record, but the potential for divisiveness over the choice of a particular member of the clergy to conduct the ceremony is apparent. . . .

The State's role did not end with the decision to include a prayer and with the choice of clergyman. Principal Lee provided Rabbi Gutterman with a copy of the "Guidelines for Civic Occasions," and advised him that his prayers should be nonsectarian. Through these means the principal directed and controlled the content of the prayer. Even if the only sanction for ignoring the instructions were that the rabbi would not be invited back, we think no religious representative who valued his or her continued reputation and effectiveness in the community would incur the State's displeasure in this regard. It is a cornerstone principle of our Establishment Clause jurisprudence that "it is no part of the business of government to compose official prayers for any group of the American people to recite as a part of a religious program carried on by government," *Engel v. Vitale,* 370 U.S. 421, 425 (1962), and that is what the school officials attempted to do.

Petitioners argue, and we find nothing in the case to refute it, that the directions for the content of the prayers were a good-faith attempt by the school to ensure that the sectarianism which is so often the flashpoint for religious animosity be removed from the graduation ceremony. The concern is understandable, as a prayer which uses ideas or images identified with a particular religion may foster a different sort of sectarian rivalry than an invocation or benediction in terms more neutral. The school's explanation, however, does not resolve the dilemma caused by its participation. The question is not the good faith of the school in attempting to make the prayer acceptable to most persons, but the legitimacy of its undertaking that enterprise at all when the object is to produce a prayer to be used in a formal religious exercise which students, for all practical purposes, are obliged to attend. . . .

The First Amendment's Religion Clauses mean that religious beliefs and religious expression are too precious to be either proscribed or prescribed by the State. The design of the Constitution is that preservation and transmission of religious beliefs and worship is a responsibility and a choice committed to the private sphere, which itself is promised freedom to pursue that mission. It must not be forgotten then, that while concern must be given to define the protection granted to an objector or a dissenting non-believer, these same Clauses exist to protect religion from government interference. James Madison, the principal author of the Bill of Rights, did not rest his opposition to a religious establishment on the sole ground of its effect on the minority. A principal ground for his view was: "[E]xperience witnesseth that ecclesiastical establishments, instead of maintaining the purity and efficacy of Religion, have had a contrary operation." Memorial and Remonstrance Against Religious Assessments (1785), in 8 Papers of James Madison 301 (W. Rachal, R. Rutland, B. Ripel, & F. Teute eds. 1973).

These concerns have particular application in the case of school officials, whose effort to monitor prayer will be perceived by the students as inducing a participation they might otherwise reject. Though the efforts of the school officials in this case to find common ground appear to have been a good-faith attempt to recognize the common aspects of religions and not the divisive ones, our precedents do not permit school officials to assist in composing prayers as an incident to a formal exercise for their students. *Engel v. Vitale, supra,* at 425. And these same precedents caution us to measure the idea of a civic religion against the central meaning of the Religion Clauses of the First Amendment, which is that all creeds must be tolerated and none favored. The suggestion that government may establish an official or civic religion as a means of avoiding the establishment of a religion with more specific creeds strikes us as a contradiction that cannot be accepted.

The degree of school involvement here made it clear that the graduation prayers bore the imprint of the State and thus put school-age children who objected in an untenable position. We turn our attention now to consider the position of the students, both those who desired the prayer and she who did not. . . .

The lessons of the First Amendment are as urgent in the modern world as in the 18th Century when it was written. One timeless lesson is that if citizens are subjected to state-sponsored religious exercises, the State disavows its own duty to guard and respect that sphere of inviolable conscience and belief which is the mark of a free people. To compromise that principle today would be to deny our own tradition and forfeit our standing to urge others to secure the protections of that tradition for themselves.

As we have observed before, there are heightened concerns with protecting freedom of conscience from subtle coercive pressure in the elementary and secondary public schools. See, e.g., *Abington School District v. Schempp,* 374 U.S. 203, 307 (1963) (Goldberg, J., concurring); *Edwards v. Aguillard,* 482 U.S. 578, 584 (1987); *Westside Community Bd. of Ed. v. Mergens,* 496 U.S. 226, 261–262 (1990) (Kennedy, J., concurring). Our decisions in *Engel v. Vitale,* 370 U.S. 421 (1962), and *Abington School District, supra,* recognize, among other things, that prayer exercises in public schools carry a particular risk of indirect coercion. The concern may not be limited to the context of schools, but it is most pronounced there. What to most believers may seem nothing more than a reasonable request that the nonbeliever respect their religious practices, in a school context may appear to the non-believer or dissenter to be an attempt to employ the machinery of the State to enforce a religious orthodoxy.

We need not look beyond the circumstances of this case to see the phenomenon at work. The undeniable fact is that the school district's supervision and control of a high school graduation ceremony places public pressure, as well as peer pressure, on attending students to stand as a group or, at least, maintain respectful silence during the Invocation and Benediction. This pressure, though subtle and indirect, can be as real as any overt compulsion. Of course, in our culture standing or remaining silent can signify adherence to a view or simple respect for the views of others. And no doubt some persons who have no desire to join a prayer have little objection to standing as a sign of respect for those who do. But for the dissenter of high school age, who has a reasonable perception that she is being forced by the State to pray in a manner her conscience will not allow, the injury is no less real. There can be no doubt that for many, if not most, of the students at the graduation, the act of standing or remaining silent was an expression of participation in the Rabbi's prayer. That was the very point of the religious exercise. It is of little comfort to a dissenter, then, to be told that for her the act of standing or remain-

ing in silence signifies mere respect, rather than participation. What matters is that, given our social conventions, a reasonable dissenter in this milieu could believe that the group exercise signified her own participation or approval of it.

Finding no violation under these circumstances would place objectors in the dilemma of participating, with all that implies, or protesting. We do not address whether that choice is acceptable if the affected citizens are mature adults, but we think the State may not, consistent with the Establishment Clause, place primary and secondary school children in this position. Research in psychology supports the common assumption that adolescents are often susceptible to pressure from their peers towards conformity, and that the influence is strongest in matters of social convention. To recognize that the choice imposed by the State constitutes an unacceptable constraint only acknowledges that the government may no more use social pressure to enforce orthodoxy than it may use more direct means.

The injury caused by the government's action, and the reason why Daniel and Deborah Weisman object to it, is that the State, in a school setting, in effect required participation in a religious exercise. It is, we concede, a brief exercise during which the individual can concentrate on joining its message, meditate on her own religion, or let her mind wander. But the embarrassment and the intrusion of the religious exercise cannot be refuted by arguing that these prayers, and similar ones to be said in the future, are of a *de minimis* character. To do so would be an affront to the Rabbi who offered them and to all those for whom the prayers were an essential and profound recognition of divine authority. And for the same reason, we think that the intrusion is greater than the two minutes or so of time consumed for prayers like these. Assuming, as we must, that the prayers were offensive to the student and the parent who now object, the intrusion was both real and, in the context of a secondary school, a violation of the objectors' rights. That the intrusion was in the course of promulgating religion that sought to be civic or nonsectarian rather than pertaining to one sect does not lessen the offense or isolation to the objectors. At best it narrows their number, at worst increases their sense of isolation and affront.

There was a stipulation in the District Court that attendance at graduation and promotional ceremonies is voluntary. Petitioners and the United States, as *amicus*, made this a center point of the case, arguing that the option of not attending the graduation excuses any inducement or coercion in the ceremony itself. The argument lacks all persuasion. Law reaches past formalism. And to say a teenage student has a real choice not to attend her high school graduation is formalistic in the extreme. True, Deborah could elect not to attend commencement without renouncing her diploma; but we shall not allow the case to turn on this point. Everyone knows that in our society and in our culture high school graduation is one of life's most significant occasions. A school rule which excuses attendance is beside the point. Attendance may not be required by official decree, yet it is apparent that a student is not free to absent herself from the graduation exercise in any real sense of the term "voluntary," for absence would require forfeiture of those intangible benefits which have motivated the student through youth and all her high school

years. Graduation is a time for family and those closest to the student to celebrate success and express mutual wishes of gratitude and respect, all to the end of impressing upon the young person the role that it is his or her right and duty to assume in the community and all of its diverse parts.

The importance of the event is the point the school district and the United States rely upon to argue that a formal prayer ought to be permitted, but it becomes one of the principal reasons why their argument must fail. Their contention, one of considerable force were it not for the constitutional constraints applied to state action, is that the prayers are an essential part of these ceremonies because for many persons an occasion of this significance lacks meaning if there is no recognition, however brief, that human achievements cannot be understood apart from their spiritual essence. We think the Government's position that this interest suffices to force students to choose between compliance or forfeiture demonstrates fundamental inconsistency in its argumentation. It fails to acknowledge that what for many of Deborah's classmates and their parents was a spiritual imperative was for Daniel and Deborah Weisman religious conformance compelled by the State. While in some societies the wishes of the majority might prevail, the Establishment Clause of the First Amendment is addressed to this contingency and rejects the balance urged upon us. The Constitution forbids the State to exact religious conformity from a student as the price of attending her own high school graduation. This is the calculus the Constitution commands.

The Government's argument gives insufficient recognition to the real conflict of conscience faced by the young student. The essence of the Government's position is that with regard to a civic, social occasion of this importance it is the objector, not the majority, who must take unilateral and private action to avoid compromising religious scruples, here by electing to miss the graduation exercise. This turns conventional First Amendment analysis on its head. It is a tenet of the First Amendment that the State cannot require one of its citizens to forfeit his or her rights and benefits as the price of resisting conformance to state-sponsored religious practice. To say that a student must remain apart from the ceremony at the opening invocation and closing benediction is to risk compelling conformity in an environment analogous to the classroom setting, where we have said the risk of compulsion is especially high. Just as in *Engel v. Vitale*, 370 U.S., at 430, and *Abington School District v. Schempp*, 374 U.S., at 224–225, we found that provisions within the challenged legislation permitting a student to be voluntarily excused from attendance or participation in the daily prayers did not shield those practices from invalidation, the fact that attendance at the graduation ceremonies is voluntary in a legal sense does not save the religious exercise.

Inherent differences between the public school system and a session of a State Legislature distinguish this case from *Marsh v. Chambers*, 463 U.S. 783 (1983). The considerations we have raised in objection to the invocation and benediction are in many respects similar to the arguments we considered in *Marsh*. But there are also obvious differences. The atmosphere at the opening of a session of a state legislature where adults are free to enter and leave with little comment and for any number of reasons cannot compare with the constraining potential of the one school event most important for the student to attend. The influence and force of a formal exercise in a school graduation are far greater than the prayer exercise we condoned in *Marsh*. The *Marsh* majority in fact gave specific recognition to this distinction and placed particular reliance on it in upholding the prayers at issue there. Today's case is different. At a high school graduation, teachers and principals must and do retain a high degree of control over the precise contents of the program, the speeches, the timing, the movements, the dress, and the decorum of the students. In this atmosphere the state-imposed character of an invocation and benediction by clergy selected by the school combine to make the prayer a state-sanctioned religious exercise in which the student was left with no alternative but to submit. This is different from *Marsh* and suffices to make the religious exercise a First Amendment violation. Our Establishment Clause jurisprudence remains a delicate and fact-sensitive one, and we cannot accept the parallel relied upon by petitioners and the United States between the facts of *Marsh* and the case now before us. Our decisions in *Engel v. Vitale, supra*, and *Abington School District v. Schempp, supra*, require us to distinguish the public school context.

We do not hold that every state action implicating religion is invalid if one or a few citizens find it offensive. People may take offense at all manner of religious as well as nonreligious messages, but offense alone does not in every case show a violation. We know too that sometimes to endure social isolation or even anger may be the price of conscience or nonconformity. But, by any reading of our cases, the conformity required of the student in this case was too high an exaction to withstand the test of the Establishment Clause. The prayer exercises in this case are especially improper because the State has in every practical sense compelled attendance and participation in an explicit religious exercise at an event of singular importance to every student, one the objecting student had no real alternative to avoid.

Our jurisprudence in this area is of necessity one of line-drawing, of determining at what point a dissenter's rights of religious freedom are infringed by the State. . . .

Our society would be less than true to its heritage if it lacked abiding concern for the values of its young people, and we acknowledge the profound belief of adherents to many faiths that there must be a place in the student's life for precepts of a morality higher even than the law we today enforce. We express no hostility to those aspirations, nor would our oath permit us to do so. A relentless and all-pervasive attempt to exclude religion from every aspect of public life could itself become inconsistent with the Constitution. We recognize that, at graduation time and throughout the course of the educational process, there will be instances when religious values, religious practices, and religious persons will have some interaction with the public schools and their students. But these matters, often questions of accommodation of religion, are not before us. The sole question presented is whether a religious exercise may be conducted at a graduation ceremony in circumstances where, as we have found, young graduates who object are induced to conform. No holding by this Court suggests that a school can persuade or compel a student to participate in a religious exercise. That is being done here, and it is forbidden by the Establishment Clause of the First Amendment.

For the reasons we have stated, the judgment of the Court of Appeals is *Affirmed.*

NO

Antonin Scalia

DISSENTING OPINION OF ANTONIN SCALIA

JUSTICE SCALIA, with whom THE CHIEF JUSTICE, JUSTICE WHITE, and JUSTICE THOMAS join, dissenting.

. . . In holding that the Establishment Clause prohibits invocations and benedictions at public-school graduation ceremonies, the Court—with nary a mention that it is doing so—lays waste a tradition that is as old as public-school graduation ceremonies themselves, and that is a component of an even more longstanding American tradition of nonsectarian prayer to God at public celebrations generally. As its instrument of destruction, the bulldozer of its social engineering, the Court invents a boundless, and boundlessly manipulable, test of psychological coercion, which promises to do for the Establishment Clause what the *Durham* rule did for the insanity defense. See *Durham v. United States*, 94 U.S. App. D. C. 228, 214 F.2d 862 (1954). Today's opinion shows more forcefully than volumes of argumentation why our Nation's protection, that fortress which is our Constitution, cannot possibly rest upon the changeable philosophical predilections of the Justices of this Court, but must have deep foundations in the historic practices of our people.

I

Justice Holmes' aphorism that "a page of history is worth a volume of logic," *New York Trust Co. v. Eisner*, 256 U.S. 345, 349 (1921), applies with particular force to our Establishment Clause jurisprudence. As we have recognized, our interpretation of the Establishment Clause should "compor[t] with what history reveals was the contemporaneous understanding of its guarantees." *Lynch v. Donnelly*, 465 U.S. 668, 673 (1984). "[T]he line we must draw between the permissible and the impermissible is one which accords with history and faithfully reflects the understanding of the Founding Fathers." *Abington School District v. Schempp*, 374 U.S. 203, 294 (1963) (Brennan, J., concurring). "[H]istorical evidence sheds light not only on what the draftsmen intended

From *Robert E. Lee et al. v. Daniel Weisman et al.*, 60 L.W. 4737 (1992). Some case citations omitted.

the Establishment Clause to mean, but also on how they thought that Clause applied" to contemporaneous practices. *Marsh v. Chambers*, 463 U.S. 783, 790 (1983). Thus, "[t]he existence from the beginning of the Nation's life of a practice, [while] not conclusive of its constitutionality . . ., is a fact of considerable import in the interpretation" of the Establishment Clause. *Walz v. Tax Comm'n of New York City*, 397 U.S. 664, 681 (1970) (Brennan, J., concurring).

The history and tradition of our Nation are replete with public ceremonies featuring prayers of thanksgiving and petition. Illustrations of this point have been amply provided in our prior opinions, but since the Court is so oblivious to our history as to suggest that the Constitution restricts "preservation and transmission of religious beliefs . . . to the private sphere," it appears necessary to provide another brief account.

From our Nation's origin, prayer has been a prominent part of governmental ceremonies and proclamations. The Declaration of Independence, the document marking our birth as a separate people, "appeal[ed] to the Supreme Judge of the world for the rectitude of our intentions" and avowed "a firm reliance on the protection of divine Providence." In his first inaugural address, after swearing his oath of office on a Bible, George Washington deliberately made a prayer a part of his first official act as President:

"it would be peculiarly improper to omit in this first official act my fervent supplications to that Almighty Being who rules over the universe, who presides in the councils of nations, and whose providential aids can supply every human defect, that His benediction may consecrate to the liberties and happiness of the people of the United States

a Government instituted by themselves for these essential purposes." Inaugural Addresses of the Presidents of the United States 2 (1989).

Such supplications have been a characteristic feature of inaugural addresses ever since. Thomas Jefferson, for example, prayed in his first inaugural address: "may that Infinite Power which rules the destinies of the universe lead our councils to what is best, and give them a favorable issue for your peace and prosperity." *Id.*, at 17. . . .

Most recently, President Bush, continuing the tradition established by President Washington, asked those attending his inauguration to bow their heads, and made a prayer his first official act as President. *Id.*, at 346.

Our national celebration of Thanksgiving likewise dates back to President Washington. As we recounted in *Lynch*,

"The day after the First Amendment was proposed, Congress urged President Washington to proclaim 'a day of public thanksgiving and prayer, to be observed by acknowledging with grateful hearts the many and signal favours of Almighty God.' President Washington proclaimed November 26, 1789, a day of thanksgiving to 'offe[r] our prayers and supplications to the Great Lord and Ruler of Nations, and beseech him to pardon our national and other transgressions. . . .' " 465 U.S., at 675, n. 2 (citations omitted).

This tradition of Thanksgiving Proclamations—with their religious theme of prayerful gratitude to God—has been adhered to by almost every President.

The other two branches of the Federal Government also have a long-established practice of prayer at public events. As we detailed in *Marsh*, Congressional sessions have opened with a chaplain's prayer ever since the First Congress. 463 U.S., at 787–788. And this Court's own sessions have opened with the invocation "God save the United States and this Honorable Court" since the days of Chief Justice Marshall. 1 C. Warren, The Supreme Court in United States History 469 (1922).

In addition to this general tradition of prayer at public ceremonies, there exists a more specific tradition of invocations and benedictions at public-school graduation exercises. By one account, the first public-high-school graduation ceremony took place in Connecticut in July 1868—the very month, as it happens, that the Fourteenth Amendment (the vehicle by which the Establishment Clause has been applied against the States) was ratified—when "15 seniors from the Norwich Free Academy marched in their best Sunday suits and dresses into a church hall and waited through majestic music and long prayers." Brodinsky, Commencement Rites Obsolete? Not At All, A 10-Week Study Shows, Updating School Board Policies, Vol. 10, p. 3 (Apr. 1979). As the Court obliquely acknowledges in describing the "customary features" of high school graduations, *ante*, at 3–4, and as respondents do not contest, the invocation and benediction have long been recognized to be "as traditional as any other parts of the [school] graduation program and are widely established." H. McKown, Commencement Activities 56 (1931).

II

The Court presumably would separate graduation invocations and benedictions from other instances of public "preservation and transmission of religious beliefs" on the ground that they involve "psychological coercion." I find it a suffi-

cient embarrassment that our Establishment Clause jurisprudence regarding holiday displays, see *Allegheny County v. Greater Pittsburgh ACLU*, 492 U.S. 573 (1989), has come to "requir[e] scrutiny more commonly associated with interior decorators than with the judiciary." *American Jewish Congress v. Chicago*, 827 F.2d 120, 129 (Easterbrook, J., dissenting). But interior decorating is a rock-hard science compared to psychology practiced by amateurs. A few citations of "[r]esearch in psychology" that have no particular bearing upon the precise issue here, cannot disguise the fact that the Court has gone beyond the realm where judges know what they are doing. The Court's argument that state officials have "coerced" students to take part in the invocation and benediction at graduation ceremonies is, not to put too fine a point on it, incoherent.

The Court identifies two "dominant facts" that it says dictate its ruling that invocations and benedictions at public-school graduation ceremonies violate the Establishment Clause. Neither of them is in any relevant sense true.

A

The Court declares that students' "attendance and participation in the [invocation and benediction] are in a fair and real sense obligatory." But what exactly is this "fair and real sense"? According to the Court, students at graduation who want "to avoid the fact or appearance of participation" in the invocation and benediction are *psychologically* obligated by "public pressure, as well as peer pressure, . . . to stand as a group or, at least, maintain respectful silence" during those prayers. This assertion—*the very linchpin of the Court's opinion*—is almost as intriguing for what it does not say as for what it says. It does not say, for example, that students are psychologically coerced to bow their heads, place their hands in a Drüer-like prayer position, pay attention to the prayers, utter "Amen," or in fact pray. (Perhaps further intensive psychological research remains to be done on these matters.) It claims only that students are psychologically coerced "to stand . . . or, at least, maintain respectful silence" (emphasis added). Both halves of this disjunctive (*both* of which must amount to the fact or appearance of participation in prayer if the Court's analysis is to survive on its own terms) merit particular attention.

To begin with the latter: The Court's notion that a student who simply *sits* in "respectful silence" during the invocation and benediction (when all others are standing) has somehow joined—or would somehow be perceived as having joined—in the prayers is nothing short of ludicrous. We indeed live in a vulgar age. But surely "our social conventions" have not coarsened to the point that anyone who does not stand on his chair and shout obscenities can reasonably be deemed to have assented to everything said in his presence. Since the Court does not dispute that students exposed to prayer at graduation ceremonies retain (despite "subtle coercive pressures") the free will to sit, there is absolutely no basis for the Court's decision. It is fanciful enough to say that "a reasonable dissenter," standing head erect in a class of bowed heads, "could believe that the group exercise signified her own participation or approval of it." It is beyond the absurd to say that she could entertain such a belief while pointedly declining to rise.

But let us assume the very worst, that the nonparticipating graduate is "subtly

coerced" . . . to stand! Even that half of the disjunctive does not remotely establish a "participation" (or an "appearance of participation") in a religious exercise. The Court acknowledges that "in our culture standing . . . can signify adherence to a view or simple respect for the views of others." (Much more often the latter than the former, I think, except perhaps in the proverbial town meeting, where one votes by standing.) But if it is a permissible inference that one who is standing is doing so simply out of respect for the prayers of others that are in progress, then how can it possibly be said that a "reasonable dissenter . . . could believe that the group exercise signified her own participation or approval"? Quite obviously, it cannot. I may add, moreover, that maintaining respect for the religious observances of others is a fundamental civic virtue that government (including the public schools) can and should cultivate—so that even if it were the case that the displaying of such respect might be mistaken for taking part in the prayer, I would deny that the dissenter's interest in avoiding *even the false appearance of participation* constitutionally trumps the government's interest in fostering respect for religion generally.

The opinion manifests that the Court itself has not given careful consideration to its test of psychological coercion. For if it had, how could it observe, with no hint of concern or disapproval, that students stood for the Pledge of Allegiance, which immediately preceded Rabbi Gutterman's invocation? The government can, of course, no more coerce political orthodoxy than religious orthodoxy. *West Virginia Board of Education v. Barnette*, 319 U.S. 624, 642 (1943). Moreover, since the Pledge of Allegiance has been revised since *Barnette* to include the phrase "under God," recital of the Pledge would appear to raise the same Establishment Clause issue as the invocation and benediction. If students were psychologically coerced to remain standing during the invocation, they must also have been psychologically coerced, moments before, to stand for (and thereby, in the Court's view, take part in or appear to take part in) the Pledge. Must the Pledge therefore be barred from the public schools (both from graduation ceremonies and from the classroom)? In *Barnette* we held that a public-school student could not be compelled to *recite* the Pledge; we did not even hint that she could not be compelled to observe respectful silence—indeed, even to *stand* in respectful silence—when those who wished to recite it did so. Logically, that ought to be the next project for the Court's bulldozer.

I also find it odd that the Court concludes that high school graduates may not be subjected to this supposed psychological coercion, yet refrains from addressing whether "mature adults" may. I had thought that the reason graduation from high school is regarded as so significant an event is that it is generally associated with transition from adolescence to young adulthood. Many graduating seniors, of course, are old enough to vote. Why, then, does the Court treat them as though they were first-graders? Will we soon have a jurisprudence that distinguishes between mature and immature adults?

B

The other "dominant fac[t]" identified by the Court is that "[s]tate officials direct the performance of a formal religious exercise" at school graduation ceremo-

nies. "Direct[ing] the performance of a formal religious exercise" has a sound of liturgy to it, summoning up images of the principal directing acolytes where to carry the cross, or showing the rabbi where to unroll the Torah. A Court professing to be engaged in a "delicate and fact-sensitive" line-drawing would better describe what it means as "prescribing the content of an invocation and benediction." But even that would be false. All the record shows is that principals of the Providence public schools, acting within their delegated authority, have invited clergy to deliver invocations and benedictions at graduations; and that Principal Lee invited Rabbi Gutterman, provided him a two-page flyer, prepared by the National Conference of Christians and Jews, giving general advice on inclusive prayer for civic occasions, and advised him that his prayers at graduation should be nonsectarian. How these facts can fairly be transformed into the charges that Principal Lee "directed and controlled the content of [Rabbi Gutterman's] prayer," that school officials "monitor prayer" and attempted to " 'compose official prayers,' " and that the "government involvement with religious activity in this case is pervasive," is difficult to fathom. The Court identifies nothing in the record remotely suggesting that school officials have ever drafted, edited, screened or censored graduation prayers, or that Rabbi Gutterman was a mouthpiece of the school officials.

These distortions of the record are, of course, not harmless error: without them the Court's solemn assertion that the school officials could reasonably be perceived to be "enforc[ing] a religious orthodoxy" would ring as hollow as it ought.

III

The deeper flaw in the Court's opinion does not lie in its wrong answer to the question whether there was state-induced "peer-pressure" coercion; it lies, rather, in the Court's making violation of the Establishment Clause hinge on such a precious question. The coercion that was a hallmark of historical establishments of religion was coercion of religious orthodoxy and of financial support *by force of law and threat of penalty.* Typically, attendance at the state church was required; only clergy of the official church could lawfully perform sacraments; and dissenters, if tolerated, faced an array of civil disabilities. L. Levy, The Establishment Clause 4 (1986). Thus, for example, in the colony of Virginia, where the Church of England had been established, ministers were required by law to conform to the doctrine and rites of the Church of England; and all persons were required to attend church and observe the Sabbath, were tithed for the public support of Anglican ministers, and were taxed for the costs of building and repairing churches. *Id.*, at 3–4.

The Establishment Clause was adopted to prohibit such an establishment of religion at the federal level (and to protect state establishments of religion from federal interference). I will further acknowledge for the sake of argument that, as some scholars have argued, by 1790 the term "establishment" had acquired an additional meaning—"financial support of religion generally, by public taxation"—that reflected the development of "general or multiple" establishments, not limited to a single church. *Id.*, at 8–9. But that would still be an establishment coerced *by force of law.* And I will further concede that our constitutional tradition,

from the Declaration of Independence and the first inaugural address of Washington, quoted earlier, down to the present day, has, with a few aberrations, see *Holy Trinity Church v. United States,* 143 U.S. 457 (1892), ruled out of order government-sponsored endorsement of religion—even when no legal coercion is present, and indeed even when no ersatz, "peer-pressure" psycho-coercion is present—where the endorsement is sectarian, in the sense of specifying details upon which men and women who believe in a benevolent, omnipotent Creator and Ruler of the world, are known to differ (for example, the divinity of Christ). But there is simply no support for the proposition that the officially sponsored nondenominational invocation and benediction read by Rabbi Gutterman—with no one legally coerced to recite them—violated the Constitution of the United States. To the contrary, they are so characteristically American they could have come from the pen of George Washington or Abraham Lincoln himself. . . .

This historical discussion places in revealing perspective the Court's extravagant claim that the State has "for all practical purposes" and "in every practical sense" compelled students to participate in prayers at graduation. Beyond the fact, stipulated to by the parties, that attendance at graduation is voluntary, there is nothing in the record to indicate that failure of attending students to take part in the invocation or benediction was subject to any penalty or discipline. Contrast this with, for example, the facts of *Barnette:* Schoolchildren were required by law to recite the Pledge of Allegiance; failure to do so resulted in expulsion, threatened the expelled child with the prospect of being sent to a reformatory for criminally inclined juveniles, and subjected his parents to prosecution (and incarceration) for causing delinquency. 319 U.S., at 629–630. To characterize the "subtle coercive pressures" allegedly present here as the "practical" equivalent of the legal sanctions in *Barnette* is . . . well, let me just say it is not a "delicate and fact-sensitive" analysis.

The Court relies on our "school prayer" cases, *Engel v. Vitale*, 370 U.S. 421 (1962), and *Abington School District v. Schempp*, 374 U.S. 203 (1963). But whatever the merit of those cases, they do not support, much less compel, the Court's psycho-journey. In the first place, *Engel* and *Schempp* do not constitute an exception to the rule, distilled from historical practice, that public ceremonies may include prayer; rather, they simply do not fall within the scope of the rule (for the obvious reason that school instruction is not a public ceremony). Second, we have made clear our understanding that school prayer occurs within a framework in which legal coercion to attend school (i.e., coercion under threat of penalty) provides the ultimate backdrop. In *Schempp*, for example, we emphasized that the prayers were "prescribed as part of the curricular activities of students who are *required by law* to attend school." 374 U.S., at 223 (emphasis added). *Engel's* suggestion that the school-prayer program at issue there—which permitted students "to remain silent or be excused from the room," 370 U.S., at 430—involved "indirect coercive pressure," *id.*, at 431, should be understood against this backdrop of legal coercion. The question whether the opt-out procedure in *Engel* sufficed to dispel the coercion resulting from the mandatory attendance requirement is quite different from the question whether forbidden coercion exists in an environment *utterly devoid of legal compulsion*. And finally, our school-prayer cases turn in part on the fact that the classroom is inherently an instructional setting, and daily prayer there—where parents are not present to counter "the students' emulation of teachers as role models and the children's susceptibility to peer pressure," *Edwards v. Aguillard*, 482 U.S. 578, 584 (1987)—might be thought to raise special concerns regarding state interference with the liberty of parents to direct the religious upbringing of their children: "Families entrust public schools with the education of their children, but condition their trust on the understanding that the classroom will not purposely be used to advance religious views that may conflict with the private beliefs of the student and his or her family." *Ibid.*; see *Pierce v. Society of Sisters*, 268 U.S. 510, 534–535 (1925). Voluntary prayer at graduation—a one-time ceremony at which parents, friends and relatives are present—can hardly be thought to raise the same concerns.

IV

Our religion-clause jurisprudence has become bedeviled (so to speak) by reliance on formulaic abstractions that are not derived from, but positively conflict with, our long-accepted constitutional traditions. Foremost among these has been the so-called *Lemon* test, see *Lemon v. Kurtzman*, 403 U.S. 602, 612–613 (1971), which has received well-earned criticism from many members of this Court. The Court today demonstrates the irrelevance of *Lemon* by essentially ignoring it, and the interment of that case may be the one happy byproduct of the Court's otherwise lamentable decision. Unfortunately, however, the Court has replaced *Lemon* with its psycho-coercion test, which suffers the double disability of having no roots whatever in our people's historic practice, and being as infinitely expandable as the reasons for psychotherapy itself.

Another happy aspect of the case is that it is only a jurisprudential disaster and not a practical one. Given the odd basis for the Court's decision, invocations and benedictions will be able to be given at public-school graduations next June, as they have for the past century and a half, so long as school authorities make clear that anyone who abstains from screaming in protest does not necessarily participate in the prayers. All that is seemingly needed is an announcement, or perhaps a written insertion at the beginning of the graduation Program, to the effect that, while all are asked to rise for the invocation and benediction, none is compelled to join in them, nor will be assumed, by rising, to have done so. That obvious fact recited, the graduates and their parents may proceed to thank God, as Americans have always done, for the blessings He has generously bestowed on them and on their country.

The reader has been told much in this case about the personal interest of Mr. Weisman and his daughter, and very little about the personal interests on the other side. They are not inconsequential. Church and state would not be such a difficult subject if religion were, as the Court apparently thinks it to be, some purely personal avocation that can be indulged entirely in secret, like pornography, in the privacy of one's room. For most believers it is *not* that, and has never been. Religious men and women of almost all denominations have felt it necessary to acknowledge and beseech the blessing of God as a people, and not just as individuals, because they believe in the "protection of divine Providence," as the Declaration of Independence put it, not just for individuals but for societies; because they believe God to be, as Washington's first Thanksgiving Proclamation put it, the "Great Lord and Ruler of Nations." One can believe in the effectiveness of such public worship, or one can deprecate and deride it. But the long-standing American tradition of prayer at official ceremonies displays with unmistakable clarity that the Establishment Clause does not forbid the government to accommodate it.

The narrow context of the present case involves a community's celebration of one of the milestones in its young citizens' lives, and it is a bold step for this Court to seek to banish from that occasion, and from thousands of similar celebrations throughout this land, the expression of gratitude to God that a majority of the community wishes to make. The issue before us today is not the abstract philosophical question whether the alternative of frustrating this desire of a religious majority is to be preferred over the alternative of imposing "psychological coercion," or a feeling of exclusion, upon nonbelievers. Rather, the question is *whether a mandatory choice in favor of the former has been imposed by the United States Constitution*. As the age-old practices of our people show, the answer to that question is not at all in doubt.

I must add one final observation: The founders of our Republic knew the fearsome potential of sectarian religious belief to generate civil dissension and civil strife. And they also knew that nothing, absolutely nothing, is so inclined to foster among religious believers of various faiths a toleration—no, an affection—for one another than voluntarily joining in prayer together, to the God whom they all worship and seek. Needless to say, no one should be compelled to do that, but it is a shame to deprive our public culture of the opportunity, and indeed the encouragement, for people to do it voluntarily. The Baptist or Catholic who heard and joined in the simple and inspiring prayers of Rabbi Gutterman on this official and patriotic occasion was inoculated from religious bigotry and prejudice in a manner that can not be replicated. To deprive our society of that important unifying mechanism, in order to spare the nonbeliever what seems to me the minimal inconvenience of standing or even sitting in respectful nonparticipation, is as senseless in policy as it is unsupported in law.

For the foregoing reasons, I dissent.

POSTSCRIPT

Do Prayers at Public School Graduation Ceremonies Violate the Constitution?

Why should church and state be separate? Is there any danger to be feared from public religious displays? It is probably fair to say that behind the debates over this issue and the ongoing controversy over prayer in the schools are differing interpretations of the history of religion. Does religion bring us to a higher level of existence, or is it a system that oppresses dissidents, nonbelievers, and members of minority faiths? Almost everyone has an opinion on this question, and most can find some historical support for their positions. Ironically, the same historical circumstances may even be used to support opposing points of view. For example, at a congressional hearing on school prayer, the following testimony was introduced:

> When I was educated in German public schools, they provided as part of the regular curriculum separate religious instruction for children of the three major faiths. At that time, all children in public schools from the ages of 6 to 18 were required not merely to recite a prayer at the beginning of each school session but to receive religious instruction twice a week. That system continued in the following decades.
>
> Did that program effectively teach morality to the German people? If it did, it would be difficult to explain the rise of Hitler and the total moral collapse and even depravity of the German people, which resulted in the torture and death of millions of Jews and Christians. (Statement by Joachim Prinz, quoted in testimony of Nathan Dershowitz, before the Committee on the Judiciary, U.S. House, *Hearings on Prayer in Public Schools and Buildings*, August 19, 1980)

Yet another witness, however, testifying in support of prayer in the schools, quoted the report of the President's Commission on the Holocaust, which said that "the Holocaust could not have occurred without the collapse of certain religious norms; increasing secularity fueled a devaluation of the image of the human being created in the likeness of God" (Statement of Judah Glasner before the Committee on the Judiciary, U.S. House, *Hearings on Prayer in Public Schools and Buildings*, July 30, 1980).

Relevant cases concerning religion in the public schools are *McCollum v. Board of Education*, 333 U.S. 203 (1948); *Zorach v. Clauson*, 343 U.S. 306 (1952); and *Board of Education of the Westside Community Schools v. Mergens*, 110 S. Ct. 2356 (1990). The pro-prayer lobby has had its greatest failure in cases involving schools or children, the area where it would probably most like to see change. See, for example, *Wallace v. Jaffree*, 105 S. Ct. 2479 (1985), which ruled the Alabama moment of silence statute unconstitutional, or *Edwards v. Aquillard*, 107 S. Ct. 2573 (1987), prohibiting the teaching of "creation science."

ISSUE 7

Is Abortion Protected by the Constitution?

YES: Sandra Day O'Connor, from Majority Opinion, *Planned Parenthood of Southeastern Pennsylvania et al. v. Robert P. Casey et al.,* U.S. Supreme Court (1992)

NO: William H. Rehnquist, from Dissenting Opinion, *Planned Parenthood of Southeastern Pennsylvania et al. v. Robert P. Casey et al.,* U.S. Supreme Court (1992)

ISSUE SUMMARY

YES: Supreme Court justice Sandra Day O'Connor upholds a woman's constitutional right to abortion under most circumstances and reaffirms the central holding of *Roe v. Wade.*
NO: Chief Justice William H. Rehnquist argues that Pennsylvania regulations on abortion should be upheld and that it is appropriate to overrule *Roe v. Wade.*

One of the strengths of the American judicial process, lawyers often claim, is that it encourages logical and objective solutions to problems and reduces the influence of emotion and whim. By proceeding slowly, by applying abstract legal rules, by relying on professional lawyers and restricting the layperson's role, it is asserted that impartiality and neutrality will be achieved and that explosive issues will be defused. The legal process works this kind of magic often, but it has clearly failed to do so with regard to the issue of abortion. Abortion remains as newsworthy and important a subject today as it was when the landmark case of *Roe v. Wade* was decided in 1973.

Perceptions of the abortion issue differ. For the courts, it is a constitutional issue, meaning that the focus is on whether or not laws restricting abortion deny a woman due process of law under the Fourteenth Amendment. Part of the reason courts have been unable to defuse the abortion issue is that they have not persuaded the public to see the subject only in these terms. How we define or categorize an issue frequently determines our conclusions about the subject.

For example, do we view abortion as an issue primarily affecting women, and thus see outlawing it as an example of sex discrimination? Or do we think firstly of the fetus, and thus conclude that abortion is murder?

Do we look at abortion from a religious perspective, thinking of how the legal codes of Western religions treat the subject? Or is it a question of privacy and of preventing the state from intruding into the affairs and personal decisions of citizens? Is it a matter of health, of preventing injuries and death to women who undergo illegal abortions? Is it an issue of discrimination against the poor, who may need the state to subsidize abortions, or even racial discrimination, because a higher proportion of poor women are black? How abortion is described can be all-important. One writer, for example, has written, "The real question is not, 'How can we justify abortion?' but, 'How can we justify compulsory childbearing?' " See Cisler, "Unfinished Business: Birth Control and Women's Liberation," in Morgan, ed., *Sisterhood is Powerful: An Anthology of Writings from the Women's Movement* (Random House, 1970).

The landmark decision of *Roe v. Wade*, 410 U.S. 113 (1973) was handed down on January 23, 1973. In the majority opinion, Justice Harry A. Blackmun wrote that states may not prohibit abortions during the first trimester, that some abortions may be regulated but not prohibited during the second trimester, and that abortions may be prohibited during the last trimester.

In the years since *Roe v. Wade* there have been many attempts to circumvent, narrow, delay, or avoid the Court's ruling. In *Harris v. McCrae*, 100 S. Ct. 2671 (1980), for example, in a 5–4 decision, the Supreme Court upheld a federal law that prohibited the federal government from reimbursing states for providing Medicaid abortions to women, except under specified circumstances. The majority held that the law did not illegally discriminate against the poor, nor did it violate the doctrines of separation of church and state merely because the restrictions coincided with Roman Catholic religious beliefs. In 1991, further limits on the use of federal funds were approved by the Court in *Rust v. Sullivan*, 111 S. Ct. 1759 (1991). In that case, regulations prohibiting abortion counseling in programs receiving federal funds for family planning were upheld.

More recently, in *Webster v. Reproductive Health Services*, 109 S. Ct. 3040 (1989), the Court refused to overturn *Roe v. Wade*, but it allowed states to impose more restrictions, such as one that required doctors, when a woman is more than 20 weeks pregnant, to perform tests "to determine if the unborn child is viable." The five-member majority included four votes to overturn *Roe*. Justice Sandra Day O'Connor, the critical fifth vote, was unwilling to overturn *Roe* but felt the Missouri law was constitutional since it did not place an "undue burden" on the woman's abortion rights.

The following readings are from the most recent and, in all likelihood, the most significant abortion decision since *Roe v. Wade*. The majority refused to overturn *Roe* but was also willing to allow some Pennsylvania restrictions involving parental notification and waiting periods. It also parted ways with the trimester model of *Roe*. The decision was neither a clear victory nor a clear defeat for either the pro-choice or pro-life movements. And as you read, you should ask whether or not the Court has finally articulated a position that will be an acceptable middle ground.

YES

Sandra Day O'Connor

MAJORITY OPINION

PLANNED PARENTHOOD v. CASEY

JUSTICE O'CONNOR, JUSTICE KENNEDY, and JUSTICE SOUTER announced the judgment of the Court.

I

Liberty finds no refuge in a jurisprudence of doubt. Yet 19 years after our holding that the Constitution protects a woman's right to terminate her pregnancy in its early stages, *Roe v. Wade*, 410 U.S. 113 (1973), that definition of liberty is still questioned. Joining the respondents as *amicus curiae*, the United States, as it has done in five other cases in the last decade, again asks us to overrule *Roe*.

At issue in these cases are five provisions of the Pennsylvania Abortion Control Act of 1982 as amended in 1988 and 1989. 18 Pa. Cons. Stat. Sec. 3203–3220 (1990). The Act requires that a woman seeking an abortion give her informed consent prior to the abortion procedure, and specifies that she be provided with certain information at least 24 hours before the abortion is performed. For a minor to obtain an abortion, the Act requires the informed consent of one of her parents, but provides for a judicial bypass option if the minor does not wish to or cannot obtain a parent's consent. Another provision of the Act requires that, unless certain exceptions apply, a married woman seeking an abortion must sign a statement indicating that she has notified her husband of her intended abortion. The Act exempts compliance with these three requirements in the event of a "medical emergency," which is defined in Sec. 3203 of the Act. In addition to the above provisions regulating the performance of abortions, the Act imposes certain reporting requirements on facilities that provide abortion services.

Before any of these provisions took effect, the petitioners, who are five abortion clinics and one physician representing himself as well as a class of physicians who provide abortion services, brought this suit seeking declar-

From *Planned Parenthood of Southeastern Pennsylvania et al. v. Robert P. Casey et al.*, 60 L.W. 4795 (1992). Some case citations omitted.

atory and injunctive relief. Each provision was challenged as unconstitutional on its face. The District Court entered a preliminary injunction against the enforcement of the regulations, and, after a 3-day bench trial, held all the provisions at issue here unconstitutional, entering a permanent injunction against Pennsylvania's enforcement of them. 744 F. Supp 1323 (ED Pa. 1990). The Court of Appeals for the Third Circuit affirmed in part and reversed in part, upholding all of the regulations except for the husband notification requirement. 947 F.2d 682 (1991). We granted certiorari.

. . . [A]t oral argument in this Court, the attorney for the parties challenging the statute took the position that none of the enactments can be upheld without overruling *Roe v. Wade*. We disagree with that analysis; but we acknowledge that our decisions after *Roe* cast doubt upon the meaning and reach of its holding. Further, the Chief Justice admits that he would overrule the central holding of *Roe* and adopt the rational relationship test as the sole criterion of constitutionality. State and federal courts as well as legislatures throughout the Union must have guidance as they seek to address this subject in conformance with the Constitution. Given these premises, we find it imperative to review once more the principles that define the rights of the woman and the legitimate authority of the State respecting the termination of pregnancies by abortion procedures.

After considering the fundamental constitutional questions resolved by *Roe*, principles of institutional integrity, and the rule of *stare decisis*, we are led to conclude this: the essential holding of *Roe v. Wade* should be retained and once again reaffirmed.

It must be stated at the outset and with clarity that *Roe*'s essential holding, the holding we reaffirm, has three parts. First is a recognition of the right of the woman to choose to have an abortion before viability and to obtain it without undue interference from the State. Before viability, the State's interests are not strong enough to support a prohibition of abortion or the imposition of a substantial obstacle to the woman's effective right to elect the procedure. Second is a confirmation of the State's power to restrict abortions after fetal viability, if the law contains exceptions for pregnancies which endanger a woman's life or health. And third is the principle that the State has legitimate interests from the outset of the pregnancy in protecting the health of the woman and the life of the fetus that may become a child. These principles do not contradict one another; and we adhere to each.

II

. . . Men and women of good conscience can disagree, and we suppose some always shall disagree, about the profound moral and spiritual implications of terminating a pregnancy, even in its earliest stage. Some of us as individuals find abortion offensive to our most basic principles of morality, but that cannot control our decision. Our obligation is to define the liberty of all, not to mandate our own moral code. The underlying constitutional issue is whether the State can resolve these philosophic questions in such a definitive way that a woman lacks all choice in the matter, except perhaps in those rare circumstances in which the pregnancy is itself a danger to her own life or health, or is the result of rape or incest. . . .

Our law affords constitutional protection to personal decisions relating to marriage, procreation, contraception, family relationships, child rearing, and education. *Carey v. Population Services International,* 431 U.S., at 685. Our cases recognize "the right of the *individual,* married or single, to be free from unwarranted governmental intrusion into matters so fundamentally affecting a person as the decision whether to bear or beget a child." *Eisenstadt v. Baird, supra,* at 453. Our precedents "have respected the private realm of family life which the state cannot enter." *Prince v. Massachusetts,* 321 U.S. 158, 166 (1944). These matters, involving the most intimate and personal choices a person may make in a lifetime, choices central to personal dignity and autonomy, are central to the liberty protected by the Fourteenth Amendment. At the heart of liberty is the right to define one's own concept of existence, of meaning, of the universe, and of the mystery of human life. Beliefs about these matters could not define the attributes of personhood were they formed under compulsion of the State.

These considerations begin our analysis of the woman's interest in terminating her pregnancy but cannot end it, for this reason: though the abortion decision may originate within the zone of conscience and belief, it is more than a philosophic exercise. Abortion is a unique act. It is an act fraught with consequences for others: for the woman who must live with the implications of her decision; for the persons who perform and assist in the procedure; for the spouse, family, and society which must confront the knowledge that these procedures exist, procedures some deem nothing short of an act of violence against innocent human life; and, depending on one's be-

liefs, for the life or potential life that is aborted. Though abortion is conduct, it does not follow that the State is entitled to proscribe it in all instances. That is because the liberty of the woman is at stake in a sense unique to the human condition and so unique to the law. The mother who carries a child to full term is subject to anxieties, to physical constraints, to pain that only she must bear. That these sacrifices have from the beginning of the human race been endured by woman with a pride that ennobles her in the eyes of others and gives to the infant a bond of love cannot alone be grounds for the State to insist she make the sacrifice. Her suffering is too intimate and personal for the State to insist, without more, upon its own vision of the woman's role, however dominant that vision has been in the course of our history and our culture. The destiny of the woman must be shaped to a large extent on her own conception of her spiritual imperatives and her place in society.

It should be recognized, moreover, that in some critical respects the abortion decision is of the same character as the decision to use contraception, to which *Griswold v. Connecticut, Eisenstadt v. Baird,* and *Carey v. Population Services International,* afford constitutional protection. We have no doubt as to the correctness of those decisions. They support the reasoning in *Roe* relating to the woman's liberty because they involve personal decisions concerning not only the meaning of procreation but also human responsibility and respect for it. As with abortion, reasonable people will have differences of opinion about these matters. One view is based on such reverence for the wonder of creation that any pregnancy ought to be welcomed and carried to full term no matter how difficult it will be to provide for the child and ensure its well-being. Another is that the inability to provide for the nurture and care of the infant is a cruelty to the child and an anguish to the parent. These are intimate views with infinite variations, and their deep, personal character underlay our decisions in *Griswold, Eisenstadt,* and *Carey.* The same concerns are present when the woman confronts the reality that, perhaps despite her attempts to avoid it, she has become pregnant.

It was this dimension of personal liberty that *Roe* sought to protect, and its holding invoked the reasoning and the tradition of the precedents we have discussed, granting protection to substantive liberties of the person. *Roe* was, of course, an extension of those cases and, as the decision itself indicated, the separate States could act in some degree to further their own legitimate interests in protecting prenatal life. The extent to which the legislatures of the States might act to outweigh the interests of the woman in choosing to terminate her pregnancy was a subject of debate both in *Roe* itself and in decisions following it.

While we appreciate the weight of the arguments made on behalf of the State in the case before us, arguments which in their ultimate formulation conclude that *Roe* should be overruled, the reservations any of us may have in reaffirming the central holding of *Roe* are outweighed by the explication of individual liberty we have given combined with the force of *stare decisis.* We turn now to that doctrine.

III
A

... [W]hen this Court reexamines a prior holding, its judgment is custom-arily informed by a series of prudential and pragmatic considerations designed to test the consistency of overruling a prior decision with the ideal of the rule of law, and to gauge the respective costs of reaffirming and overruling a prior case. Thus, for example, we may ask whether the rule has proved to be intolerable simply in defying practical workability; whether the rule is subject to a kind of reliance that would lend a special hardship to the consequences of overruling and add inequity to the cost of repudiation; whether related principles of law have so far developed as to have left the old rule no more than a remnant of abandoned doctrine; or whether facts have so changed or come to be seen so differently, as to have robbed the old rule of significant application or justification.

So in this case we may inquire whether *Roe*'s central rule has been found unworkable; whether the rule's limitation on state power could be removed without serious inequity to those who have relied upon it or significant damage to the stability of the society governed by the rule in question; whether the law's growth in the intervening years has left *Roe*'s central rule a doctrinal anachronism discounted by society; and whether *Roe*'s premises of fact have so far changed in the ensuing two decades as to render its central holding somehow irrelevant or unjustifiable in dealing with the issue it addressed.

1

Although *Roe* has engendered opposition, it has in no sense proven "unworkable," see *Garcia v. San Antonio Metropolitan Transit Authority,* 469 U.S. 528, 546 (1985), representing as it does a simple limitation beyond which a state law is unenforceable. While *Roe* has, of course, required judicial assessment of state laws affecting the exercise of the choice guaranteed against government infringement, and although the need for such review will remain as a consequence of today's decision, the required determinations fall within judicial competence.

2

. . . [F]or two decades of economic and social developments, people have organized intimate relationships and made choices that define their views of themselves and their places in society, in reliance on the availability of abortion in the event that contraception should fail. The ability of women to participate equally in the economic and social life of the Nation has been facilitated by their ability to control their reproductive lives. See, e.g., R. Petchesky, Abortion and Woman's Choice 109, 133, n. 7 (rev. ed. 1990). The Constitution serves human values, and while the effect of reliance on *Roe* cannot be exactly measured, neither can the certain cost of overruling *Roe* for people who have ordered their thinking and living around that case be dismissed.

3

No evolution of legal principle has left *Roe's* doctrinal footings weaker than they were in 1973. No development of constitutional law since the case was decided has implicitly or explicitly left *Roe* behind as a mere survivor of obsolete constitutional thinking.

It will be recognized, of course, that *Roe* stands at an intersection of two lines of decisions, but in whichever doctrinal category one reads the case, the result for present purposes will be the same. The

Roe Court itself placed its holding in the succession of cases most prominently exemplified by *Griswold v. Connecticut*, 381 U.S. 479 (1965), see *Roe*, 410 U.S., at 152–153. When it is so seen, *Roe* is clearly in no jeopardy, since subsequent constitutional developments have neither disturbed, nor do they threaten to diminish, the scope of recognized protection accorded to the liberty relating to intimate relationships, the family, and decisions about whether or not to beget or bear a child. See, e.g., *Carey v. Population Services International*, 431 U.S. 678 (1977); *Moore v. East Cleveland*, 431 U.S. 678 (1977).

Roe, however, may be seen not only as an exemplar of *Griswold* liberty but as a rule (whether or not mistaken) of personal autonomy and bodily integrity, with doctrinal affinity to cases recognizing limits on governmental power to mandate medical treatment or to bar its rejection. If so, our cases since *Roe* accord with *Roe's* view that a State's interest in the protection of life falls short of justifying any plenary override of individual liberty claims. . . .

4

We have seen how time has overtaken some of *Roe's* factual assumptions: advances in maternal health care allow for abortions safe to the mother later in pregnancy than was true in 1973, and advances in neonatal care have advanced viability to a point somewhat earlier. But these facts go only to the scheme of time limits on the realization of competing interests, and the divergences from the factual premises of 1973 have no bearing on the validity of *Roe's* central holding, that viability marks the earliest point at which the State's interest in fetal life is constitutionally adequate to justify a legislative ban on nontherapeutic abortions. The soundness or unsoundness of that constitutional judgment in no sense turns on whether viability occurs at approximately 28 weeks, as was usual at the time of *Roe*, at 23 to 24 weeks, as it sometimes does today, or at some moment even slightly earlier in pregnancy, as it may if fetal respiratory capacity can somehow be enhanced in the future. Whenever it may occur, the attainment of viability may continue to serve as the critical fact, just as it has done since *Roe* was decided; which is to say that no change in *Roe*'s factual underpinning has left its central holding obsolete, and none supports an argument for overruling it.

5

The sum of the precedential inquiry to this point shows *Roe*'s underpinnings unweakened in any way affecting its central holding. While it has engendered disapproval, it has not been unworkable. An entire generation has come of age free to assume *Roe*'s concept of liberty in defining the capacity of women to act in society, and to make reproductive decisions; no erosion of principle going to liberty or personal autonomy has left *Roe*'s central holding a doctrinal remnant; *Roe* portends no developments at odds with other precedent for the analysis of personal liberty; and no changes of fact have rendered viability more or less appropriate as the point at which the balance of interests tips. Within the bounds of normal *stare decisis* analysis, then, and subject to the considerations on which it customarily turns, the stronger argument is for affirming *Roe*'s central holding, with whatever degree of personal

reluctance any of us may have, not for overruling it. . . .

Our analysis would not be complete. . . without explaining why overruling *Roe*'s central holding would not only reach an unjustifiable result under principles of *stare decisis*, but would seriously weaken the Court's capacity to exercise the judicial power and to function as the Supreme Court of a Nation dedicated to the rule of law. To understand why this would be so it is necessary to understand the source of this Court's authority, the conditions necessary for its preservation, and its relationship to the country's understanding of itself as a constitutional Republic.

The root of American governmental power is revealed most clearly in the instance of the power conferred by the Constitution upon the Judiciary of the United States and specifically upon this Court. As Americans of each succeeding generation are rightly told, the Court cannot buy support for its decisions by spending money and, except to a minor degree, it cannot independently coerce obedience to its decrees. The Court's power lies, rather, in its legitimacy, a product of substance and perception that shows itself in the people's acceptance of the Judiciary as fit to determine what the Nation's law means and to declare what it demands.

The underlying substance of this legitimacy is of course the warrant for the Court's decisions in the Constitution and the lesser sources of legal principle on which the Court draws. That substance is expressed in the Court's opinions, and our contemporary understanding is such that a decision without principled justification would be no judicial act at all. But even when justification is furnished by apposite legal principle, something more is required. Because not every conscientious claim of principled justification will be accepted as such, the justification claimed must be beyond dispute. The Court must take care to speak and act in ways that allow people to accept its decisions on the terms the Court claims for them, as grounded truly in principle, not as compromises with social and political pressures having, as such, no bearing on the principled choices that the Court is obliged to make. Thus, the Court's legitimacy depends on making legally principled decisions under circumstances in which their principled character is sufficiently plausible to be accepted by the Nation.

The need for principled action to be perceived as such is implicated to some degree whenever this, or any other appellate court, overrules a prior case. This is not to say, of course, that this Court cannot give a perfectly satisfactory explanation in most cases. People understand that some of the Constitution's language is hard to fathom and that the Court's Justices are sometimes able to perceive significant facts or to understand principles of law that eluded their predecessors and that justify departures from existing decisions. However upsetting it may be to those most directly affected when one judicially derived rule replaces another, the country can accept some correction of error without necessarily questioning the legitimacy of the Court.

In two circumstances, however, the Court would almost certainly fail to receive the benefit of the doubt in overruling prior cases. There is, first, a point beyond which frequent overruling would overtax the country's belief in the Court's good faith. Despite the variety of reasons that may inform and justify a decision to overrule, we cannot forget that such a

decision is usually perceived (and perceived correctly) as, at the least, a statement that a prior decision was wrong. There is a limit to the amount of error that can plausibly be imputed to prior courts. If that limit should be exceeded, disturbance of prior rulings would be taken as evidence that justifiable reexamination of principle had given way to drives for particular results in the short term. The legitimacy of the Court would fade with the frequency of its vacillation.

That first circumstance can be described as hypothetical; the second is to the point here and now. Where, in the performance of its judicial duties, the Court decides a case in such a way as to resolve the sort of intensely divisive controversy reflected in *Roe* and those rare, comparable cases, its decision has a dimension that the resolution of the normal case does not carry. It is the dimension present whenever the Court's interpretation of the Constitution calls the contending sides of a national controversy to end their national division by accepting a common mandate rooted in the Constitution.

The Court is not asked to do this very often, having thus addressed the Nation only twice in our lifetime, in the decisions of *Brown* and *Roe*. But when the Court does act in this way, its decision requires an equally rare precedential force to counter the inevitable efforts to overturn it and to thwart its implementation. Some of those efforts may be mere unprincipled emotional reactions; others may proceed from principles worthy of profound respect. But whatever the premises of opposition may be, only the most convincing justification under accepted standards of precedent could suffice to demonstrate that a later decision overruling the first was anything but a surrender to political pressure, and an unjustified repudiation of the principle on which the Court staked its authority in the first instance. So to overrule under fire in the absence of the most compelling reason to reexamine a watershed decision would subvert the Court's legitimacy beyond any serious question. . . .

The Court's duty in the present case is clear. In 1973, it confronted the already-divisive issue of governmental power to limit personal choice to undergo abortion, for which it provided a new resolution based on the due process guaranteed by the Fourteenth Amendment. Whether or not a new social consensus is developing on that issue, its divisiveness is no less today than in 1973, and pressure to overrule the decision, like pressure to retain it, has grown only more intense. A decision to overrule *Roe*'s essential holding under the existing circumstances would address error, if error there was, at the cost of both profound and unnecessary damage to the Court's legitimacy, and to the Nation's commitment to the rule of law. It is therefore imperative to adhere to the essence of Roe's original decision, and we do so today.

IV

From what we have said so far it follows that it is a constitutional liberty of the woman to have some freedom to terminate her pregnancy. We conclude that the basic decision in *Roe* was based on a constitutional analysis which we cannot now repudiate. The woman's liberty is not so unlimited, however, that from the outset the State cannot show its concern for the life of the unborn, and at a later point in fetal development the State's interest in life has sufficient force so that

the right of the woman to terminate the pregnancy can be restricted.

That brings us, of course, to the point where much criticism has been directed at *Roe*, a criticism that always inheres when the Court draws a specific rule from what in the Constitution is but a general standard. We conclude, however, that the urgent claims of the woman to retain the ultimate control over her destiny and her body, claims implicit in the meaning of liberty, require us to perform that function. Liberty must not be extinguished for want of a line that is clear. And it falls to us to give some real substance to the woman's liberty to determine whether to carry her pregnancy to full term.

We conclude the line should be drawn at viability, so that before that time the woman has a right to choose to terminate her pregnancy. We adhere to this principle for two reasons. First, as we have said, is the doctrine of *stare decisis*. Any judicial act of line-drawing may seem somewhat arbitrary, but *Roe* was a reasoned statement, elaborated with great care. We have twice reaffirmed it in the face of great opposition. See *Thornburgh v. American College of Obstetricians & Gynecologists*, 476 U.S., at 759; *Akron I*, 462 U.S., at 419–420. Although we must overrule those parts of *Thornburgh* and *Akron I* which, in our view, are inconsistent with *Roe*'s statement that the State has a legitimate interest in promoting the life or potential life of the unborn, the central premise of those cases represents an unbroken commitment by this Court to the essential holding of *Roe*. It is that premise which we reaffirm today.

The second reason is that the concept of viability, as we noted in *Roe*, is the time at which there is a realistic possibility of maintaining and nourishing a life outside the womb, so that the independent existence of the second life can in reason and all fairness be the object of state protection that now overrides the rights of the woman. See *Roe v. Wade*, 410 U.S., at 163. Consistent with other constitutional norms, legislatures may draw lines which appear arbitrary without the necessity of offering a justification. But courts may not. We must justify the lines we draw. And there is no line other than viability which is more workable. To be sure, as we have said, there may be some medical developments that affect the precise point of viability, but this is an imprecision within tolerable limits given that the medical community and all those who must apply its discoveries will continue to explore the matter. The viability line also has, as a practical matter, an element of fairness. In some broad sense it might be said that a woman who fails to act before viability has consented to the State's intervention on behalf of the developing child.

The woman's right to terminate her pregnancy before viability is the most central principle of *Roe v. Wade*. It is a rule of law and a component of liberty we cannot renounce.

On the other side of the equation is the interest of the State in the protection of potential life. The *Roe* Court recognized the State's "important and legitimate interest in protecting the potentiality of human life." *Roe, supra*, at 162. The weight to be given this state interest, not the strength of the woman's interest, was the difficult question faced in *Roe*. We do not need to say whether each of us, had we been Members of the Court when the valuation of the State interest came before it as an original matter, would have concluded, as the *Roe* Court did, that its weight is insufficient to justify a ban on abortions prior to viability even when it is subject to certain exceptions. The matter is not before us in the first instance, and coming as it does after nearly 20 years of litigation in *Roe's* wake we are satisfied that the immediate question is not the soundness of *Roe's* resolution of the issue, but the precedential force that must be accorded to its holding. And we have concluded that the essential holding of *Roe* should be reaffirmed.

Yet it must be remembered that *Roe v. Wade* speaks with clarity in establishing not only the woman's liberty but also the State's "important and legitimate interest in potential life." *Roe, supra*, at 163. That portion of the decision in *Roe* has been given too little acknowledgement and implementation by the Court in its subsequent cases. . . .

Roe established a trimester framework to govern abortion regulations. Under this elaborate but rigid construct, almost no regulation at all is permitted during the first trimester of pregnancy; regulations designed to protect the woman's health, but not to further the State's interest in potential life, are permitted during the second trimester; and during the third trimester, when the fetus is viable, prohibitions are permitted provided the life or health of the mother is not at stake. *Roe v. Wade, supra*, at 163–166. Most of our cases since *Roe* have involved the application of rules derived from the trimester framework.

The trimester framework no doubt was erected to ensure that the woman's right to choose not become so subordinate to the State's interest in promoting fetal life that her choice exists in theory but not in fact. We do not agree, however, that the trimester approach is necessary to accomplish this objective. A framework of this rigidity was unnecessary and in its later interpretation sometimes contradicted the State's permissible exercise of its powers.

Though the woman has a right to choose to terminate or continue her pregnancy before viability, it does not at all follow that the State is prohibited from taking steps to ensure that this choice is thoughtful and informed. Even in the earliest stages of pregnancy, the State may enact rules and regulations designed to encourage her to know that there are philosophic and social arguments of great weight that can be brought to bear in favor of continuing the pregnancy to full term and that there are procedures and institutions to allow adoption of unwanted children as well as a certain degree of state assistance if the mother chooses to raise the child herself. " '[T]he Constitution does not forbid a State or city, pursuant to democratic processes, from expressing a preference for normal childbirth.' " *Webster v. Reproductive Health Services*, 492 U.S., at 511 (opinion of the Court) (quoting *Poelker v. Doe*, 432 U.S. 519, 521 (1977)). It follows that States are free to enact laws to provide a reasonable framework for a woman to make a decision that has such profound and lasting meaning. This, too, we find consistent with *Roe's* central premises, and indeed the inevitable consequence of our holding that the State has an interest in protecting the life of the unborn.

We reject the trimester framework, which we do not consider to be part of the essential holding of *Roe*. Measures aimed at ensuring that a woman's choice contemplates the consequences for the fetus do not necessarily interfere with the right recognized in *Roe*, although those measures have been found to be inconsistent with the rigid trimester framework announced in that case. A logical reading of the central holding in *Roe* itself, and a necessary reconciliation of the liberty of the woman and the interest of the State in promoting prenatal life, require, in our view, that we abandon the trimester framework as a rigid prohibition on all previability regulation aimed at the protection of fetal life. The trimester framework suffers from these basic flaws: in its formulation it misconceives the nature of the pregnant woman's interest; and in practice it undervalues the State's interest in potential life, as recognized in *Roe*.

As our jurisprudence relating to all liberties save perhaps abortion has recognized, not every law which makes a right more difficult to exercise is, *ipso facto*, an infringement of that right. An example clarifies the point. We have held that not every ballot access limitation amounts to an infringement of the right to vote. Rather, the States are granted substantial flexibility in establishing the framework within which voters choose the candidates for whom they wish to vote. *Anderson v. Celebrezze*, 460 U.S. 780, 788 (1983); *Norman v. Reed*, 502 U.S. _____ (1992).

The abortion right is similar. Numerous forms of state regulation might have the incidental effect of increasing the cost or decreasing the availability of medical care, whether for abortion or any other medical procedure. The fact that a law which serves a valid purpose, one not designed to strike at the right itself, has the incidental effect of making it more difficult or more expensive to procure an abortion cannot be enough to invalidate it. Only where state regulation imposes an undue burden on a woman's ability to make this decision does the power of the State reach into the heart of the liberty protected by the Due Process Clause. . . .

A finding of an undue burden is a shorthand for the conclusion that a state regulation has the purpose or effect of placing a substantial obstacle in the path of a woman seeking an abortion of a nonviable fetus. A statute with this purpose is invalid because the means chosen by the State to further the interest in potential life must be calculated to inform the woman's free choice, not hinder it. And a statute which, while furthering the interest in potential life or some other valid state interest, has the effect of placing a substantial obstacle in the path of a woman's choice cannot be considered a permissible means of serving its legitimate ends. To the extent that the opinions of the Court or of individual Justices use the undue burden standard in a manner that is inconsistent with this analysis, we set out what in our view should be the controlling standard. . . . Understood another way, we answer the question, left open in previous opinions discussing the undue burden formulation, whether a law designed to further the State's interest in fetal life which imposes an undue burden on the woman's decision before fetal viability could be constitutional. The answer is no.

Some guiding principles should emerge. What is at stake is the woman's right to make the ultimate decision, not a right to be insulated from all others in doing so. Regulations which do no more than create a structural mechanism by which the State, or the parent or guardian of a minor, may express profound respect for the life of the unborn are permitted, if they are not a substantial obstacle to the woman's exercise of the right to choose. Unless it has that effect on her right of choice, a state measure designed to persuade her to choose childbirth over abortion will be upheld if reasonably related to that goal. Regulations designed to foster the health of a woman seeking an abortion are valid if they do not constitute an undue burden.

Even when jurists reason from shared premises, some disagreement is inevitable. That is to be expected in the application of any legal standard which must accommodate life's complexity. We do not expect it to be otherwise with respect to the undue burden standard. We give this summary:

(a) To protect the central right recognized by *Roe v. Wade* while at the same time accommodating the State's profound interest in potential life, we will employ the undue burden analysis as explained in this opinion. An undue burden exists, and therefore a provision of law is invalid, if its purpose or effect is to place a substantial obstacle in the path of a woman seeking an abortion before the fetus attains viability.

(b) We reject the rigid trimester framework of *Roe v. Wade*. To promote the State's profound interest in potential life, throughout pregnancy the State may take measures to ensure that the woman's choice is informed, and measures designed to advance this interest will not be invalidated as long as their purpose is to persuade the woman to choose childbirth over abortion. These measures must not be an undue burden on the right.

(c) As with any medical procedure, the State may enact regulations to further the health or safety of a woman seeking an abortion. Unnecessary health regulations that have the purpose or effect of presenting a substantial obstacle to a woman seeking an abortion impose an undue burden on the right.

(d) Our adoption of the undue burden analysis does not disturb the central holding of *Roe v. Wade*, and we reaffirm that holding. Regardless of whether exceptions are made for particular circumstances, a State may not prohibit any woman from making the ultimate decision to terminate her pregnancy before viability.

(e) We also reaffirm *Roe's* holding that "subsequent to viability, the State in promoting its interest in the potentiality of human life may, if it chooses, regulate, and even proscribe, abortion except where it is necessary, in appropriate medical judgment, for the preservation of the life or health of the mother." *Roe v. Wade*, 410 U.S., at 164–165.

NO

William H. Rehnquist

DISSENTING OPINION OF WILLIAM H. REHNQUIST

CHIEF JUSTICE REHNQUIST, with whom JUSTICE WHITE, JUSTICE SCALIA, and JUSTICE THOMAS join, concurring in the judgment in part and dissenting in part.

. . . We believe that *Roe* was wrongly decided, and that it can and should be overruled consistently with our traditional approach to *stare decisis* in constitutional cases. We would adopt the approach of the plurality in *Webster v. Reproductive Health Services*, 492 U.S. 490 (1989), and uphold the challenged provisions of the Pennsylvania statute in their entirety.

I

. . . In *Roe v. Wade*, the Court recognized a "guarantee of personal privacy" which "is broad enough to encompass a woman's decision whether or not to terminate her pregnancy." 410 U.S., at 152–153. We are now of the view that, in terming this right fundamental, the Court in *Roe* read the earlier opinions upon which it based its decision much too broadly. Unlike marriage, procreation and contraception, abortion "involves the purposeful termination of potential life." *Harris v. McRae*, 448 U.S. 297, 325 (1980). The abortion decision must therefore "be recognized as *sui generis*, different in kind from the others that the Court has protected under the rubric of personal or family privacy and autonomy." *Thornburgh v. American College of Obstetricians and Gynecologists, supra*, at 792 (White, J., dissenting). One cannot ignore the fact that a woman is not isolated in her pregnancy, and that the decision to abort necessarily involves the destruction of a fetus. *See Michael H. v. Gerald D., supra*, at 124, n. 4 (To look "at the act which is assertedly the subject of a liberty interest in isolation from its effect upon other people [is] like inquiring whether there is a liberty interest in firing a gun where the case at hand happens to involve its discharge into another person's body").

Nor do the historical traditions of the American people support the view that the right to terminate one's pregnancy is "fundamental." The common law which we inherited from England made abortion after "quickening" an

From *Planned Parenthood of Southeastern Pennsylvania et al. v. Robert P. Casey et al.*, 60 L.W. 4826 (1992). Notes and some case citations omitted.

offense. At the time of the adoption of the Fourteenth Amendment, statutory prohibitions or restrictions on abortion were commonplace; in 1868, at least 28 of the then-37 States and 8 Territories had statutes banning or limiting abortion. J. Mohr, Abortion in America 200 (1978). By the turn of the century virtually every State had a law prohibiting or restricting abortion on its books. By the middle of the present century, a liberalization trend had set in. But 21 of the restrictive abortion laws in effect in 1868 were still in effect in 1973 when *Roe* was decided, and an overwhelming majority of the States prohibited abortion unless necessary to preserve the life or health of the mother. *Roe v. Wade*, 410 U.S., at 139–140; *id.*, at 176–177, n. 2 (Rehnquist, J., dissenting). On this record, it can scarcely be said that any deeply rooted tradition of relatively unrestricted abortion in our history supported the classification of the right to abortion as "fundamental" under the Due Process Clause of the Fourteenth Amendment.

We think, therefore, both in view of this history and of our decided cases dealing with substantive liberty under the Due Process Clause, that the Court was mistaken in *Roe* when it classified a woman's decision to terminate her pregnancy as a "fundamental right" that could be abridged only in a manner which withstood "strict scrutiny." In so concluding, we repeat the observation made in *Bowers v. Hardwick*, 478 U.S. 186 (1986):

"Nor are we inclined to take a more expansive view of our authority to discover new fundamental rights imbedded in the Due Process Clause. The Court is most vulnerable and comes nearest to illegitimacy when it deals with judge-made constitutional law having little or no cognizable roots in

the language or design of the Constitution." *Id.*, at 194.

We believe that the sort of constitutionally imposed abortion code of the type illustrated by our decisions following Roe is inconsistent "with the notion of a Constitution cast in general terms, as ours is, and usually speaking in general principles, as ours does." *Webster v. Reproductive Health Services*, 492 U.S., at 518 (plurality opinion). The Court in *Roe* reached too far when it analogized the right to abort a fetus to the rights involved in *Pierce, Meyer, Loving,* and *Griswold*, and thereby deemed the right to abortion fundamental.

II

The joint opinion of Justices O'Connor, Kennedy, and Souter cannot bring itself to say that *Roe* was correct as an original matter, but the authors are of the view that "the immediate question is not the soundness of *Roe's* resolution of the issue, but the precedential force that must be accorded to its holding." Instead of claiming that *Roe* was correct as a matter of original constitutional interpretation, the opinion therefore contains an elaborate discussion of *stare decisis*. This discussion of the principle of *stare decisis* appears to be almost entirely dicta, because the joint opinion does not apply that principle in dealing with *Roe*. *Roe* decided that a woman had a fundamental right to an abortion. The joint opinion rejects that view. *Roe* decided that abortion regulations were to be subjected to "strict scrutiny" and could be justified only in the light of "compelling state interests." The joint opinion rejects that view. *Roe* analyzed abortion regulation under a rigid trimester framework, a framework which has guided this Court's decisionmaking for 19 years. The joint opinion rejects that framework. . . .

In our view, authentic principles of *stare decisis* do not require that any portion of the reasoning in *Roe* be kept intact. "*Stare decisis* is not . . . a universal, inexorable command," especially in cases involving the interpretation of the Federal Constitution. *Burnet v. Coronado Oil & Gas Co.*, 285 U.S. 393, 405 (1932) (Brandeis, J., dissenting). Erroneous decisions in such constitutional cases are uniquely durable, because correction through legislative action, save for constitutional amendment, is impossible. It is therefore our duty to reconsider constitutional interpretations that "depar[t] from a proper understanding" of the Constitution. . . . Our constitutional watch does not cease merely because we have spoken before on an issue; when it becomes clear that a prior constitutional interpretation is unsound we are obliged to reexamine the question.

The joint opinion discusses several *stare decisis* factors which, it asserts, point toward retaining a portion of *Roe*. Two of these factors are that the main "factual underpinning" of *Roe* has remained the same, and that its doctrinal foundation is no weaker now than it was in 1973. Of course, what might be called the basic facts which gave rise to *Roe* have remained the same—women become pregnant, there is a point somewhere, depending on medical technology, where a fetus becomes viable, and women give birth to children. But this is only to say that the same facts which gave rise to *Roe* will continue to give rise to similar cases. It is not a reason, in and of itself, why those cases must be decided in the same incorrect manner as was the first case to deal with the question. And surely there is no requirement, in considering whether to depart from *stare decisis* in a constitutional case, that a decision be more wrong now than it was at the time it was rendered. If that were true, the most outlandish constitutional decision could survive forever, based simply on the fact that it was no more outlandish later than it was when originally rendered.

Nor does the joint opinion faithfully follow this alleged requirement. The opinion frankly concludes that *Roe* and its progeny were wrong in failing to recognize that the State's interests in maternal health and in the protection of unborn human life exist throughout pregnancy. But there is no indication that these components of *Roe* are any more incorrect at this juncture than they were at its inception. . . .

The joint opinion thus turns to what can only be described as an unconventional—and unconvincing—notion of reliance, a view based on the surmise that the availability of abortion since *Roe* has led to "two decades of economic and social developments" that would be undercut if the error of *Roe* were recognized. The joint opinion's assertion of this fact is undeveloped and totally conclusory. In fact, one can not be sure to what economic and social developments the opinion is referring. Surely it is dubious to suggest that women have reached their "places in society" in reliance upon *Roe*, rather than as a result of their determination to obtain higher education and compete with men in the job market, and of society's increasing recognition of their ability to fill positions that were previously thought to be reserved only for men.

In the end, having failed to put forth any evidence to prove any true reliance, the joint opinion's argument is based solely on generalized assertions about the national psyche, on a belief that the people of this country have grown accustomed to the *Roe* decision over the last 19 years and have "ordered their thinking and living around" it. As an initial matter, one might inquire how the joint opinion can view the "central holding" of *Roe* as so deeply rooted in our constitutional culture, when it so casually uproots and disposes of that same decision's trimester framework. Furthermore, at various points in the past, the same could have been said about this Court's erroneous decisions that the Constitution allowed "separate but equal" treatment of minorities, see *Plessy v. Ferguson*, 163 U.S. 537 (1896), or that "liberty" under the Due Process Clause protected "freedom of contract." See *Adkins v. Children's Hospital of D. C.*, 261 U.S. 525 (1923); *Lochner v. New York*, 198 U.S. 45 (1905). The "separate but equal" doctrine lasted 58 years after *Plessy*, and *Lochner*'s protection of contractual freedom lasted 32 years. However, the simple fact that a generation or more had grown used to these major decisions did not prevent the Court from correcting its errors in those cases, nor should it prevent us from correctly interpreting the Constitution here.

Apparently realizing that conventional *stare decisis* principles do not support its position, the joint opinion advances a belief that retaining a portion of *Roe* is necessary to protect the "legitimacy" of this Court. Because the Court must take care to render decisions "grounded truly in principle," and not simply as political and social compromises, the joint opinion properly declares it to be this Court's duty to ignore the public criticism and protest that may arise as a result of a decision. Few would quarrel with this statement, although it may be doubted that Members of this Court, holding their

tenure as they do during constitutional "good behavior," are at all likely to be intimidated by such public protests. . . .

The joint opinion also agrees that the Court acted properly in rejecting the doctrine of "separate but equal" in *Brown*. In fact, the opinion lauds *Brown* in comparing it to *Roe*. This is strange, in that under the opinion's "legitimacy" principle the Court would seemingly have been forced to adhere to its erroneous decision in *Plessy* because of its "intensely divisive" character. To us, adherence to *Roe* today under the guise of "legitimacy" would seem to resemble more closely adherence to *Plessy* on the same ground. Fortunately, the Court did not choose that option in *Brown*, and instead frankly repudiated *Plessy*. The joint opinion concludes that such repudiation was justified only because of newly discovered evidence that segregation had the effect of treating one race as inferior to another. But it can hardly be argued that this was not urged upon those who decided *Plessy*, as Justice Harlan observed in his dissent that the law at issue "puts the brand of servitude and degradation upon a large class of our fellow-citizens, our equals before the law." *Plessy v. Ferguson*, 163 U.S., at 562 (Harlan, J., dissenting). It is clear that the same arguments made before the Court in *Brown* were made in *Plessy* as well. The Court in *Brown* simply recognized, as Justice Harlan had recognized beforehand, that the Fourteenth Amendment does not permit racial segregation. The rule of *Brown* is not tied to popular opinion about the evils of segregation; it is a judgment that the Equal Protection Clause does not permit racial segregation, no matter whether the public might come to believe that it is beneficial. On that ground it stands, and on that ground alone the Court was justified in properly concluding that the *Plessy* Court had erred. . . .

There are other reasons why the joint opinion's discussion of legitimacy is unconvincing as well. In assuming that the Court is perceived as "surrender[ing] to political pressure" when it overrules a controversial decision, the joint opinion forgets that there are two sides to any controversy. The joint opinion asserts that, in order to protect its legitimacy, the Court must refrain from overruling a controversial decision lest it be viewed as favoring those who oppose the decision. But a decision to *adhere* to prior precedent is subject to the same criticism, for in such a case one can easily argue that the Court is responding to those who have demonstrated in favor of the original decision. The decision in *Roe* has engendered large demonstrations, including repeated marches on this Court and on Congress, both in opposition to and in support of that opinion. A decision either way on *Roe* can therefore be perceived as favoring one group or the other. But this perceived dilemma arises only if one assumes, as the joint opinion does, that the Court should make its decisions with a view toward speculative public perceptions. If one assumes instead, as the Court surely did in both *Brown* and *West Coast Hotel,* that the Court's legitimacy is enhanced by faithful interpretation of the Constitution irrespective of public opposition, such self-engendered difficulties may be put to one side.

Roe is not this Court's only decision to generate conflict. Our decisions in some recent capital cases, and in *Bowers v. Hardwick,* 478 U.S. 186 (1986), have also engendered demonstrations in opposition. The joint opinion's message to such protesters appears to be that they must cease their activities in order to serve their cause, because their protests will only cement in place a decision which by normal standards of *stare decisis* should be reconsidered. Nearly a century ago, Justice David J. Brewer of this Court, in an article discussing criticism of its decisions, observed that "many criticisms may be, like their authors, devoid of good taste, but better all sorts of criticism than no criticism at all." Justice Brewer on "The Nation's Anchor," 57 Albany L.J. 166, 169 (1898). This was good advice to the Court then, as it is today. Strong and often misguided criticism of a decision should not render the decision immune from reconsideration, lest a fetish for legitimacy penalize freedom of expression.

The end result of the joint opinion's paeans of praise for legitimacy is the enunciation of a brand new standard for evaluating state regulation of a woman's right to abortion—the "undue burden" standard. As indicated above, *Roe v. Wade* adopted a "fundamental right" standard under which state regulations could survive only if they met the requirement of "strict scrutiny." While we disagree with that standard, it at least had a recognized basis in constitutional law at the time *Roe* was decided. The same cannot be said for the "undue burden" standard, which is created largely out of whole cloth by the authors of the joint opinion. It is a standard which even today does not command the support of a majority of this Court. And it will not, we believe, result in the sort of "simple limitation," easily applied, which the joint opinion anticipates. In sum, it is a standard which is not built to last. . . .

The sum of the joint opinion's labors in the name of *stare decisis* and "legitimacy" is this: *Roe v. Wade* stands as a sort of judicial Potemkin Village, which may be pointed out to passers by as a monument to the importance of adhering to precedent. But behind the facade, an entirely new method of analysis, without any roots in constitutional law, is imported to decide the constitutionality of state laws regulating abortion. Neither *stare decisis* nor "legitimacy" are truly served by such an effort. . . .

III . . .
E

Finally, petitioners challenge the medical emergency exception provided for by the Act. The existence of a medical emergency exempts compliance with the Act's informed consent, parental consent, and spousal notice requirements. See 18 Pa. Cons. Stat. sec. 3205(a), 3206(a), 3209(c) (1990). The Act defines a "medical emergency" as

"[t]hat condition which, on the basis of the physician's good faith clinical judgment, so complicates the medical condition of a pregnant woman as to necessitate the immediate abortion of her pregnancy to avert her death or for which a delay will create serious risk of substantial and irreversible impairment of major bodily function." sec. 3203.

Petitioners argued before the District Court that the statutory definition was inadequate because it did not cover three serious conditions that pregnant women can suffer—preeclampsia, inevitable abortion, and prematurely ruptured membrane. The District Court agreed with petitioners that the medical emergency exception was inadequate, but the Court of Appeals reversed this holding. In construing the medical emergency provision, the Court of Appeals first observed that all three conditions do indeed present the risk of serious injury or death when an abortion is not performed, and noted that the medical profession's uniformly prescribed treatment for each of the three conditions is an immediate abortion. See 947 F.2d, at 700–701. Finding that "[t]he Pennsylvania legislature did not choose the wording of its medical emergency exception in a vacuum," the court read the exception as intended "to assure that compliance with its abortion regulations would not in any way pose a significant threat to the life or health of a woman." *Id.*, at 701. It thus concluded that the exception encompassed each of the three dangerous conditions pointed to by petitioners.

We observe that Pennsylvania's present definition of medical emergency is almost an exact copy of that State's definition at the time of this Court's ruling in *Thornburgh*, one which the Court made reference to with apparent approval. 476 U.S., at 771 ("It is clear that the Pennsylvania Legislature knows how to provide a medical-emergency exception when it chooses to do so"). We find that the interpretation of the Court of Appeals in this case is eminently reasonable, and that the provision thus should be upheld. When a woman is faced with any condition that poses a "significant threat to [her] life or health," she is exempted from the Act's consent and notice requirements and may proceed immediately with her abortion.

IV

For the reasons stated, we therefore would hold that each of the challenged provisions of the Pennsylvania statute is consistent with the Constitution. It bears emphasis that our conclusion in this regard does not carry with it any necessary approval of these regulations. Our task is, as always, to decide only whether the challenged provisions of a law comport with the United States Constitution. If, as we believe, these do, their wisdom as a matter of public policy is for the people of Pennsylvania to decide.

POSTSCRIPT

Is Abortion Protected by the Constitution?

In spite of the majority's refusal to overturn *Roe*, the constitutional right to an abortion remains on shaky ground. This was a 5–4 decision and, as Justice Harry A. Blackmun wrote, "I am 83 years old. I cannot remain on this Court forever, and when I do step down, the confirmation process for my successor well may focus on the issue before us today." Whether *Roe v. Wade* is overturned is, therefore, only partly a matter of legal analysis. It is also a matter of politics, of personality, of values, and of judicial philosophy.

What would be the consequences of a decision overturning *Roe*? The current state of great controversy over abortion would certainly not decline. Quite the contrary. The reason for this is that reversing *Roe* would mean that each state could permit or restrict abortion as it wished. The main contention of the justices who wish to overturn *Roe* is not necessarily that abortion should be banned, but that this decision should be left to the states, and that it is not a constitutional issue. Such a position means that the political process will have to deal with the issue more than it does now, which is not likely to defuse the issue.

Even without overturning *Roe*, conflict will continue. Courts will be faced with determining whether or not state regulations constitute an "undue burden." Congress will wrestle with federal legislation that would restrict state regulations, such as the Freedom of Choice Act. New technologies, such as RU-486, the so-called abortion pill, which is approved for use in Europe but not in the United States, will raise legal challenges as will groups, such as Operation Rescue, that employ methods that are at the boundary of permissible protests.

Recent writings about abortion include Tribe, *Abortion: The Clash of Absolutes* (W. W. Norton, 1990); Note, "Judicial Restraint and the Non-Decision in *Webster v. Reproductive Health Services*," 13 *Harvard Journal of Law and Public Policy* 263 (1990); Novick, "Justice Holmes and *Roe v. Wade*," 25 *Trial* 58 (December 1989); and Symposium on Abortion, *University of Pennsylvania Law Review* (vol. 138, 1989). The story of the *Roe* case is recounted in Faux, *Roe v. Wade: The Untold Story of the Landmark Supreme Court Decision That Made Abortion Legal* (NAL, 1988).

ISSUE 8

Should Pornography Be Protected by the First Amendment?

YES: Sarah Evans Barker, from *American Booksellers Association, Inc. v. William H. Hudnut III*, U.S. Court of Appeals for the Seventh Circuit (1984)

NO: Andrea Dworkin, from *Amicus Curiae, American Booksellers Association, Inc. v. William H. Hudnut III*, U.S. Court of Appeals for the Seventh Circuit (1984)

ISSUE SUMMARY

YES: Judge Sarah Evans Barker argues that the ordinances banning pornography as a violation of the civil rights of women are unconstitutional infringements on freedom of speech.

NO: Author Andrea Dworkin maintains that pornography should not be constitutionally protected because it is destructive, abusive, and detrimental to women, and it violates their civil rights.

In April 1984, the city of Indianapolis, urged on by an unusual alliance between feminists and the conservative right, passed an ordinance banning the distribution of pornography within the city limits. Several groups in Indianapolis went to court, arguing that the new law interfered with their rights of free speech and free press as guaranteed by the First Amendment. In November 1984, Judge Sarah Evans Barker of the Federal District Court ruled that the law was indeed a violation of the Constitution. Her decision was affirmed by the Court of Appeals, 771 F.2d 323 (1984), and sustained by the Supreme Court, 106 S. Ct. 1172 (1986). The following readings contain Barker's opinion and a brief filed by Andrea Dworkin in the Court of Appeals arguing that Barker was wrong in declaring the law unconstitutional.

From a legal point of view, what is perhaps most significant about the pornography litigation is that the courts refused to recognize another exception to the First Amendment. The First Amendment does not provide absolute protection to everything that is spoken or printed. The most common example of unprotected speech is obscenity. Obscene publications have been deemed to contribute so little to society that the courts have held the First Amendment to be essentially irrelevant to obscene publications. Similarly, "fighting words," in which someone advocates illegal acts "where such advocacy is directed to inciting or producing imminent lawless action and is likely to incite or produce such action," can sometimes be punished. In general, however, constitutional theory holds that the solution to speech that someone does not like is more speech. According to the Supreme Court,

> a function of speech . . . is to invite dispute. It may indeed best serve its high purpose when it induces a condition of unrest, creates dissatisfaction with conditions as they are, or even stirs people to anger. Speech is often provocative and challenging. It may strike at prejudices and preconceptions and have profound unsettling effects.

The main issue, in obscenity cases that are brought to court, is whether or not the material meets the standards that have been developed to define obscenity. The conclusion that obscene expression is constitutionally unprotected was affirmed more than 30 years ago. The struggle for judges since then has been to construct a precise definition of obscenity so that judges, authors, and publishers will know when a publication is legally obscene and when it is not. This has been a mighty and not particularly successful struggle, and you will see mention in the following readings of the various definitions that have been tried and then abandoned by the Supreme Court.

The legal assault on pornography, in order for it to be successful, must not only define pornography in a clear manner but must also persuade the courts that pornography is so damaging and contributes so little to our society that nothing will be lost if it is suppressed. It would have been surprising if the antipornography movement had won a complete victory in its first lawsuit. What will be worth noting is whether or not other judges, even if they reject the approach used in Indianapolis, suggest that the sale and production of pornography might be restricted in some other way.

While the courts have generally resisted attempts to restrict offensive art and expression, political pressure to combat pornography has been increasing. In 1989 and 1990, there were frequent newsworthy attempts to suppress a wide variety of forms of expression, such as the exhibit of sexually explicit photographs by the late Robert Mapplethorpe and the records of the rap music group 2 Live Crew. Efforts were made to require special warning labels on record albums that contain explicit lyrics, to prosecute some television executives for transmitting allegedly obscene films by satellite to Alabama, and to impose restrictions on artists who receive grants from the National Endowment for the Arts. These examples suggest that courts will continue to be very busy trying to distinguish protected from unprotected forms of expression.

YES

Sarah Evans Barker

PORNOGRAPHY AND FIRST AMENDMENT RIGHTS

This case comes to the Court amidst heated public and private debate over the problems of pornography and sex discrimination in American society. In apparent response to the perceived urgency and seriousness of these issues, the Indianapolis City-County Council debated and enacted an ordinance with subsequent amendments which sought to deal with both of these conditions by limiting the availability in Indianapolis of materials which depict the sexually explicit subordination of women. The Council defined pornography as the graphic depiction of the sexually explicit subordination of women and then declared pornography a discriminatory practice. By way of outlawing this practice, it then forbade most of the specific acts necessary to produce, sell, or distribute such material.

It is difficult to quarrel either with the Council's underlying concern (that pornography and sex discrimination are harmful, offensive, and inimical to and inconsistent with enlightened approaches to equality) or with its premise that some legislative controls are in order. But beyond that, it is in fact outside the rightful purview of this Court to enter the public debate over whether and to what extent these conditions constitute a real social harm. It is also beyond the purview of the Court to substitute its judgment for that of the legislative body, either in defining the acceptable community standards in these areas or in imposing appropriate sanctions for behavior which violate those standards.

Thus, the Court's duty in this circumstance is a narrow one. That duty is to assess the constitutionality of the legislative enactment: to determine whether the Ordinance, however well-motivated or otherwise meritorious it may be, unconstitutionally diminishes, violates, or otherwise derrogates our fundamental freedoms as a people.

This litigation, therefore, requires the Court to weigh and resolve the conflict between the First Amendment guarantees of free speech, on the one hand, and the Fourteenth Amendment right to be free from sex-based discrimination, on the other hand. In addition, the Court must determine

From U.S. Court of Appeals for the Seventh Circuit, *American Booksellers Association, Inc. v. William H. Hudnut III*, 598 F.Supp. 1316, 106 S.Ct. 1172 (1984).

whether the Indianapolis enactment meets the due process requirements of the Fifth and Fourteenth Amendments.

The plaintiffs in this lawsuit request the Court "to preliminarily and permanently enjoin enforcement of, and to declare facially unconstitutional, void and of no effect, City County General Ordinances No. 24 and 35, 1984 (together hereinafter referred to as the "Ordinance"), on the grounds that it is unconstitutional under the United States Constitution." . . .

Plaintiffs have cited numerous reasons to support their claim for relief. They first contend that the Ordinance severely restricts the availability, display and distribution of constitutionally protected, non-obscene materials, in violation of the First and Fourteenth Amendments. More specifically, they claim that the regulatory restraints of the Ordinance are not limited merely to unprotected speech, such as obscenity. As a result, plaintiffs contend that they will be forced under the Ordinance to remove from availability in Indianapolis materials which are in fact protected by the First Amendment.

Plaintiffs also contend that in seeking to ban speech directed to the general public because it is highly offensive to many, the Ordinances violate established Supreme Court precedents which preclude the banning of speech simply because its contents may be socially or politically offensive to the majority. . . .

The defendants admit in their answer that the scope of the Ordinance goes beyond regulating obscene materials. However, they assert, such action does not violate the Constitution. Defendants deny every other allegation that the plaintiffs' rights as guaranteed by the United States Constitution are violated by this Ordinance. . . .

FIRST AMENDMENT REQUIREMENTS

This Ordinance cannot be analyzed adequately without first recognizing this: the drafters of the Ordinance have used what appears to be a legal term of art, "pornography," but have in fact given the term a specialized meaning which differs from the meanings ordinarily assigned to that word in both legal and common parlance. In Section 16–3(v) (page 6), the Ordinance states:

> "Pornography shall mean the sexually explicit subordination of women, graphically depicted, whether in pictures or in words, that includes one or more of the following . . . "

There follows at that point a listing of five specific presentations of women in various settings which serve as examples of "pornography" and as such further define and describe that term under the Ordinance.

As is generally recognized, the word "pornography" is usually associated, and sometimes synonomous, with the word, "obscenity." "Obscenity" not only has its own separate and specialized meaning in the law, but in laymen's use also, and it is a much broader meaning than the definition given the word "pornography" in the Ordinance which is at issue at this action. There is thus a considerable risk of confusion in analyzing this ordinance unless care and precision are used in that process.

The Constitutional analysis of this Ordinance requires a determination of several underlying issues: first, the Court must determine whether the Ordinance imposes restraints on speech or behavior (content versus conduct); if the Ordinance is found to regulate speech, the

Court must next determine whether the subject speech is protected or not protected under the First Amendment; if the speech which is regulated by this Ordinance is protected speech under the Constitution, the Court must then decide whether the regulation is constitutionally permissible as being based on a compelling state interest justifying the removal of such speech from First Amendment protections.

Do the Ordinances Regulate Speech or Behavior (Content or Conduct)?

It appears to be central to the defense of the Ordinance by defendants that the Court accept their premise that the City-County Council has not attempted to regulate speech, let alone protected speech. Defendants repeat throughout the briefs the incantation that their Ordinance regulates conduct, not speech. They contend (one senses with a certain sleight of hand) that the production, dissemination, and use of sexually explicit words and pictures *is* the actual subordination of women and not an expression of ideas deserving of First Amendment protection. . . .

Defendants claim support for their theory by analogy, arguing that it is an accepted and established legal distinction that has allowed other courts to find that advocacy of a racially "separate but equal" doctrine in a civil rights context is protected speech under the First Amendment though "segregation" is not constitutionally protected behavior. Accordingly, defendants characterize their Ordinance here as a civil rights measure, through which they seek to prevent the distribution, sale, and exhibition of "pornography," as defined in the Ordinance, in order to regulate and control the underlying unacceptable conduct.

The content-versus-conduct approach espoused by defendants is not persuasive, however, and is contrary to accepted First Amendment principles. Accepting as true the City-County Council's finding that pornography conditions society to subordinate women, the means by which the Ordinance attempts to combat this sex discrimination is nonetheless through the regulation of speech.

For instance, the definition of pornography, the control of which is the whole thrust of the Ordinance, states that it is "the sexually explicit subordination of women, graphically *depicted*, whether in *pictures* or in *words*, that includes one or more of the following:" (emphasis supplied) and the following five descriptive subparagraphs begin with the words, "Women are *presented* . . ." (emphasis supplied).

The unlawful acts and discriminatory practices under the Ordinance are set out in Section 16-3(g):

"(4) Trafficking in pornography: the production, sale, exhibition, or distribution of pornography. [Subparagraphs omitted here]
(5) Coercion into pornographic performance: coercing, intimidating or fraudulently inducing any person . . . into performing for pornography. . . . [Subparagraphs omitted here]
(6) Forcing pornography on a person: . . .
(7) Assault or physical attack due to pornography: the assault, physical attack, or injury of any woman, man, child or transsexual in a way that is directly caused by specific pornography. . . . "

Section (7), *supra*, goes on to provide a cause of action in damages against the perpetrators, makers, distributors, sellers and exhibitors of pornography and injunctive relief against the further exhibition, distribution or sale of pornography.

In summary, therefore, the Ordinance establishes through the legislative findings that pornography causes a tendency to commit these various harmful acts, and outlaws the pornography (that is, the "depictions"), the activities involved in the production of pornography, and the behavior caused by or resulting from pornography.

Thus, though the purpose of the Ordinance is cast in civil rights terminology—"to prevent and prohibit all discriminatory practices of sexual subordination or inequality through pornography" (Section 16-1(b)(8))—it is clearly aimed at controlling the content of the speech and ideas which the City-County Council has found harmful and offensive. Those words and pictures which depict women in sexually subordinate roles are banned legislation. Despite defendants' attempt to redefine offensive speech as harmful action, the clear wording of the Ordinance discloses that they seek to control speech, and those restrictions must be analyzed in light of applicable constitutional requirements and standards.

Is the Speech Regulated by the Ordinance Protected or Unprotected Speech Under the First Amendment?

The First Amendment provides that government shall make no law abridging the freedom of speech. However, "the First and Fourteenth Amendments have never been thought to give absolute protection to every individual to speak whenever or wherever he pleases or to use any form of address in any circumstances that he chooses." *Cohen v. California*, 403 U.S. 15, 19, 91 S.Ct. 1780, 1785, 29 L.Ed.2d 284 (1971). Courts have recognized only a "relatively few categories of

instances," *id.* at 19–20, 91 S.Ct. at 1785, where the government may regulate certain forms of individual expression. The traditional categories of speech subject to permissible government regulation include "the lewd and obscene, the profane, the libelous, and the insulting or 'fighting' words—those which by their very utterance inflict injury or tend to incite an immediate breach of the peace." *Chaplinsky v. State of New Hampshire*, 315 U.S. 568, 572, 62 S.Ct. 766, 769, 86 L.Ed. 1031 (1942). In addition, the Supreme Court has recently upheld legislation prohibiting the dissemination of material depicting children engaged in sexual conduct. *New York v. Ferber*, 458 U.S. 747, 102 S.Ct. 3348, 73 L.Ed.2d 1113 (1982).

Having found that the Ordinance at issue here seeks to regulate speech (and not conduct), the next question before the Court is whether the Ordinance, which seeks to restrict the distribution, sale, and exhibition of "pornography" as a form of sex discrimination against women, falls within one of the established categories of speech subject to permissible government regulation, that is, speech deemed to be unprotected by the First Amendment.

It is clear that this case does not present issues relating to profanity, libel, or "fighting words." In searching for an analytical "peg," the plaintiffs argue that the Ordinance most closely resembles obscenity, and is, therefore, subject to the requirements set forth in *Miller v. California*, 413 U.S. 15, 93 S.Ct. 2607, 37 L.Ed.2d 419 (1973). . . . But the defendants admit that the scope of the Ordinance is not limited to the regulation of legally obscene material as defined in *Miller*. . . . In fact, defendants concede that the "pornography" they seek to control goes beyond obscenity, as defined by the Supreme Court and excepted from First Amendment protections. Accordingly, the parties agree that the materials encompassed in the restrictions set out in the Ordinance include to some extent what have traditionally been protected materials.

The test under *Miller* for determining whether material is legal obscenity is:

"(a) whether 'the average person, applying contemporary community standards would find that the work, taken as a whole, appeals to the prurient interest, . . . ; (b) whether the work depicts or describes, in a patently offensive way a sexual conduct specifically defined by the applicable state law; and (c) whether the work, taken as a whole, lacks serious literary, artistic, political, or scientific value.". . .

It is obvious that this three-step test is not directly applicable to the present case, because, as has been noted, the Ordinance goes beyond legally obscene material in imposing its controls. The restrictions in the Indianapolis ordinance reach what has otherwise traditionally been regarded as protected speech under the *Miller* test. Beyond that, the Ordinance does not speak in terms of a "community standard" or attempt to restrict the dissemination of material that appeals to the "prurient interest." Nor has the Ordinance been drafted in a way to limit only distributions of "patently offensive" materials. Neither does it provide for the dissemination of works which, though "pornographic," may have "serious literary, artistic, political or scientific value." Finally, the Ordinance does not limit its reach to "hard core sexual conduct," though conceivably "hard core" materials may be included in its proscriptions.

Because the Ordinance spans so much more broadly in its regulatory scope than merely "hard core" obscenity by limiting the distribution of "pornography," the proscriptions in the Ordinance intrude with defendants' explicit approval into areas of otherwise protected speech. Under ordinary constitutional analysis, that would be sufficient grounds to overturn the Ordinance, but defendants argue that this case is not governed by any direct precedent, that it raises a new issue for the Court and even though the Ordinance regulates protected speech, it does so in a constitutionally permissible fashion.

Does Established First Amendment Law Permit the Regulation Provided for in the Ordinance of Otherwise Protected Speech?
In conceding that the scope of this Ordinance extends beyond constitutional limits, it becomes clear that what defendants actually seek by enacting this legislation is a newly-defined class of constitutionally unprotected speech, labeled "pornography" and characterized as sexually discriminatory.

Defendants vigorously argue that *Miller* is not the " 'constitutional divide' separating protected from unprotected expression in this area." . . . Defendants point to three cases which allegedly support their proposition that *Miller* is not the exclusive guideline for disposing of pornography/obscenity cases, and that the traditional obscenity test should not be applied in the present case. *See New York v. Ferber*, 458 U.S. 747, 102 S.Ct. 3348, 73 L.Ed.2d 1113 (1982); *FCC v. Pacifica Foundation*, 438 U.S. 726, 98 S.Ct. 3026, 57 L.Ed.2d 1073 (1978); *Young v. American Mini Theatres, Inc.*, 427 U.S. 50, 96 S.Ct. 2440, 49 L.Ed.2d 310 (1976).

Defendants first argue that the Court must use the same reasoning applied by the Supreme Court in *New York v. Ferber, supra,* which upheld a New York statute prohibiting persons from promoting child pornography by distributing material which depicted such activity, and carve out another similar exception to protected speech under the First Amendment.

Defendants can properly claim some support for their position in *Ferber.* There the Supreme Court allowed the states "greater leeway" in their regulation of pornographic depictions of children in light of the State's compelling interest in protecting children who, without such protections, are extraordinarily vulnerable to exploitation and harm. The Court stated in upholding the New York statute:

> "The prevention of sexual exploitation and abuse of children constitutes a government objective of surpassing importance. The legislative findings accompanying passage of the New York laws reflect this concern. . . ."

The Supreme Court continued in *Ferber* by noting that the *Miller* standard for legal obscenity does not satisfy the unique concerns and issues posed by child pornography where children are involved; it is irrelevant, for instance, that the materials sought to be regulated contain serious literary, artistic, political or scientific value. In finding that some speech, such as that represented in depictions of child pornography, is outside First Amendment protections, the *Ferber* court stated:

> "When a definable class of material, such as that covered by § 263.15, bears so heavily and pervasively on the welfare of children engaged in its production, we think the balance of competing

interests is clearly struck and that it is permissible to consider these materials as without the protection of the First Amendment.". . .

Defendants, in the case at bar, argue that the interests of protecting women from sex-based discrimination are analogous to and every bit as compelling and fundamental as those which the Supreme Court upheld in *Ferber* for the benefit of children. But *Ferber* appears clearly distinguishable from the instant case on both the facts and law.

As has already been shown, the rationale applied by the Supreme Court in *Ferber* appears intended to apply solely to child pornography cases. In *Ferber,* the court recognized "that a state's interest in 'safeguarding the physical and psychological well-being of a minor' is 'compelling.' *Globe Newspaper v. Superior Court,* 457 U.S. 596, 607, 102 S.Ct. 2613, 2621, 73 L.Ed.2d 248 (1982)." 102 S.Ct. at 3354. *See also, FCC v. Pacifica Foundation, supra; Prince v. Massachusetts,* 321 U.S. 158, 168, 64 S.Ct. 438, 443, 88 L.Ed. 645 (1944); *Ginsberg v. New York,* 390 U.S. 629, 88 S.Ct. 1274, 20 L.Ed.2d 195 (1968). Also, the obscenity standard in *Miller* is appropriately abandoned in child pornography cases because it "[does] not reflect the State's particular and more compelling interest in prosecuting those who promote the sexual exploitations of children." *Id.* Since a state's compelling interest in preventing child pornography outweighs an individual's First Amendment rights, the Supreme Court held that "the states are entitled to greater leeway in the regulation of pornographic depictions of children." *Id.* 102 S.Ct. at 3354.

In contrast, the case at bar presents issues more far reaching than those in *Ferber.* Here, the City-County Council found that the distribution, sale, and exhibition of words and pictures depicting the subordination of women is a form of sex discrimination and as such is appropriate for governmental regulation. The state has a well-recognized interest in preventing sex discrimination, and, defendants argue, it can regulate speech to accomplish that end.

But the First Amendment gives primacy to free speech and any other state interest (such as the interest of sex based equality under law) must be so compelling as to be fundamental; only then can it be deemed to outweigh the interest of free speech. This Court finds no legal authority or public policy argument which justifies so broad an incursion into First Amendment freedoms as to allow that which defendants attempt to advance here. *Ferber* does not open the door to allow the regulation contained in the Ordinance for the reason that adult women as a group do not, as a matter of public policy or applicable law, stand in need of the same type of protection which has long been afforded children. This is true even of women who are subject to the sort of inhuman treatment defendants have described and documented to the Court in support of this Ordinance. The Supreme Court's finding in *Ferber* of the uncontroverted state interest in "safeguarding the physical and psychological well being of a minor" and its resultant characterization of that interest as "compelling," 102 S.Ct. 3348, 3354, is an interest which inheres to children and is not an interest which is readily transferrable to adult women as a class. Adult women generally have the capacity to protect themselves from participating in and being personally victimized by pornography, which makes the State's interest in safeguarding the physical and

psychological well-being of women by prohibiting "the sexually explicit subordination of women, graphically depicted, whether in pictures or in words" not so compelling as to sacrifice the guarantees of the First Amendment. . . .

The second case relied upon by defendants to support their contention that *Miller* is not controlling in the present case is *FCC v. Pacifica Foundation*, 438 U.S. 726, 98 S.Ct. 3026, 57 L.Ed.2d 1073 (1978). According to defendants, *Pacifica* exemplifies the Supreme Court's refusal to make obscenity the sole legal basis for regulating sexually explicit conduct.

In *Pacifica*, the Supreme Court was faced with the question of whether a broadcast of patently offensive words dealing with sex and excretion may be regulated on the basis of their content. 438 U.S. at 745, 98 S.Ct. at 3038. The Court held that this type of speech was not entitled to absolute constitutional protection in every context. *Id.* at 747, 98 S.Ct. at 3039. Since the context of the speech in *Pacifica* was broadcasting, it was determined only to be due "the most limited First Amendment protection." *Id.* at 748, 98 S.Ct. at 3040. The reason for such treatment was twofold:

"First, the broadcast media have established a uniquely pervasive presence in all the lives of all Americans. Patently offensive, indecent material presented over the airwaves confronts the citizen, not only in public, but also in the privacy of the home, where the individual's right to be left alone plainly outweighs the First Amendment rights of an intruder. Second, broadcasting is uniquely accessible to children, even those too young to read . . ."

Although the defendants correctly point out that the Supreme Court did not use the traditional obscenity test in *Pacif-*

ica, this Court is not persuaded that the rule enunciated there is applicable to the facts of the present case. The Ordinance does not attempt to regulate the airwaves; in terms of its restrictions, it is not even remotely concerned with the broadcast media. The reasons for the rule in *Pacifica,* that speech in certain contexts should be afforded minimal First Amendment protection, are not present here, since we are not dealing with a medium that "invades" the privacy of the home. In contrast, if an individual is offended by "pornography," as defined in the Ordinance, the logical thing to do is avoid it, an option frequently not available to the public with material disseminated through broadcasting.

In addition, the Ordinance is not written to protect children from the distribution of pornography, in contrast to the challenged FCC regulation in *Pacifica.* Therefore, the peculiar state interest in protecting the "well being of its youth," *id.* at 649, 98 S.Ct. at 3040 (quoting *Ginsberg v. New York,* 390 U.S. 629, 88 S.Ct. 1274, 20 L.Ed.2d 195 (1968)), does not underlie this Ordinance and cannot be called upon to justify a decision by this Court to uphold the Ordinance.

The third case cited by defendants in support of their proposition that the traditional obscenity standard in *Miller* should not be used to overrule the Ordinance is *Young v. American Mini Theatres, Inc.,* 427 U.S. 50, 96 S.Ct. 2440, 49 L.Ed.2d 310 (1976). In *Young* the Supreme Court upheld a city ordinance that restricted the location of movie theatres featuring erotic films. The Court, in a plurality opinion, stated that "[e]ven though the First Amendment protects communication in this area from total suppression, we hold that the State may legitimately use the content of these ma-

terials as the basis for placing them in a different classification from other motion pictures." 427 U.S. at 71–72, 96 S.Ct. at 2452. The Court concluded that the city's interest in preserving the character of its neighborhoods justified the ordinance which required that adult theaters be separated, rather than concentrated, in the same areas as it is permissible for other theaters to do without limitation. *Id.* at 71, 96 S.Ct. at 2452–53.

Young is distinguishable from the present case because we are not here dealing with an attempt by the City-County Council to restrict the time, place, and manner in which "pornography" may be distributed. Instead, the Ordinance prohibits completely the sale, distribution, or exhibition of material depicting women in a sexually subordinate role, at all times, in all places and in every manner.

The Ordinance's attempt to regulate speech beyond one of the well-defined exceptions to protected speech under the First Amendment is not supported by other Supreme Court precedents. The Court must, therefore, examine the underlying premise of the Ordinance: that the State has so compelling an interest in regulating the sort of sex discrimination imposed and perpetuated through "pornography" that it warrants an exception to free speech.

Is Sex Discrimination a Compelling State Interest Justifying an Exception to First Amendment Protections?

It is significant to note that the premise of the Ordinance is the sociological harm, *i.e.,* the discrimination, which results from "pornography" to degrade women as a class. The Ordinance does not presume or require specifically defined, identifiable victims for most of its proscriptions. The Ordinance seeks to protect adult women, as a group, from the diminution of their legal and sociological status as women, that is, from the discriminatory stigma which befalls women as *women* as a result of "pornography." On page one of the introduction to defendants' *Amicus* Brief, counsel explicitly argues that the harm which underlies this legislation is the "harm to the treatment and *status* of women . . . on the basis of sex." . . .

This is a novel theory advanced by the defendants, an issue of first impression in the courts. If this Court were to accept defendants' argument—that the State's interest in protecting women from the humiliation and degradation which comes from being depicted in a sexually subordinate context is so compelling as to warrant the regulation of otherwise free speech to accomplish that end—one wonders what would prevent the City-County Council (or any other legislative body) from enacting protections for other equally compelling claims against exploitation and discrimination as are presented here. Legislative bodies, finding support, here, could also enact legislation prohibiting other unfair expression —the publication and distribution of racist material, for instance, on the grounds that it causes racial discrimination,[1] or legislation prohibiting ethnic or religious slurs on the grounds that they cause discrimination against particular ethnic or religious groups, or legislation barring literary depictions which are uncomplimentary or oppressive to handicapped persons on the grounds that they cause discrimination against that group of people, and so on. If this Court were to extend to this case the rationale in *Ferber* to uphold the Amendment, it would signal so great a potential encroachment

upon First Amendment freedoms that the precious liberties reposed within those guarantees would not survive. The compelling state interest, which defendants claim gives constitutional life to their Ordinance, though important and valid as that interest may be in other contexts, is not so fundamental an interest as to warrant a broad intrusion into otherwise free expression.

Defendants contend that pornography is not deserving of constitutional protection because its harms victimize all women. It is argued that "pornography" not only negatively effects [sic] women who risk and suffer the direct abuse of its production,[2] but also, those on whom violent pornography is forced through such acts as compelled performances of "dangerous acts such as being hoisted upside down by ropes, bound by ropes and chains, hung from trees and scaffolds or having sex with animals. . . ." Defendants' Memorandum In Support To Plaintiffs' Motion For Summary Judgment, pp. 3–4. It is also alleged that exposure to pornography produces a negative impact on its viewers, causing in them an increased willingness to aggress toward women, *ibid.* at p. 4, and experience self-generated rape fantasies, increases in sexual arousal and a rise in the self-reported possibility of raping. *Ibid.* at p. 6. In addition, it causes discriminatory attitudes and behavior toward all women. *Ibid.*, at pp. 11–12. The City-County Council, after considering testimony and social research studies, enacted the Ordinance in order to "combat" pornography's "concrete and tangible harms to women." *Ibid.* at p. 13.

Defendants rely on *Paris Adult Theatre I v. Slaton*, 413 U.S. 49, 93 S.Ct. 2628, 37 L.Ed.2d 446 (1973), to justify their regulation of "pornography." In that case the

Supreme Court held "that there are legitimate state interests at stake in stemming the tide of commercialized obscenity . . . [which] include the interest of the public in the quality of life and the total community environment, the tone of commerce in the great city centers, and, possibly, the public safety itself." 413 U.S. at 57–58, 93 S.Ct. at 2635.

The Georgia Legislature had determined that in that case exposure to obscene material adversely affected men and women, that is to say, society as a whole. Although the petitioners argued in that case that there was no scientific data to conclusively prove that proposition, the Court said, "[i]t is not for us to resolve empirical uncertainties underlying state legislation, save in the exceptional case where that legislation plainly impinges upon rights protected by the constitution itself." *Id.* at 60, 93 S.Ct. at 2636–37 (footnote omitted).

In *Slaton*, the Georgia Legislature sought to regulate "obscenity," an accepted area of unprotected speech. *See Miller v. California*, 413 U.S. 15, 93 S.Ct. 2607, 37 L.Ed.2d 419 (1973). The Court specifically found that "nothing precludes the State of Georgia from the regulation of the allegedly obscene material exhibited in *Paris Adult Theatre I or II*, provided that the applicable Georgia law, as written or authoritatively interpreted by the Georgia courts, meets the First Amendment standards set forth in *Miller v. California* . . ." 413 U.S. at 69, 93 S.Ct. at 2642 (citations omitted).

Based on this reasoning, defendants argue that there is more than enough "empirical" evidence in the case at bar to support the City-County Council's conclusion that "pornography" harms women in the same way obscenity harms people, and, therefore, this Court should not question the legislative finding. As has already been acknowledged, it is not the Court's function to question the City-County Council's legislative finding. The Court's solitary duty is to ensure that the Ordinance accomplishes its purpose without violating constitutional standards or impinging upon constitutionally protected rights. In applying those tests, the Court finds that the Ordinance cannot withstand constitutional scrutiny.

It has already been noted that the Ordinance does not purport to regulate legal obscenity, as defined in *Miller*. Thus, although the City-County Council determined that "pornography" harms women, this Court must and does declare the Ordinance invalid without being bound by the legislative findings because "pornography," as defined and regulated in the Ordinance, is constitutionally protected speech under the First Amendment and such an exception to the First Amendment protections is constitutionally unwarranted.[3] This Court cannot legitimately embark on judicial policymaking, carving out a new exception to the First Amendment simply to uphold the Ordinance, even when there may be many good reasons to support legislative action. To permit every interest group, especially those who claim to be victimized by unfair expression, their own legislative exceptions to the First Amendment so long as they succeed in obtaining a majority of legislative votes in their favor demonstrates the potentially predatory nature of what defendants seek through this Ordinance and defend in this lawsuit.

It ought to be remembered by defendants and all others who would support such a legislative initiative that, in terms of altering sociological patterns, much as alteration may be necessary and desirable, free speech, rather than being the enemy, is a long-tested and worthy ally. To deny free speech in order to engineer social change in the name of accomplishing a greater good for one sector of our society erodes the freedoms of all and, as such, threatens tyranny and injustice for those subjected to the rule of such laws. The First Amendment protections presuppose the evil of such tyranny and prevent a finding by this Court upholding the Ordinance. . . .

SUMMARY

For the foregoing reasons, the Court finds that the Ordinance regulates speech protected by the First Amendment and is, therefore, in violation of the United States Constitution. The Ordinance's proscriptions are not limited to categories of speech, such as obscenity or child pornography, which have been excepted from First Amendment protections and permit some governmental regulation. The City-County Council, in defining and outlawing "pornography" as the graphically depicted subordination of women, which it then characterizes as sex discrimination, has sought to regulate expression, that is, to suppress speech. And although the State has a recognized interest in prohibiting sex discrimination, that interest does not outweigh the constitutionally protected interest of free speech. For these reasons the Ordinance does not withstand this constitutional challenge.

NOTES

1. In *Beauharnais v. Illinois*, 343 U.S. 250, 72 S.Ct. 725, 96 L.Ed. 919 (1952), the Supreme Court upheld an Illinois libel statute prohibiting the dissemination of materials promoting racial or religious hatred and which tended to produce a breach of the peace and riots. It has been recognized that "the rationale of that decision turns quite plainly on the strong tendency of the prohibited utterances to cause violence and disorder." *Collin v. Smith*, 578 F.2d 1197, 1204 (7th Cir. 1978). The Supreme Court has recognized breach of the peace as the traditional justification for upholding a criminal libel statute. *Beauharnais*, 343 U.S. at 254, 72 S.Ct. at 729. Therefore, a law preventing the distribution of material that causes racial discrimination, an attitude, would be upheld under this analysis. Further, the underlying reasoning of the *Beauharnais* opinion, that the punishment of libel raises no constitutional problems, has been questioned in many recent cases. *See Collin, supra*, 578 F.2d at 1205, and cases cited therein.

2. The defendants point to social research data, as well as graphic personal accounts of individuals, in support of their position that "women are recruited into all forms of sexual exploitation through physical force, psychological coercion, drugs and economic exigencies." Defendants' Memorandum In Support To Plaintiffs' Motion For Summary Judgment, p. 2.

3. Defendants again rely on *Young v. American Mini Theatres, Inc.*, 427 U.S. 50, 96 S.Ct. 2440, 49 L.Ed.2d 310 (1976), contending that since the legislation in that case was upheld upon a single affidavit of a sociologist that the location of adult movie theatres had a disruptive impact on the community, the Ordinance should be upheld because there is more than enough data to demonstrate that pornography harms women. As discussed above in subpart B, however, the legislation in *Young* sought to regulate the place where pornography could be distributed, not to completely ban its distribution. Thus *Young* is not controlling.

NO

Andrea Dworkin

THE OPPRESSION OF PORNOGRAPHY

I am co-author with Catharine A. MacKinnon of the Indianapolis legislation defining pornography as a violation of women's civil rights; the author of *Pornography: Men Possessing Women* (1981), *Woman Hating* (1974), and many articles on pornography; a lecturer at universities on pornography; a speaker at rallies protesting pornography; and an organizer involved in demonstrating against pornography. I have spent the last thirteen years analyzing the impact of pornography on women's social status and the role of pornography in sexual abuse. . . .

PORNOGRAPHY IS A CENTRAL ELEMENT
IN THE OPPRESSION OF WOMEN

Judge Barker says that pornography as defined in the Ordinance is constitutionally protected speech. This means that the abuse of women in pornography, the trafficking in women that constitutes the bulk of pornography, the coercion of women required to make pornography, the abuses of women inevitably resulting from pornography, and the inequality created by pornography all have constitutional protection. Women cannot function as citizens in this world of social and sexual predation.

The Ordinance characterizes pornography as "a discriminatory practice based on sex." Speech and action are meshed in this discrimination, which is a system of sexual exploitation constructed on sex-based powerlessness and which generates sex-based abuse. The presence of speech cannot be used to immunize discrimination and sexual abuse from legal remedy.

When pornography is photographic, it is indisputably action. It gets perceived as speech because the woman in the photograph is effectively rendered an object or commodity by the pornography; the perception of the photograph as speech in itself denies the human status of the woman in it. The so-called speech belongs to whomever took or sold the photograph—the pornographer—not to the woman used in it, to whom things were done as if she were an object or commodity, and who indeed continues to be sold as an

From U.S. Court of Appeals for the Seventh Circuit, *American Booksellers Association, Inc. v. William H. Hudnut III*, 598 F.Supp. 1316, 106 S.Ct. 1172 (1984).

object or commodity. The woman is excluded from recognizably human dialogue by the uses to which she is put. The courts reify this injustice when they take the photograph to be real speech and do not recognize the woman in it as a real person who, by virtue of being human, is necessarily being used in ways antagonistic to full human status. The court accepts the pornographers' misogyny as its own if it holds that the pornographers' exploitation of a woman's body is an appropriate use of her: that what she is entitled to as a human being is properly expressed in these uses to which she is put.

The actions immortalized in pornography are not ideas, thoughts, or fantasies. The vocabulary of "sexual fantasy," often applied to pornography as a genre, is in fact the language of prostitution, where the act that the man wants done and pays to get done is consistently referred to as his "fantasy," as if it never happens in the real world. He goes to a prostitute and pays her money so that she will do what he tells her to do, and it is this *act* that is called "fantasy."

Similarly, in pornography, *acts* done to or by women are called "speech," even though the woman is doing an act dictated by what is required to sexually gratify men. Her body is a commodity in itself. Her body is also the literal language of the so-called publisher, who in reality is a pimp trafficking in women. Because the pimp introduces a camera into the trafficking, his whole process of exploiting the woman's body is protected as "speech."

The First Amendment predated the invention of the camera. The founding fathers could never have considered that there might be physical rights of people trampled on by rights of speech: that in

protecting a photograph, for instance, one might be protecting an actual act of torture. In pornography, photographs are made with real women. These photographs are then used on real women, to get them to do the acts the real women in the photographs are doing.

The hostility and discrimination produced by written pornography is just as real. In written pornography, the vocabularies of sex and violence are inextricably combined, so that erection and orgasm are produced as pleasurable responses to sexual abuse. This behaviorally conditions men to sex as dominance over and violence against women. The nature of written pornography is definable and distinct enough from all other written material that it can be isolated as well as recognized. Sexually explicit and abusive male dominance, conveyed in repeated acts of rape, torture, and humiliation, is the entire substance of written pornography. *See* Smith, *The Social Content of Pornography*, 26 J. Communication 16 (1976). It is impossible, however, to separate the effects of written pornography from the effects of photographic pornography.

Obscenity law recognizes the incredible physical impact of this kind of sexually explicit material, written and photographic, on men—an impact so different from the impact of any known form of "speech" that the Supreme Court has repeatedly held that obscenity is not speech, even though it is words and pictures. *See*, e.g., *Roth v. United States*, 354 U.S. 476, 485 (1957). The standard of "prurient interest" suggests the kind of line that the Court wants to draw between "speech" and "not speech" even with regard to words and pictures. "Prurient" means "itch" or "itching"; it is derived from the Sanscrit "he burns."

If he itches, let alone burns, the power and urgency of his response is not socially innocuous. Pornography creates the physiologically real conviction in men that women want abuse; that women are whores by nature; that women want to be raped and humiliated; that women get sexual pleasure from pain; even that women get sexual pleasure from being maimed or killed. . . . Obscenity law is premised on the inevitability of male sexual response to sexually explicit verbal and visual stimuli; it occurs in a world of concrete male dominance, obscenity law itself originating in a context of legalized male ownership of women.

Judicial decisions reflect and perpetuate the focus on male response, by wholly ignoring women, both in and outside the pornography. The statutory definition of pornography in the Ordinance articulates for the first time in the law how pornography both uses and impacts on women in particular, which is what distinguishes it as a uniquely destructive phenomenon. Pornography is appropriately recognized as an energetic agent of male domination over women. Pornography creates a devastating relationship between the status of some women, who are particularly powerless and vulnerable to abuse, and the status of all women. The vicious exploitation through sex of some women in pornography as entertainment establishes a sexual imperative in which forcing sex on any woman is justified. The bad treatment of some women in pornography justifies the second-class status of all women in society, because the bad treatment is presented as an appropriate response to the human worthlessness of women as such. Only *some* Christians had to be slaughtered as public entertainment in Roman circuses for all Christians and all Romans to

understand who could be hurt, harassed, and persecuted with *de facto* impunity.

Pornographers draw on and benefit from particularly cruel aspects of women's vulnerability. Incest and child sexual abuse produce between two-thirds and three-quarters of the women who get exploited in pornography. *See* James and Heyerding, *Early Sexual Experiences and Prostitution*, 134 Am. J. Psychiatry 1381 (1977); Silbert and Pines, *Pornography and Sexual Abuse of Women*, 10 Sex Roles 857 (1984); Senate Committee on the Judiciary, Subcommittee on Juvenile Justice, *A Hearing to Consider the Effects of Pornography on Children and Women* (Aug. 8, 1984) (testimony of Katherine Brady). The ownership of a girl by her father or other adult male, including sexual ownership of her, is deeply implicated in the continuing vulnerability of adult women to the sexual abuse of pornography. It is not possible to draw a firm line between the uses of children in pornography, recognized in *New York v. Ferber*, 458 U.S. 747 (1982), and the uses of women in pornography, since so many of the women are habituated to sexual abuse, even first used in pornography, as children. The court must not accept the pornographers' propaganda, which insists that these women have made a career choice as free and equal adults for pornographic exploitation. The ownership of women and children by adult men is historically linked (for example, in the power of the Roman *paterfamilias*); and it is empirically and sociologically linked in the abuse of women and children in pornography.

Pornography is deeply implicated in rape, *see* Minneapolis Hearings, Sess. III (Dec. 13, 1983) at 11 (testimony of Bill Neiman), 14 (testimony of Susan Graack),

18 *et seq.* (testimony of Carol LaFavor); in battery, *see id.* at 21 (testimony of Wanda Richardson), 27 *et seq.* (testimony of Donna Dunn); in incest, *see id.* at 69 *et seq.* (testimony of Charlotte Castle); in forced prostitution, *see id.* at 75 *es seq.* (testimony of Sue Santa). Pornography is also a consistent phenomenon in the lives of serial killers. *See* S. Michaud and J. Aynesworth, *The Only Living Witness* 104, 105, 115, 118, 130 (1983) (Ted Bundy); T. Schwarz, *The Hillside Strangler* 152–153 (1982); T. Sullivan and P. Maiken, *Killer Clown: The John Wayne Gacy Murders* 28, 29, 218, 223; P. Johnson, *On Iniquity* 39, 52, 80, 81 (1967) (Moors murders); E. Williams, *Beyond Belief* 135, 143, 148–156 (1968) (Moors murders); G. Burn, ' . . . *somebody's husband, somebody's son': The Story of Peter Sutcliffe* 113–116, 123 (1984) (Yorkshire Ripper).

Pornography presents the rape and torture of women as entertainment. This is surely the nadir of social worthlessness.

PORNOGRAPHERS' RIGHTS OF EXPRESSION ARE OUTWEIGHED BY WOMEN'S RIGHTS TO EQUALITY

The Expression of Ideas Through Injurious Acts Is Not Constitutionally Protected

It is wrong to say, as Judge Barker did, that pornography as defined in the Ordinance expresses ideas and is therefore protected speech, unless one is prepared to say that murder or rape or torture with an ideology behind it also expresses ideas and might well be protected on that account. Most acts express ideas. Most systems of exploitation or inequality express ideas. Segregation expressed an idea more eloquently than any book about the inferiority of black people ever did. Yet the Supreme Court overturned segregation—after protecting it for a very long time—because the Court finally grasped its harm to people. The difference between the Court's view in *Plessy v. Ferguson*, 163 U.S. 537, 551 (1896), that segregation harmed blacks "solely because the colored race chooses to put that construction upon it," and its view in *Brown v. Bd. of Education of Topeka*, 347 U.S. 483, 494 (1954) that segregation "generates a feeling of inferiority as to their status in the community that may affect their hearts and minds in a way unlikely ever to be undone," is dramatic and instructive. The fact that the idea segregation expressed would suffer because the idea required the practice for much of its persuasive power did not afford segregation constitutional protection: attempts to invoke First Amendment justifications have been thoroughly repudiated. . . . An effort to claim that segregation was protected as first amendment "speech" because it has a point of view and an ideology would be a transparent use of the First Amendment to shield a practice of inequality; and such a claim for pornography is similarly transparent. Exploitation cannot be protected because it expresses the idea that the people being exploited are inferior or worthless as human beings or deserve to be exploited. All exploitation fundamentally expresses precisely that idea.

The Sexual Exploitation of Women Perpetuated by Pornography Negates Women's Rights to Equality

In her decision, Judge Barker says that "[a]dult women generally have the capacity to protect themselves from participating in and being personally victimized by pornography." The fault, she suggests, is with the individual who is hurt, and no legal remedy is justified. Adult men generally have the capacity to protect themselves from being murdered; yet murderers are not excused because they only succeed in murdering men who are dumb enough, weak enough, or provocative enough to get killed. Indeed, no one ever thinks of male victims of violence in those terms at all. Yet that valuation of women hurt by pornography is implicit in Judge Barker's misogynistic logic.

It is not true that women can protect ourselves from being victimized by pornography. Pornography's effect on our civil status—the way it creates attitudes and behaviors of discrimination against us—is beyond personal remedy. Pornography's role in generating sexual abuse is beyond our capacities as individuals to stop or moderate, especially with no legal recourse against its production, sale, exhibition, or distribution. Sexual abuse is endemic in this country. One-fifth to one-third of all women have an unwanted sexual encounter with an adult male as children; one woman in a hundred has had a sexual experience as a child with her father or step-father; it is estimated that 16,000 new cases of father-daughter incest are initiated each year. See J. Herman, *Father-Daughter Incest* 12–14 (1982). Studies and police and hospital records in different localities suggest that battery occurs in one-third to one-half of all marriages. See R. Langley and R. Levy, *Wife Beating* 4–11 (1977); D. Russell, *Rape in Marriage* 98–100 (1982). A documented forcible rape occurs every seven minutes; and rape remains one of the most underreported violent crimes. See Federal Bureau of Investigation, *Uni-form Crime Reports for the United States* at 5, 14 (1983). Studies continue to be done in all areas of sexual abuse, including sexual harassment, marital rape, and prostitution; and the figures showing frequency of abuse increase as the descriptions of violence become more precise and the political efforts of feminists provide a context in which to comprehend the abuse.

The place of pornography in actually producing the scenarios and behaviors that constitute that mass of sexual abuse is increasingly documented, especially by victims. Coercion of women into pornography is expanding as the market for live women expands, especially in video pornography. Women in homes do not have the real social and economic power to keep men from using pornography on them or making them participate in it. There has been an increased use of cameras in actual rapes, with the subsequent appearance of the photographs on the commercial pornography market. Pornography itself is also being used as a form of sexual assault: the public violation of a woman—photographs made against her will or by fraud or without her knowledge, then published as public rape. Her forced exposure, like rape, is an act of hostility and humiliation. With the normalization of pornography, women who have pictures of themselves used against them as sexual abuse have no social or legal credibility to assert that rights of privacy were violated, because they appear indistinguishable from other women in similar photographs whose active compliance is presumed.

The statutory definition of pornography in the Ordinance, far from being "vague," delineates the structure of actual, concrete material produced and sold as pornography by the $8-billion-a-year pornography industry. *See U.S. News and World Report,* June 4, 1984, at 84–85. No adult bookstore has any problem knowing what to stock. No consumer has any problem knowing what to buy. No pornography theatre has any trouble knowing what to show. The so-called books are produced by formula, and they do not vary ever in their nature, content, or impact. They cannot be confused with the language of any writer I have ever read, including Jean Genet and Jerzy Kosinski, who are particularly graphic about rape and hate women. It may be difficult to believe that the definition is accurate and clear, because it may be difficult to believe that we are actually living in a country where the material described in the statutory definition is being produced, especially with live people. Nevertheless, we do. Or perhaps one effect of using $8 billion of pornography a year is that the basic premise of this law appears bizarre by contrast with the pornography: that women are human beings with rights of equality; and that being hurt by pornography violates those rights.

The Elimination of Sex Discrimination Is a Compelling State Interest That Is Furthered by the Ordinance

Sex discrimination keeps more than half the population from being able to enjoy the full benefits of free speech, because they are too poor to buy speech, too silenced through sexual abuse to articulate in a credible way their own experiences, too despised because of their sex to be able to achieve the public significance required to exercise speech in a technologically advanced society. The First Amendment protects speech al-ready articulated and published from state interference. It does nothing to empower those who have been systematically excluded—especially on the bases of sex and race—from pragmatic access to the means of speech.

The First Amendment is nearly as old as this country. The eradication of sex discrimination is new as a compelling state interest, perhaps causing Judge Barker to underestimate its importance. . . . Without vigorous action in behalf of equality, women will never be able to exercise the speech that the First Amendment would then protect.

State governments were not held to the proscriptions on government in the First Amendment until the Supreme Court held that the due process clause of the Fourteenth Amendment incorporated First Amendment standards. *See,* e.g., *Fiske v. Kansas,* 274 U.S. 380 (1927). Nevertheless, the simple reality is that the First Amendment and its values of free speech existed in harmony with both legal slavery and legal segregation. No effective legal challenge to those systems of racial subordination was mounted under the rubric of freedom of expression, even though in both systems reading and writing were at issue. In slavery, laws prohibited teaching slaves to read or write. *See* K. Stampp, *The Peculiar Institution* 208 (1956). In segregation, separate-but-equal education assured that blacks remained widely illiterate; then literacy tests were used to screen voters, so that blacks could not qualify to vote. *See Oregon v. Mitchell,* 400 U.S. 112, 132–33 (1970) (Black, J.); *Gaston County v. United States,* 395 U.S. 285 (1969). *Cf. Griggs v. Duke Power Company,* 401 U.S. 424, 430 (1971) (inferior segregated education hurts blacks where employer uses non-job-related educational criteria for employment decisions). Rights of speech, association, and religion (being kept out of certain churches, for instance, by state law), were simply denied blacks. The Civil War Amendments are an institutional acknowledgment that powerlessness is not cured simply by "more speech"; first amendment values alone could not fulfill constitutional ambitions for dignity and equity that reside in principles of justice not abrogated even by sadistic political institutions like slavery. The Fourteenth Amendment, however, purposefully used the word "male" in its guarantee of voting rights, U.S. Const. amend. XIV, §2, to rule out any possible application of equality rights to women's social and political condition. The right to vote, won in 1920, gave women the most mundane recognition of civil existence as citizens. U.S. Const., amend. XIX. The equality principles underlying the Fourteenth Amendment were even then not applied to women until 1971. *Reed v. Reed*, 404 U.S. 71 (1971).

The absolute, fixed, towering importance of the First Amendment and the absolute, fixed insignificance of sex discrimination and of equality of interests in Judge Barker's decision is a direct consequence of how late women came into this legal system as real citizens. Equality must be the legal priority for any group excluded from constitutional protections for so long and stigmatized as inferior. Yet the historical worthlessness of women—which is why our interests are not as old as this country—undermines any claim we make to having rights that must be taken as fundamental: equality for women is seen as trivial, faddish. The First Amendment, by contrast, is fundamental—a behemoth characterized by longevity, constancy, and familiarity. Because women have been silenced, and

because women have been second-class, our equality claims are seen as intrinsically inferior. The opposite should be the case. Those whom the law has helped to keep out by enforcing conditions of inferiority, servitude, and debasement should, by virtue of that involuntary but intensely destructive exclusion, have the court's full attention when asserting any equality claim.

This must certainly be true when speech rights are asserted in behalf of pornographers, since the speech of the pornographers is exercised largely through sexual abuse and is intricately interwoven with physical assault and injury. The First Amendment here is clearly being used to shield those who are not only powerful but also cruel and cynical. The victims, targeted on the basis of sex, must ask for relief from systematic sexual predation through a recognition of equality rights, because only equality stands up against the injury of longstanding exclusion from constitutional protections. Judge Barker holds that only expression matters, even when the expression is trafficking in women; equality does not matter, and the systematic harms of inequality and abuse suffered by women on a massive scale do not matter. This view of the First Amendment relies on historical inequities to establish modern constitutional priorities.

The courts must, instead, give real weight to equality interests, because of their historical exclusion from the original Bill of Rights. The deformities of the social system caused by that exclusion destroy justice, which requires symmetry, equity, and balance. By refusing to give equality values any weight when in conflict with free speech values, Judge Barker allows speech to function as if it were a military arsenal: hoarded by men for over two centuries, it is now used to bludgeon women, who have been without it and have none in reserve; we do not even have slingshots against Goliath. If equality interests can never matter against first amendment challenges, then speech becomes a weapon used by the haves against the have-nots; and the First Amendment, not balanced against equality rights of the have-nots, becomes an intolerable instrument of dispossession, not a safeguard of human liberty. The real exclusion of women from public discourse has allowed men to accumulate speech as a resource of power; and with that power, men have articulated values and furthered practices that have continued to debase women and to justify that debasement. The First Amendment, then, in reality, operates to the extreme detriment of those who do not have the power of socially and politically real speech. In this case, Judge Barker is saying that real people being tortured are properly not persons with rights of equality that are being violated; but, because a picture has been taken, are the abstract speech of those who exploit them. She is saying that the victim in the photograph is properly silent, even if gagged; that the victim's historical exclusion from speech need not, cannot, and should not be changed by vigorous legislative and judicial commitments to equality. She is saying that the woman's body is properly seen as the man's speech; and, in this corrupt logic, that the picture that in fact documents the abuse of a human being is to be dignified as an idea that warrants legal protection. Equality is indeed meaningless in this arrangement of power; and speech is a nightmare with a victim whose humanity is degraded by both the pornographers and the court.

The Pornographers Degrade the First Amendment

The pornographers also degrade the First Amendment by using it as a shield to protect sexual abuse and sexual trafficking. If the court allows these parasites an impenetrable shield of absolute protection because they use pictures and words as part of the sexual abuse they perpetrate and promote, there is really no end to the possible manipulations of the First Amendment to protect like forms of exploitation. All any exploiter has to do is to interject speech into any practice of exploitation, however malignant, and hide the whole practice behind the First Amendment. By isolating the speech elements in other practices of discrimination and asserting their absolute protection, the discrimination could be made to disappear. Consider, for example, a common situation in sexual harassment in employment, where a "speech" element—a sexual proposition from a supervisor—is part of a chain of events leading to an adverse employment consequence. *See*, e.g., *Tomkins v. Public Serv. Elec. & Gas Co.*, 568 F.2d 1044, 1045 (3d Cir. 1977), in which a conversation over lunch was a crucial component of the Title VII violation. No court has held that the mere presence of words in the process of discrimination turns the discrimination into protected activity. The speech is part of the discrimination. The Constitution places no value on discrimination. . . .

If the First Amendment is not to protect those who have power against the just claims of those who need equality; if pornography is sexual exploitation and produces sexual abuse and discrimination; then the Ordinance is more than justified. It saves our constitutional system from the indignity of protecting sex-based abuse. It exonerates principles of equity by allowing them vitality and potency. It shows that law can actively help the powerless and not be paralyzed by the cynical manipulations of sadists and profiteers. It is an appropriate and care- fully balanced response to a social harm of staggering magnitude.

CONCLUSION

For the foregoing reasons, the judgment of the District Court should be reversed.

POSTSCRIPT

Should Pornography Be Protected by the First Amendment?

The antipornography forces have not been very successful in the courts, but they may have won at least one battle in the war. The pornography issue has attracted the attention of politicians, and attempts to regulate content seem destined to continue. It will be very interesting to follow the continuing clashes between First Amendment rights and those favoring restrictions on pornographic material to see whether or not the process of law will be influenced by the public debate.

It is also worth keeping in mind that the problem is no longer mainly one of books, magazines, and film. Pornography is one of the fastest growing segments of the videotape market. The growth in this market has undoubtedly influenced many of those who fear the effects of pornography. Should different standards apply to tapes? Should the fact that they can be viewed in the privacy of one's home make them less or more of a public concern? Congress and the Federal Communications Commission have attempted to establish penalties recently for both phone sex services and for "indecent" speech on radio and television. The ease of making and copying videotapes makes pornographic tapes a more difficult regulatory target. The relationship between the development of new communications technologies and the pornography explosion is discussed in E. Katsh, *The Electronic Media and The Transformation of Law* (Oxford University Press, 1989). The Supreme Court addressed the phone sex issue in *Sable Communications of California, Inc. v. FCC*, 109 S. Ct. 2829 (1989).

The *Hudnut* case is discussed in Brest and Vandenberg, "Politics, Feminism, and the Constitution: The Anti-Pornography Movement in Minneapolis," 39 *Stanford Law Review* 607 (1987); Benson, "Pornography and the First Amendment: *American Booksellers v. Hudnut*," 9 *Harvard Women's Law Journal* 153 (1986); *Final Report of the Attorney General's Commission on Pornography* (1986); Downs, *The New Politics of Pornography* (University of Chicago Press, 1989); C. MacKinnon, *Toward a Feminist Theory of the State* (Harvard University Press, 1989); and C. MacKinnon, *Feminism Unmodified: Discourses on Life and Law* (Harvard University Press, 1989).

Recent writings on the problem of pornography include Symposium, *Law and Contemporary Problems* (Winter 1988); Hawkins and Zimring, *Pornography in a Free Society* (Cambridge University Press, 1989); C. McKinnion, "Pornography, Civil Rights, and Speech," 20 *Harvard Civil Rights–Civil Liberties Law Review* 1 (1985); A. Dworkin, *Pornography: Men Possessing Women* (E. P. Dutton, 1981); A. Dworkin, "Against The Male Flood: Censorship, Pornography and Equality," 8 *Harvard Women's Law Journal* 1 (1985); Note, "Feminism, Pornography and the Law," 133 *University of Pennsylvania Law Review* 497 (1985); and Note, "Anti-Pornography Laws and First Amendment Values," 98 *Harvard Law Review* 460 (1984). Child pornography was dealt with by the Supreme Court in *New York v. Ferber*, 458 U.S. 747. The most relevant obscenity case is *Miller v. California*, 413 U.S. 15 (1973).

ISSUE 9

Is Affirmative Action Constitutional?

YES: Thurgood Marshall, from Dissenting Opinion, *Regents of the University of California v. Allan Bakke,* U.S. Supreme Court (1978)

NO: Potter Stewart, from Dissenting Opinion, *H. Earl Fullilove v. Philip M. Klutznick,* U.S. Supreme Court (1980)

ISSUE SUMMARY

YES: Supreme Court justice Thurgood Marshall points to past discrimination and argues that we must find a way to compensate for the years of disadvantage.

NO: Justice Potter Stewart contends that the law and the Constitution must not discriminate on the basis of race, for whatever reason.

The most widely publicized Supreme Court case of the late 1970s was that of the *Regents of the University of California v. Allan Bakke,* 438 U.S. 265 (1978). Bakke had been denied admission to the medical school of the University of California, Davis, even though he had ranked higher than some minority applicants who were admitted to the school. He sued, asserting that the affirmative action program, which reserved 16 of 100 places for minority students, discriminated against him because of his race and that "reverse discrimination" of this sort violated his constitutional right to equal protection of the laws.

In its decision, the Supreme Court held that Bakke should prevail and be admitted to the medical school. Rigid quotas, it ruled, were indeed prohibited by the Constitution. More importantly, however, the Court also indicated that affirmative action programs that did not impose quotas would be permissible. Thus, if the University of California had an admissions program that gave some preference to an ethnic or racial group and that took race or sex into account along with test scores, geographical origins, extracurricular activities, and so on, it would have been upheld. It is fair to say, therefore, that although Bakke won, the principle of affirmative action without rigid quotas also won.

The *Bakke* case, as is often the case with Supreme Court decisions, raised as many questions as it answered. It inevitably led to cases involving the validity of affirmative action programs in contexts different from that in *Bakke.* In *United Steelworkers v. Weber,* 443 U.S. 193 (1979), the Steelworkers

Union and the Kaiser Aluminum and Chemical Company negotiated a collective bargaining agreement that set aside 50 percent of trainee positions for blacks, until their low percentage (2 percent) among Kaiser craft employees rose to approximate their percentage (39 percent) in the local labor force. This case included a strict quota, but the Supreme Court upheld the program since it did not involve state action and was, according to Justice Lewis F. Powell, Jr., "adopted voluntarily" (even though it was begun in response to criticism by the Federal Office of Contract Compliance).

In 1989, in a case that did involve government, the Court ruled that a municipal public works program that allotted 30 percent of its funds for minority contractors was unconstitutional (*City of Richmond v. J. A. Croson Co.*, 109 S. Ct. 706, 1989). In the absence of some specific evidence of discrimination, such a program was held to violate the white contractors' rights to equal protection of the law. The case has been a major blow to local governmental efforts to increase minority involvement in construction, although similar programs mandated by Congress are still constitutional.

Should the law permit otherwise equal applicants to be treated differently on the basis of sex, race, or ethnic background? In the following excerpt from his dissenting opinion in the *Bakke* case, Justice Thurgood Marshall argues that such a practice is necessary to remedy past injuries. In his dissent in the *Fullilove* case, Justice Potter Stewart asserts that such preferences are impermissible and unconstitutional forms of discrimination.

In their opinions, the justices outline the legal reasons and principles for and against affirmative action programs. Yet, more is involved in these cases than the development of a consistent body of law. Affirmative action is an experiment that tests the power of law. In his exceptional book about the 1954 school desegregation cases, *Simple Justice* (Alfred A. Knopf, 1976), Richard Kluger describes discussions in 1929 about what strategies could be used to promote the legal rights of southern blacks. At that time, Roger Baldwin of the American Civil Liberties Union expressed some skepticism that the law could be used to this end "because forces that keep the Negro under subjection will find some way of accomplishing their purposes, law or no law." Such an attitude toward affirmative action programs and their real impact upon institutions might not be inappropriate today. Affirmative action is legally required of public institutions and many private ones, but it is not yet clear that any substantial change has resulted. Nor is it clear that the judges of the Supreme Court agree on standards that would govern affirmative action plans that differ from the ones already ruled upon.

YES

Thurgood Marshall

COMPENSATION FOR PAST
DISCRIMINATION

Mr. Justice Marshall dissenting.

I do not agree that petitioner's admissions program violates the Constitution. For it must be remembered that, during most of the past 200 years, the Constitution as interpreted by this Court did not prohibit the most ingenious and pervasive forms of discrimination against the Negro. Now, when a State acts to remedy the effects of that legacy of discrimination, I cannot believe that this same Constitution stands as a barrier.

I

A. Three hundred and fifty years ago, the Negro was dragged to this country in chains to be sold into slavery. Uprooted from his homeland and thrust into bondage for forced labor, the slave was deprived of all legal rights. It was unlawful to teach him to read; he could be sold away from his family and friends at the whim of his master; and killing or maiming him was not a crime. The system of slavery brutalized and dehumanized both master and slave.[1]

The denial of human rights was etched into the American Colonies' first attempts at establishing self-government. When the colonists determined to seek their independence from England, they drafted a unique document cataloguing their grievances against the King and proclaiming as "self-evident" that "all men are created equal" and are endowed "with certain unalienable Rights," including those to "Life, Liberty and the pursuit of Happiness." The self-evident truths and the unalienable rights were intended, however, to apply only to white men. An earlier draft of the Declaration of Independence, submitted by Thomas Jefferson to the Continental Congress, had included among the charges against the King that

"[h]e has waged cruel war against human nature itself, violating its most sacred rights of life and liberty in the persons of a distant people who never

From *Regents of the University of California v. Allan Bakke*, 98 S.Ct. 2733, 438 U.S. 265, 57 L.Ed. 2d 750 (1978).

offended him, captivating and carrying them into slavery in another hemisphere, or to incur miserable death in their transportation thither." Franklin 88.

The Southern delegation insisted that the charge be deleted; the colonists themselves were implicated in the slave trade, and inclusion of this claim might have made it more difficult to justify the continuation of slavery once the ties to England were severed. Thus, even as the colonists embarked on a course to secure their own freedom and equality, they ensured perpetuation of the system that deprived a whole race of those rights.

The implicit protection of slavery embodied in the Declaration of Independence was made explicit in the Constitution, which treated a slave as being equivalent to three-fifths of a person for purposes of apportioning representatives and taxes among the States. Art. I, § 2. The Constitution also contained a clause ensuring that the "Migration or Importation" of slaves into the existing States would be legal until at least 1808, Art. I, § 9, and a fugitive slave clause requiring that when a slave escaped to another State, he must be returned on the claim of the master, Art. IV, § 2. In their declaration of the principles that were to provide the cornerstone of the new Nation, therefore, the Framers made it plain that "we the people," for whose protection the Constitution was designed, did not include those whose skins were the wrong color. As Professor John Hope Franklin has observed, Americans "proudly accepted the challenge and responsibility of their new political freedom by establishing the machinery and safeguards that insured the continued enslavement of blacks." Franklin 100.

The individual States likewise established the machinery to protect the system of slavery through the promulgation of the Slave Codes, which were designed primarily to defend the property interest of the owner in his slave. The position of the Negro slave as mere property was confirmed by this Court in *Dred Scott v. Sandford*, 19 How. 393, 15 L.Ed. 691 (1857), holding that the Missouri Compromise—which prohibited slavery in the portion of the Louisiana Purchase Territory north of Missouri—was unconstitutional because it deprived slave owners of their property without due process. The Court declared that under the Constitution a slave was property, and "[t]he right to traffic in it, like an ordinary article of merchandise and property, was guaranteed to the citizens of the United States. . . ." *Id.*, at 451. The Court further concluded that Negroes were not intended to be included as citizens under the Constitution but were "regarded as beings of an inferior order . . . altogether unfit to associate with the white race, either in social or political relations; and so far inferior, that they had no rights which the white man was bound to respect. . . ." *Id.*, at 407.

B. The status of the Negro as property was officially erased by his emancipation at the end of the Civil War. But the long-awaited emancipation, while freeing the Negro from slavery, did not bring him citizenship or equality in any meaningful way. Slavery was replaced by a system of "laws which imposed upon the colored race onerous disabilities and burdens, and curtailed their rights in the pursuit of life, liberty, and property to such an extent that their freedom was of little value." *Slaughter-House Cases*, 16 Wall 36, 70, 21 L.Ed. (1873). Despite the passage of the Thirteenth, Fourteenth, and Fifteenth Amendments, the Negro was systematically denied the rights those Amendments were supposed to secure. The combined actions and inactions of the State and Federal Governments maintained Negroes in a position of legal inferiority for another century after the Civil War.

The Southern States took the first steps to re-enslave the Negroes. Immediately following the end of the Civil War, many of the provisional legislatures passed Black Codes, similar to the Slave Codes, which, among other things, limited the rights of Negroes to own or rent property and permitted imprisonment for breach of employment contracts. Over the next several decades, the South managed to disenfranchise the Negroes in spite of the Fifteenth Amendment by various techniques, including poll taxes, deliberately complicated balloting processes, property and literacy qualifications, and finally the white primary.

Congress responded to the legal disabilities being imposed in the Southern States by passing the Reconstruction Acts and the Civil Rights Acts. Congress also responded to the needs of the Negroes at the end of the Civil War by establishing the Bureau of Refugees, Freedmen, and Abandoned Lands, better known as the Freedmen's Bureau, to supply food, hospitals, land, and education to the newly freed slaves. Thus, for a time it seemed as if the Negro might be protected from the continued denial of his civil rights and might be relieved of the disabilities that prevented him from taking his place as a free and equal citizen.

That time, however, was short-lived. Reconstruction came to a close, and, with the assistance of this Court, the Negro was rapidly stripped of his new civil rights. In the words of C. Vann Woodward: "By narrow and ingenious interpretation [the Supreme Court's] decisions over a period of years had whittled away a great part of the authority presumably given the government for protection of civil rights." Woodward 139.

The Court began by interpreting the Civil War Amendments in a manner that sharply curtailed their substantive protections. See, e.g., *Slaughter-House Cases, supra; United States v. Reese,* 92 U.S. 214, 23 L.Ed. 563 (1876); *United States v. Cruikshank,* 92 U.S. 542, 23 L.Ed. 588 (1876). Then in the notorious *Civil Rights Cases,* 109 U.S. 3, 3 S.Ct. 18, 27 L.Ed. 835 (1883), the Court strangled Congress' efforts to use its power to promote racial equality. In those cases the Court invalidated sections of the Civil Rights Act of 1875 that made it a crime to deny equal access to "inns, public conveyances, theatres and other places of public amusement." *Id.,* at 10, 3 S.Ct., at 20. According to the Court, the Fourteenth Amendment gave Congress the power to proscribe only discriminatory action by the State. The Court ruled that the Negroes who were excluded from public places suffered only an invasion of their social rights at the hands of private individuals, and Congress had no power to remedy that. *Id.,* at 24–25, 3 S.Ct., at 31. "When a man has emerged from slavery, and by the aid of beneficent legislation has shaken off the inseparable concomitants of that state," the Court concluded, "there must be some stage in the progress of his elevation when he takes the rank of a mere citizen, and ceases to be the special favorite of the laws. . . ." *Id.,* at 25, 3 S.Ct., at 31. As Mr. Justice Harlan noted in dissent, however, the Civil War Amendments and Civil Rights Acts did not make the Negroes the "special favorite" of the laws but instead "sought to accomplish in reference to that race . . . —what had already been done in every State of the Union for the white race—to secure and protect rights belonging to them as freemen and citizens; nothing more." *Id.*, at 61, 3 S.Ct., at 57.

The Court's ultimate blow to the Civil War Amendments and to the equality of Negroes came in *Plessy v. Ferguson*, 163 U.S. 537, 16 S.Ct. 1138, 41 L.Ed. 256 (1896). In upholding a Louisiana law that required railway companies to provide "equal but separate" accommodations for whites and Negroes, the Court held that the Fourteenth Amendment was not intended "to abolish distinctions based upon color, or to enforce social, as distinguished from political equality, or a commingling of the two races upon terms unsatisfactory to either." *Id.*, at 544, 16 S.Ct., at 1140. Ignoring totally the realities of the positions of the two races, the Court remarked:

> "We consider the underlying fallacy of the plaintiff's argument to consist in the assumption that the enforced separation of the two races stamps the colored race with a badge of inferiority. If this be so, it is not by reason of anything found in the act, but solely because the colored race chooses to put that construction upon it." *Id.*, at 551, 16 S.Ct., at 1143.

Mr. Justice Harlan's dissenting opinion recognized the bankruptcy of the Court's reasoning. He noted that the "real meaning" of the legislation was "that colored citizens are so inferior and degraded that they cannot be allowed to sit in public coaches occupied by white citizens." *Id.*, at 560, 16 S.Ct., at 1147. He expressed his fear that if like laws were enacted in other States, "the effect would be in the highest degree mischievous." *Id.*, at 563, 16 S.Ct., at 1148. Although slavery would

have disappeared, the States would retain the power "to interfere with the full enjoyment of the blessings of freedom; to regulate civil rights, common to all citizens, upon the basis of race; and to place in a condition of legal inferiority a large body of American citizens. . . ." *Ibid.*

The fears of Mr. Justice Harlan were soon to be realized. In the wake of *Plessy*, many States expanded their Jim Crow laws, which had up until that time been limited primarily to passenger trains and schools. The segregation of the races was extended to residential areas, parks, hospitals, theaters, waiting rooms, and bathrooms. These were even statutes and ordinances which authorized separate phone booths for Negroes and whites, which required that textbooks used by children of one race be kept separate from those used by the other, and which required that Negro and white prostitutes be kept in separate districts. In 1898, after *Plessy*, the Charlestown News and Courier printed a parody of Jim Crow laws:

> " 'If there must be Jim Crow cars on the railroads, there should be Jim Crow cars on the street railways. Also on all passenger boats. . . . If there are to be Jim Crow cars, moreover, there should be Jim Crow waiting saloons at all stations, and Jim Crow eating houses. . . . There should be Jim Crow sections of the jury box, and a separate Jim Crow dock and witness stand in every court—and a Jim Crow Bible for colored witnesses to kiss.' " Woodward 68.

The irony is that before many years had passed, with the exception of the Jim Crow witness stand, "all the improbable applications of the principle suggested by the editor in derision had been put into practice—down to and including the Jim Crow Bible." *Id.*, at 69.

Nor were the laws restricting the rights of Negroes limited solely to the Southern States. In many of the Northern States, the Negro was denied the right to vote, prevented from serving on juries, and excluded from theaters, restaurants, hotels, and inns. Under President Wilson, the Federal Government began to require segregation in government buildings; desks of Negro employees were curtained off; separate bathrooms and separate tables in the cafeterias were provided; and even the galleries of the Congress were segregated. When his segregationist policies were attacked, President Wilson responded that segregation was "not humiliating but a benefit" and that he was "rendering [the Negroes] more safe in their possession of office and less likely to be discriminated against." Kluger 91.

The enforced segregation of the races continued into the middle of the 20th century. In both World Wars, Negroes were for the most part confined to separate military units; it was not until 1948 that an end to segregation in the military was ordered by President Truman. And the history of the exclusion of Negro children from white public schools is too well known and recent to require repeating here. That Negroes were deliberately excluded from public graduate and professional schools—and thereby denied the opportunity to become doctors, lawyers, engineers, and the like—is also well established. It is of course true that some of the Jim Crow laws (which the decisions of this Court had helped to foster) were struck down by this Court in a series of decisions leading up to *Brown v. Board of Education*, 347 U.S. 483, 74 S.Ct. 686, 98 L.Ed. 873 (1954). See, e.g., *Morgan v. Virginia*, 328 U.S. 373, 66 S.Ct. 1050, 90 L.Ed. 1317 (1946); *Sweatt v. Painter*, 339 U.S. 629, 70 S.Ct. 848, 94 L.Ed. 1114 (1950); *McLaurin v. Oklahoma State Regents*, 339 U.S. 637, 70 S.Ct. 851, 94 L.Ed. 1149 (1950). Those decisions, however, did not automatically end segregation, nor did they move Negroes from a position of legal inferiority to one of equality. The legacy of years of slavery and of years of second-class citizenship in the wake of emancipation could not be so easily eliminated.

II

The position of the Negro today in America is the tragic but inevitable consequence of centuries of unequal treatment. Measured by any benchmark of comfort or achievement, meaningful equality remains a distant dream for the Negro.

A Negro child today has a life expectancy which is shorter by more than five years than that of a white child. The Negro child's mother is over three times more likely to die of complications in childbirth, and the infant mortality rate for Negroes is nearly twice that for whites. The median income of the Negro family is only 60% that of the median of a white family, and the percentage of Negroes who live in families with incomes below the poverty line is nearly four times greater than that of whites.

When the Negro child reaches working age, he finds that America offers him significantly less than it offers his white counterpart. For Negro adults, the unemployment rate is twice that of whites, and the unemployment rate for Negro teenagers is nearly three times that of white teenagers. A Negro male who completes four years of college can expect a median annual income of merely $110 more than a white male who has only a high school diploma. Although Negroes represent 11.5% of the population, they are only 1.2% of the lawyers, and judges, 2% of the physicians, 2.3% of the dentists, 1.1% of the engineers and 2.6% of the college and university professors.

The relationship between those figures and the history of unequal treatment afforded to the Negro cannot be denied. At every point from birth to death the impact of the past is reflected in the still disfavored position of the Negro.

In light of the sorry history of discrimination and its devastating impact on the lives of Negroes, bringing the Negro into the mainstream of American life should be a state interest of the highest order. To fail to do so is to ensure that America will forever remain a divided society.

III

I do not believe that the Fourteenth Amendment requires us to accept that fate. Neither its history nor our past cases lend any support to the conclusion that a university may not remedy the cumulative effects of society's discrimination by giving consideration to race in an effort to increase the number and percentage of Negro doctors.

A. This Court long ago remarked that

> "in any fair and just construction of any section or phrase of these [Civil War] amendments, it is necessary to look to the purpose which we have said was the pervading spirit of them all, the evil which they were designed to remedy. . . ." *Slaughter-House Cases*, 16 Wall., at 72.

It is plain that the Fourteenth Amendment was not intended to prohibit measures designed to remedy the effects of the Nation's past treatment of Negroes. The Congress that passed the Fourteenth Amendment is the same Congress that passed the 1866 Freedmen's Bureau Act, an Act that provided many of its benefits only to Negroes. Act of July 16, 1866, ch. 200, 14 Stat. 173; see *supra*, at 2800. Although the Freedmen's Bureau legislation provided aid for refugees, thereby including white persons within some of the relief measures, 14 Stat. 174; see also Act of Mar. 3, 1865, ch. 90, 13 Stat. 507, the bill was regarded, to the dismay of many Congressmen, as "solely and entirely for the freedmen, and to the exclusion of all other persons. . . ." Cong. Globe, 39th Cong., 1st Sess., 544 (1866) (remarks of Rep. Taylor). See also *id.*, at 634–635 (remarks of Rep. Chanler). Indeed, the bill was bitterly opposed on the ground that it "undertakes to make the Negro in some respects . . . superior . . . and gives them favors that the poor white boy in the North cannot get." *Id.*, at 401 (remarks of Sen. McDougall). See also *id.*, at 319 (remarks of Sen. Hendricks); *id.*, at 362 (remarks of Sen. Saulsbury); *id.*, at 397 (remarks of Sen. Willey); *id.*, at 544 (remarks of Rep. Taylor). The bill's supporters defended it—not by rebutting the claim of special treatment—but by pointing to the need for such treatment:

> "The very discrimination it makes between 'destitute and suffering' Negroes, and destitute and suffering white paupers, proceeds upon the distinction that, in the omitted case, civil rights and immunities are already sufficiently protected by the possession of political power, the absence of which in the case provided for necessitates governmental protection." *Id.*, at App. 75 (remarks of Rep. Phelps).

Despite the objection to the special treatment the bill would provide for Negroes, it was passed by Congress. *Id.*, at 421, 688. President Johnson vetoed this bill and also a subsequent bill that contained some modifications; one of his principle objections to both bills was that they gave special benefits to Negroes. 8 Messages and Papers of the Presidents 3596, 3599, 3620, 3623 (1897). Rejecting the concerns of the President and the bill's opponents, Congress overrode the President's second veto. Cong. Globe, 39th Cong., 1st Sess., 3842, 3850 (1866).

Since the Congress that considered and rejected the objections to the 1866 Freedmen's Bureau Act concerning special relief to Negroes also proposed the Fourteenth Amendment, it is inconceivable that the Fourteenth Amendment was intended to prohibit all race-conscious relief measures. It "would be a distortion of the policy manifested in that amendment, which was adopted to prevent state legislation designed to perpetuate discrimination on the basis of race or color." *Railway Mail Assn. v. Corsi,* 326 U.S. 88, 94, 65 S.Ct. 1483, 1487, 89 L.Ed. 2072 (1945), to hold that it barred state action to remedy the effects of that discrimination. Such a result would pervert the intent of the Framers by substituting abstract equality for the genuine equality the Amendment was intended to achieve.

B. As has been demonstrated in our joint opinion, this Court's past cases establish the constitutionality of race-conscious remedial measures. Beginning with the school desegregation cases, we recognized that even absent a judicial or legislative finding of constitutional violation, a school board constitutionally could consider the race of students in making school-assignment decisions. See

Swann v. Charlotte-Mecklenburg Board of Education, 402 U.S. 1, 16, 91 S.Ct. 1267, 1276, 28 L.Ed.2d 554 (1971); *McDaniel v. Barresi,* 402 U.S. 39, 41, 91 S.Ct. 1287, 1288, 28 L.Ed.2d 582 (1971). We noted, moreover, that a

> "flat prohibition against assignment of students for the purpose of creating a racial balance must inevitably conflict with the duty of school authorities to disestablish dual school systems. As we have held in *Swann,* the Constitution does not compel any particular degree of racial balance or mixing, but when past and continuing constitutional violations are found, some ratios are likely to be useful as starting points in shaping a remedy. An absolute prohibition against use of such a device—even as a starting point—contravenes the implicit command of *Green v. County School Board,* 391 U.S. 430 [88 S.Ct. 1689, 20 L.Ed.2d 716] (1968), that all reasonable methods be available to formulate an effective remedy." *Board of Education v. Swann,* 402 U.S. 43, 46, 91 S.Ct. 1284, 1286, 28 L.Ed.2d 586 (1971).

As we have observed, "[a]ny other approach would freeze the status quo that is the very target of all desegregation processes." *McDaniel v. Barresi, supra,* 402 U.S. at 41, 91 S.Ct. at 1289.

Only last Term, in *United Jewish Organizations v. Carey,* 430 U.S. 144, 97 S.Ct. 996, 51 L.Ed. 229 (1977), we upheld a New York reapportionment plan that was deliberately drawn on the basis of race to enhance the electoral power of Negroes and Puerto Ricans; the plan had the effect of diluting the electoral strength of the Hasidic Jewish community. We were willing in *UJO* to sanction the remedial use of a racial classification even though it disadvantaged otherwise "innocent" individuals. In another case last Term, *Califano v. Webster,* 430 U.S. 313,

97 S.Ct. 1192, 51 L.Ed.2d 360 (1977), the Court upheld a provision in the Social Security laws that discriminated against men because its purpose was "the permissible one of redressing our society's longstanding disparate treatment of women.' " *Id.*, at 317, 97 S.Ct. at 1195, quoting *Califano v. Goldfarb*, 430 U.S. 199, 209, n. 8, 97 S.Ct. 1021, 1028, 51 L.Ed.2d 270 (1977) (plurality opinion). We thus recognized the permissibility of remedying past societal discrimination through the use of otherwise disfavored classifications. . . .

IV

While I applaud the judgment of the Court that a university may consider race in its admissions process, it is more than a little ironic that, after several hundred years of class-based discrimination against Negroes, the Court is unwilling to hold that a class-based remedy for that discrimination is permissible. In declining to so hold, today's judgment ignores the fact that for several hundred years Negroes have been discriminated against, not as individuals, but rather solely because of the color of their skins. It is unnecessary in 20th-century America to have individual Negroes demonstrate that they have been victims of racial discrimination; the racism of our society has been so pervasive that none, regardless of wealth or position, has managed to escape its impact. The experience of Negroes in America has been different in kind, not just in degree, from that of other ethnic groups. It is not merely the history of slavery alone but also that a whole people were marked as inferior by the law. And that mark has endured. The dream of America as the great melting pot has not been realized for the Negro; be-

cause of his skin color he never even made it into the pot.

These differences in the experiences of the Negro make it difficult for me to accept that Negroes cannot be afforded greater protection under the Fourteenth Amendment where it is necessary to remedy the effects of past discrimination. In the *Civil Rights Cases, supra,* the Court wrote that the Negro emerging from slavery must cease "to be the special favorite of the laws." 109 U.S., at 25, 3 S.Ct., at 31, see *supra,* at 2800. We cannot in light of the history of the last century yield to that view. Had the Court in that decision and others been willing to "do for human liberty and the fundamental rights of American citizenship, what it did . . . for the protection of slavery and the rights of the masters of fugitive slaves," 109 U.S., at 53, 3 S.Ct., at 51 (Harlan, J., dissenting), we would not need now to permit the recognition of any "special wards."

Most importantly, had the Court been willing in 1896, in *Plessy v. Ferguson,* to hold that the Equal Protection Clause forbids differences in treatment based on race, we would not be faced with this dilemma in 1978. We must remember, however, that the principle that the "constitution is color-blind" appeared only in the opinion of the lone dissenter. 163 U.S., at 559, 16 S.Ct., at 1146. The majority of the Court rejected the principle of color-blindness, and for the next 58 years, from *Plessy* to *Brown v. Board of Education,* ours was a Nation where, *by law,* an individual could be given "special" treatment based on the color of his skin.

It is because of a legacy of unequal treatment that we now must permit the institutions of this society to give consideration to race in making decisions about who will hold the positions of influence, affluence, and prestige in America. For far too long, the doors to those positions have been shut to Negroes. If we are ever to become a fully integrated society, one in which the color of a person's skin will not determine the opportunities available to him or her, we must be willing to take steps to open those doors. I do not believe that anyone can truly look into America's past and still find that a remedy for the effects of that past is impermissible.

It has been said that this case involves only the individual, Bakke, and this University. I doubt, however, that there is a computer capable of determining the number of persons and institutions that may be affected by the decision in this case. For example, we are told by the Attorney General of the United States that at least 27 federal agencies have adopted regulations requiring recipients of federal funds to take "affirmative action to overcome the effects of conditions which resulted in limiting participation . . . by persons of a particular race, color, or national origin." Supplemental Brief for United States as *Amicus Curiae* 16 (emphasis added). I cannot even guess the number of state and local governments that have set up affirmative-action programs, which may be affected by today's decision.

I fear that we have come full circle. After the Civil War our Government started several "affirmative action" programs. This Court in the *Civil Rights Cases* and *Plessy v. Ferguson* destroyed the movement toward complete equality. For almost a century no action was taken, and this nonaction was with the tacit approval of the courts. Then we had *Brown v. Board of Education* and the Civil Rights Acts of Congress, followed by numerous affirmative-action programs. *Now,* we have this Court again stepping in, this time to stop affirmative-action programs of the type used by the University of California.

NOTES

1. The history recounted here is perhaps too well known to require documentation. But I must acknowledge the authorities on which I rely in retelling it. J. Franklin, *From Slavery to Freedom* (4th ed. 1974) (hereinafter Franklin); R. Kluger, *Simple Justice* (1975) (hereinafter Kluger); C. Woodward, *The Strange Career of Jim Crow* (3d ed. 1974) (hereinafter Woodward).

NO
Potter Stewart

THE CONSTITUTION AND DISCRIMINATION

Mr. Justice Stewart, with whom Mr. Justice Rehnquist joins, dissenting.

"Our Constitution is color-blind, and neither knows nor tolerates classes among citizens. . . . The law regards man as man, and takes no account of his surroundings or of his color. . . ." Those words were written by a Member of this Court 84 years ago. *Plessy v. Ferguson*, 163 U.S. 537, 16 S.Ct. 1138, 1146, 41 L.Ed. 256 (Harlan, J., dissenting). His colleagues disagreed with him, and held that a statute that required the separation of people on the basis of their race was constitutionally valid because it was a "reasonable" exercise of legislative power and had been "enacted in good faith for the promotion [of] the public good. . . ." *Id.*, at 550, 16 S.Ct., at 1143. Today, the Court upholds a statute that accords a preference to citizens who are "Negroes, Spanish-speaking, Orientals, Indians, Eskimos, and Aleuts," for much the same reasons. I think today's decision is wrong for the same reason that *Plessy v. Ferguson* was wrong, and I respectfully dissent.

A

The equal protection standard of the Constitution has one clear and central meaning—it absolutely prohibits invidious discrimination by government. That standard must be met by every State under the Equal Protection Clause of the Fourteenth Amendment. . . . And that standard must be met by the United States itself under the Due Process Clause of the Fifth Amendment. . . . Under our Constitution, any official action that treats a person differently on account of his race or ethnic origin is inherently suspect and presumptively invalid. . . .

The hostility of the Constitution to racial classifications by government has been manifested in many cases decided by this Court. . . . And our cases have made clear that the Constitution is wholly neutral in forbidding such racial discrimination, whatever the race may be of those who are its victims. In *Anderson v. Martin*, 375 U.S. 399, 84 S.Ct. 454, 11 L.Ed.2d 430, for instance,

From *H. Earl Fullilove v. Philip M. Klutznick*, 100 S.Ct. 2758, 448 U.S. 448, 65 L.Ed. 2d 902 (1980).

the Court dealt with a state law that required that the race of each candidate for election to public office be designated on the nomination papers and ballots. Although the law applied equally to candidates of whatever race, the Court held that it nonetheless violated the constitutional standard of equal protection. "We see *no relevance*," the Court said, "in the State's pointing up the race of the candidate as bearing upon his qualifications for office." *Id.*, at 403, 84 S.Ct., at 456 (emphasis added). Similarly, in *Loving v. Virginia, supra,* and *McLaughlin v. Florida, supra,* the Court held that statutes outlawing miscegenation and interracial cohabitation were constitutionally invalid, even though the laws penalized all violators equally. The laws were unconstitutional for the simple reason that they penalized individuals solely because of their race, whatever their race might be. . . .

This history contains one clear lesson. Under our Constitution, the government may never act to the detriment of a person solely because of that person's race. The color of a person's skin and the country of his origin are immutable facts that bear no relation to ability, disadvantage, moral culpability, or any other characteristics of constitutionally permissible interest to government. "Distinctions between citizens solely because of their ancestry are by their very nature odious to a free people whose institutions are founded upon the doctrine of equality." *Hirabayashi v. United States,* 320 U.S. 81, 100, 63 S.Ct. 1375, 1385, 87 L.Ed. 1774, quoted in *Loving v. Virginia, supra,* 388 U.S., at 11, 87 S.Ct., at 1823. In short, racial discrimination is by definition invidious discrimination.

The rule cannot be any different when the persons injured by a racially biased law are not members of a racial minority. The guarantee of equal protection is "universal in [its] application, to all persons . . . without regard to any differences of race, of color, or of nationality." *Yick Wo v. Hopkins,* 118 U.S. 356, 369, 6 S.Ct. 1064, 1070, 30 L.Ed. 220. . . . The command of the equal protection guarantee is simple but unequivocal: In the words of the Fourteenth Amendment, "No State shall . . . deny to *any* person . . . the equal protection of the laws." Nothing in this language singles out some "persons" for more "equal" treatment than others. Rather, as the Court made clear in *Shelley v. Kraemer,* 334, U.S. 1, 22, 68 S.Ct. 836, 846, 92 L.Ed. 1161 the benefits afforded by the Equal Protection Clause "are, by its terms, guaranteed to the individual. [They] are personal rights." From the perspective of a person detrimentally affected by a racially discriminatory law, the arbitrariness and unfairness is entirely the same, whatever his skin color and whatever the law's purpose, be it purportedly "for the promotion of the public good" and otherwise.

No one disputes the self-evident proposition that Congress has broad discretion under its Spending Power to disburse the revenues of the United States as it deems best and to set conditions on the receipt of the funds disbursed. No one disputes that Congress has the authority under the Commerce Clause to regulate contracting practices on federally funded public works projects, or that it enjoys broad powers under § 5 of the Fourteenth Amendment "to enforce by appropriate legislation" the provisions of that Amendment. But these self-evident truisms do not begin to answer the question before us in this case. For in the exercise of its powers,

Congress must obey the Constitution just as the legislatures of all the States must obey the Constitution in the exercise of their powers. If a law is unconstitutional, it is no less unconstitutional just because it is a product of the Congress of the United States.

B

On its face, the minority business enterprise (MBE) provision at issue in this case denies the equal protection of the law. The Public Works Employment Act of 1977 directs that all project construction shall be performed by those private contractors who submit the lowest competitive bids and who meet established criteria of responsibility. 42 U.S.C. § 6705(e)(1) (1976 ed. Supp. I). One class of contracting firms—defined solely according to the racial and ethnic attributes of their owners—is, however, excepted from the full rigor of these requirements with respect to a percentage of each federal grant. The statute, on its face and in effect, thus bars a class to which the petitioners belong from having the opportunity to receive a government benefit, and bars the members of that class solely on the basis of their race or ethnic background. This is precisely the kind of law that the guarantee of equal protection forbids.

The Court's attempt to characterize the law as a proper remedial measure to counteract the effects of past or present racial discrimination is remarkably unconvincing. The Legislative Branch of government is not a court of equity. It has neither the dispassionate objectivity nor the flexibility that are needed to mold a race-conscious remedy around the single objective of eliminating the effects of past or present discrimination.

But even assuming that Congress has the power, under § 5 of the Fourteenth Amendment or some other constitutional provision, to remedy previous illegal racial discrimination, there is no evidence that Congress has in the past engaged in racial discrimination in its disbursement of federal contracting funds. The MBE provision thus pushes the limits of any such justification far beyond the equal protection standard of the Constitution. Certainly, nothing in the Constitution gives Congress any greater authority to impose detriments on the basis of race than is afforded the Judicial Branch. And a judicial decree that imposes burdens on the basis of race can be upheld only where its sole purpose is to eradicate the actual effects of illegal race discrimination. . . .

The provision at issue here does not satisfy this condition. Its legislative history suggests that it had at least two other objectives in addition to that of counteracting the effects of past or present racial discrimination in the public works construction industry. One such purpose appears to have been to assure to minority contractors a certain percentage of federally funded public works contracts. But, since the guarantee of equal protection immunizes from capricious governmental treatment "persons"—not "races," it can never countenance laws that seek racial balance as a goal in and of itself. "Preferring members of any group for no reason other than race or ethnic origin is discrimination for its own sake. This the Constitution forbids." *Regents of the University of California v. Bakke*, 438 U.S. 265, 307, 98 S.Ct. 2733, 2757, 57 L.Ed.2d 750 (opinion of Powell, J.). Second, there are indications that the MBE provision may have been enacted to compensate for the effects of social, educational, and economic disadvantage. No race, however, has a monopoly on social, educational, or economic disadvantage, and any law that indulges in such a presumption clearly violates the constitutional guarantee of equal protection. Since the MBE provision was in whole or in part designed to effectuate objectives other than the elimination of the effects of racial discrimination, it cannot stand as a remedy that comports with the strictures of equal protection, even if it otherwise could.

C

The Fourteenth Amendment was adopted to ensure that every person must be treated equally by each State regardless of the color of his skin. The Amendment promised to carry to its necessary conclusion a fundamental principle upon which this Nation had been founded—that the law would honor no preference based on lineage. Tragically, the promise of 1868 was not immediately fulfilled, and decades passed before the States and the Federal Government were finally directed to eliminate detrimental classifications based on race. Today, the Court derails this achievement and places its imprimatur on the creation once again by government of privileges based on birth.

The Court, moreover, takes this drastic step without, in my opinion, seriously considering the ramifications of its decision. Laws that operate on the basis of race require definitions of race. Because of the Court's decision today, our statute books will once again have to contain laws that reflect the odious practice of delineating those qualities that make one person a Negro and make another white. Moreover, racial discrimination, even "good faith" racial discrimination, is inevitably a two-edged sword. "[P]referential programs may only reinforce common stereotypes holding that certain groups are unable to achieve success without special protection based on a factor having no relationship to individual worth." *University of California Regents v. Bakke, supra*, 438 U.S., at 298, 98 S.Ct., at 2753 (opinion of Powell, J.). Most importantly, by making race a relevant criterion once again in its own affairs, the Government implicitly teaches the public that the apportionment of rewards and penalties can legitimately be made according to race—rather than according to merit or ability—and that people can, and perhaps should, view themselves and others in terms of their racial characteristics. Notions of "racial entitlement" will be fostered, and private discrimination will necessarily be encouraged. . . .

There are those who think that we need a new Constitution, and their views may someday prevail. But under the Constitution we have, one practice in which government may never engage is the practice of racism—not even "temporarily" and not even as an "experiment."

POSTSCRIPT

Is Affirmative Action Constitutional?

The most significant development of the last two years has not been a court decision but the appointment of Judge Clarence Thomas to the Supreme Court. Judge Thomas has been an outspoken opponent of affirmative action. The justice he replaced was Justice Marshall, who, as the first reading in this issue indicates, was a forceful advocate for affirmative action.

The study of the question of affirmative action calls for an interdisciplinary approach. Justices Marshall and Stewart focus primarily on the legal issue of whether or not such programs violate the Fourteenth Amendment guarantee of equal protection of the laws. Yet beyond the legal issue are philosophical problems of morality and justice, economic issues involving employment and the distribution of scarce resources, and sociological and psychological analyses of racism and sexism.

Affirmative action programs force us to take an honest look at our own attitudes and at the nature of our society. What are the attitudes and practices of our institutions with respect to race and sex? What would we like such attitudes and practices to be in the future? What means should be employed to move us from the current state of affairs to where we would like to be?

Recent litigation in the affirmative action area is discussed in Devins, "Affirmative Action After Reagan," 68 *Texas Law Review* 353 (1989); "Constitutional Scholars' Statement on Affirmative Action After *City of Richmond v. J. A. Croson Co.*," 98 *Yale Law Journal* 1711 (1989); Fried, "Affirmative Action After *City of Richmond v. J. A. Croson Co.*: A Response to the Scholars' Statement," 99 *Yale Law Journal* 155 (1989); and Schwartz, "The 1986 and 1987 Affirmative Action Cases: It's All Over But the Shouting," 86 *Michigan Law Review* 524 (1987). One of the most enlightening law review articles defending affirmative action is Wasserstrom, "Racism, Sexism and Preferential Treatment: An Approach to the Topics," 24 *UCLA Law Review*, pp. 581–622 (1977). A history of the *Bakke* case is found in Dreyfuss and Lawrence, *The Bakke Case: The Politics of Inequality* (Harcourt Brace Jovanovich, 1979). An interesting recent book is Stephen Carter, *Reflections of an Affirmative Action Baby* (Basic Books, 1991).

ISSUE 10

Can States Restrict the Right to Die?

YES: William H. Rehnquist, from Majority Opinion, *Nancy Beth Cruzan v. Director, Missouri Department of Health,* U.S. Supreme Court (1990)

NO: William J. Brennan, Jr., from Dissenting Opinion, *Nancy Beth Cruzan v. Director, Missouri Department of Health,* U.S. Supreme Court (1990)

ISSUE SUMMARY

YES: Supreme Court chief justice William H. Rehnquist recognizes that a competent individual may refuse medical treatment but believes a showing of clear and convincing proof of the individual's wishes is required before allowing the termination of feeding to an incompetent person.
NO: Justice William J. Brennan, Jr., argues that the Court is erecting too high a standard for allowing an individual's wishes to be followed and that Nancy Cruzan did indeed wish to have her feeding discontinued.

To please no one will I prescribe a deadly drug, nor give advice which may cause death.

—Oath of Hippocrates

When a dispute gets to court, the issues before the court tend to be framed differently from the way they are stated in the popular press or in discussions among individuals. Legal discussions in court emphasize different issues from discussions among lay people even when the topic is the same. For example, the substantive question of what the result should be in a particular case, the kind of debate that one often finds on editorial pages of newspapers, may not be the main question in a legal case. Instead, the legal question for the court may be what is the proper procedure to follow or who has the right or authority to do something, leaving the decision of whether or not to perform the act up to the person who has won the case.

One of the most publicized cases of the 1970s involved 21-year-old Karen Ann Quinlan. Quinlan was in a coma, her doctors did not believe she would ever come out of the coma, and all believed, erroneously it turned out, that if her respirator were removed she would stop breathing. The question the court focused on was who had authority over the respirator and who should be responsible for deciding what to do with it. The court did not answer the question of whether or not the respirator should be disconnected but left this tormenting problem to the party that prevailed in the case. Soon after the decision, Quinlan's parents authorized the removal of the respirator. Contrary to what had been predicted, this did not result in her death. She survived another nine years before succumbing in 1985.

The process followed in the Quinlan case, and in the Cruzan case that follows, illustrates a basic distinction made by the law. The law prohibits active euthanasia, in which death results from some positive act, such as a lethal injection. "Mercy killings" fall into this category and can be prosecuted as acts of homicide. The law is more tolerant of passive euthanasia, in which death results from the failure to act or on the removal of life-saving equipment. As you read the following opinions, you should consider whether or not this is a reasonable distinction to make.

While modern debates about euthanasia can be traced back more than 100 years, the necessity for the legal system to become involved is more recent. Not all of these cases raise the same issues. The Quinlan case involved a person who was neither legally dead nor, according to medical opinion, ever likely to regain consciousness. She was unable to make the decision herself and the key questions were whose interests needed to be given priority and how the interests of the individual should be protected. The following case, in that it involves the termination of feeding rather than the removal of life support equipment, is more difficult. Or is it? Due to advances in medical technology, some of the traditional distinctions made in this area are not as clear as they once were. As Alexander Capron, a professor of law at the University of Southern California and a knowledgeable observer in this area, has written,

> The growing medicalization of death also meant that human interventions replaced natural processes. If pneumonia was once the old man's friend, his companion now is an antibiotic; if cardiopulmonary arrest once meant inevitable death, now the cries of 'Code Blue' echo down hospital corridors, as nurses and physicians race to the bedside to jump-start hearts with drugs and electric paddles, and to reinflate lungs with artificial pumps. We have gotten to the point . . . when in the age of miracle drugs and surgical derring-do, no illness can be said to have a natural course. There is no such thing as a 'natural' death. Somewhere along the way for just about every patient, death is forestalled by human choice and human action, or death is allowed to occur because of human choice. Life-support techniques make death a matter of human choice and hence a matter that provokes ethical concern. Who should make the choice? When? And on what grounds?

The *Cruzan* case that follows was probably the most discussed Supreme Court decision of the 1989–90 term. Nancy Cruzan, age 32, had been in a coma for seven years. She was one of an estimated 10,000 persons in the United States in a "vegetative state." She had left no explicit directions on whether or not she would like to continue to be fed and receive treatment if she were ever to be in such a condition. Should her parents be allowed to make this decision under such circumstances? How clear should an incompetent person's wishes be before the parents are allowed to make a decision?

YES

William H. Rehnquist

MAJORITY OPINION

CRUZAN v. MISSOURI DEPARTMENT OF HEALTH

CHIEF JUSTICE REHNQUIST delivered the opinion of the Court.

Petitioner Nancy Beth Cruzan was rendered incompetent as a result of severe injuries sustained during an automobile accident. Co-petitioners Lester and Joyce Cruzan, Nancy's parents and co-guardians, sought a court order directing the withdrawal of their daughter's artificial feeding and hydration equipment after it became apparent that she had virtually no chance of recovering her cognitive faculties. The Supreme Court of Missouri held that because there was no clear and convincing evidence of Nancy's desire to have life-sustaining treatment withdrawn under such circumstances, her parents lacked authority to effectuate such a request. We granted certiorari, and now affirm.

On the night of January 11, 1983, Nancy Cruzan lost control of her car as she traveled down Elm Road in Jasper County, Missouri. The vehicle overturned, and Cruzan was discovered lying face down in a ditch without detectable respiratory or cardiac function. Paramedics were able to restore her breathing and heartbeat at the accident site, and she was transported to a hospital in an unconscious state. An attending neurosurgeon diagnosed her as having sustained probable cerebral contusions, compounded by significant anoxia (lack of oxygen). The Missouri trial court in this case found that permanent brain damage generally results after 6 minutes in an anoxic state; it was estimated that Cruzan was deprived of oxygen from 12 to 14 minutes. She remained in a coma for approximately three weeks and then progressed to an unconscious state in which she was able to orally ingest some nutrition. In order to ease feeding and further the recovery, surgeons implanted a gastrostomy feeding and hydration tube in Cruzan with the consent of her then husband. Subsequent rehabilitative efforts proved unavailing. She now lies in a Missouri state hospital in what is commonly referred to as a persistent vegetative state: generally, a condition in which a person exhibits motor reflexes but evinces no indications of significant cognitive function.[1]

From *Nancy Beth Cruzan v. Director, Missouri Department of Health*, 58 L.W. 4916 (1990). Some notes and case citations omitted.

The State of Missouri is bearing the cost of her care.

After it had become apparent that Nancy Cruzan had virtually no chance of regaining her mental faculties her parents asked hospital employees to terminate the artificial nutrition and hydration procedures. All agree that such a removal would cause her death. The employees refused to honor the request without court approval. The parents then sought and received authorization from the state trial court for termination. The court found that a person in Nancy's condition had a fundamental right under the State and Federal Constitutions to refuse or direct the withdrawal of "death prolonging procedures." The court also found that Nancy's "expressed thoughts at age twenty-five in somewhat serious conversation with a housemate friend that if sick or injured she would not wish to continue her life unless she could live at least halfway normally suggests that given her present condition she would not wish to continue on with her nutrition and hydration."

The Supreme Court of Missouri reversed by a divided vote. The court recognized a right to refuse treatment embodied in the common-law doctrine of informed consent, but expressed skepticism about the application of that doctrine in the circumstances of this case. *Cruzan v. Harmon*, 760 S. W. 2d 408, 416–417 (Mo. 1988) (en banc). The court also declined to read a broad right of privacy into the State Constitution which would "support the right of a person to refuse medical treatment in every circumstance," and expressed doubt as to whether such a right existed under the United States Constitution. *Id.*, at 417–418. It then decided that the Missouri Living Will statute, Mo. Rev. State. §

459.010 *et seq.* (1986), embodied a state policy strongly favoring the preservation of life. 760 S. W. 2d, at 419–420. The court found that Cruzan's statements to her roommate regarding her desire to live or die under certain conditions were "unreliable for the purpose of determining her intent," *id.*, at 424, "and thus insufficient to support the co-guardians claim to exercise substituted judgment on Nancy's behalf." *Id.*, at 426. It rejected the argument that Cruzan's parents were entitled to order the termination of her medical treatment, concluding that "no person can assume that choice for an incompetent in the absence of the formalities required under Missouri's Living Will statutes or the clear and convincing, inherently reliable evidence absent here." *Id.*, at 425. The court also expressed its view that "[b]road policy questions bearing on life and death are more properly addressed by representative assemblies" than judicial bodies. *Id.*, at 426.

We granted certiorari to consider the question of whether Cruzan has a right under the United States Constitution which would require the hospital to withdraw life-sustaining treatment from her under these circumstances. . . .

Before the turn of the century, this Court observed that "[n]o right is held more sacred, or is more carefully guarded, by the common law, than the right of every individual to the possession and control of his own person, free from all restraint or interference of others, unless by clear and unquestionable authority of law." *Union Pacific R. Co. v. Botsford*, 141 U.S. 250, 251 (1891). This notion of bodily integrity has been embodied in the requirement that informed consent is generally required for medical treatment. Justice Cardozo, while on the Court of Appeals of New York, aptly described this doctrine: "Every human being of adult years and sound mind has a right to determine what shall be done with his own body; and a surgeon who performs an operation without his patient's consent commits an assault, for which he is liable in damages." *Schloendorff v. Society of New York Hospital*, 211 N. Y. 125, 129–30, 105 N. E. 92, 93 (1914). The informed consent doctrine has become firmly entrenched in American tort law.

The logical corollary of the doctrine of informed consent is that the patient generally possesses the right not to consent, that is, to refuse treatment. Until about 15 years ago and the seminal decision in *In re Quinlan*, 70 N. J. 10, 355 A. 2d 647, cert. denied *sub nom.*, *Garger v. New Jersey*, 429 U.S. 922 (1976), the number of right-to-refuse-treatment decisions were relatively few.[2] Most of the earlier cases involved patients who refused medical treatment forbidden by their religious beliefs, thus implicating First Amendment rights as well as common law rights of self-determination.[3] More recently, however, with the advance of medical technology capable of sustaining life well past the point where natural forces would have brought certain death in earlier times, cases involving the right to refuse life-sustaining treatment have burgeoned. See 760 S. W. 2d, at 412, n. 4 (collecting 54 reported decisions from 1976–1988).

In the *Quinlan* case, young Karen Quinlan suffered severe brain damage as the result of anoxia, and entered a persistent vegetative state. Karen's father sought judicial approval to disconnect his daughter's respirator. The New Jersey Supreme Court granted the relief, holding that Karen had a right of privacy grounded in the Federal Constitution to terminate treatment. *In re Quinlan*, 70 N. J., at 38–42, 355 A. 2d at 662–664. Recog-

nizing that this right was not absolute, however, the court balanced it against asserted state interests. Noting that the State's interest "weakens and the individual's right to privacy grows as the degree of bodily invasion increases and the prognosis dims," the court concluded that the state interests had to give way in that case. *Id.*, at 41, 355 A. 2d, at 664. The court also concluded that the "only practical way" to prevent the loss of Karen's privacy right due to her incompetence was to allow her guardian and family to decide "whether she would exercise it in these circumstances." *Ibid.*

After *Quinlan*, however, most courts have based a right to refuse treatment either solely on the common law right to informed consent or on both the common law right and a constitutional privacy right. See L. Tribe, American Constitutional Law § 15–11, p. 1365 (2d ed. 1988). In *Superintendent of Belchertown State School v. Saikewicz*, 373 Mass. 728, 370 N. E. 2d 417 (1977), the Supreme Judicial Court of Massachusetts relied on both the right of privacy and the right of informed consent to permit the withholding of chemotherapy from a profoundly-retarded 67-year-old man suffering from leukemia. *Id.*, at 737–738, 370 N. E. 2d, at 424. Reasoning that an incompetent person retains the same rights as a competent individual "because the value of human dignity extends to both," the court adopted a "substituted judgment" standard whereby courts were to determine what an incompetent individual's decision would have been under the circumstances. *Id.*, at 745, 752–753, 757–758, 370 N. E. 2d, at 427, 431, 434. Distilling certain state interests from prior case law—the preservation of life, the protection of the interests of innocent third parties, the prevention of suicide, and the maintenance of the ethical integrity of the medical profession—the court recognized the first interest as paramount and noted it was greatest when an affliction was curable, "as opposed to the State interest where, as here, the issue is not whether, but when, for how long, and at what cost to the individual [a] life may be briefly extended." *Id.*, at 742, 370 N. E. 2d, at 426.

In *In re Storar* 52 N. Y. 2d 363, 420 N. E. 2d 64, cert. denied, 454 U.S. 858 (1981), the New York Court of Appeals declined to base a right to refuse treatment on a constitutional privacy right. Instead, it found such a right "adequately supported" by the informed consent doctrine. *Id.*, at 376–377, 420 N. E. 2d, at 70. In *In re Eichner* (decided with *In re Storar, supra*) an 83-year-old man who had suffered brain damage from anoxia entered a vegetative state and was thus incompetent to consent to the removal of his respirator. The court, however, found it unnecessary to reach the question of whether his rights could be exercised by others since it found the evidence clear and convincing from statements made by the patient when competent that he "did not want to be maintained in a vegetable coma by use of a respirator." *Id.*, at 380, 420 N. E. 2d, at 72. In the companion *Storar* case, a 52-year-old man suffering from bladder cancer had been profoundly retarded during most of his life. Implicitly rejecting the approach taken in *Saikewicz, supra*, the court reasoned that due to such life-long incompetency, "it is unrealistic to attempt to determine whether he would want to continue potentially life prolonging treatment if he were competent." 52 N. Y. 2d, at 380, 420 N. E. 2d, at 72. As the evidence showed that the patient's required blood transfusions did not involve excessive pain and without them his mental and physical abilities would deteriorate, the court concluded that it should not "allow an incompetent patient to bleed to death because someone, even someone as close as a parent or sibling, feels that this is best for one with an incurable disease." *Id.*, at 382, 420 N. E. 2d, at 73.

Many of the later cases build on the principles established in *Quinlan, Saikewicz* and *Storar/Eichner*. For instance, in *In re Conroy*, 98 N. J. 321, 486 A. 2d 1209 (1985), the same court that decided *Quinlan* considered whether a nasogastric feeding tube could be removed from an 84-year-old incompetent nursing-home resident suffering irreversible mental and physical ailments. While recognizing that a federal right of privacy might apply in the case, the court, contrary to its approach in *Quinlan*, decided to base its decision on the common-law right to self-determination and informed consent. 98 N. J., at 348, 486 A. 2d, at 1223. "On balance, the right to self-determination ordinarily outweighs any countervailing state interests, and competent persons generally are permitted to refuse medical treatment, even at the risk of death. Most of the cases that have held otherwise, unless they involved the interest in protecting innocent third parties, have concerned the patient's competency to make a rational and considered choice." *Id.*, at 353–354, 486 A. 2d, at 1225.

Reasoning that the right of self-determination should not be lost merely because an individual is unable to sense a violation of it, the court held that incompetent individuals retain a right to refuse treatment. It also held that such a right could be exercised by a surrogate decisionmaker using a "subjective" standard when there was clear evidence that the incompetent person would have exercised it. Where such evidence was lacking, the court held that an individual's right could still be involved in certain circumstances under objective "best interest" standards. *Id.*, at 361–368, 486 A. 2d, at 1229–1233. Thus, if some trustworthy evidence existed that the individual would have wanted to terminate treatment, but not enough to clearly establish a person's wishes for purposes of the subjective standard, and the burden of a prolonged life from the experience of pain and suffering markedly outweighed its satisfactions, treatment could be terminated under a "limited-objective" standard. Where no trustworthy evidence existed, and a person's suffering would make the administration of life-sustaining treatment inhumane, a "pure-objective" standard could be used to terminate treatment. If none of these conditions obtained, the court held it was best to err in favor of preserving life. *Id.*, at 364–368, 486 A. 2d, at 1231–1233.

The court also rejected certain categorical distinctions that had been drawn in prior refusal-of-treatment cases as lacking substance for decision purposes: the distinction between actively hastening death by terminating treatment and passively allowing a person to die of a disease; between treating individuals as an initial matter versus withdrawing treatment afterwards; between ordinary versus extraordinary treatment; and between treatment by artificial feeding versus other forms of life-sustaining medical procedures. *Id.*, at 369–374, 486 N. E. 2d, at 1233–1237. As to the last item, the court acknowledged the "emotional significance" of food, but noted that feeding by implanted tubes is a "medical procedur[e] with inherent risks and possible side effects, instituted by skilled health-care providers to compensate for impaired physical functioning"

which analytically was equivalent to artificial breathing using a respirator. *Id.*, at 373, 486 A. 2d, at 1236.[4]

In contrast to *Conroy*, the Court of Appeals of New York recently refused to accept less than the clearly expressed wishes of a patient before permitting the exercise of her right to refuse treatment by a surrogate decisionmaker. *In re Westchester County Medical Center on behalf of O'Connor*, 531 N. E. 2d 607 (1988) (*O'Connor*). There, the court, over the objection of the patient's family members, granted an order to insert a feeding tube into a 77-year-old woman rendered incompetent as a result of several strokes. While continuing to recognize a common-law right to refuse treatment, the court rejected the substituted judgment approach for asserting it "because it is inconsistent with our fundamental commitment to the notion that no person or court should substitute its judgment as to what would be an acceptable quality of life for another. Consequently, we adhere to the view that, despite its pitfalls and inevitable uncertainties, the inquiry must always be narrowed to the patient's expressed intent, with every effort made to minimize the opportunity for error." *Id.*, at 530, 531 N. E. 2d, at 613 (citation omitted). The court held that the record lacked the requisite clear and convincing evidence of the patient's expressed intent to withhold life-sustaining treatment. *Id.*, at 531–534, 531 N. E. 2d, at 613–615. . . .

In *In re Estate of Longeway*, 123 Ill. 2d 33, 549 N. E. 2d 292 (1989), the Supreme Court of Illinois considered whether a 76-year-old woman rendered incompetent from a series of strokes had a right to the discontinuance of artificial nutrition and hydration. Noting that the boundaries of a federal right of privacy were uncertain, the court found a right to refuse treatment in the doctrine of informed consent. *Id.*, at 43–45, 549 N. E. 2d, at 296–297. The court further held that the State Probate Act impliedly authorized a guardian to exercise a ward's right to refuse artificial sustenance in the event that the ward was terminally ill and irreversibly comatose. *Id.*, at 45–47, 549 N. E. 2d, at 298. Declining to adopt a best interests standard for deciding when it would be appropriate to exercise a ward's right because it "lets another make a determination of a patient's quality of life," the court opted instead for a substituted judgment standard. *Id.*, at 49, 549 N. E. 2d, at 299. Finding the "expressed intent" standard utilized in *O'Connor, supra,* too rigid, the court noted that other clear and convincing evidence of the patient's intent could be considered. 133 Ill. 2d, at 50–51, 549 N. E. 2d, at 300. The court also adopted the "consensus opinion [that] treats artificial nutrition and hydration as medical treatment." *Id.*, at 42, 549 N. E. 2d, at 296. Cf. *McConnell v. Beverly Enterprises-Connecticut, Inc.*, 209 Conn. 692, 705, 553 A. 2d 596, 603 (1989) (right to withdraw artificial nutrition and hydration found in the Connecticut Removal of Life Support Systems Act, which "provid[es] functional guidelines for the exercise of the common law and constitutional rights of self-determination"; attending physician authorized to remove treatment after finding that patient is in a terminal condition, obtaining consent of family, and considering expressed wishes of patient).[5]

As these cases demonstrate, the common-law doctrine of informed consent is viewed as generally encompassing the right of a competent individual to refuse medical treatment. Beyond that, these decisions demonstrate both similarity and diversity in their approach to deci-

sion of what all agree is a perplexing question with unusually strong moral and ethical overtones. State courts have available to them for decision a number of sources—state constitutions, statutes, and common law—which are not available to us. In this Court, the question is simply and starkly whether the United States Constitution prohibits Missouri from choosing the rule of decision which it did. This is the first case in which we have been squarely presented with the issue of whether the United States Constitution grants what is in common parlance referred to as a "right to die." We follow the judicious counsel of our decision in *Twin City Bank v. Nebeker,* 167 U.S. 197, 202 (1897), where we said that in deciding "a question of such magnitude and importance . . . it is the [better] part of wisdom not to attempt, by any general statement, to cover every possible phase of the subject."

The Fourteenth Amendment provides that no State shall "deprive any person of life, liberty, or property, without due process of law." The principle that a competent person has a constitutionally protected liberty interest in refusing unwanted medical treatment may be inferred from our prior decisions. In *Jacobson v. Massachusetts,* 197 U.S. 11, 24–30 (1905), for instance, the Court balanced an individual's liberty interest in declining an unwanted smallpox vaccine against the State's interest in preventing disease. . . .

Just this Term, in the course of holding that a State's procedures for administering antipsychotic medication to prisoners were sufficient to satisfy due process concerns, we recognized that prisoners possess "a significant liberty interest in avoiding the unwanted administration of antipsychotic drugs under the Due Process Clause of the Fourteenth Amendment." *Washington v. Harper,* (1990) ("The forcible injection of medication into a nonconsenting person's body represents a substantial interference with that person's liberty"). Still other cases support the recognition of a general liberty interest in refusing medical treatment. *Vitek v. Jones,* 445 U.S. 480, 494 (1980) (transfer to mental hospital coupled with mandatory behavior modification treatment implicated liberty interests); *Parham v. J.R.,* 442 U.S. 584, 600 (1979) ("a child, in common with adults, has a substantial liberty interest in not being confined unnecessarily for medical treatment").

But determining that a person has a "liberty interest" under the Due Process Clause does not end the inquiry; "whether respondent's constitutional rights have been violated must be determined by balancing his liberty interests against the relevant state interests." *Youngberg v. Romeo,* 457 U.S. 307, 321 (1982). See also *Mills v. Rogers,* 457 U.S. 291, 299 (1982).

Petitioners insist that under the general holdings of our cases, the forced administration of life-sustaining medical treatment, and even of artificially-delivered food and water essential to life, would implicate a competent person's liberty interest. Although we think the logic of the cases discussed above would embrace such a liberty interest, the dramatic consequences involved in refusal of such treatment would inform the inquiry as to whether the deprivation of that interest is constitutionally permissible. But for purposes of this case, we assume that the United States Constitution would grant a competent person a constitutionally protected right to refuse lifesaving hydration and nutrition.

Petitioners go on to assert that an incompetent person should possess the same right in this respect as is possessed by a competent person. They rely primarily on our decisions in *Parham v. J. R., supra,* and *Youngberg v. Romeo,* 457 U.S. 307 (1982). In *Parham,* we held that a mentally disturbed minor child had a liberty interest in "not being confined unnecessarily for medical treatment," 442 U.S. at 600, but we certainly did not intimate that such a minor child, after commitment, would have a liberty interest in refusing treatment. In *Youngberg,* we held that a seriously retarded adult had a liberty interest in safety and freedom from bodily restraint, 457 U.S., at 320. *Youngberg,* however, did not deal with decisions to administer or withhold medical treatment.

The difficulty with petitioners' claim is that in a sense it begs the question: an incompetent person is not able to make an informed and voluntary choice to exercise hypothetical right to refuse treatment or any other right. Such a "right" must be exercised for her, if at all, by some sort of surrogate. Here, Missouri has in effect recognized that under certain circumstances a surrogate may act for the patient in electing to have hydration and nutrition withdrawn in such a way as to cause death, but it has established a procedural safeguard to assure that the action of the surrogate conforms as best it may to the wishes expressed by the patient while competent. Missouri requires that evidence of the incompetent's wishes as to the withdrawal of treatment be proved by clear and convincing evidence. The question, then, is whether the United States Constitution forbids the establishment of this procedural requirement by the State. We hold that it does not.

Whether or not Missouri's clear and convincing evidence requirement comports with the United States Constitution depends in part on what interests the State may properly seek to protect in this situation. Missouri relies on its interest in the protection and preservation of human life, and there can be no gainsaying this interest. As a general matter, the States—indeed, all civilized nations—demonstrate their commitment to life by treating homicide as serious crime. Moreover, the majority of States in this country have laws imposing criminal penalties on one who assists another to commit suicide. We do not think a State is required to remain neutral in the face of an informed and voluntary decision by a physically-able adult to starve to death.

But in the context presented here, a State has more particular interests at stake. The choice between life and death is a deeply personal decision of obvious and overwhelming finality. We believe Missouri may legitimately seek to safeguard the personal element of this choice through the imposition of heightened evidentiary requirements. It cannot be disputed that the Due Process Clause protects an interest in life as well as an interest in refusing life-sustaining medical treatment. Not all incompetent patients will have loved ones available to serve as surrogate decisionmakers. And even where family members are present, "[t]here will, of course, be some unfortunate situations in which family members will not act to protect a patient." *In re Jobes*, 108 N. J. 394, 419, 529 A. 2d 434, 477 (1987). A State is entitled to guard against potential abuses in such situations. Similarly, a State is entitled to consider that a judicial proceeding to make a determination regarding an incompetent's wishes may very well not be an adversarial one, with the added guarantee of accurate factfinding that the adversary process brings with it. Finally, we think a State

may properly decline to make judgments about the "quality" of life that a particular individual may enjoy, and simply assert an unqualified interest in the preservation of human life to be weighed against the constitutionally protected interests of the individual.

In our view, Missouri has permissibly sought to advance these interests through the adoption of a "clear and convincing" standard of proof to govern such proceedings. "The function of a standard of proof, as that concept is embodied in the Due Process Clause and in the realm of factfinding, is to 'instruct the factfinder concerning the degree of confidence our society thinks he should have in the correctness of factual conclusions for a particular type of adjudication.' " *Addington v. Texas*, 441 U.S. 418, 423 (1979) (quoting *In re Winship*, 397 U.S. 358, 370 (1970) (Harlan, J., concurring)). "This Court has mandated an intermediate standard of proof—'clear and convincing evidence'—when the individual interests at stake in a state proceeding are both 'particularly important' and 'more substantial than mere loss of money.' " *Santosky v. Kramer*, 455 U.S. 745, 756 (1982) (quoting *Addington, supra*, at 424). Thus, such a standard has been required in deportation proceedings, *Woodby v. INS*, 385 U.S. 276 (1966), in denaturalization proceedings, *Schneiderman v. United States*, 320 U.S. 118 (1943), in civil commitment proceedings, *Addington, supra*, and in proceedings for the termination of parental rights. *Santosky, supra*,[6] Further, this level of proof, "or an even higher one, has traditionally been imposed in cases involving allegations of civil fraud, and in a variety of other kinds of civil cases involving such issues as . . . lost wills, oral contracts to make bequests, and the like." *Woodby, supra*, at 285, n. 18.

We think it self-evident that the interests at stake in the instant proceedings are more substantial, both on an individual and societal level, than those involved in a run-of-the-mine civil dispute. But not only does the standard of proof reflect the importance of a particular adjudication, it also serves as "a societal judgment about how the risk of error should be distributed between the litigants." *Santosky, supra,* 455 U.S. at 755; *Addington, supra,* at 423. The more stringent the burden of proof a party must bear, the more that party bears the risk of an erroneous decision. We believe that Missouri may permissibly place an increased risk of an erroneous decision on those seeking to terminate an incompetent individual's life-sustaining treatment. An erroneous decision not to terminate results in a maintenance of the status quo; the possibility of subsequent developments such as advancments in medical science, the discovery of new evidence regarding the patient's intent, changes in the law, or simply the unexpected death of the patient despite the administration of life-sustaining treatment, at least create the potential that a wrong decision will eventually be corrected or its impact mitigated. An erroneous decision to withdraw life-sustaining treatment, however, is not susceptible of correction. In *Santosky,* one of the factors which led the Court to require proof by clear and convincing evidence in a proceeding to terminate parental rights was that a decision in such a case was final and irrevocable. *Santosky, supra,* at 759. The same must be said of the decision to discontinue hydration and nutrition of a patient such as Nancy Cruzan, which all agree will result in her death.

It is also worth noting that most, if not all, States simply forbid oral testimony entirely in determining the wishes of parties in transactions which, while important, simply do not have the consequences that a decision to terminate a person's life does. At common law and by statute in most States, the parole evidence rule prevents the variations of the terms of a written contract by oral testimony. The statute of frauds makes unenforceable oral contracts to leave property by will, and statutes regulating the making of wills universally require that those instruments be in writing. See 2 A. Corbin, Contracts § 398, pp. 360–361 (1950); 2 W. Page, Law of Wills § § 19.3–19.5, pp. 61–71 (1960). There is no doubt that statutes requiring wills to be in writing, and statutes of frauds which require that a contract to make a will be in writing, on occasion frustrate the effectuation of the intent of a particular decedent, just as Missouri's requirement of proof in this case may have frustrated the effectuation of the not-fully-expressed desires of Nancy Cruzan. But the Constitution does not require general rules to work faultlessly; no general rule can.

In sum, we conclude that a State may apply a clear and convincing evidence standard in proceedings where a guardian seeks to discontinue nutrition and hydration of a person diagnosed to be in a persistent vegetative state. We note that many courts which have adopted some sort of substituted judgment procedure in situations like this, whether they limit consideration of evidence to the prior expressed wishes of the incompetent individual, or whether they allow more general proof of what the individual's decision would have been, require a clear and convincing standard of proof for such evidence.

The Supreme Court of Missouri held that in this case the testimony adduced at trial did not amount to clear and convincing proof of the patient's desire to have hydration and nutrition withdrawn. In so doing, it reversed a decision of the Missouri trial court which had found that the evidence "suggest[ed]" Nancy Cruzan would not have desired to continue such measures, but which had not adopted the standard of "clear and convincing evidence" enunciated by the Supreme Court. The testimony adduced at trial consisted primarily of Nancy Cruzan's statements made to a housemate about a year before her accident that she would not want to live should she face life as a "vegetable," and other observations to the same effect. The observations did not deal in terms with withdrawal of medical treatment or of hydration and nutrition. We cannot say that the Supreme Court of Missouri committed constitutional error in reaching the conclusion that it did.[7]

Petitioners alternatively contend that Missouri must accept the "substituted judgment" of close family members even in the absence of substantial proof that their views reflect the views of the patient. They rely primarily upon our decisions in *Michael H. v. Gerald D.*, 491 U.S.——(1989), and *Parham v. J. R.*, 442 U.S. 584 (1979). But we do not think these cases support their claim. In *Michael H.*, we *upheld* the constitutionality of California's favored treatment of traditional family relationships; such a holding may not be turned around into a constitutional requirement that a State *must* recognize the primacy of those relationships in a situation like this. And in *Parham*, where the patient was a minor, we also *upheld* the constitutionality of a state scheme in which parents made certain decisions for mentally ill minors. Here again petitioners would seek to turn a decision which allowed a State to rely on family decisionmaking into a constitutional requirement that the State recognize such decisionmaking. But constitutional law does not work that way.

No doubt is engendered by anything in this record but that Nancy Cruzan's mother and father are loving and caring parents. If the State were required by the United States Constitution to repose a right of "substituted judgment" with anyone, the Cruzans would surely qualify. But we do not think the Due Process Clause requires the State to repose judgment on these matters with anyone but the patient herself. Close family members may have a strong feeling—a feeling not at all ignoble or unworthy, but not entirely disinterested, either—that they do not wish to witness the continuation of the life of a loved one which they regard as hopeless, meaningless, and even degrading. But there is no automatic assurance that the view of close family members will necessarily be the same as the patient's would have been had she been confronted with the prospect of her situation while competent. All of the reasons previously discussed for allowing Missouri to require clear and convincing evidence of the patient's wishes lead us to conclude that the state may choose to defer only to those wishes, rather than confide the decision to close family members.[8]

The judgment of the Supreme Court of Missouri is

Affirmed.

NOTES

1. The State Supreme Court, adopting much of the trial court's findings, described Nancy Cruzan's medical condition as follows:
" . . .(1) [H]er respiration and circulation are not artificially maintained and are within the normal

limits of a thirty-year-old female; (2) she is oblivious to her environment except for reflexive responses to sound and perhaps painful stimuli; (3) she suffered anoxia of the brain resulting in a massive enlargement of the ventricles filling with cerebrospinal fluid in the area where the brain has degenerated and [her] cerebral cortical atrophy is irreversible, permanent, progressive and ongoing; (4) her highest cognitive brain function is exhibited by her grimacing perhaps in recognition of ordinarily painful stimuli, indicating the experience of pain and apparent response to sound; (5) she is a spastic quadriplegic; (6) her four extremities are contracted with irreversible muscular and tendon damage to all extremities; (7) she has no cognitive or reflexive ability to swallow food or water to maintain her daily essential needs and . . . she will never recover her ability to swallow sufficient [sic] to satisfy her needs. In sum, Nancy is diagnosed as in a persistent vegetative state. She is not dead. She is not terminally ill. Medical experts testified that she could live another thirty years." *Cruzan v. Harmon*, 760 S. W. 2d 408, 411 (Mo. 1989) (en banc) (quotations omitted; footnote omitted).

In observing that Cruzan was not dead, the court referred to the following Missouri statute: "For all legal purposes, the occurrence of human death shall be determined in accordance with the usual and customary standards of medical practice, provided that death shall not be determined to have occurred unless the following minimal conditions have been met:

"(1) When respiration and circulation are not artificially maintained, there is an irreversible cessation of spontaneous respiration and circulation; or

"(2) When respiration and circulation are artificially maintained, and there is total irreversible cessation of all brain function, including the brain stem and that such determination is made by a licensed physician." Mo. Rev. Stat. § 194.005 (1986).

Since Cruzan's respiration and circulation were not being artificially maintained, she obviously fit within the first proviso of the statute.

Dr. Fred Plum, the creator of the term "persistent vegetative state" and a renowned expert on the subject, has described the "vegetative state" in the following terms:

" 'Vegetative state describes a body which is functioning entirely in terms of its internal controls. It maintains temperature. It maintains heart beat and pulmonary ventilation. It maintains digestive activity. It maintains reflex activity of muscles and nerves for low level conditioned responses. But there is no behavioral evidence of either self-awareness or awareness of the surroundings in a learned manner.' " *In re Jobes*, 108 N. J. 394, 403, 529 A. 2d 434, 438 (1987).

See also Brief for American Medical Association et al., as *Amici Curiae*, 6 ("The persistent vegetative state can best be understood as one of the conditions in which patients have suffered a loss of consciousness").

2. See generally Karnezis, Patient's Right to Refuse Treatment Allegedly Necessary to Sustain Life, 93 A. L. R. 3d 67 (1979) (collecting cases); Cantor, A Patient's Decision to Decline Life-Saving Medical Treatment: Bodily Integrity Versus the Preservation of Life, 26 Rutgers L. Rev. 228, 229, and n. 5 (1973) (noting paucity of cases).

3. See Chapman, The Uniform Rights of the Terminally Ill Act: Too Little, Too Late?, 42 Ark. L. Rev. 319, 324, n. 15 (1989); see also F. Rozovsky, Consent to Treatment, A Practical Guide 415–423 (2d ed. 1984).

4. In a later trilogy of cases, the New Jersey Supreme Court stressed that the analytic framework adopted in *Conroy* was limited to elderly, incompetent patients with shortened life expectancies, and established alternative approaches to deal with a different set of situations. See *In re Farrell*, 108 N. J. 335, 529 A. 2d 404 (1987) (37-year-old competent mother with terminal illness had right to removal of respirator based on common law and constitutional principles which overrode competing state interests); *In re Peter*, 108 N.J. 365, 529 A. 2d 419 (1987) (65-year-old woman in persistent vegetative state had right to removal of nasogastric feeding tube—under *Conroy* subjective test, power of attorney and hearsay testimony constituted clear and convincing proof of patient's intent to have treatment withdrawn); *In re Jobes*, 108 N. J. 394, 529 A. 2d 434 (1987) (31-year-old woman in persistent vegetative state entitled to removal of jejunostomy feeding tube—even though hearsay testimony regarding patient's intent insufficient to meet clear and convincing standard of proof, under *Quinlan*, family or close friends entitled to make a substituted judgment for patient).

5. Besides the Missouri Supreme Court in *Cruzan* and the courts in *McConnell, Longeway, Drabick, Bouvia, Barber, O'Connor, Conroy, Jobes,* and *Peter, supra,* appellate courts of at least four other States and one Federal District Court have specifically considered and discussed the issue of withholding or withdrawing artificial nutrition and hydration from incompetent individuals. See *Gray v. Romeo,* 697 F. Supp. 580 (RI 1988); *In re Gardner,* 534 A. 2d 947 (Me. 1987); *In re Grant,* 109 Wash. 2d 545, 747 P. 2d 445 (Wash. 1987); *Brophy v. New England Sinai Hospital, Inc.,* 398 Mass. 417, 497 N. E. 2d 626 (1986); *Corbett v. D'Alessandro,* 487 So. 2d 368 (Fla. App. 1986). All of these courts permitted or would permit the termination of such measures based on rights

grounded in the common law, or in the State or Federal Constitution.

6. We recognize that these cases involved instances where the government sought to take action against an individual. See *Price Waterhouse v. Hopkins*, 490 U.S.___ , ___(1989) (plurality opinion). Here, by contrast, the government seeks to protect the interests of an individual, as well as its own institutional interests, in life. We do not see any reason why important individual interests should be afforded less protection simply because the government finds itself in the position of defending them. "[W]e find it significant that . . . the defendant rather than the plaintiff" seeks the clear and convincing standard of proof—"suggesting that this standard ordinarily serves as a shield rather than . . . a sword." *Id.*, at ___ . That it is the government that has picked up the shield should be of no moment.

7. The clear and convincing standard of proof has been variously defined in this context as "proof sufficient to persuade the trier of fact that the patient held a firm and settled commitment to the termination of life supports under the circumstances like those presented," *In re Westchester County Medical Center on behalf of O'Connor*, 72 N. Y. 2d 517, 531, N. E. 2d 607, 613 (1988) (*O'Connor*), and as evidence which "produces in the mind of the trier of fact a firm belief or conviction as to the truth of the allegations sought to be established, evidence so clear, direct and weighty and convincing as to enable [the factfinder] to come to a clear conviction, without hesitancy, of the truth of the precise facts in issue." *In re Jobes*, 108 N. J. at 407–408, 529 A. 2d, at 441 (quotation omitted). In both of these cases the evidence of the patient's intent to refuse medical treatment was arguably stronger than that presented here. The New York Court of Appeals and the Supreme Court of New Jersey, respectively, held that the proof failed to meet a clear and convincing threshold. See *O'Connor, supra*, at 526–534, 531 N. E. 2d, at 610–615; *Jobes, supra*, at 442–443.

8. We are not faced in this case with the question of whether a State might be required to defer to the decision of a surrogate if competent and probative evidence established that the patient herself had expressed a desire that the decision to terminate life-sustaining treatment be made for her by that individual. Petitioners also adumbrate in their brief a claim based on the Equal Protection Clause of the Fourteenth Amendment to the effect that Missouri has impermissibly treated incompetent parties differently from competent ones, citing the statement in *Cleburne v. Cleburne Living Center, Inc.*, 473 U.S. 432, 439 (1985), that the clause is "essentially a direction that all persons similarly situated should be treated alike." The differences between the choice made *by* a competent person to refuse medical treatment, and the choice made *for* an incompetent person by someone else to refuse medical treatment, are so obviously different that the State is warranted in establishing rigorous procedures for the latter class of cases which do not apply to the former class.

NO

William J. Brennan, Jr.

DISSENTING OPINION OF
WILLIAM J. BRENNAN, JR.

. . . JUSTICE BRENNAN, . . . dissenting.

"Medical technology has effectively created a twilight zone of suspended animation where death commences while life, in some form, continues. Some patients, however, want no part of a life sustained only by medical technology. Instead, they prefer a plan of medical treatment that allows nature to take its course and permits them to die with dignity."[1]

Nancy Cruzan has dwelt in that twilight zone for six years. She is oblivious to her surroundings and will remain so. Her body twitches only reflexively, without consciousness. The areas of her brain that once thought, felt, and experienced sensations have degenerated badly and are continuing to do so. The cavities remaining are filling with cerebrospinal fluid. The " 'cerebral cortical atrophy is irreversible, permanent, progressive and ongoing.' " "Nancy will never interact meaningfully with her environment again. She will remain in a persistent vegetative state until her death." Because she cannot swallow, her nutrition and hydration are delivered through a tube surgically implanted in her stomach.

A grown woman at the time of the accident, Nancy had previously expressed her wish to forgo continuing medical care under circumstances such as these. Her family and her friends are convinced that this is what she would want. A guardian ad litem appointed by the trial court is also convinced that this is what Nancy would want. See 760 S. W. 2d, at 444 (Higgins, J., dissenting from denial of rehearing). Yet the Missouri Supreme Court, alone among state courts deciding such a question, has determined that an irreversibly vegetative patient will remain a passive prisoner of medical technology—for Nancy, perhaps for the next 30 years. See id., at 424, 427.

Today the Court, while tentatively accepting that there is some degree of constitutionally protected liberty interest in avoiding unwanted medical treatment, including life-sustaining medical treatment such as artificial

From *Nancy Beth Cruzan v. Director, Missouri Department of Health*, 58 L.W. 4916 (1990). Some notes and case citations omitted.

nutrition and hydration, affirms the decision of the Missouri Supreme Court. The majority opinion, as I read it, would affirm that decision on the ground that a State may require "clear and convincing" evidence of Nancy Cruzan's prior decision to forgo life-sustaining treatment under circumstances such as hers in order to ensure that her actual wishes are honored. Because I believe that Nancy Cruzan has a fundamental right to be free of unwanted artificial nutrition and hydration, which right is not outweighed by any interests of the State, and because I find that the improperly biased procedural obstacles imposed by the Missouri Supreme Court impermissibly burden that right, I respectfully dissent. Nancy Cruzan is entitled to choose to die with dignity.

I

A

"[T]he timing of death—once a matter of fate—is now a matter of human choice." Office of Technology Assessment Task Force, Life Sustaining Technologies and the Elderly 41 (1988). Of the approximately two million people who die each year, 80% die in hospitals and long-term care institutions,[2] and perhaps 70% of those after a decision to forgo life-sustaining treatment has been made.[3] Nearly every death involves a decision whether to undertake some medical procedure that could prolong the process of dying. Such decisions are difficult and personal. They must be made on the basis of individual values, informed by medical realities, yet within a framework governed by law. The role of the courts is confined to defining that framework, delineating

the ways in which government may and may not participate in such decisions.

The question before this Court is a relatively narrow one: whether the Due Process Clause allows Missouri to require a now-incompetent patient in an irreversible persistent vegetative state to remain on life-support absent rigorously clear and convincing evidence that avoiding the treatment represents the patient's prior, express choice. If a fundamental right is at issue, Missouri's rule of decision must be scrutinized under the standards this Court has always applied in such circumstances. As we said in *Zablocki v. Redhail*, 434 U.S. 374, 388 (1978), if a requirement imposed by a State "significantly interferes with the exercise of a fundamental right, it cannot be upheld unless it is supported by sufficiently important state interests and is closely tailored to effectuate only those interests." . . .

B

The starting point of our legal analysis must be whether a competent person has a constitutional right to avoid unwanted medical care. Earlier this Term, this Court held that the Due Process Clause of the Fourteenth Amendment confers a significant liberty interest in avoiding unwanted medical treatment. *Washington v. Harper*, (1990). Today, the Court concedes that our prior decisions "support the recognition of a general liberty interest in refusing medical treatment." The Court, however, avoids discussing either the measure of that liberty interest or its application by assuming, for purposes of this case only, that a competent person has a constitutionally protected liberty interest in being free of unwanted artificial nutrition and hydration. JUSTICE

O'CONNOR's opinion is less parsimonious. She openly affirms that "the Court has often deemed state incursions into the body repugnant to the interests protected by the Due Process Clause," that there is a liberty interest in avoiding unwanted medical treatment and that it encompasses the right to be free of "artificially delivered food and water."

But if a competent person has a liberty interest to be free of unwanted medical treatment, as both the majority and JUSTICE O'CONNOR concede, it must be fundamental. "We are dealing here with [a decision] which involves one of the basic civil rights of man." *Skinner v. Oklahoma ex rel. Williamson*, 316 U.S. 535, 541 (1942) (invalidating a statute authorizing sterilization of certain felons). Whatever other liberties protected by the Due Process Clause are fundamental, "those liberties that are 'deeply rooted in this Nation's history and tradition' " are among them. *Bowers v. Hardwick*, 478 U.S. 186, 192 (1986) (quoting *Moore v. East Cleveland, supra*, at 503 (plurality opinion).

The right to be free from medical attention without consent, to determine what shall be done with one's own body, *is* deeply rooted in this Nation's traditions, as the majority acknowledges. This right has long been "firmly entrenched in American tort law" and is securely grounded in the earliest common law. *Ibid.* See also *Mills v. Rogers*, 457 U.S. 291, 294, n. 4 (1982) ("the right to refuse any medical treatment emerged from the doctrines of trespass and battery, which were applied to unauthorized touchings of a physician"). " 'Anglo-American law starts with the premise of thoroughgoing self determination. It follows that each man is considered to be master of his own body, and he may, if he be of sound mind, expressly prohibit the performance of lifesaving surgery, or other medical treatment.' " *Natanson v. Kline*, 186 Kan. 393, 406–407, 350 P. 2d 1093, 1104 (1960). "The inviolability of the person" has been held as "sacred" and "carefully guarded" as any common law right. *Union Pacific R. Co. v. Botsford*, 141 U.S. 250, 251–252 (1891). Thus, freedom from unwanted medical attention is unquestionably among those principles "so rooted in the traditions and conscience of our people as to be ranked as fundamental." *Snyder v. Massachusetts*, 291 U.S. 97, 105 (1934).

That there may be serious consequences involved in refusal of the medical treatment at issue here does not vitiate the right under our common law tradition of medical self-determination. It is "a well-established rule of general law . . . that it is the patient, not the physician, who ultimately decides if treatment—any treatment—is to be given at all. . . . The rule has never been qualified in its application by either the nature or purpose of the treatment, or the gravity of the consequences of acceding to or foregoing it." *Tune v. Walter Reed Army Medical Hospital*, 602 F. Supp. 1452, 1455 (DC 1985). See also *Downer v. Veilleux*, 322 A. 2d 82, 91 (Me. 1974). . . .

No material distinction can be drawn between the treatment to which Nancy Cruzan continues to be subject—artificial nutrition and hydration—and any other medical treatment. The artificial delivery of nutrition and hydration is undoubtedly medical treatment. The technique to which Nancy Cruzan is subject—artificial feeding through a gastrostomy tube—involves a tube implanted surgically into her stomach through incisions in her abdominal wall. It may obstruct the intestinal tract, erode and pierce the stomach wall or cause leakage of the stomach's contents into the abdominal cavity. See Page, Andrassy, & Sandler, Techniques in Delivery of Liquid Diets, in Nutrition in Clinical Surgery 66–67 (M. Deitel 2d ed. 1985). The tube can cause pneumonia from reflux of the stomach's contents into the lung. See Bernard & Forlaw, Complications and Their Prevention, in Enteral and Tube Feeding 553 (J. Rombeau & M. Caldwell eds. 1984). Typically, and in this case, commercially prepared formulas are used, rather than fresh food. The type of formula and method of administration must be experimented with to avoid gastrointestinal problems. The patient must be monitored daily by medical personnel as to weight, fluid intake and fluid output; blood tests must be done weekly.

Artificial delivery of food and water is regarded as medical treatment by the medical profession and the Federal Government.[4] According to the American Academy of Neurology, "[t]he artificial provision of nutrition and hydration is a form of medical treatment . . . analogous to other forms of life-sustaining treatment, such as the use of the respirator. When a patient is unconscious, both a respirator and an artificial feeding device serve to support or replace normal bodily functions that are compromised as a result of the patient's illness." Position of the American Academy of Neurology on Certain Aspects of the Care and Management of the Persistent Vegetative State Patient, 39 Neurology 125 (Jan. 1989). See also Council on Ethical and Judicial Affairs of the American Medical Association, Current Opinions, Opinion 2.20 (1989) ("Life-prolonging medical treatment includes medication and artificially or technologically supplied respiration, nutrition or hydration"); President's Commission 88 (life-sustaining treatment includes respirators, kidney dialysis machines, special feeding procedures). The Federal Government permits the cost of the medical devices and formulas used in enteral feeding to be reimbursed under Medicare. The formulas are regulated by the Federal Drug Administration as "medical foods," and the feeding tubes are regulated as medical devices.

Nor does the fact that Nancy Cruzan is now incompetent deprive her of her fundamental rights. See Youngberg v. Romeo, 457 U.S. 307, 315–316, 319 (1982) (holding that severely retarded man's liberty interests in safety, freedom from bodily restraint and reasonable training survive involuntary commitment); Parham v. J. R., 442 U.S. 584, 600 (1979) (recognizing a child's substantial liberty interest in not being confined unnecessarily for medical treatment); Jackson v. Indiana, 406 U.S. 715, 730, 738 (1972) (holding that Indiana could not violate the due process and equal protection rights of a mentally retarded deaf mute by committing him for an indefinite amount of time simply because he was incompetent to stand trial on the criminal charges filed against him). As the majority recognizes, the question is not whether an incompetent has constitutional rights, but how such rights may be exercised. As we explained in Thompson v. Oklahoma, 487 U.S. 815 (1988), "[t]he law must often adjust the manner in which it affords rights to those whose status renders them unable to exercise choice freely and rationally. Children, the insane, and those who are irreversibly ill with loss of brain function, for instance, all retain 'rights,' to be sure, but often such rights are only meaningful as they are exercised by agents acting with the best interests of their principals in mind." Id., at 825, n. 23 (emphasis added). "To deny [its] exercise because the patient is unconscious or incompetent would be to deny the right." *Foody v. Manchester Memorial Hospital*, 40 Conn. Super. 127, 133, 482 A. 2d 713, 718 (1984). . . .

III

This is not to say that the State has no legitimate interests to assert here. As the majority recognizes, Missouri has a *parens patriae* interest in providing Nancy Cruzan, now incompetent, with as accurate as possible a determination of how she would exercise her rights under these circumstances. Second, if and when it is determined that Nancy Cruzan would want to continue treatment, the State may legitimately assert an interest in providing that treatment. But *until* Nancy's wishes have been determined, the only state interest that may be asserted is an interest in safeguarding the accuracy of that determination.

Accuracy, therefore, must be our touchstone. Missouri may constitutionally impose only those procedural requirements that serve to enhance the accuracy of a determination of Nancy Cruzan's wishes or are at least consistent with an accurate determination. The Missouri "safeguard" that the Court upholds. today does not meet that standard. The determination needed in this context is whether the incompetent person would choose to live in a persistent vegetative state on life-support or to avoid this medical treatment. Missouri's rule of decision imposes a markedly asymmetrical evidentiary burden. Only evidence of specific statements of treatment choice made by the patient when competent is admissible to support a finding that the patient, now in a persistent vegetative state, would wish to avoid further medical treatment. Moreover, this evidence

must be clear and convincing. No proof is required to support a finding that the incompetent person would wish to continue treatment.

A

The majority offers several justifications for Missouri's heightened evidentiary standard. First, the majority explains that the State may constitutionally adopt this rule to govern determinations of an incompetent's wishes in order to advance the State's substantive interests, including its unqualified interest in the preservation of human life. Missouri's evidentiary standard, however, cannot rest on the State's own interest in a particular substantive result. To be sure, courts have long erected clear and convincing evidence standards to place the greater risk of erroneous decisions on those bringing disfavored claims. In such cases, however, the choice to discourage certain claims was a legitimate, constitutional policy choice. In contrast, Missouri has not such power to disfavor a choice by Nancy Cruzan to avoid medical treatment, because Missouri has no legitimate interest in providing Nancy with treatment until it is established that this represents her choice. Just as a State may not override Nancy's choice directly, it may not do so indirectly through the imposition of a procedural rule. . . .

The majority claims that the allocation of the risk of error is justified because it is more important not to terminate life-support for someone who would wish it continued than to honor the wishes of someone who would not. An erroneous decision to terminate life-support is irrevocable, says the majority, while an erroneous decision not to terminate "results in a maintenance of the status quo." But, from the point of view of the patient, an erroneous decision in either direction is irrevocable. An erroneous decision to terminate artificial nutrition and hydration, to be sure, will lead to failure of that last remnant of physiological life, the brain stem, and result in complete brain death. An erroneous decision not to terminate life-support, however, robs a patient of the very qualities protected by the right to avoid unwanted medical treatment. His own degraded existence is perpetuated; his family's suffering is protracted; the memory he leaves behind becomes more and more distorted.

Even a later decision to grant him his wish cannot undo the intervening harm. But a later decision is unlikely in an event. "[T]he discovery of new evidence," to which the majority refers, is more hypothetical than plausible. The majority also misconceives the relevance of the possibility of "advancements in medical science," by treating it as a reason to force someone to continue medical treatment against his will. The possibility of a medical miracle is indeed part of the calculus, but it is a part of the *patient's* calculus. If current research suggests that some hope for cure or even moderate improvement is possible within the lifespan projected, this is a factor that should be and would be accorded significant weight in assessing what the patient himself would choose.[5] . . .

C

I do not suggest that States must sit by helplessly if the choices of incompetent patients are in danger of being ignored. Even if the Court had ruled that Missouri's rule of decision is unconstitutional, as I believe it should have, States would nevertheless remain free to fash-

ion procedural protections to safeguard the interests of incompetents under these circumstances. The Constitution provides merely a framework here: protections must be genuinely aimed at ensuring decisions commensurate with the will of the patient, and must be reliable as instruments to that end. Of the many states which have instituted such protections, Missouri is virtually the only one to have fashioned a rule that lessens the likelihood of accurate determinations. In contrast, nothing in the Constitution prevents States from reviewing the advisability of a family decision, by requiring a court proceeding or by appointing an impartial guardian ad litem. . . .

D

Finally, I cannot agree with the majority that when it is not possible to determine what choice an incompetent patient would make, a State's role as *parens patriae* permits the State automatically to make that choice itself. . . . Under fair rules of evidence, it is improbable that a court could not determine what the patient's choice would be. Under the rule of decision adopted by Missouri and upheld today by this Court, such occasions might be numerous. But in neither case does it follow that it is constitutionally acceptable for the State invariably to assume the role of deciding for the patient. A State's legitimate interest in safeguarding a patient's choice cannot be furthered by simply appropriating it.

The majority justifies its position by arguing that, while close family members may have a strong feeling about the question, "there is no automatic assurance that the view of close family members will necessarily be the same as the patient's would have been had she been confronted with the prospect of her situation while competent." I cannot quarrel with this observation. But it leads only to another question: Is there any reason to suppose that a State is *more* likely to make the choice that the patient would have made than someone who knew the patient intimately? To ask this is to answer it. As the New Jersey Supreme Court observed: "Family members are best qualified to make substituted judgments for incompetent patients not only because of their peculiar grasp of the patient's approach to life, but also because of their special bonds with him or her. . . . It is . . . they who treat the patient as a person, rather than a symbol of a cause." *In re Jobes*, 108 N. J. 394, 416, 529 A. 2d 434, 445 (1987). The State, in contrast, is a stranger to the patient.

A State's inability to discern an incompetent patient's choice still need not mean that a State is rendered powerless to protect that choice. But I would find that the Due Process Clause prohibits a State from doing more than that. A State may ensure that the person who makes the decision on the patient's behalf is the one whom the patient himself would have selected to make that choice for him. And a State may exclude from consideration anyone having improper motives. But a State generally must either repose the choice with the person whom the patient himself would most likely have chosen as proxy or leave the decision to the patient's family.[6]

IV

As many as 10,000 patients are being maintained in persistent vegetative states in the United States, and the number is expected to increase significantly in the near future. Medical technology, developed over the past 20 or so years, is often capable of resuscitating people after they have stopped breathing or their hearts have stopped beating. Some of those people are brought fully back to life. Two decades ago, those who were not and could not swallow and digest food, died. Intravenous solutions could not provide sufficient calories to maintain people for more than a short time. Today, various forms of artificial feeding have been developed that are able to keep people metabolically alive for years, even decades. See Spencer & Palmisano, Specialized Nutritional Support of Patients— A Hospital's Legal Duty?, 11 Quality Rev. Bull. 160, 160–161 (1985). In addition, in this century, chronic or degenerative ailments have replaced communicable diseases as the primary causes of death. See R. Weir, Abating Treatment with Critically Ill Patients 12–13 (1989); President's Commission 15–16. The 80% of Americans who die in hospitals are "likely to meet their end . . . 'in a sedated or comatose state; betubed nasally, abdominally and intravenously; and far more like manipulated objects than like moral subjects.' "[7] A fifth of all adults surviving to age 80 will suffer a progressive dementing disorder prior to death. See Cohen & Eisdorfer, Dementing Disorders, in The Practice of Geriatrics 194 (E. Calkins, P. Davis, & A, Ford eds. 1986).

"[L]aw, equity and justice must not themselves quail and be helpless in the face of modern technological marvels presenting questions hitherto unthought of." *In re Quinlan*, 70 N. J. 10, 44, 355 A. 2d 647, 665, cert. denied, 429 U.S. 922 (1976). The new medical technology can reclaim those who would have been irretrievably lost a few decades ago and restore them to active lives. For Nancy Cruzan, it failed, and for others with wasting incurable disease it may be doomed to failure. In these unfortunate situations, the bodies and preferences and memories of the victims do not escheat to the State; nor does our Constitution permit the State or any other government to commandeer them. No singularity of feeling exists upon which such a government might confidently rely as *parens patriae*. The President's Commission, after years of research, concluded:

> "In few areas of health care are people's evaluations of their experiences so varied and uniquely personal as in their assessments of the nature and value of the processes associated with dying. For some, every moment of life is of inestimable value; for others, life without some desired level of mental or physical ability is worthless or burdensome. A moderate degree of suffering may be an important means of personal growth and religious experience to one person, but only frightening or despicable to another." President's Commission 276.

Yet Missouri and this Court have displaced Nancy's own assessment of the processes associated with dying. They have discarded evidence of her will, ignored her values, and deprived her of the right to a decision as closely approximating her own choice as humanly possible. They have done so disingenuously in her name, and openly in Missouri's own. That Missouri and this Court may truly be motivated only by concern for incompetent patients makes no matter. As one of our most prominent jurists warned us decades ago: "Experience should teach us to be most on our guard to protect liberty when the government's

purposes are beneficent. . . . The greatest dangers to liberty lurk in insidious encroachment by men of zeal, well meaning but without understanding." *Olmstead v. United States*, 277 U.S. 438, 479 (1928) (Brandeis, J., dissenting).

I respectfully dissent.

NOTES

1. *Rasmussen v. Fleming*, 154 Arix. 207, 211, 741 P. 2d 674, 678 (1987) (en banc).
2. See President's Commission for the Study of Ethical Problems in Medicine and Biomedical and Behavioral Research, Deciding to Forego Life Sustaining Treatment 15, n. 1, and 17–18 (1983) (hereafter President's Commission).
3. See Lipton, Do-Not-Resuscitate Decisions in a Community Hospital: Incidence, Implications and Outcomes, 256 JAMA 1164, 1168 (1986).
4. The Missouri court appears to be alone among state courts to suggest otherwise, 760 S. W. 2d, at 419 and 423, although the court did not rely on a distinction between artificial feeding and other forms of medical treatment. *Id.*, at 423. See, e. g., *Delio v. Westchester County Medical Center*, 129 App. Div. 2d 1, 19, 516 N. Y. S. 2d 677, 689 (1987) ("review of the decisions in other jurisdictions . . . failed to uncover a single case in which a court confronted with an application to discontinue feeding by artificial means has evaluated medical procedures to provide nutrition and hydration differently from other types of life-sustaining procedures").
5. For Nancy Cruzan, no such cure or improvement is in view. So much of her brain has deteriorated and been replaced by fluid, that apparently the only medical advance that could restore consciousness to her body would be a brain transplant.
6. Only in the exceedingly rare case where the State cannot find any family member or friend who can be trusted to endeavor genuinely to make the treatment choice the patient would have made does the State become the legitimate surrogate decisionmaker.
7. Fadiman, The Liberation of Lolly and Gronky, Life Magazine, Dec. 1986, p. 72 (quoting medical ethicist Joseph Fletcher).

POSTSCRIPT

Can States Restrict the Right to Die?

Nancy Cruzan died six months after the U.S. Supreme Court's ruling on her right to die. Two months after the Court's decision, the Cruzans asked for a court hearing to present new evidence from three of their daughter's co-workers. At the hearing, the co-workers testified that they recalled her saying she would never want to live "like a vegetable." At the same hearing, Cruzan's doctor called her existence a "living hell" and recommended removal of the tube. Her court-appointed guardian concurred. The judge then ruled that there was clear evidence of Cruzan's wishes and gave permission for the feeding tube to be removed. She died on December 26, 1990.

The fundamental concern in right to die cases, indeed in most civil liberties cases, is the fear of what will happen in the next case. In other words, a judge may avoid doing what seems reasonable in one case if his ruling could be used to reach a less desirable result in a future case with slightly different facts. Lawyers refer to this as the "slippery slope." If euthanasia is justified in a case where the patient is terminally ill and in severe pain, it may be allowed in a later case where, as in *Cruzan*, the patient is in an unrecoverable state but not in pain. Perhaps euthanasia would be extended to handicapped newborns or to the senile.

Underlying the slippery slope argument in these cases, as in the abortion cases, is the fear of what might happen if life in some instances is not considered to be sacred. A member of the prosecution staff at the Nuremberg trials of Nazi doctors who participated in the killing of "incurables" and the "useless" traced the origin of Nazi policy to

> a subtle shift in emphasis in the basic attitude of the physicians. It started with the acceptance of the attitude, basic in the euthanasia movement, that there is such a thing as the life not worthy to be lived. This attitude in its early stages concerned itself merely with the severely and chronically sick. Gradually, the sphere of those to be included in this category was enlarged to encompass the socially unproductive, the ideologically unwanted, the racially unwanted and finally all non-Germans. But it is important to realize that the infinitely small wedged-in lever from which this entire trend received its impetus was the attitude toward the unrehabilitatable sick. (Kamisar, "Some Non-Religious Views Against Proposed 'Mercy Killing' Legislation," 42 *Minnesota Law Review* 969 [1958])

Considering the decisions in the *Cruzan* case, how do you feel about the slippery slope argument? Does the majority opinion, by allowing alert and competent patients to choose to remove feeding tubes, start us down the slippery slope? Does establishing a "clear and convincing" standard effectively halt the slide down the slope? Even if you feel that the slide down the slope has not begun, it is also true that there will be more cases to follow *Cruzan*. For example, what if there is disagreement between hospital and family officials about whether or not the patient's wishes are "clear and convincing"? What happens if the patient is conscious but in great pain and receiving large doses of pain medication? Which parties should be entitled to be heard if a case gets to court? What is to be done if there is disagreement among family members?

One effect of the Court's opinion is to encourage the use of living wills. Forty states and the District of Columbia have statutes permitting living wills, which allow individuals to specify in advance what treatment they would wish to receive. Most of these statutes apply only in cases of terminal illness, but the statutes are likely to be changed in the light of the *Cruzan* decision. Since less than half of the U.S. population have regular wills, the living will is unlikely to provide a total solution to the problem.

Other recent cases involving the withdrawal of treatment are *In the matter of Mary O'Connor*, 72 N.Y.2d 517 (1988); *Brophy v. New England Sinai Hospital*, 497 N.E.2d 626 (1986); *In re Conroy*, 486 A.2d 1209 (1985); *Bovia v. The Superior Court of Los Angeles County*, 225 Cal. 297 (1986); and *In re Quinlan*, 355 A.2d 647 (1976). Recent analyses include "The Care of the Dying: A Symposium on the Case of Betty Wright," 17 *Law, Medicine and Health Care*, pp. 207–233 (1989); Weir, *Abating Treatment with Critically Ill Patients* (Oxford University Press, 1989); Wennberg, *Terminal Choices: Euthanasia, Suicide, and the Right to Die* (Wm. B. Eerdmans, 1989); Rhoden, "Litigating Life and Death," 102 *Harvard Law Review* 375 (1988); Note, "Judicial Postponement of Death Recognition: The Tragic Case of Mary O'Connor," 15 *American Journal of Law and Medicine* 301 (1990); Capron, "Legal and Ethical Problems in Decisions for Death," 14 *Law, Medicine and Health Care* 141 (1987); Cantor, *Legal Frontiers of Death and Dying* (Indiana University Press, 1987); and *Guidelines on the Termination of Life-Sustaining Treatment and the Care of the Dying: A Report by the Hastings Center* (Indiana University Press, 1987).

Further worthwhile reading on euthanasia and the right to die may be found in *President's Commission for the Study of Ethical Problems in Medicine, Deciding to Forgo Lifesaving Treatment* (Washington, 1983); J. Lyon, *Playing God in the Nursery* (W. W. Norton, 1985); R. Weir, *Selective Nontreatment of Handicapped Newborns: Moral Dilemmas in Neonatal Medicine* (Oxford University Press, 1984); Note, "Physician-Assisted Suicide and the Right to Die With Assistance," 105 *Harvard Law Review* 2021 (1992); Kamisar, "When Is There a Constitutional 'Right to Die'? When Is There No Constitutional 'Right to Live'?" 25 *Georgia Law Review* 1203 (1991); Robertson, "Assessing Quality of Life: A Response to Professor Kamisar," 25 *Georgia Law Review* 1243 (1991); and A. W. Alschuler, "The Right to Die," 141 *New Law Journal* 1637 (November 29, 1991).

ISSUE 11

Should Homosexuality Bar a Parent from Being Awarded Custody of a Child?

YES: Hewitt P. Tomlin, Jr., from Concurring Opinion, *Leonard Arthur Collins v. Beverly Jo Clendenan Collins*, Court of Appeals of Tennessee (1988)

NO: Melvin P. Antell, from Majority Opinion, *M. P. v. S. P.*, Superior Court of New Jersey, Appellate Division (1979)

ISSUE SUMMARY

YES: Judge Hewitt P. Tomlin, Jr., argues that an award of child custody to a homosexual parent cannot be in the best interests of the child.
NO: Justice Melvin P. Antell refuses to allow one parent's homosexuality to be a deciding factor in the custody decision of the court.

> Parental rights are comprehensive, and they operate against the state, against third parties, and against the child. Parents have the right to custody of their child; to discipline the child; and to make decisions about education, medical treatment, and religious upbringing. Parents assign the child a name. They have a right to the child's earnings and services. They decide where the child shall live. Parents have a right to information gathered by others about the child and may exclude others from that information. They may speak for the child and may assert or waive the child's rights. Parents have the right to determine who may visit the child and to place their child in another's care.
> —Katharine Bartlett

In *Bowers v. Hardwick*, 478 U.S. 186 (1986) the Supreme Court upheld a Georgia law that made acts of sodomy performed by anyone in any place a crime. The 5–4 decision was one of the most controversial and widely publicized Supreme Court decisions of 1986. The Georgia law had been challenged by Michael Hardwick, a homosexual who had been arrested for acts performed in his own home. The Supreme Court refused to find that such acts, even when performed in private places, were protected by the Constitution and ruled that there was no "fundamental right to engage in homosexual sodomy."

Bowers v. Hardwick was a considerable blow to the cause of gay rights. Privacy law had been relied upon, sometimes unsuccessfully, in earlier cases that involved the legality of gay sexual activity and undoubtedly would have been used in future cases. Yet, it is also true that there are many legal protections sought by homosexuals for which privacy law is largely irrelevant. These include conflicts involving nonsexual conduct or conduct in public—acts that involve the ability to live one's life without state interference or discrimination. As one gay rights activist has stated, "For many gay people the most important 'gay rights' issues are simply human issues—their rights to a job, a place to live, or custody of a child."

The following readings ask whether or not a person's sexual orientation should be considered in a hearing to determine which parent will be awarded custody of a child. Only one jurisdiction in the United States, the District of Columbia, prohibits a judge from making sexual orientation the sole criteria in granting custody to a father or a mother. Even this law, however, does not prohibit the court from taking sexual orientation into account.

The general standard for awarding custody of a child is "the best interests of the child." There is no single definition or set of criteria for this standard, but it typically includes all or most of the following:

1. the wishes of the child's parent or parents as to his custody;
2. the wishes of the child as to his custodian;
3. the interaction and interrelationship of the child with his parent or parents, his siblings, and any other person who may significantly affect the child's best interest;
4. the child's adjustment to his home, school, and community;
5. the mental and physical health of all individuals involved;
6. the length of time the child has lived in a stable, satisfactory environment and the desirability of maintaining continuity;
7. the permanence, as a family unit, of the existing or proposed custodial home;
8. the capacity and disposition of the parties to give the child love, affection, and guidance, and to continue educating and raising the child in the child's culture and religion or creed, if any.

As you read the following cases, try to evaluate how much weight should be given to each of the above criteria and whether or not the sexual orientation of a party relates to any of these factors.

YES

Hewitt P. Tomlin, Jr.

OPINION OF HEWITT P. TOMLIN, JR.

COLLINS v. COLLINS

[The parents in this case were divorced in 1978 on the grounds of irreconcilable differences. Their only child, a daughter, was less than a year old at that time. Both parties agreed that the mother would have custody of the child and the father would have reasonable visitation privileges and pay child support of $160 per month. The child was nine years old at the time of this custody hearing.

In 1984, the father filed a petition for custody. At trial he stated that he sought this change of custody solely on the basis of the mother's homosexuality.

The mother admitted that she is a practicing homosexual. She has had four serious lesbian relationships since the divorce in 1978, the first beginning when her daughter was approximately one-and-one-half years of age. The duration of these relationships ranged from eight months to three-and-one-half years. The current relationship began about one year prior to the hearing. —Ed.]

Judge P.J. Tomlin concurring:

While I agree with the results reached by my colleagues in affirming the trial court, I feel constrained to write this separate concurring opinion for the reasons that I feel that the majority did not address the issue of the homosexuality of the former custodial parent as directly as it should be addressed. It is my opinion that in the future, the courts of this state oftentimes are going to be faced with the issue of the homosexuality of a custodial parent or one desiring to be a custodial parent. For this reason adequate ground rules need to be laid down.

The majority approached the custody issue on the basis of the comparative fitness of the two parents and concluded that the father was more fit than the mother, noting that the mother was a fit parent as well. This issue was not

From *Leonard Arthur Collins v. Beverly Jo Clendenan Collins*, Court of Appeals of Tennessee, Western Section (1988). Notes and some case citations omitted.

presented to us as a matter of comparative fitness. The issue, clearly stated, is whether a child's best interests are promoted by an award of custody to a parent who carries on an active, open homosexual relationship in the family home. As noted in the majority opinion, the father stated at trial that he sought change of custody from the mother to himself solely on the basis of the mother's homosexuality.

The facts in the case at bar present a clear picture of a homosexual mother who has actively practiced lesbianism for the past eight years. The mother's commitment to homosexuality can best be described in her own words:

Q Okay. In that regard, you would agree that you are a practicing homosexual?
A Yes.
Q All right. During the time that you have had custody of the child, and her name is J . . ., is it not?
A Yes, it is.
Q And she is how old?
A Nine.
Q Nine years old?
A Yes.
Q Have you had several relationships that were primary relationships with other homosexual women?
A Yes. I've had three serious relationships and I am currently in a relationship.
Q Okay. You are currently in a relationship?
A Yes.
Q By serious relationships, exactly what do you mean?
A I mean one where someone would share my home and my life, and would actually live there. . . .
Q Going back to that first person and to the first primary relationship that you had in your home and as a significant

other person in your life; when did that person move into your home, that person being number one? . . .
A J . . . was around two years old and I lived with that person for a year and a half. . . .
Then the second person that I was with was a short or shorter relationship because that person left me and went to Houston. That lasted for about eight months. Then when J . . . was five, I was with somebody for three and a half years. . . .
And then I was [with] the third person from the time J . . . was three until she was about eight and a half. The person that I am with now I have been seeing for about a year. . . .
Q And you are now in a fourth relationship?
A Yes.
Q Does that individual, the fourth person, also reside in the house there with you and with J . . .?
A No.
Q Did Lois Rainey reside there in the house with you and J . . .?
A Yes.
Q Were you in love with Lois Rainey?
A Yes. . . .
Q Did you or do you, as a matter of practice, and this is a two-part question. Did you or do you express your affection by way of embracing these other persons?
A Only if one or the other of us would be gone for a week or two, we might hug upon returning to each other. . . .
Q Do you currently share the same bed with this other person, number four?
A Yes.
Q Did you share the same bed with number two?
A Yes, sir.
Q And number three?
A Yes, sir.

Q And number one?

A Yes, sir.

Q How large a home do you occupy?

A Three bedrooms.

Q And do you know how many square feet are in that home?

A Fifteen hundred. . . .

Q Does Lois still see J . . .?

A Yes, sir.

Q Under what circumstances?

A She is out of town and she has parents here and when she comes into town she often asks if she can see J . . . and she and J . . . will go over to her parents. They have adopted her as a grandchild of their own. . . .

Q Are most of your friends homosexual?

A Yes, sir.

Q Are they mostly female homosexuals or are they also males?

A Mostly female.

Q Do you ever have parties?

A Twice a year, maybe around holidays.

Q Are your female homosexual friends the primary core of the invited guests?

A Yes.

Q Would J . . . not be present at any of these parties?

A I make it a strict rule with any of my friends to abide by the same values, same restrictions as I do, myself. They love J . . . and she is there up until her bedtime and then she goes to bed. . . .

Q You aren't around all the time that your friends are around J . . ., are you?

A I am not around?

Q That is the question. Are you around all the time that they are?

A The entire time?

Q Yes.

A No, but I have trust in them.

Q And you are not around all the time when Lois takes J . . . from the house, are you?

A No, but I also trust her.

Q Have you recently started to discuss with J . . . your sexual preferences and what that means to you.

A For a long time, I put it off but knowing that this court date was going to actually occur then yes, I sat down and explained it to her.

Q What did you tell her?

A I told her that being gay meant that you cared and loved—gay, that you loved another woman and that love is love and there are all kinds of different loves. You know, at the same time, I also had to explain to her what her father had against that and I explained that to the best of my ability. All that I could sense from her was that I am her mother and that it doesn't matter to her whether I am gay.

Q Have you distinguished between the love that exists between you and your friends and the kind of love that exists between a man and a woman, if any?

A I explained to her that it is the same type of love. . . .

Q I noticed in your statements that you take J . . . with you when you spend the night with Barbara, and Barbara meaning number four?

A Yes.

Q What are the sleeping arrangements there at Barbara's house?

A There is a downstairs bedroom. She only has two bedrooms. There's the downstairs bedroom that J . . . sleeps in and she and I stay upstairs in her bedroom.

In addition, the daughter's testimony sheds additional light on the nature and extent of Mother's activities. Daughter testified as follows:

Q Do they [Mother and lesbian lover] sleep together in the same bed as well as in the same bedroom?

A Yes.

Q They said they love each other. As far as you know, how do they express that with each other? Do they hug each other?

A Yes.

Q Do they kiss each other?

A Yes.

Q Do they tell each other that they love each other?

A Yes.

While we are dealing with lesbianism, there is no ground for a gender-based distinction. Therefore, I shall speak to this issue solely in terms of homosexuality. Homosexuality has been considered contrary to the morality of man for well over two thousand years. It has been and is considered to be an unnatural, immoral act. Since 1858, sexual acts connected with homosexuality have been labeled a crime. T.C.A. § 39-2-612 reads as follows:

Crimes against nature—Crimes against nature, either with mankind or any beast, are punishable by imprisonment in the penitentiary not less than five (5) years nor more than fifteen (15) years.

There are many compelling reasons for a state to regulate homosexuality. Writing in the Cornell Law Review, J. Harvey Wilkinson and G. Edward White stated in an article entitled "Constitutional Protection for Personal Lifestyles," Vol. 62, pp. 593, 595–596 as follows:

[S]tate interests of significant strength support a prohibition of homosexuality. First, a state may be interested in discouraging public behavior that gives widespread offense.

. . . The most threatening aspect of homosexuality is its potential to become a viable alternative to heterosexual intimacy. . . .

This state concern, in our view, should not be minimized. The nuclear, heterosexual family is charged with several of society's most essential functions. It has served as an important means of educating the young; it has often provided economic support and psychological comfort to family members; and it has operated as the unit upon which basic governmental policies in such matters as taxation, conscription, and inheritance have been based. Family life has been a central unifying experience throughout American society. Preserving the strength of this basic, organic unit is a central and legitimate end of the police power. The state ought to be concerned that if allegiance to traditional family arrangements declines, society as a whole may well suffer. . . .

In seeking to regulate homosexuality, the state takes as a basic premise that social and legal attitudes play an important and interdependent role in the individual's formation of his or her sexual destiny. A shift on the part of the law from opposition to neutrality arguably makes homosexuality appear a more acceptable sexual lifestyle, particularly to younger persons whose sexual preferences are as yet unformed. Young people form their sexual identity partly on the basis of models they see in society. If homosexual behavior is legalized, and thus partly legitimized, an adolescent may question whether he or she should "choose" heterosexuality. At the time their sexual feelings begin to develop many young people have more interests in common with members of their own sex; sexual attraction rather than genuine interest often first draws adolescents to members of the opposite sex. If society accorded more legitimacy to expressions of homosexual attraction, attachment to the opposite sex might be postponed or diverted for some time, perhaps until after the establishment of sexual patterns that would hamper development of traditional heterosexual family relationships. For those persons who eventually choose the heterosexual model, the existence of conflicting models might provide further sexual tension destructive to the traditional marital unit.

This writer's research has turned up only two opinions by appellate courts of this state addressing this issue. The unreported case of *Dettwiller v. Dettwiller* from the Middle Section of this Court is of little if any value for the principal reason that the *Dettwiller* opinion fails to reveal any specific homosexual activities of the mother, although she entertained male homosexuals in her home.

The sole reported Tennessee case to address the homosexual-custodial parent issue is that of *Dailey v. Dailey*, 625 S.W.2d 391 (Tenn. App. 1981), decided by the Eastern Section. While some distinctions might be made between *Dailey* and the case at bar, we characterize them as distinctions without substance. These distinctions are found on both sides of the scale. The record in *Dailey* presented a lesbian relationship that was more flagrant insofar as sexual activities were concerned than in the case at bar. However, in both *Dailey* and this case there was evidence that the two women slept together in the same bedroom in the house where the child was, and that they would hug and kiss each other and express their love for one another. On the other hand, the child in *Dailey* suffered from cerebral palsy and was described as being "somewhat handicapped physically

and as mentally slow." He was only five years old at the time of trial. It was likely that with these physical and mental handicaps he would not be as aware of what was going on as the normal nine-year-old in the case at bar.

Admittedly, there was conflicting expert testimony as to the effects of a minor child being raised in a homosexual environment. In the case at bar, the only expert testimony was that offered on behalf of the lesbian mother. The expert stated essentially that the child appeared to demonstrate no harmful effects caused from living in this environment up to the time of trial, and that none was anticipated. The trial court has the privilege of passing upon the credibility of expert testimony, whether it stand unopposed or whether it be in conflict. *Gibson v. Ferguson*, 562 S.W.2d 188 (Tenn. 1976).

In affirming the action of the trial court changing custody from a lesbian mother to the father, the *Dailey* court quoted with approval from two cases from neighboring states. We quote:

> However, we think it appropriate to refer to a recent Kentucky case of *S v. S*, Ky. App., 608 S.W.2d 64 (1980) where the facts were similar to the case at bar. The court of appeals reversed the trial court for not granting a change of custody from a lesbian mother to the father. In that opinion the court said:

> "This Court would call attention to an article entitled 'Children of lesbians: their point of view' contained in the Journal of the National Association of Social Workers, Vol. 25, Number 3, May, 1980, p. 198, et seq. This article points out the fact that the lesbianism of the mother, because of the failure of the community to accept and support such a condition, forces on the child a need for secrecy and the isolation imposed

by such a secret, thus separating the child from his or her peers." *Id.* at 394.

The second case was concerned with child rearing and moral values. Again we quote:

In the case of *Jarrett v. Jarrett,* 78 Ill.2d 337, 36 Ill.Dec. 1, 400 N.E.2d 421, the Supreme Court of Illinois had occasion to address the question of the adverse effects that might be had on three young children by virtue of the mother's having a "live in" boy friend. In that case the mother was awarded the custody of three small children. Shortly thereafter her boy friend moved into the home to live with the mother. The father filed a petition for a change of custody based upon a change in circumstances. The trial court denied the petition. The Supreme Court reversed, holding that such living arrangements were not in the best interest of the children. There the Court said 36 Ill. Dec. at 5, 400 N.E.2d at 425:

"At the time of this hearing, however, and even when this case was argued orally to this court, Jacqueline continued to cohabit with Wayne Hammon and had done nothing to indicate that this relationship would not continue in the future. Thus the moral values which Jacqueline currently represents to her children, and those which she may be expected to portray to them in the future, contravene statutorily declared standards of conduct and endanger the children's moral development. . . .

"At the time of the hearing the three Jarrett children, who were then 12, 10 and 7 years old, were obviously incapable of emulating their mother's moral indiscretions. To wait until later years to determine whether Jacqueline had inculcated her moral values in the children would be to await a demonstration that the very harm which the statute seeks to avoid had occurred. Measures

to safeguard the moral well-being of children, whose lives have already been disrupted by the divorce of their parents, cannot have been intended to be delayed until there are tangible manifestations of damage to their character.

"While our comments have focused upon the moral hazards, we are not convinced that open cohabitation does not also affect the mental and emotional health of the children." *Id.* at 394-95.

In this writer's opinion, as a case of first impression in this state *Dailey* has erected the signpost for the direction that this Court should follow. Here we are dealing with one of our more precious, if not most precious, commodities—the life of a young child. Parents are given wide discretion in the raising of their children without state interferences. However, when they seek to dissolve the marriage relationship when children are involved, the court must assert itself as the guardian of the moral and physical welfare of these children. The rights of the children take precedence over the rights of the parents.

Other jurisdictions have reached similar conclusions. In *Roberts v. Roberts,* 489 N.E.2d 1067 (Ohio App. 1985), the Ohio Court of Appeals reversed the action of the trial court in modifying visitation rights of three minor children with their homosexual father on the ground that the modifications made did not go far enough to protect the children. The Court said:

Actually, given its concern for perpetuating the values associated with conventional marriage and the family as the basic unit of society, the state has a substantial interest in viewing homosexuality as errant sexual behavior which threatens the social fabric, and in endeavoring to protect minors from being influenced by those who advocate homosexual lifestyles. See, e.g., *Doe v. Commonwealth's Attorney* (E.D.Va.1975), 403 F.Supp. 1199, affirmed (1976), 425 U.S. 901, 96 S.Ct. 1489, 47 L.Ed.2d 751. See, also, *Dronenburg v. Zech* (C.A.D.C.1984), 741 F.2d 1388. *Id.* at 1170.

In the case of *S.E.G. v. R.A.G.*, 735 S.W.2d 164 (Mo. App. 1987), a lesbian mother sought to gain custody of the parties' four minor children in a divorce action wherein custody was granted to father. The record therein reflected that wife's lesbian relationship had been ongoing for but six months when husband obtained a modification of the divorce decree granting custody to wife. Wife and her lover showed affection toward one another in front of the children; they slept together in the same bed at the family home; when wife and the children traveled to St. Louis to see her lover, they slept together there. Both sides presented evidence as to the effects of a parent's homosexuality on the minor children in his or her custody. In affirming the trial court, the Missouri Court of Appeals stated:

> Since it is our duty to protect the moral growth and the best interests of the minor children, we find Wife's arguments lacking. . . . [H]omosexuality is not openly accepted or widespread. We wish to protect the children from peer pressure, teasing, and possible ostracizing they may encounter as a result of the "alternative life style" their mother has chosen. . . .
> All of these factors present an unhealthy environment for minor children. Such conduct can never be kept private enough to be a neutral factor in the development of a child's values and character. We will not ignore such con-

duct by a parent which may have an effect on the children's moral development. *Id.* at 166.

In *Jacobson v. Jacobson*, 314 N.W.2d 78 (N.D. 1981), the North Dakota Supreme Court reversed a judgment of the lower court awarding custody of the parties' children to the wife, who was admittedly involved in a homosexual relationship with another woman at the time of trial. In so doing, the Court stated:

> [W]e cannot lightly dismiss the fact that living in the same house with their mother and her lover may well cause the children to "suffer from the slings and arrows of a disapproving society" to a much greater extent than would an arrangement wherein the children were placed in the custody of their father with visitation rights in the mother. Although we agree with the trial court that the children will be required to deal with the problem regardless of which parent has custody, it is apparent to us that requiring the children to live, day-to-day, in the same residence with the mother and her lover means that the children will have to confront the problem to a significantly greater degree than they would if living with their father. We agree with the trial court that we cannot determine whether or not the fact the custodial parent is homosexual or bisexual will result in an increased likelihood that the children will become homosexual or bisexual. There is insufficient expert testimony to make that determination. However, that issue does not control our conclusion. Rather, we believe that because of the mores of today's society, because Sandra is engaged in a homosexual relationship in the home in which she resides with the children, and because of the lack of legal recognition of the status of a homosexual relationship, the best inter-

ests of the children will be better served by placing custody of the children with Duane. *Id.* 81-82.

In *M. J. P. v. J. G. P.*, 640 P.2d 966 (Okla. 1982), the Supreme Court of Oklahoma held that an open homosexual relationship involving custodial parents was sufficient change of circumstances to warrant a modification of a child custody order giving custody of the parties' two-and-a-half-year-old son to mother. Shortly after the divorce, the mother moved in with a female lover and her twelve-year-old son. The mother admitted that she had established a homosexual relationship with her lover, and that they engaged in certain lovers' caresses in the presence of the young boy. The mother testified that she had told her lover's son that there was nothing immoral about two women being lovers and living together, and that it was not immoral for two men to have a homosexual relationship. She also told him that one day she would express those same thoughts to her own son, stating that an explanation of the strong commitment and love that she and her lover had for one another would be in her son's best welfare.

The writer is not impressed by the attempt of wife to assert a constitutional argument couched upon the Fourteenth Amendment. The cases cited by wife are not in point. Furthermore, homosexuals are not offered the constitutional protection that race, national origin and alienage have been afforded. *Anderson v. Martin*, 375 U.S. 399, 84 S.Ct. 454, 11 L.Ed.2d 430 (1964) (race); *Castaneda v. Partida*, 430 U.S. 482, 97 S.Ct. 1272, 51 L.Ed.2d 498 (1977) (national origin); and *Graham v. Richardson*, 403 U.S. 365, 91 S.Ct. 1848, 29 L.Ed.2d 534 (1971) (alienage). *Bowers v. Hardwick,*—U.S.—, 106 S.Ct. 2841, 92 L.Ed.2d 140 (1986). By the

same token, I find no persuasion in wife's citation of cases from other jurisdictions that favor homosexual parental custody. *S.N.E. v. R.L.B.*, 699 P.2d 875 (Alaska 1985); *M. P. v. S. P.*, 404 A.2d 1256 (N.J. App. 1979); *D. H. v. J. H.*, 418 N.E.2d 286 (Ind. App. 1981).

The record before this Court presents a mother who seeks to have the courts of this state afford her the privilege of raising to adulthood the parties' nine-year-old daughter, notwithstanding the fact that during the eight years prior to trial she had been involved in not one but four ongoing homosexual relationships. Each relationship was carried on in the family home where she would hug and kiss her female lover, as well as telling her that she loved her. During the period that she had custody, Mother and her lover slept in the same bed in the same bedroom in the custodial home. In addition, Mother informed her daughter that she was a homosexual, stating that homosexual love is the same as heterosexual love. Nonetheless, the daughter has been counseled by her mother not to discuss her homosexuality with the daughter's friends.

The courts of this state have a duty to perpetuate the values and morals associated with the family and conventional marriage, inasmuch as homosexuality is and should be treated as errant and deviant social behavior. I would have this Court declare under this or a similar set of facts that a practicing homosexual parent be disqualified from obtaining legal custody of one's minor child or children. While a child the age of parties' daughter is too young to emulate her mother's conduct, to hold otherwise would be adopting a "wait and see" attitude and would endanger the child's moral development. It is too great a risk to postpone taking action to safeguard the moral well being of children until one sees tangible manifestations of harm to their characters.

In so holding, this Court would not be deciding that Mother could never obtain custody of the child. While Mother's homosexuality may be beyond her control, submitting to it and living with a person of the same sex in a sexual relationship is not. Just as an alcoholic overcomes the habit and becomes a nondrinker, so this mother should attempt to dissolve her "alternate life style" of homosexual living. Such is not too great a sacrifice to expect of a parent in order to gain or retain custody of his or her child. This Court can take judicial notice of the fact that throughout the ages, dedicated, loving parents have countless times made much greater sacrifices for their children.

NO

Melvin P. Antell

MAJORITY OPINION

M. P. *v.* S. P.

The opinion of the court was delivered by Judge Antell.

Defendant (former wife) was awarded a divorce for sexual cruelty by judgment dated September 11, 1969 after a six-year marriage from which two children were born, Franceen (fictitious name) on June 8, 1964 and Joy (fictitious name) on July 15, 1968. She received custody of the daughters, and until the determination before us for review they have always resided with their mother, a period of about seven years after the divorce.

On May 20, 1975 the Chancery Division ordered defendant to show cause why custody of the children should not be transferred to plaintiff on the ground that defendant "is an unfit mother." The order was signed on plaintiff's application, his first since the judgment of divorce. After a number of hearings, the last of which was on January 22, 1976, the trial judge, by letter opinion dated August 30, 1976, awarded custody to the father, directing that the "provision for custody shall take effect immediately and shall be explained at length in my opinion to follow as soon as possible." The judge's oral opinion was delivered September 23, 1977 and his order, transferring custody and granting defendant rights of visitation, was filed on October 3, 1977. We have not been told of any valid reason for the lengthy delays in the foregoing sequence of procedural events. Our concern is that this unexplained delay on the trial judge's part should not be the basis for denying defendant relief if she is otherwise entitled thereto. Defendant appeals on the ground that the trial judge erred in modifying the judgment and divesting her of custody.

Central to this appeal is the fact that defendant is an admitted practicing homosexual. She argues that the action below was taken because of this fact alone and is therefore not legally sustainable. Plaintiff expressly disavows any claim that defendant is an unfit mother by reason of her homosexuality. He concedes that her right to custody of the children cannot be denied,

From *M. P. v. S. P.*, 169 N.J.Super. 425, 404 A.2d 1256 (1979). Notes and some case citations omitted.

limited or restricted on the basis of her sexual orientation alone—a proposition with which we are in accord. Furthermore, compatibly with the uncontradicted expert testimony, plaintiff disclaims being concerned with "any threat that the children's sexual development will be in any way altered by the fact that defendant is a homosexual." Rather, he relies for affirmance exclusively upon a claim of changed circumstances since the date of the original custody award such that the best interests of the children dictate modification of that determination.

At the outset it is noted that the trial judge made no finding, nor in any way concerned himself with the issue, of changed circumstances.

The evidence discloses that from the beginning this marriage was afflicted by sexual discord. Although the record is burdened with detailed testimony in which each party blames the other for their disastrous relationship, much is irrelevant except to demonstrate that at least from the time of their separation in 1967 plaintiff has been aware of defendant's homosexual propensities. As he knew when they separated, defendant was involved in an affair with another woman (Barbara), one which continued through and beyond the date of the divorce.

After the divorce defendant moved into a small apartment and plaintiff exercised weekly visitation rights with respect to the older daughter, Franceen, but refused to acknowledge Joy as his child. He persisted in this refusal, failing even to visit her when she was hospitalized, until adjudicated the father and ordered to pay for her support. It was as a result of defendant's persuasion that he eventually included Joy in his visits.

On October 14, 1970 defendant voluntarily admitted herself to Ancora State Hospital to be treated for a depressive neurosis. Plaintiff made no attempt to obtain custody at that time, and the daughters were cared for by defendant's parents. After defendant left the hospital on December 17, 1970 she and the girls lived with her parents until the summer of 1974. During this time defendant worked full-time and attended counseling sessions.

In the fall of 1974 Joy developed emotional problems that impaired her learning abilities, and defendant reduced her work to a part-time basis. She observed Joy's work in school, met frequently with her teachers, met with the school psychologist and helped with remediating Joy's motor coordination skills. The child was also enrolled in a county guidance center where mother and daughter attended sessions together, and Joy was thereafter returned to regular classes.

The evidence shows that defendant has been equally concerned with the needs of Franceen.

In late 1974, upon the advice of school officials, defendant and the girls left the household where they had been residing. For three months thereafter they resided with "Joyce," defendant's lesbian companion. This arrangement was unworkable, however, since Joyce lived in a school district different from where defendant's daughters were enrolled. Therefore, in the interests of her children defendant returned to her parents' home. During the foregoing period defendant and Joyce slept apart and the children had their own room.

No specific findings were made in connection therewith, but the record is uncontradicted that defendant is an attentive mother who fed and dressed her children well, provided them with medical and dental care, and arranged for surgery, allergy tests and orthodonture. She has done all that can be expected of a dutiful mother.

Although he determined to alter the custody arrangement, the trial judge found that defendant was "a very warm, loving mother," that she "cares for her children and generally within her means, at least at a level deemed minimally adequate, has provided for them." Recognizing, however, that plaintiff was "equally concerned" with the children, the judge decided to "examine into the question of homosexuality as a disqualifying effect on a parent."

The trial judge apparently weighed against defendant the fact that she was caught up "in an attempt to find her own identity and to deal with the problems" arising from her sexual status. However, he did not explain what problems he had in mind or in what way her problems or her quest for identity were different from those of most ordinary people; more importantly, he made no attempt to articulate a relationship between any of this and the welfare of the children. The judge also noted that defendant's ongoing liaison with her lesbian companion had "materially upset the older child and will have a slight influence in all probability, from the credible evidence, on the younger child." On an earlier occasion the judge had ordered that defendant not share Joyce's company at any time when the children were present, and this order has not been violated. Furthermore, there is nothing in the record to show any nexus between defendant's sexual companionship and the older girl's reaction.

Nowhere do we find documented in the record any specific instances of sex-

ual misconduct by defendant or evidence that she tried in any way to inculcate the girls with her sexual attitudes. To the contrary, the evidence is affirmatively to the effect that she never displayed any sexual behavior in the presence of her children, and that she refrains from any demonstration of affection toward other women when the girls are present. Moreover, she is not a member of any homosexual organization. As we said in *De Vita v. De Vita*, 145 N.J. Super. 120 (App. Div. 1976):

> When dealing with custody the burden of proof required to show that a mother is guilty of gross sexual misconduct to the detriment of her children is a heavy one. [at 124]

It is well settled that the best interests of the child are of primary concern to the court in any matter involving the custody of minor children. Since the conditions which would satisfy the best interests of a child during all of its minority cannot be conclusively determined in a single decree, custody orders are always held to be modifiable upon a showing of changed circumstances that would affect the welfare of the child. The party seeking the modification bears the burden of showing sufficient changed circumstances so as to require modification.

In assessing a claim of changed circumstances deference is given to the length and stability of the existing custody relationship. The potential for damage which resides in removing a child from its psychological parent has been recognized in a number of cases. In *In re P, and wife*, 114 N.J. Super. 584, 592–93, 595 (App. Div. 1971), we held that although neither set of parents was obviously better fit than the other, the best interests of the child mandated that custody remain with the psychological foster parents, rather than the biological parents. So important is this factor that our Supreme Court pointedly stated in *Sorentino v. Family & Children's Soc. of Elizabeth*, 72 N.J. 127 (1976), that one seeking to change the child's custodial status quo

> . . . will have the burden of proving by a preponderance of the credible evidence that the potentiality for serious psychological harm accompanying or resulting from such a move will not become a reality. [at 133]

Not only did plaintiff offer no proof to meet this formidable burden, but, as we noted earlier, the trial judge made no findings which pointed to a change of circumstances. The only conclusion to be drawn is, as defendant claims, that the custody order was modified for the sole reason that she is a homosexual and without regard to the welfare of the children. This conclusion gains added support from our further analysis of the record and the determinations before us for review.

In awarding custody to plaintiff the trial judge did so on the reasoning that plaintiff

> . . . may provide a more stable atmosphere for the custody, maintenance and welfare of these children. His home is more stable. He is financially secure and is able to provide the children with the best type of care, custody, maintenance and it is in their best interest that the Court feels that custody should reside in the father.

However, absent from the record is any factual basis for the judge's belief that the father's home is more stable than the defendant's or that he is "financially secure and is able to provide the children with the best type of care, custody, maintenance. . . ." Actually, at the time of the

hearing plaintiff was in arrears on his child support obligations in the amount of almost $ 5,000, a fact which has caused defendant to apply for welfare assistance. When asked by the trial judge why he had not been making the payments, he explained only, "I imagine it is a combination of things," and stated that support would be "easier having the children with you." As to his sincerity of purpose in seeking custody, we note again that plaintiff initially denied that he was Joy's father, and in the course of the judicial proceedings which followed he admittedly testified falsely in denying that he had had sexual relations with defendant during certain critical times. The inference is at least reasonable that if defendant had not brought proceedings in aid of execution to compel plaintiff to meet his support obligations, plaintiff's custody application would not have been made.

Nor are we shown any factual support for the trial judge's evident belief that the children are being harmed or are likely to be harmed by continued custody with defendant. The only findings offered for this purpose are that defendant's homosexuality has "affected" Franceen, that it has "materially upset" her, and that it "will have a slight influence in all probability" on Joy. Against this the report of Dr. Yaskin, the psychiatrist appointed by the court at the recommendation of plaintiff's attorney, concludes that the younger child, Joy,

> . . . is seriously in need of her mother's continuing emotional support. Her ongoing deep identification and dependency is with the mother and it is my clinical opinion that any attempt, at this time, to separate [Joy] from her mother will result in serious psychological consequences to the child.

Reporting on Franceen he comments that she is "rather well poised" and "that she has no ongoing emotional or behavioral problems." Further,

. . . [T]here is no question that she loves her mother. She states, without hesitation, that her mother has always shown an adequate concern re the nutrition and their dress. She also states her mother has always been kind to her and has never abused her. She adds, "I know she loves me." I asked her if there was anything in her ongoing relationship with her mother that she objected to and she answers, "No—Mother is a good person."

Dr. Yaskin took account of Franceen's expressed desire to live with her father, but concluded that her reasons were "puerile," i.e., that she could "go fishing and everything" with her cousins who lived nearby, that she feels sorry for her father sometimes, and that she has feelings of affection for her baby stepbrother. The doctor found that Franceen had no "real ongoing concern or realistic knowledge as to what the term homosexuality connotes" and "just considers it as a type of relationship." His report left no doubt that she "has a deep maternal attachment and identification."

In dismissing this testimony the trial judge said nothing more than that he would "totally reject" the expert evidence which fully supported continued custody in defendant mother because he did "not find it credible in its postulates and conclusions." In doing so he overlooked the fact that the assistance of experts as an aid in resolving the difficult questions presented was clearly desirable. We emphasize that it was the trial judge himself who, evidently recognizing his own lack of expertise, requested the examination and report from Dr.

Yaskin, whose name was recommended to him by plaintiff's own attorney. As we have noted elsewhere, the testimony of child study specialists is properly relied on by the courts. These witnesses were qualified, their opinions were unrefuted and were not inherently implausible. . . . [W]e see no reason why they should have been ignored in this case. See, too, Sorentino v. Family & Children's Soc. of Elizabeth, 74 N.J. 313, 320 (1977).

Apparently the trial judge placed greater credence in what the children told him during in camera hearings, some of which was recorded, some not. For example, he concluded that Franceen disliked defendant's companion, Joyce, "almost to the point of hatred," but there is nothing in Franceen's recorded testimony to support such a belief. If it was based on something he was privately told by the child, it was not memorialized in the manner suggested in State v. Green, 129 N.J. Super. 157, 166 (App. Div. 1974). Except for the conclusion which he drew therefrom, there is nothing to show what he was told off the record, and without some disclosure to the parties on the record it should not have been allowed to influence his decision. In effect, defendant was denied an opportunity to be heard on the facts. Callen v. Gill, 7 N.J. 312, 319 (1951).

In modifying custody the trial judge rejected the "tender years" doctrine as "an obsolete, untenable, antediluvian theory." We disagree that he was free to disregard in this manner the ages of the children as a factor in determining where custody should lie. Although our personal views may be contrary, the Supreme Court has still not displaced the doctrine that custody of a young child "is normally placed with the mother, if fit." Esposito v. Esposito, 41 N.J. 143, 154

(1963). Also see *Mayer v. Mayer*, 150 N.J. Super. 556, 563–64 (Ch. Div. 1977). That the children were still of tender years was something which should have been weighed in this case in favor of preserving the custodial arrangement, and the trial judge erred in failing to do so.

We have already noted that the trial judge made no finding of changed circumstances as a reason for modifying the custody provision. However, plaintiff argues that a change of circumstance may`nevertheless be found in the fact that defendant's variant sexual orientation now causes embarrassment to the girls in the eyes of their peers. We address ourselves to this final contention.

It is first observed that the trial judge made no finding of fact which lends support to plaintiff's claim. All he said was that Franceen had been "upset" by Joyce, defendant's lesbian friend, a problem earlier resolved by banishing Joyce from the presence of the children. The only evidence of "embarrassment" is to be found in Franceen's testimony about conversations with her friends, in which she was asked why her mother dated other women. Nothing therein suggests that these were in any way traumatizing. We know of no finding by the trial judge that Franceen is "pressured by her peers," nor how such a finding could be supported by the proofs. In fact, we do not understand the sense in which this expression is used in the dissenting opinion or the weight which such a finding could be accorded within the context of this case.

Plaintiff's argument overlooks, too, the fact that the children's exposure to embarrassment is not dependent upon the identity of the parent with whom they happen to reside. Their discomfiture, if any, comes about not because of living with defendant, but because she is their mother, because she is a lesbian, and because the community will not accept her. Neither the prejudices of the small community in which they live nor the curiosity of their peers about defendant's sexual nature will be abated by a change of custody. Hard facts must be faced. These are matters which courts cannot control, and there is little to gain by creating an artificial world where the children may dream that life is different than it is.

Furthermore, the law governing grants of custody does not yield to such narrow considerations. Of overriding importance is that within the context of a loving and supportive relationship there is no reason to think that the girls will be unable to manage whatever anxieties may flow from the community's disapproval of their mother. In *Commonwealth ex rel. Lucas v. Kreischer*, 450 Pa. 352, 299 A.2d 243 (Sup. Ct. 1973), the trial court awarded custody of the children, whose mother had entered into an interracial marriage, to their father because of the "almost universal prejudice and intolerance of interracial marriage." In reversing, the Supreme Court of Pennsylvania rested its determination upon the following observation, which we deem pertinent, made by the dissenting judge of the intermediate appellate court:

> "[I]n a multiracial society such as ours racial prejudice and tension are inevitable. If . . . children are raised in a happy and stable home, they will be able to cope with prejudice and hopefully learn that people are unique individuals who should be judged as such." [299 A.2d at 246]

Mistaken also, in our view, is plaintiff's assumption that the welfare of the children cannot be served unless they are sheltered from all the adversities that are inherent to their basic life situation. Regrettably, the decision as to where custody shall lie must be made in terms of available alternatives, and in this case neither holds out the promise of a completely unguent environment. While one is troubled by the possible problems that may arise from defendant's homosexual bent, the evidence also strongly features a disturbed and abrasive personal relationship between Joy and plaintiff's present wife which has resulted in the administration of unduly harsh discipline to this child. She also dislikes and fears plaintiff. . . .

If defendant retains custody, it may be that because the community is intolerant of her differences these girls may sometimes have to bear themselves with greater than ordinary fortitude. But this does not necessarily portend that their moral welfare or safety will be jeopardized. It is just as reasonable to expect that they will emerge better equipped to search out their own standards of right and wrong, better able to perceive that the majority is not always correct in its moral judgments, and better able to understand the importance of conforming their beliefs to the requirements of reason and tested knowledge, not the constraints of currently popular sentiment or prejudice.

Taking the children from defendant can be done only at the cost of sacrificing those very qualities they will find most sustaining in meeting the challenges inevitably ahead. Instead of forbearance and feelings of protectiveness, it will foster in them a sense of shame for their mother. Instead of courage and the precept that people of integrity do not shrink from bigots, it counsels the easy option of shirking difficult problems and following the course of expedience. Lastly, it diminishes their regard for the rule of human behavior, everywhere accepted, that we do not forsake those to whom we are indebted for love and nurture merely because they are held in low esteem by others.

We conclude that the children's best interests will be disserved by undermining in this way their growth as mature and principled adults. Extensive evidence in the record upon which we have not commented amply confirms the trial judge's finding that defendant is a worthy mother. Nothing suggests that her homosexual preference in itself presents any threat of harm to her daughters or that in the ordinary course of their development they will be unable to deal with whatever vexation may be caused to their spirits by the community.

Careful attention has been given to the nature of the relief to be awarded. Although advantages are evident in remanding for further hearings by which the current status of the matter may be ascertained, after a thorough examination of the entire record we are satisfied that the welfare of the children will only be impaired without corresponding benefit by prolonging any further these already protracted proceedings. The order under review is therefore reversed and the custody provision contained in the judgment of divorce dated September 11, 1969 is reinstated.

POSTSCRIPT

Should Homosexuality Bar a Parent from Being Awarded Custody of a Child?

The custody issue discussed here involves both gay rights and the larger issue of what the legal definition of a family should be. Families have been changing and the law is struggling to come to grips with these changes. The proportion of American households consisting of a married couple and their own minor children, for example, declined from 44.2 percent in 1960 to 27.0 percent in 1988. In 1988, single parents with their own minor children constituted 27.3 percent of American households, more than double the number of single-parent families in 1970. More children are living with a stepparent. The number of households consisting of two unrelated adults of the opposite sex (with or without children under 15 years old) was five times greater in 1990 than 1970.

While there are no reliable statistics on gay households, it is probably a fair assessment to say that it has become clear that the 1980s have witnessed the emergence of an entirely new family structure, unparalleled in human history. For the first time ever in any society we know about, gay people in large numbers are setting out consciously, deliberately, proudly, and openly to bear or adopt children.

These new living arrangements challenge the law in many areas. Unmarried couples who live together, for example, often do not receive the same health and death benefits as legally married employees receive for their spouses. The current legal definition of *family* may also deny benefits to stepfamilies, foster families, grandparents, and parents of children born through new reproductive technologies. Surrogate motherhood, for example, has been a continuously controversial and challenging legal topic since the Baby M case in 1988.

The issue of redefining the family is considered in M. Minow, "Redefining Families: Who's In and Who's Out?" 62 *Colorado Law Review* 269 (1991); Note, "Looking for a Family Resemblance: The Limits of the Functional Approach to the Legal Definition of Family," 104 *Harvard Law Review* 1640 (1991); M. Glendon, *State, Law and Family: Family Law in Transition in the United States and Western Europe* (1977); and Bartlett, "Rethinking Parenthood as an Exclusive Status: The Need for Legal Alternatives When the Promise of the Nuclear Family Has Failed," 70 *Virginia Law Review* 879 (1984). In *Braschi v. Stahl Associates*, 543 N.E.2d 49, 55 (1989), a New York court held that a homosexual partnership could be considered a "family" for purposes of New York City's rent control law. Changes in family law are discussed in "Beyond No-Fault: New Directions in Divorce Reform," in Sugarman and Kay, eds., *Divorce Reform at the Crossroads* (1990). Readings on gay rights include "Developments in the Law—Sexual Orientation and the Law," 102 *Harvard Law Review* 1508 (1989).

Photo courtesy of the IBM Corporation

PART 3

Law and Crime

Crime is a fact of life for many citizens in the United States, and the social, economic, and psychological costs are high for individual victims and society as a whole. Every society has to contend with those members who refuse to adhere to the established rules of behavior; how criminals are treated is often one standard for judging a society's fairness and compassion.

The debates in this section address issues concerning the treatment of criminals and the legal rights of the accused as well as the rights of citizens to be free from fear.

Should the Death Penalty
  Be Abolished?
  _____

Should the Exclusionary Rule
  Be Abolished?
  _____

Should "Battered Wife Syndrome" Be
  Barred as a Defense in a Murder
  Case?
  _____

Should a National Gun Control Policy
  Be Established?
  _____

Does Caller ID Invade Privacy?
  _____

Should the Insanity Defense Be
  Abolished?

ISSUE 12

Should the Death Penalty Be Abolished?

YES: Jack Greenberg, from "Against the American System of Capital Punishment," *Harvard Law Review* (1986)

NO: Ernest van den Haag, from "The Ultimate Punishment: A Defense," *Harvard Law Review* (1986)

ISSUE SUMMARY

YES: Law professor Jack Greenberg argues that capital punishment should be banned because it is applied erratically and in a racially and regionally biased manner.
NO: Law professor Ernest van den Haag responds that the death penalty is moral and just and should be employed against those who commit murder.

Unlike some of the issues in this book, capital punishment has a long history. For example, in 428 B.C., Thucydides recorded the following arguments by Cleon, in support of the death penalty:

> Punish them as they deserve, and teach your other allies by a striking example that the penalty of rebellion is death. Let them once understand this and you will not so often have to neglect your enemies while you are fighting with your confederates.

In response, Diodotus wrote:

> All states and individuals are alike prone to err, and there is no law that will prevent them, or why should men have exhausted the list of punishments in search of enactments to protect them from evil doers? It is probable that in early times the penalties for the greatest offenses were less severe, and that as these were disregarded, the penalty of death has been by degrees in most cases arrived at, which is itself disregarded in like manner. Either some means of terror more terrible than this must be discovered, or it must be owned that this restraint is useless. . . .
>
> We must make up our minds to look for our protection not to legal terrors but to careful administration. . . . Good policy against an adversary is superior to the blind attacks of brute force.

During the last two decades, the Supreme Court has been confronted with death penalty cases almost every year. The most significant decision was that of *Furman v. Georgia*, 408 U.S. 238, decided in 1972. Furman, a 26-year-old black man, had killed a homeowner during a break-in and was sentenced to death. In a 5–4 decision, the Court overturned the sentence. It held that the procedure used by Georgia (and most other states at that time) was "cruel and unusual" and therefore a violation of the Eighth Amendment of the Constitution. At the heart of the case was the fact that Georgia law left it up to the discretion of the jury to decide whether or not the death penalty was appropriate in a particular case. Two justices, Thurgood Marshall and William J. Brennan, Jr., believed that the death penalty under any circumstances violated the cruel and unusual punishment clause. The three other justices in the majority, however, felt that the death penalty was not in itself unconstitutional but that the manner in which it was applied in this case was unlawful. They felt that leaving the sentence up to the jury led it to be "wantonly" and "freakishly" imposed and "pregnant with discrimination."

The short-term impact of the *Furman* case was to remove all individuals sentenced under pre-*Furman* laws from death row. The long-term message of the decision, however, was that the death penalty was lawful if the procedure that was employed limited the discretion of the person(s) meting out the punishment.

Since 1972, 36 states have enacted new death penalty statutes. The following cases illustrate some of the difficulties involved in developing a consistent standard through a case-by-case approach.

1. *Gregg v. Georgia*, 428 U.S. 153 (1976) After *Furman*, Georgia enacted a new statute retaining the death penalty for murder and five other crimes. Guilt or innocence was determined at a trial and then a second hearing or trial was held for the jury to determine whether the death penalty should be applied. The law set up procedures that were intended to limit the jury's discretion and that required higher court review of the sentence with the hope that this would reduce the incidence of discrimination and prejudice. In a 7–2 decision, this law was upheld by the Supreme Court.

2. *Lockett v. Ohio*, 438 U.S. 586 (1978) Ohio law prevented the jury from considering any mitigating circumstances other than those specifically enumerated in the statute. The Supreme Court held that this law was unconstitutional.

3. *Coker v. Georgia*, 433 U.S. 584 (1977) The Supreme Court held that the death penalty may not be imposed on persons convicted of rape. The case suggests that the death penalty is unconstitutional if a death did not take place as a result of the defendant's actions.

What these cases indicate is that the death penalty is lawful and not "cruel and unusual" if the victim has been killed, if the statute provides the defendant the opportunity to present mitigating circumstances, if the statute lists aggravating circumstances that must be considered, and if it requires appellate review. These procedural requirements have been imposed mainly to reduce the possibility of discriminatory application of the death penalty.

YES
Jack Greenberg

AGAINST THE AMERICAN SYSTEM
OF CAPITAL PUNISHMENT

Over and over, proponents of the death penalty insist that it is right and useful. In reply abolitionists argue that it is morally flawed and cite studies to demonstrate its failure to deter. Were the subject not so grim and compelling, the exchanges would, by now, be tiresome.

Yet all too frequently, the debate has been off the mark. Death penalty proponents have assumed a system of capital punishment that simply does not exist: a system in which the penalty is inflicted on the most reprehensible criminals and meted out frequently enough both to deter and to perform the moral and utilitarian functions ascribed to retribution. Explicitly or implicitly, they assume a system in which certainly the worst criminals, Charles Manson or a putative killer of one's parent or child, for example, are executed in an even-handed manner. But this idealized system is *not* the American system of capital punishment. Because of the goals that our criminal justice system must satisfy—deterring crime, punishing the guilty, acquitting the innocent, avoiding needless cruelty, treating citizens equally, and prohibiting oppression by the state—America simply does not have the kind of capital punishment system contemplated by death penalty partisans.

Indeed, the reality of American capital punishment is quite to the contrary. Since at least 1967, the death penalty has been inflicted only rarely, erratically, and often upon the least odious killers, while many of the most heinous criminals have escaped execution. Moreover, it has been employed almost exclusively in a few formerly slaveholding states, and there it has been used almost exclusively against killers of whites, not blacks, and never against white killers of blacks. This is the American system of capital punishment. It is this system, not some idealized one, that must be defended in any national debate on the death penalty. I submit that this system is deeply incompatible with the proclaimed objectives of death penalty proponents.

From Jack Greenberg, "Against the American System of Capital Punishment," *Harvard Law Review,* vol. 99 (May 1986). Copyright © 1986 by the Harvard Law Review Association. Reprinted by permission. Some notes omitted.

I. THE AMERICAN SYSTEM OF CAPITAL PUNISHMENT

Here is how America's system of capital punishment really works today. Since 1967, the year in which the courts first began to grapple in earnest with death penalty issues, the death penalty has been frequently imposed but rarely enforced. Between 1967 and 1980, death sentences or convictions were reversed for 1889 of the 2402 people on death row, a reversal rate of nearly eighty percent.[1] These reversals reflected, among other factors, a 1968 Supreme Court decision dealing with how juries should be chosen in capital cases,[2] a 1972 decision declaring capital sentences unconstitutional partly because they were imposed arbitrarily and "freakishly,"[3] and a 1976 decision holding mandatory death sentences unconstitutional.[4] Many death sentences were also invalidated on a wide variety of commonplace state-law grounds, such as hearsay rule violations or improper prosecutorial argument.

This judicial tendency to invalidate death penalties proved resistant to change. After 1972, in response to Supreme Court decisions, many states adopted new death penalty laws, and judges developed a clearer idea of the requirements that the Court had begun to enunciate a few years earlier. By 1979, the efforts of state legislatures finally paid off when John Spenkelink[5] became the first person involuntarily[6] executed since 1967.[7] Nevertheless, from 1972 to 1980, the death penalty invalidation rate declined to "only" sixty percent. In contrast, ordinary noncapital convictions and sentences were almost invariably upheld.[8]

Today, the death row population has grown to more than 1600 convicts. About 300 prisoners per year join this group, while about 100 per year leave death row mainly by reason of judicial invalidations but also by execution and by death from other causes. Following Spenkelink's execution, some states began to put some of these convicted murderers to death. Five persons were executed involuntarily in 1983, twenty-one in 1984, and fourteen in 1985. . . . Yet even if this number doubled, or increased fivefold, executions would not be numerous either in proportion to the nation's homicides (approximately 19,000 per year) or to its death row population (over 1600).

One reason for the small number of executions is that the courts continue to upset capital convictions at an extraordinarily high rate, albeit not so high as earlier. Between January 1, 1982 and October 1, 1985, state supreme courts invalidated thirty-five percent of all capital judgments. State post-appellate process undid a few more. The federal district and appeals courts overturned another ten percent, and last Term the Supreme Court reversed three of the four capital sentences it reviewed. Altogether, about forty-five percent of capital judgments which were reviewed during this period were set aside by one court or another. One index of the vitality of litigation to reverse executions is that while legal attacks on capital punishment began as a coordinated effort by civil rights lawyers, they now come from a variety of segments of the bar.[9]

States not only execute convicted killers rarely, but they do so erratically. Spenkelink's execution, the nation's first involuntary execution since 1967, did not augur well for new systems of guided discretion designed to produce evenhanded capital justice in which only the worst murderers would be executed.

Spenkelink was a drifter who killed a traveling companion who had sexually abused him. The Assistant Attorney General of Florida in charge of capital cases described him as "probably the least obnoxious individual on death row in terms of the crime he committed." . . .

[O]ne major difference exists between the period 1982 to 1985 and earlier years: increasingly, the death penalty has been concentrated geographically, not applied evenly across the United States. In the most recent period, there were forty-three involuntary executions. Quite strikingly, all occurred in the states of the Old Confederacy. Thirty-four of the forty-three were in four states, and more than a quarter were in a single state, Florida, with thirteen. In all but four cases, the defendants killed white persons. In no case was a white executed for killing a black person.

Why are there so few executions? Convictions and sentences are reversed, cases move slowly and states devote relatively meager resources to pursuing *actual* executions. Even Florida, which above all other states has shown that it can execute almost any death row inmate it wants to, had killed only 13 of 221 inmates since 1979, 12 since 1982. (It now has 233 convicts on death row.) Outside the former slave-holding states, more than half the states are now abolitionist either de jure (fourteen states) or de facto (five states have no one on death row). Moreover, past experience suggests that the execution level will not go very high. Before the 1967–76 moratorium, the number of executions exceeded fifty only once after 1957—fifty-six in 1960. At that time there were fewer abolitionist states and more capital crimes. This experience suggests that executions will not deplete the death row population.

The limited number of actual executions seems to me to reflect the very deep ambivalence that Americans feel about capital punishment. We are the only nation of the Western democratic world that has not abolished capital punishment. By contrast, countries with whose dominant value systems we ordinarily disagree, like the Soviet Union, China, Iran, and South Africa, execute prisoners in great numbers.

II. THE FAILURES OF CAPITAL PUNISHMENT

We have a system of capital punishment that results in infrequent, random, and erratic executions, one that is structured to inflict death neither on those who have committed the worst offenses nor on defendants of the worst character. This is the "system"—if that is the right descriptive term—of capital punishment that must be defended by death penalty proponents. *This* system may not be justified by positing a particularly egregious killer like Charles Manson. Our commitment to the rule of law means that we need an acceptable *general* system of capital justice if we are to have one at all. However, the real American system of capital punishment clearly fails when measured against the most common justifications for the infliction of punishment, deterrence, and retribution.

If capital punishment can be a deterrent greater than life imprisonment at all, the American system is at best a feeble one. Studies by Thorsten Sellin showed no demonstrable deterrent effect of capital punishment even during its heyday. Today's death penalty, which is far less frequently used, geographically localized, and biased according to the race of the victim, cannot possibly upset that conclusion. The forty-three persons who were involuntarily executed from 1982 to 1985 were among a death row population of more than 1600 condemned to execution out of about 20,000 who committed non-negligent homicides per year. While forty-three percent of the victims were black, the death penalty is so administered that it overwhelmingly condemns and executes those who have killed whites.

Very little reason exists to believe that the present capital punishment system deters the conduct of others any more effectively than life imprisonment. Potential killers who rationally weigh the odds of being killed themselves must conclude that the danger is nonexistent in most parts of the country and that in the South the danger is slight, particularly if the proposed victim is black. Moreover, the paradigm of this kind of murderer, the contract killer, is almost by definition a person who takes his chances like the soldier of fortune he is.

But most killers do not engage in anything like a cost-benefit analysis. They are impulsive, and they kill impulsively. If capital punishment is to deter them, it can do so only indirectly: by impressing on potential killers a standard of right and wrong, a moral authority, an influence on their superegos that, notwithstanding mental disorder, would inhibit homicide. This conception of general deterrence seems deeply flawed because it rests upon a quite implausible conception of how this killer population internalizes social norms. Although not mentally disturbed enough to sustain insanity as a defense, they are often highly disturbed, of low intelligence, and addicted to drugs or alcohol. In any event, the message, if any, that the real American system of capital punishment sends to the psyches of would-be killers is quite limited: you may in a rare case be executed if you murder in the deepest South and kill a white person.

The consequences of the real American system of capital justice are no more favorable as far as retribution is concerned. Retributive theories of criminal punishment draw support from several different moral theories that cannot be adequately elaborated here. While some of the grounds of retribution arguments resemble the conscience-building argument underlying general deterrence theory, all retribution theories insist that seeking retribution constitutes a morally permissible use of governmental power. To retribution theorists, the death penalty makes a moral point: it holds up as an example worthy of the most severe condemnation one who has committed the most opprobrious crime.

As with many controversies over moral issues, these purely moral arguments may appear to end any real possibility for further discussion. For those who believe in them, they persuade, just as the moral counter-arguments persuade abolitionists. But discussion should not end at this point. Those who claim a moral justification for capital punishment must reconcile that belief with other moral considerations. To my mind, the moral force of any retribution argument is radically undercut by the hard facts of the actual American system of capital punishment. This system violates fundamental norms because it is haphazard, and because it is regionally and racially biased. To these moral flaws, I would add another: the minuscule number of executions nowadays cannot achieve the grand moral aims that are presupposed by a serious societal commitment to retribution.

Some retribution proponents argue that it is the pronouncement of several hundred death sentences followed by lengthy life imprisonment, not the actual imposition of a few executions, that satisfies the public's demand for retribution. Of course, the public has not said that it wants the death penalty as it exists—widely applicable but infrequently used. Nor, to the best of my knowledge, is there any solid empirical basis for such a claim. Like other statutes, death penalty laws are of general applicability, to be employed according to their terms.[10] Nothing in their language or legislative history authorizes the erratic, occasional, racially biased use of these laws. But my objections to this argument go much deeper. I find morally objectionable a system of many pronounced death sentences but few actual executions, a system in which race and region are the only significant variables in determining who actually dies. My objection is not grounded in a theory that posits any special moral rights for the death row population. The decisive point is my understanding of the basic moral aspirations of American civilization, particularly its deep commitment to the rule of law. I cannot reconcile an erratic, racially and regionally biased system of executions with my understanding of the core values of our legal order.

Death penalty proponents may respond to this argument by saying that if there is not enough capital punishment, there should be more. If only killers of whites are being executed, then killers of blacks should be killed too; and if many sentences are being reversed, standards of review should be relaxed. In the meantime, they might urge, the death penalty should go on. But this argument is unavailing, because it seeks to change the terms of the debate in a fundamental way. It seeks to substitute an imaginary system for the real American system of capital punishment. If there were a different kind of system of death penalty administration in this country or even a reasonable possibility that one might emerge, we could debate its implications. But any current debate over the death penalty cannot ignore the deep moral deficiencies of the present system.

III. THE CONSTITUTION AND THE DEATH PENALTY

This debate about whether we should have a death penalty is a matter on which the Supreme Court is unlikely to have the last say now or in the near future. Yet, the Court's decisions have some relevance. The grounds that the Court has employed in striking down various forms of the death penalty resemble the arguments I have made. Freakishness was a ground for invalidating the death penalty as it was administered throughout the country in 1972.[11] Rarity of use contributed to invalidation of the death penalty for rape[12] and felony murder,[13] and to invalidation of the mandatory death penalty.[14] That constitutional law reflects moral concerns should not be strange: concepts of cruel and unusual punishment, due process, and equal protection express contemporary standards of decency.

Moreover, the whole development of the fourteenth amendment points to the existence of certain, basic standards of decency and fairness from which no state or region can claim exemption. One such value is, of course, the racially neutral administration of justice. No one disputes that one of the fourteenth amendment's central designs was to secure the evenhanded administration of justice in the southern state courts and that the persistent failure to achieve that goal has been one of America's greatest tragedies. We cannot be blind to the fact that actual executions have taken place primarily in the South and in at least a racially suspect manner. In light of our constitutional history, the race-specific aspects of the death penalty in the South are profoundly unsettling.

Given the situation as I have described it, and as I believe it will continue so long as we have capital punishment, one could argue that the death penalty should be declared unconstitutional in all its forms. But the Court is unlikely to take that step soon. Only ten years have passed since the type of death statute now in use was upheld, and some states have had such laws for an even shorter period. Thirty-seven states have passed laws showing they want some sort of death penalty. Public opinion polls show that most Americans want capital punishment in some form. Having only recently invalidated one application of the death penalty in *Furman v. Georgia* in 1972, the Court is unlikely soon to deal with the concept wholesale again. But, if the way capital punishment works does not change materially, I think that at some point the Court will declare the overall system to be cruel and unusual. If this prediction is correct—and it is at least arguably so—an additional moral factor enters the debate. Is it right to kill death row inmates during this period of experimentation? There is, of course, an element of bootstrapping to my argument: exercising further restraint in killing death-sentenced convicts reinforces arguments of freakishness and rarity of application. But unless one can assure a full and steady stream of executions, suf-

ficient to do the jobs the death penalty proponents claim that it can do, there is further reason to kill no one at all.

NOTES

1. These statistics and the pre-1981 experience with the death penalty are reviewed more extensively in Greenberg, *Capital Punishment as a System*, 91 Yale L.J. 908, 917–18 (1982).

2. *See* Witherspoon v. Illinois, 391 U.S. 510 (1968). On the erosion of *Witherspoon*, see Wainwright v. Witt, 105 S.Ct. 844 (1985), and the perceptive comment in *The Supreme Court, 1984 Term*, 99 Harv L. Rev. 120 (1985).

3. Furman v. Georgia, 408 US. 238, 293 (1972) (Brennan, J., concurring).

4. *See* Woodson v. North Carolina, 428 U.S. 280 (1976).

5. *See* Spinkellink v. State, 313 So. 2d 666 (Fla. 1975), *cert. denied*, 428 U.S. 911 (1976). Spenkelink's name was misspelled by many of the courts that considered his case. *See* Spinkellink v. Wainwright, 578 F.2d 582, 582 n.ı (5th Cir. 1978).

6. I call an execution "involuntary" if the defendant has contested actual implementation of the death penalty. Conversely, a "voluntary" execution is one in which the defendant at some point has voluntarily ceased efforts to resist.

7. This statistic was derived from NAACP Legal Defense and Educational Fund, Death Row U.S.A. 4 (1986) and Greenberg, note I above, at 913. Other statistics set forth in this article, including the number and location of death-sentenced prisoners, whether they have been executed, and their race and the race of their victims have been obtained from the Death Row U.S.A. data bank (on file at the NAACP Legal Defense and Educational Fund in New York), which was computerized in 1984–1985. Death Row U.S.A. is frequently used as an authoritative source by courts, *see*, *e.g.*, Godfrey v. Georgia, 446 US. 420, 439 nn. 7 & 8 (1980); the media, *see*, *e.g.*, U.S. News & World Rep., May 11, 1981, at 72; and scholars, *see*, *e.g.*, Gillers, *Deciding Who Dies*, 129 U. Pa. L. Rev 1, 2 n.2 (1980).

8. For example, in the federal court system during the year ending June 30, 1980, 28,598 defendants were convicted while only 4405 convicted defendants filed appeals. Of these appeals, only 6.5% prevailed. Thus, while not all defendants appealing were convicted during the year surveyed, one can estimate that about 1% of all criminal convictions handed down during that year (290 out of 28,598) were upset on ap-

peal. *See* Administrative Office of the U.S. Courts, 1980 Annual Report of the Director 2 (table 2), 51 (table 10), 97. State court experience is similar.

9. The NAACP Legal Defense and Educational Fund, of which I was Director Counsel until 1984 and which commenced the attacks on capital punishment, has participated in virtually none of the state cases that invalidated death penalties and in very few of the recent federal cases. The American Bar Association Board of Governors, however, approved an effort to obtain $150,000 for a post-conviction death penalty representation project in December 1983, and the Florida legislature enacted a law to furnish counsel on post-conviction death penalty proceedings, *see* Fla. Stat. Ann. § 27.7001 (West Supp. 1986).

10. A few death penalty proponents say that the death penalty is the only way of "assuring" life imprisonment for the worst criminals. Recog-

nizing that most death sentences have turned into interminable prison sentences, they say this is preferable to sentences of life imprisonment from which convicts may be released on parole. But human ingenuity can fashion a sentence of life without parole. The death sentence following extensive litigation, amounting to life sentence for most while executing only a few, is an inefficient way of achieving the purpose of life imprisonment. And again, this sort of life sentencing process is not what the death penalty laws contemplate.

11. *See* Furman v. Georgia, 408 U.S. 238, 293 (1972) (Brennan, J., concurring).

12. *See* Coker v. Georgia, 433 U.S. 584, 594–97 (1977).

13. *See* Enmund v. Florida, 458 U.S. 782, 792–96 (1982).

14. *See* Woodson v. North Carolina, 428 U.S. 280, 292–303 (1976).

NO

Ernest van den Haag

THE ULTIMATE PUNISHMENT: A DEFENSE

In an average year about 20,000 homicides occur in the United States. Fewer than 300 convicted murderers are sentenced to death. But because no more than thirty murderers have been executed in any recent year, most convicts sentenced to death are likely to die of old age.[1] Nonetheless, the death penalty looms large in discussions: it raises important moral questions independent of the number of executions.

The death penalty is our harshest punishment. It is irrevocable: it ends the existence of those punished, instead of temporarily imprisoning them. Further, although not intended to cause physical pain, execution is the only corporal punishment still applied to adults. These singular characteristics contribute to the perennial, impassioned controversy about capital punishment.

I. DISTRIBUTION

Consideration of the justice, morality, or usefulness, of capital punishment is often conflated with objections to its alleged discriminatory or capricious distribution among the guilty. Wrongly so. If capital punishment is immoral *in se*, no distribution among the guilty could make it moral. If capital punishment is moral, no distribution would make it immoral. Improper distribution cannot affect the quality of what is distributed, be it punishments or rewards. Discriminatory or capricious distribution thus could not justify abolition of the death penalty. Further, maldistribution inheres no more in capital punishment than in any other punishment.

Maldistribution between the guilty and the innocent is, by definition, unjust. But the injustice does not lie in the nature of the punishment. Because of the finality of the death penalty, the most grievous maldistribution occurs when it is imposed upon the innocent. However, the frequent allegations of discrimination and capriciousness refer to maldistribution among the guilty and not to the punishment of the innocent.

Maldistribution of any punishment among those who deserve it is irrelevant to its justice or morality. Even if poor or black convicts guilty of capital

From Ernest van den Haag, "The Ultimate Punishment: A Defense," *Harvard Law Review*, vol. 99 (May 1986). Copyright © 1986 by the Harvard Law Review Association. Reprinted by permission. Some notes omitted.

offenses suffer capital punishment, and other convicts equally guilty of the same crimes do not, a more equal distribution however desirable, would merely be more equal. It would not be more just to the convicts under sentence of death.

Punishments are imposed on persons, not on racial or economic groups. Guilt is personal. The only relevant question is: does the person to be executed deserve the punishment? Whether or not others who deserved the same punishment, whatever their economic or racial group, have avoided execution is irrelevant. If they have, the guilt of the executed convicts would not be diminished, nor would their punishment be less deserved. To put the issue starkly, if the death penalty were imposed on guilty blacks, but not on guilty whites, or, if it were imposed by lottery among the guilty, this irrationally discriminatory or capricious distribution would neither make the penalty unjust, nor cause anyone to be unjustly punished, despite the undue impunity bestowed on others.

Equality, in short, seems morally less important than justice. And justice is independent of distributional inequalities. The ideal of equal justice demands that justice be equally distributed, not that it be replaced by equality. Justice requires that as many of the guilty as possible be punished, regardless of whether others have avoided punishment. To let these others escape the deserved punishment does not do justice to them, or to society. But it is not unjust to those who could not escape.

These moral considerations are not meant to deny that irrational discrimination, or capriciousness, would be inconsistent with constitutional requirements. But I am satisfied that the Supreme Court has in fact provided for adherence to the constitutional requirement of equality as much as is possible. Some inequality is indeed unavoidable as a practical matter in any system.[2] But, *ultra posse nemo obligatur.* (Nobody is bound beyond ability.)

Recent data reveal little direct racial discrimination in the sentencing of those arrested and convicted of murder. The abrogation of the death penalty for rape has eliminated a major source of racial discrimination. Concededly, some discrimination based on the race of murder victims may exist; yet, this discrimination affects criminal victimizers in an unexpected way. Murderers of whites are thought more likely to be executed than murderers of blacks. Black victims, then, are less fully vindicated than white ones. However, because most black murderers kill blacks, black murderers are spared the death penalty more often than are white murderers. They fare better than most white murderers. The motivation behind unequal distribution of the death penalty may well have been to discriminate against blacks, but the result has favored them. Maldistribution is thus a straw man for empirical as well as analytical reasons.

II. MISCARRIAGES OF JUSTICE

In a recent survey Professors Hugo Adam Bedau and Michael Radelet found that 7,000 persons were executed in the United States between 1900 and 1985 and that 25 were innocent of capital crimes. Among the innocents they list Sacco and Vanzetti as well as Ethel and Julius Rosenberg. Although their data may be questionable, I do not doubt that, over a long enough period, miscarriages of justice will occur even in capital cases.

Despite precautions, nearly all human activities, such as trucking, lighting, or construction, cost the lives of some innocent bystanders. We do not give up these activities, because the advantages, moral or material, outweigh the unintended losses. Analogously, for those who think the death penalty just, miscarriages of justice are offset by the moral benefits and the usefulness of doing justice. For those who think the death penalty unjust even when it does not miscarry, miscarriages can hardly be decisive.

III. DETERRENCE

Despite much recent work, there has been no conclusive statistical demonstration that the death penalty is a better deterrent than are alternative punishments.[3] However, deterrence is less than decisive for either side. Most abolitionists acknowledge that they would continue to favor abolition even if the death penalty were shown to deter more murders than alternatives could deter. Abolitionists appear to value the life of a convicted murderer or, at least, his non-execution, more highly than they value the lives of the innocent victims who might be spared by deterring prospective murderers.

Deterrence is not altogether decisive for me either. I would favor retention of the death penalty as retribution even if it were shown that the threat of execution could not deter prospective murderers not already deterred by the threat of imprisonment.[4] Still, I believe the death penalty, because of its finality, is more feared than imprisonment, and deters some prospective murderers not deterred by the threat of imprisonment. Sparing the lives of even a few prospec-

tive victims by deterring their murderers is more important than preserving the lives of convicted murderers because of the possibility, or even the probability, that executing them would not deter others. Whereas the lives of the victims who might be saved are valuable, that of the murderer has only negative value, because of his crime. Surely the criminal law is meant to protect the lives of potential victims in preference to those of actual murderers.

Murder rates are determined by many factors; neither the severity nor the probability of the threatened sanction is always decisive. However, for the long run, I share the view of Sir James Fitzjames Stephen: "Some men, probably, abstain from murder because they fear that if they committed murder they would be hanged. Hundreds of thousands abstain from it because they regard it with horror. One great reason why they regard it with horror is that murderers are hanged."[5] Penal sanctions are useful in the long run for the formation of the internal restraints so necessary to control crime. The severity and finality of the death penalty is appropriate to the seriousness and the finality of murder.

IV. INCIDENTAL ISSUES: COST, RELATIVE SUFFERING, BRUTALIZATION

Many nondecisive issues are associated with capital punishment. Some believe that the monetary cost of appealing a capital sentence is excessive.[6] Yet most comparisons of the cost of life imprisonment with the cost of execution, apart from their dubious relevance, are flawed at least by the implied assumption that life prisoners will generate no judicial costs during their imprisonment. At any rate, the actual monetary costs are trumped by the importance of doing justice.

Others insist that a person sentenced to death suffers more than his victim suffered, and that this (excess) suffering is undue according to the *lex talionis* (rule of retaliation). We cannot know whether the murderer on death row suffers more than his victim suffered; however, unlike the murderer, the victim deserved none of the suffering inflicted. Further, the limitations of the *lex talionis* were meant to restrain private vengeance, not the social retribution that has taken its place. Punishment—regardless of the motivation—is not intended to revenge, offset, or compensate for the victim's suffering, or to be measured by it. Punishment is to vindicate the law and the social order undermined by the crime. This is why a kidnapper's penal confinement is not limited to the period for which he imprisoned his victim; nor is a burglar's confinement meant merely to offset the suffering or the harm he caused his victim; nor is it meant only to offset the advantage he gained.[7]

Another argument heard at least since Beccaria is that, by killing a murderer, we encourage, endorse, or legitimize unlawful killing. Yet, although all punishments are meant to be unpleasant, it is seldom argued that they legitimize the unlawful imposition of identical unpleasantness. Imprisonment is not thought to be legitimize kidnapping; neither are fines thought to legitimize robbery. The difference between murder and execution, or between kidnapping and imprisonment, is that the first is unlawful and undeserved, the second a lawful and deserved punishment for an unlawful act. The physical similarities of the punishment to the crime are irrelevant. The relevant difference is not physical, but social.[8]

V. JUSTICE, EXCESS, DEGRADATION

We threaten punishments in order to deter crime. We impose them not only to make the threats credible but also as retribution (justice) for the crimes that were not deterred. Threats and punishments are necessary to deter and deterrence is a sufficient practical justification for them. Retribution is an independent moral justification.[9] Although penalties can be unwise, repulsive, or inappropriate, and those punished can be pitiable, in a sense the infliction of legal punishment on a guilty person cannot be unjust. By committing the crime, the criminal volunteered to assume the risk of receiving a legal punishment that he could have avoided by not committing the crime. The punishment he suffers is the punishment he voluntarily risked suffering and, therefore, it is no more unjust to him than any other event for which one knowingly volunteers to assume the risk. Thus, the death penalty cannot be unjust to the guilty criminal.

There remain, however, two moral objections. The penalty may be regarded as always excessive as retribution and always morally degrading. To regard the death penalty as always excessive, one must believe that no crime—no matter how heinous—could possibly justify capital punishment. Such belief can be neither corroborated nor refuted; it is an article of faith.

Alternatively, or concurrently, one may believe that everybody, the murderer no less than the victim, has an imprescriptible (natural?) right to life. The law therefore should not deprive anyone of life. I share Jeremy Bentham's view that any such "natural and imprescriptible rights" are "nonsense upon stilts."

Justice Brennan has insisted that the death penalty is "uncivilized," "inhuman," inconsistent with "human dignity" and with "the sanctity of life,"[10] that it "treats members of the human race as nonhumans, as objects to be toyed with and discarded,"[11] that it is "uniquely degrading to human dignity"[12] and "by its very nature, [involves] a denial of the executed person's humanity."[13] Justice Brennan does not say why he thinks execution "uncivilized." Hitherto most civilizations have had the death penalty, although it has been discarded in Western Europe, where it is currently unfashionable probably because of its abuse by totalitarian regimes.

By "degrading," Justice Brennan seems to mean that execution degrades the executed convicts. Yet philosophers, such as Immanuel Kant and G. F. W. Hegel, have insisted that, when deserved, execution, far from degrading the executed convict, affirms his humanity by affirming his rationality and his responsibility for his actions. They thought that execution, when deserved, is required for the sake of the convict's dignity. (Does not life imprisonment violate human dignity more than execution, by keeping alive a prisoner deprived of all autonomy?)

Common sense indicates that it cannot be death—our common fate—that is inhuman. Therefore, Justice Brennan must mean that death degrades when it comes not as a natural or accidental event, but as a deliberate social imposition. The murderer learns through his punishment that his fellow men have found him unworthy of living; that because he has murdered, he is being expelled from the community of the living. This degradation is self-inflicted. By murdering, the murderer has so dehumanized himself that he cannot remain among the living. The social recognition of his self-degradation is the punitive essence of execution. To believe, as Justice Brennan appears to, that the degradation is inflicted by the execution reverses the direction of causality.

Execution of those who have committed heinous murders may deter only one murder per year. If it does, it seems quite warranted. It is also the only fitting retribution for murder I can think of.

NOTES

1. Death row as a semipermanent residence is cruel, because convicts are denied the normal amenities of prison life. Thus, unless death row residents are integrated into the prison population, the continuing accumulation of convicts on death row should lead us to accelerate either the rate of executions or the rate of commutations. I find little objection to integration.

2. The ideal of equality, unlike the ideal of retributive justice (which can be approximated separately in each instance), is clearly unattainable unless all guilty persons are apprehended, and thereafter tried, convicted and sentenced by the same court, at the same time. Unequal justice is the best we can do; it is still better than the injustice, equal or unequal, which occurs if, for the sake of equality, we deliberately allow some who could be punished to escape.

3. For a sample of conflicting views on the subject, see Baldus & Cole, *A Comparison of the Work of Thorsten Sellin and Isaac Ehrlich on the Deterrent Effect of Capital Punishment*, 85 Yale L. J. 170 (1975); Bowers & Pierce, *Deterrence or Brutalization: What Is the Effect of Executions?*, 26 Crime & Delinq. 453 (1980); Bowers & Pierce, *The Illusion of Deterrence in Isaac Ehrlich's Research on Capital Punishment*, 85 Yale L. J. 187 (1975); Ehrlich, *Fear of Deterrence: A Critical Evaluation of the "Report of the Panel on Research on Deterrent and Incapacitative Effects,"* 6 J. Legal Stud. 293 (1977); Ehrlich, *The Deterrent Effect of Capital Punishment: A Question of Life and Death*, 65 Am. Econ. Rev. 397, 415-16 (1975); Ehrlich & Gibbons, *On the Measurement of the Deterrent Effect of Capital Punishment and the Theory of Deterrence*, 6 J. Legal Stud. 35 (1977).

4. If executions were shown to increase the murder rate in the long run, I would favor abolition. Sparing the innocent victims who would be

spared, *ex hypothesi*, by the nonexecution of murderers would be more important to me than the execution, however just, of murderers. But although there is a lively discussion of the subject, no serious evidence exists to support the hypothesis that executions produce a higher murder rate. *Cf.* Phillips, *The Deterrent Effect of Capital Punishment: New Evidence on an Old Controversy*, 86 Am. J. Soc. 139 (1980) (arguing that murder rates drop immediately after executions of criminals).

5. H. Gross, A Theory of Criminal Justice 489 (1979) attributing this passage to Sir James Fitzjames Stephen).

6. *Cf.* Kaplan, *Administering Capital Punishment*, 36 U. Fla. L. Rev. 177, 178, 190–91 (1984) (noting the high cost of appealing a capital sentence).

7. Thus restitution (a civil liability) cannot satisfy the punitive purpose of penal sanctions, whether the purpose be retributive or deterrent.

8. Some abolitionists challenge: if the death penalty is just and serves as a deterrent, why not televise executions? The answer is simple. The death even of a murderer, however well-deserved, should not serve as public entertainment. It so served in earlier centuries. But in this respect our sensibility has changed for the better, I believe. Further, television unavoidably would trivialize executions, wedged in, as they would be, between game shows, situation comedies and the like. Finally, because televised executions would focus on the physical aspects of the punishment, rather than the nature of the crime and the suffering of the victim, a televised execution would present the murderer as the victim of the state. Far from communicating the moral significance of the execution, television would shift the focus to the pitiable fear of the murderer. We no longer place in cages those sentenced to imprisonment to expose them to public view. Why should we so expose those sentenced to execution?

9. *See* van den Haag, *Punishment as a Device for Controlling the Crime Rate*, 33 Rutgers L. Rev. 706, 719 (1981) (explaining why the desire for retribution, although independent, would have to be satisfied even if deterrence were the only purpose of punishment.)

10. The Death Penalty in America 256–63 (H. Bedau ed., 3d ed. 1982) (quoting Furman v. Georgia, 408 U.S. 238, 286, 305 (1972) (Brennan, J., concurring).

11. *Id.* at 272–73; *see also* Gregg v. Georgia, 428 U.S. 153, 230 (1976) (Brennan, J., dissenting).

12. Furman v. Georgia, 408 U.S. 238, 291 (1972) (Brennan, J., concurring).

13. *Id.* at 290.

POSTSCRIPT

Should the Death Penalty Be Abolished?

We are in a new era in the history of capital punishment. The death penalty is constitutional, and almost 2,600 persons are on death row, a larger number than at any time since a national count was begun. In the first edition of this book, published in 1982, I wrote that "Although only four persons have been executed in the past fifteen years, this situation seems certain to change in the next two years as appeals in many cases are exhausted." There has indeed been an increase in executions, although the rise has not been as fast as some had predicted. One hundred and seventy-seven persons had been executed as of the summer of 1992.

Appeals still are time-consuming, a situation that some Supreme Court justices have complained about. As a result of the appeals process, the number of persons on death row is still growing by about 150 a year. When the first edition of this book was prepared, there were more than 1,000 people on death row, less than half the number today. The increase in the death row population means, of course, that there are more people sentenced to death each year than there are executions. The slow pace of executions has been a source of great frustration to some Supreme Court justices and, as a result, the Court has restricted some appeals.

The Supreme Court has made several notable and controversial decisions in recent years involving the death penalty. These include *Penry v. Lyunaugh*, 109 S. Ct. 2934 (1989), in which the Court ruled that mentally retarded murderers may be executed, and *Stanford v. Kentucky*, 109 S. Ct. 2969 (1989), in which the Court ruled that persons as young as 16 years of age may be executed.

Interesting works on capital punishment include H. Bedau, ed., *The Death Penalty in America*, 3rd ed. (Oxford University Press, 1982); F. Zimring and G. Hawkins, *Capital Punishment and the American Agenda* (Cambridge University Press, 1989); Brown and Adler, *Public Justice, Private Mercy: A Governor's Education on Death Row* (Weidenfeld & Nicolson, 1989); H. Bedau, *Death Is Different: Studies in the Morality, Law, and Politics of Capital Punishment* (Northeastern University Press, 1987); W. Berns, *For Capital Punishment: Crime and the Morality of the Death Penalty* (Basic Books, 1979); E. van den Haag and J. P. Conrad, *The Death Penalty: A Debate* (Plenum, 1983); J. M. Giarrantano, "To the Best of Our Knowledge, We Have Never Been Wrong: Fallibility vs. Finality in Capital Punishment," 100 *Yale Law Journal* 1005 (1991); W. S. White, "The Death Penalty in the Nineties: An Examination of the Modern System of Capital Punishment," 53 *University of Pittsburgh Law Review* 251 (1991); and Note, "The Madness of the Method: The Use of Electrocution and the Death Penalty," 70 *Texas Law Review* 1039 (1992).

ISSUE 13

Should the Exclusionary Rule Be Abolished?

YES: Malcolm Richard Wilkey, from "The Exclusionary Rule: Why Suppress Valid Evidence?" *Judicature* (November 1978)

NO: Yale Kamisar, from "The Exclusionary Rule in Historical Perspective: The Struggle to Make the Fourth Amendment More Than 'an Empty Blessing,' " *Judicature* (February 1979)

ISSUE SUMMARY

YES: U.S. Court of Appeals judge Malcolm Richard Wilkey raises objections to the exclusionary rule on the grounds that it may suppress evidence and allow the guilty to go free.
NO: Professor of law Yale Kamisar argues that the exclusionary rule is necessary to prevent abuses by police and to protect citizens' rights.

The Fourth Amendment to the Constitution provides that "the right of the people to be secure in their persons, houses, papers, and effects against unreasonable searches and seizures, shall not be violated, and no Warrants shall issue, but upon probable cause." Thus, if the police wish to search someone's property, they must first persuade a judge that probable cause exists that a crime has been committed and that the evidence sought will be found in the place to be searched. The warrant requirement is the key constitutional element restricting the power of the police to decide unilaterally to invade the privacy of someone's home.

What should happen if the police conduct an illegal search and, as a result, discover incriminating evidence? According to the exclusionary rule, such evidence may not be introduced at a trial or be considered by a jury in considering guilt or innocence. If no other evidence of guilt exists, therefore, the defendant will go free. If there is enough other evidence of the defendant's guilt, he may still be convicted.

The exclusionary rule is over 70 years old. It is not required by the Constitution nor mentioned in it. Rather, courts have imposed it because they felt it was the most workable and feasible way to deter illegal police conduct and maintain an honest system of law enforcement. In the following articles, Judge Malcolm Richard Wilkey asserts that society can no longer bear the costs that the rule brings, that guilty persons escape prosecution because of it, and that illegal police conduct is not deterred. Yale Kamisar, a noted criminal law scholar, argues that the rule's rationale is still valid and that the rule should be maintained.

The articles mention a number of legal cases that should be understood since they describe the historical development of the rule:

1. *Weeks v. United States,* 232 U.S. 383 (1914) The U.S. Supreme Court imposed the exclusionary rule for the first time and ruled that illegally seized evidence could not be used in the federal courts. Such evidence, however, could still be used in criminal cases in state courts unless the state decided on its own to require the exclusionary rule in its courts. Although a few states did impose the exclusionary rule, most did not. The New York Court of Appeals, for example, rejected the rule, with Judge Benjamin N. Cardozo refusing to accept the proposition that "the criminal is to go free because the constable has blundered" (*People v. Defore,* 150 N.E. 585, 1926).

2. *Wolf v. Colorado,* 338 U.S. 25 (1949) The Supreme Court ruled that due process of law under the Fourteenth Amendment is denied individuals who are illegally searched. But the Court refused to require state courts to impose or apply the exclusionary rule. Thus, the Court held that "in a prosecution in a State court for a State crime the Fourteenth Amendment does not forbid the admission of evidence obtained by an unreasonable search and seizure."

3. *Rochin v. California,* 342 U.S. 165 (1952) and *Irvine v. California,* 347 U.S. 128 (1954) These two cases involved particularly blatant Fourth Amendment violations by the police. The defendants were convicted, but the Supreme Court refused, as in *Wolf,* to require states to follow the exclusionary rule. Rochin's conviction, however, was reversed because the police action was "shocking to the conscience."

4. *Mapp v. Ohio,* 367 U.S. 643 (1961) Dollree Mapp was convicted of possession of obscene materials after the police conducted a search of her home without a search warrant. The Supreme Court decided to overrule the *Wolf* decision and require state courts to apply the exclusionary rule. The Court cited a well-known statement by Justice Louis D. Brandeis that "if the government becomes a lawbreaker, it breeds contempt for the law; it invites every man to become a law unto himself; it invites anarchy." As you read the following articles, consider whether Justice Brandeis's statement is still valid. (A fascinating description of the facts of the *Mapp* case is contained in Friendly and Elliot's *The Constitution: That Delicate Balance* [Random House, 1984].)

YES

Malcolm Richard Wilkey

WHY SUPPRESS VALID EVIDENCE?

America is now ready to confront frankly and to examine realistically both the achievements and social costs of the policies which have been so hopefully enacted in the past 40 years. That reappraisal has made the most headlines in regard to economic and fiscal matters. It is imperative that this honest reappraisal include the huge social costs which American society— alone in the civilized world—pays as a result of our unique exclusionary rule of evidence in criminal cases.

We can see that huge social cost most clearly in the distressing rate of street crimes—assaults and robberies with deadly weapons, narcotics trafficking, gambling and prostitution—which flourish in no small degree simply because of the exclusionary rule of evidence. To this high price we can rightfully add specific, pernicious police conduct and lack of discipline—the very opposite of the objectives of the rule itself. . . .

Though scholars have been shedding more and more light on this problem, few people have considered the enormous social cost of the exclusionary rule, and fewer still have thought about possible alternatives to the rule. I propose to do both those things in this article.

THE RULE'S MYSTIQUE

What is the exclusionary rule? It is a judge-made rule of evidence, originated in 1914 by the Supreme Court in *Weeks v. United States*, which bars "the use of evidence secured through an illegal search and seizure." It is not a rule required by the Constitution. No Supreme Court has ever held that it was. As Justice Black once said,

> [T]he Fourth Amendment does not itself contain any provision expressly precluding the use of such evidence and I am extremely doubtful that such a provision could properly be inferred from nothing more than the basic command against unreasonable searches and seizures.

The greatest obstacle to replacing the exclusionary rule with a rational process, which will both protect the citizenry by controlling the police and

From Malcolm Richard Wilkey, "The Exclusionary Rule: Why Suppress Valid Evidence?" *Judicature* (November 1978). Copyright © 1978 by Malcolm Richard Wilkey. Reprinted by permission.

avoid rewarding the criminal, is the powerful, unthinking emotional attachment to the rule. The mystique and misunderstanding of the rule causes not only many ordinary citizens but also judges and lawyers to feel (not think) that the exclusionary rule was enshrined in the Constitution by the Founding Fathers, and that to abolish it would do violence to the whole sacred Bill of Rights. They appear totally unaware that the rule was not employed in U.S. courts during the first 125 years of the Fourth Amendment, that it was devised by the judiciary in the assumed absence of any other method of controlling the police, and that no other country in the civilized world has adopted such a rule.

Realistically, the exclusionary rule can probably never be abolished until both the public and the Supreme Court are satisfied that there is available in our legal system a reasonably workable alternative. Unfortunately, the converse may also be true—we will never have any alternative in operation until the rule is abolished. So long as we keep the rule, the police are not going to investigate and discipline their own men, and thus sabotage prosecutions by invalidating the admissibility of vital evidence.

HOW THE RULE WORKS

The impact of the exclusionary rule may not be immediately apparent from the simple phrase of the *Wolf* decision that it bars "the use of evidence seized through an illegal search and seizure." It may help to consider three examples to see how the exclusionary rule needlessly frustrates police and prosecutors trying to do a very difficult job on the streets of our cities.

In *U.S. v. Montgomery*, two police officers on auto patrol in a residential neighborhood at 6 P.M. on a winter day saw Montgomery driving his car in a way that suggested he was "sizing up" the area. When they stopped and identified him, they learned by radio that an arrest warrant was outstanding against him. Before taking him into custody, the officers searched him for weapons and found a .38 caliber bullet in his pants pocket, a magnum revolver loaded with six rounds and an unregistered, sawed-off shotgun with shells in the car.

A trial court convicted him of illegal possession of firearms, but the Court of Appeals (2–1) reversed, holding that no probable cause existed for stopping Montgomery in the first place, and that all evidence discovered thereafter was the product of an illegal search and seizure. Applying the exclusionary rule, the court suppressed as evidence the revolver and the sawed-off shotgun, which made it impossible to convict Montgomery or to retry the case.

Montgomery is an example of typical routine police work, which many citizens would think of as needed reasonable effort to prevent crime. But now look at *U.S. v. Willie Robinson*, a similar case with a different result. A policeman stopped Robinson for a minor traffic violation and discovered that license bureau records indicated his license was probably a forgery. Four days later, the same officer spotted Robinson about 2 A.M. and arrested him for driving with a forged credential.

Since police regulations required him to take Robinson into custody, the officer began a pat down or frisk for dangerous weapons. Close inspection of the cigarette package in the outer pocket of the man's jacket revealed heroin. Robinson was convicted of heroin possession but the Court of Appeals held 5-4 that, in light of the exclusionary rule, the search of Robinson was illegal and the heroin evidence must be suppressed. The Supreme Court reversed, holding that probable cause existed for the search, the evidence was legally obtained, and it could be offered in evidence. The High Court reinstated the original conviction.

This is one search and seizure case which turned out, in my view, correctly. But it took a U.S. District Court suppression hearing, a 2-1 panel decision in the Court of Appeals, a 5-4 decision in the court *en banc*, and a 6-3 decision of the Supreme Court to confirm the validity of the on-the-spot judgment of a lone police officer exercised at 2 A.M. on a Washington Street—five years and eight months earlier.

In *Coolidge v. New Hampshire*, a 14-year-old girl was found with her throat slit and a bullet in her head eight days after she had disappeared. Police contacted the wife of a suspect whose car was like one seen near the crime, and she gave them her husband's guns. Tests proved that one of the weapons had fired the fatal bullet.

Invoking his statutory authority, the attorney general of the state issued a warrant for the arrest of the suspect and the seizure of his car. Coolidge was captured and convicted. But the Supreme Court reversed the conviction on the grounds that the warrant was defective, the search of the auto unreasonable and vacuum sweepings from the auto (which matched the victim's clothing) were inadmissible. Why? Because the attorney general who issued the warrant had personally assumed direction of the investigation and thus was not a "neutral and detached magistrate."

Observe that here the conviction was reversed because of a defect in the warrant, not because of any blunder. Errors of law by either the attorney preparing the affidavit and application for the warrant or the magistrate in issuing the warrant frequently invalidate the entire search that the police officers make, relying in good faith on the warrant; those errors cause the suppression of the evidence and the reversal of the conviction. How does the exclusionary rule improve police conduct in such cases?

THE COURT'S RATIONALE

Deterrence: During the rule's development, the Supreme Court has offered three main reasons for the rule. The principal and almost sole theory today is that excluding the evidence will punish the police officers who made the illegal search and seizure or otherwise violated the constitutional rights of the defendant, and thus deter policemen from committing the same violation again. The flaw in this theory is that there is absolutely no empirical data that excluding evidence against a defendant has anything to do with either punishing police officers or thereby deterring them from future violations.

Chief Justice Burger has flatly asserted " . . . there is no empirical evidence to support the claim that the rule actually deters illegal conduct of law enforcement officials," and the Supreme Court has never sought to adduce such empirical evidence in support of the rule. Probably such a connection can never be proved, for as a matter of logical analysis "the exclusionary rule is well tailored to deter the prosecutor from illegal conduct. But the prosecutor is not the guilty party in an illegal arrest or search and seizure, and he rarely has any measure of control over the police who are responsible."

Privacy: From *Weeks* (1914) to *Mapp* (1961) the rule was also justified as protecting the privacy of the individual against illegal searches and seizures as guaranteed by the Fourth Amendment. The Supreme Court later downgraded the protection of privacy rationale, perhaps because of the obvious defect that the rule purports to do nothing to recompense innocent victims of Fourth Amendment violations, and the gnawing doubt as to just what right of privacy guilty individuals have in illegal firearms, contraband narcotics and policy betting slips—the frequent objects of search and seizure.

Judicial integrity: A third theme of the Supreme Court's justifying rationale, now somewhat muted, is that the use of illegally obtained evidence brings the court system into disrepute. In *Mapp* Justice Clark referred to "that judicial integrity so necessary in the true administration of justice," which was reminiscent of Justice Brandeis dissenting in *Burdeau v. McDowell*, " . . . respect for law will not be advanced by resort, in its enforcement, to means which shock the common man's sense of decency and fair play."

THE IMPACT OF THE RULE

It is undeniable that, as a result of the rule, the most valid, conclusive, and irrefutable factual evidence is excluded from the knowledge of the jury or consideration by the judge. As Justice Cardozo predicted in 1926, in describing the complete irrationality of the exclusionary rule:

> The criminal is to go free because the constable has blundered. . . . A room is searched against the law, and the body

of a murdered man is found. . . . The privacy of the home has been infringed, and the murderer goes free.

Fifty years later Justice Powell wrote for the Court:

> The costs of applying the exclusionary rule even at trial and on direct review are well known: . . . the physical evidence sought to be excluded is typically reliable and often the most probative evidence bearing on the guilt or innocence of the defendant. . . . Application of the rule thus deflects the truthfinding process and often frees the guilty. The disparity in particular cases between the error committed by the police officer and the windfall afforded the guilty defendant by application of the rule is contrary to the idea of proportionality that is essential to the concept of justice.

I submit that justice is, or should be, a truth-seeking process. The court has a duty to the accused to see that he receives a fair trial; the court also has a duty to society to see that all the truth is brought out; only if all the truth is brought out can there be a fair trial. The exclusionary rule results in a complete distortion of the truth. Undeniable facts, of the greatest importance, are forever barred—facts such as Robinson's heroin, Montgomery's sawed-off shotgun and pistol, the bullet fired from Coolidge's gun and the sweepings from his car which contained items from the dead girl's clothes.

If justice is a truth-seeking process, it is all important that *there is never any question of reliability* in exclusionary rule cases involving material evidence, as the three examples illustrate. We rightly exclude evidence whenever its reliability is questionable—a coerced or induced confession, for example, or a faulty line-up for identification of the suspect. We exclude it because it is inherently unreliable, not because of the illegality of obtaining it. An illegal search in no way reduces the reliability of the evidence.

There have been several empirical studies on the effects of the exclusionary rule in five major American cities—Boston, Chicago, Cincinnati, New York and Washington, D.C.—during the period from 1950 to 1971. These have been recently collected and analyzed, along with other aspects of the exclusionary rule and its alternatives, by Professor Steven Schlesinger in his book *Exclusionary Injustice: The Problem of Illegally Obtained Evidence*.

Three of these studies concluded that the exclusionary rule was a total failure in its primary task of deterring illegal police activity and that it also produced other highly undesirable side effects. The fourth study, which said the first three were too harsh in concluding that the rule was totally ineffective, still said: "Nonetheless, the inconclusiveness of our findings is real enough; they do not nail down an argument that the exclusionary rule has accomplished its task."

Schlesinger and others regard the study by Dallin Oakes as perhaps the most comprehensive ever undertaken, both in terms of data and the breadth of analysis of the rule's effects. Oakes concluded:

As a device for directly deterring illegal searches and seizures by the police, the exclusionary rule is a failure. . . . The harshest criticism of the rule is that it is ineffective. It is the sole means of enforcing the essential guarantees of freedom from unreasonable arrests and searches and seizures by law enforcement officers, and it is a failure in that vital task.

Spiotto made a comparative study of both the American exclusionary rule and the existing Canadian tort alternative, taking Chicago and Toronto as comparable metropolitan areas. He found that an

empirical study [of narcotics and weapons cases] indicates that, over a 20-year period in Chicago, the proportion of cases in which there were motions to suppress evidence allegedly obtained illegally increased significantly. This is the opposite result of what would be expected if the rule had been efficacious in deterring police misconduct.

Three studies conducted between 1950 and 1971 show a substantial increase in motions to suppress in both narcotics and gun offenses. The increase from 1950 to 1971 can fairly be attributed to the impact of *Mapp* (1961) on search and seizure in the state courts.

CRITICISMS OF THE RULE

By this point, we should be able to see that the exclusionary rule actually produces many effects opposite from those that the Court intended to produce. No matter what rationale we consider, the rule in its indiscriminate workings does far more harm than good and, in many respects, it actually prevents us from dealing with the real problems of Fourth Amendment violations in the course of criminal investigations.

In the eyes of the Supreme Court, the first and primary rationale of the exclusionary rule is deterrence. I submit that all available facts and logic show that excluding the most reliable evidence does absolutely nothing to punish and thus deter the official wrongdoer, but the inevitable and certain result is that the guilty criminal defendant goes free.

The second—now rather distant second—rationale in the eyes of the Court has been the protection of privacy. I submit a policy of excluding incriminating evidence can never protect an innocent victim of an illegal search against whom no incriminating evidence is discovered. The only persons protected by the rule are the guilty against whom the most serious reliable evidence should be offered. It cannot be separately argued that the innocent person is protected *in the future* by excluding evidence against the criminal *now*, for this is only the deterrent argument all over again.

The third rationale found in the past opinions of the Court is that the use of illegally obtained evidence brings our court system into disrepute. I submit that the exclusion of valid, probative, undeniably truthful evidence undermines the reputation of and destroys the respect for the entire judicial system.

Ask any group of laymen if they can understand why a pistol found on a man when he is searched by an officer should not be received in evidence when the man is charged with illegal possession of a weapon, or why a heroin package found under similar circumstances should not be always received in evidence when he is prosecuted for a narcotics possession, and I believe you will receive a lecture that these are outrageous technicalities of the law which the American people should not tolerate. If you put the same issue to a representative group of lawyers and judges, I predict you would receive a strong preponderance of opinions supporting the lay view, although from those heavily imbued with a mystique of the exclusionary rule as of almost divine origin you would doubtless hear some support.

The rationale of protecting judicial integrity is also inconsistent with the behavior of the courts in other areas of the criminal law. For example, it is well settled that courts will try defendants who have been illegally seized and brought before them. In *Ker v. Illinois*, a defendant kidnapped in Peru was brought by force to Illinois for trial; in *Mahon v. Justice* the accused was forcibly abducted from West Virginia for trial in Kentucky; and in *Frisbie v. Collins*, the defendant was forcibly seized in Illinois for trial in Michigan. Said the *Frisbie* court:

> This court has never departed from the rule announced in *Ker v. Illinois* . . . that the power of the court to try a person for crime is not impaired by the fact that he had been brought within the court's jurisdiction by reason of 'forcible abduction.'

Why should there be an exclusionary rule for illegally seized evidence when there is no such exclusionary rule for illegally seized people? Why should a court be concerned about the circumstances under which the murder weapon has been obtained, while it remains unconcerned about the circumstances under which the murderer himself has been apprehended? It makes no sense to argue that the admission of illegally seized evidence somehow signals the judiciary's condonation of the violation of rights when the judiciary's trial of an illegally-seized *person* is not perceived as signaling such condonation.

OTHER DEFECTS OF THE RULE

The rule does not simply fail to meet its declared objectives; it suffers from five other defects, too. One of those defects is that it uses an undiscriminating, meat-ax approach in the most sensitive areas of the administration of justice. It totally fails to discriminate between the degrees of culpability of the officer or the degrees of harm to the victim of the illegal search and seizure.

It does not matter whether the action of the officer was grossly willful and flagrant or whether he was conscientiously using his very best judgment under difficult circumstances; the result is the same: the evidence is out. The rule likewise fails to distinguish errors of judgment which cause no harm or inconvenience to the individual whose person or premises are searched, except for the discovery of valid incriminating evidence, from flagrant violations of the Fourth Amendment as in *Mapp* or *Rochin*. Chief Justice Burger's point in *Bivens* is undeniable:

> . . . society has at least as much right to expect rationally graded responses from judges in place of the universal 'capital punishment' we inflict on all evidence when police error is shown in its acquisition.

Another defect is that the rule makes no distinction between minor offenses and more serious crimes. The teenage runner caught with policy slips in his pocket and the syndicate hit man accused of first degree murder are each automatically set free by operation of the exclusionary rule, without any consideration of the impact on the community. Customarily, however, we apply different standards to crimes which vary as to seriousness, both in granting bail before trial and in imposing sentence afterwards.

A third problem is that, strangely, a rule which is supposed to discipline and improve police conduct actually results in encouraging highly pernicious police behavior. A policeman is supposed to tell the truth, but when he knows that describing the search truthfully will taint the evidence and free the suspect, the policeman is apt to feel that he has a "higher duty" than the truth. He may perjure himself to convict the defendant.

Similarly, knowing that evidence of gambling, narcotics or prostitution is hard to obtain under the present rules of search and seizure, the policeman may feel that he can best enforce the law by stepping up the incidence of searches and seizures, making them frequent enough to be harassing, with no idea of ultimate prosecution. Or, for those policemen inclined *ab initio* to corruption, the exclusionary rule provides a fine opportunity to make phony raids on establishments, deliberately violating the standards of the Fourth Amendment and immunizing the persons and premises raided—while making good newspaper headlines for active law enforcement.

Fourth, the rule discourages internal disciplinary action by the police themselves. Even if police officials know that an officer violated Fourth Amendment standards in a particular case, few of them will charge the erring officer with a Fourth Amendment violation: it would sabotage the case for the prosecution before it even begins. The prosecutor hopes the defendant will plea bargain and thus receive some punishment, even if the full rigor of the law cannot be imposed because of the dubious validity of the search. Even after the defendant has been convicted or has pleaded guilty, it would be dangerous to discipline the officer—months or years later—because the offender might come back seeking one of the now popular post-conviction remedies.

Finally, the existence of the federally imposed exclusionary rule makes it virtually impossible for any state, not only the federal government, to experiment with any other methods of controlling police. One unfortunate consequence of *Mapp* was that it removed from the states both the incentive and the opportunity to deal with illegal search and seizure by means other than suppression. Justice Harlan, in commenting on the evil impact of the federal imposition of the exclusionary rule on the states, observed:

> Another [state], though equally solicitous of constitutional rights, may choose to pursue one purpose at a time, allowing all evidence relevant to guilt to be brought into a criminal trial, and dealing with constitutional infractions by other means.

ALTERNATIVES TO THE RULE

The excuse given for the persistence of the exclusionary rule in this country is that there is no effective alternative to make the police obey the law in regard to unreasonable searches and seizures. If this excuse did not come from such respected sources, one would be tempted to term it an expression of intellectual bankruptcy.

"No effective alternative"? How do all the other civilized countries control their police? By disciplinary measures against the erring policeman, by effective civil damage action against both the policeman and the government—not by freeing the criminal. Judging by police conduct in England, Canada and other nations, these measures work very well. Why does the United States alone rely upon the irrational exclusionary rule?

It isn't necessary. Justice Frankfurter in *Wolf* (1949) noted that none of the 10 jurisdictions in the British Commonwealth had held evidence obtained by an illegal search and seizure inadmissible, and "the jurisdictions which have rejected the *Weeks* doctrine have not left the right to privacy without other means of protection. . . ." Justice Harlan in his dissent in *Mapp* noted the wisdom of allowing all evidence to be brought in and "dealing with constitutional infractions by other means." Justice Black, concurring in *Mapp*, noted that the Fourth Amendment did not itself preclude the use of illegally obtained evidence.

In his dissent in *Bivens*, Chief Justice Burger suggested that Congress provide that Fourth Amendment violations be made actionable under the Federal Tort Claims Act, or something similar. Senator Lloyd Bentsen and other members of Congress have put forward proposals to abolish the rule and substitute the liability of the federal government toward the victims of illegal searches and seizures, both those innocent and those guilty of crimes.

THE PURPOSES OF AN ALTERNATIVE

Before examining what mechanism we might adopt in place of the exclusionary rule as a tool for enforcing the rights guaranteed by the Fourth Amendment, let us see clearly what objectives we desire to achieve by such alternatives.

The *first* objective, in sequence and perhaps in the public consciousness of those who are aware of the shortcomings of the rule, is to prevent the unquestionably guilty from going free from all punishment for their crime—to put an end to the ridiculous situation that the murderer goes free because the constable has blundered. Let me reiterate: the exclusionary rule, as applied to tangible evidence, has never prevented an innocent person from being convicted.

Second, the system should provide effective guidance to the police as to proper conduct under the Fourth Amendment. When appellate courts rule several years after the violation, their decisions are not only years too late, but usually far too obscure for the average policeman to understand. They are remote in both time and impact on the policeman at fault. Immediate guidance to the policeman as to his error, with an appropriate penalty, is obviously more effective, in contrast to simply rewarding the criminal.

Third sequentially, but first in value, the mechanism should protect citizens from Fourth Amendment violations by law enforcement officers. (I say sequentially, because it is necessary first to abolish the exclusionary rule and then to provide guidance to the police.) If police receive immediate and meaningful rulings, accompanied by prompt disciplinary penalties, they will be effectively deterred from future wrongful action and citizens will thus be effectively protected.

Fourth, the procedure should provide effective and meaningful compensation to those citizens, particularly innocent victims of illegal searches and seizures. This the present exclusionary rule totally fails to do. Only the guilty person who has suffered an illegal search and seizure receives some form of compensation—an acquittal, which is usually in gross disproportion to the injury inflicted on him by an illegal search and seizure. Thus, under the present irrational exclusionary rule system, the guilty are over-rewarded by a commutation of all penalties for crimes they did commit and the inno-

cent are never compensated for the injuries they suffered.

THE MAGNITUDE OF THE OFFENSE

Fifth, it should be an objective of any substitute for the exclusionary rule to introduce comparative values into what is now a totally arbitrary process and inflexible penalty. Under the exclusionary rule, the "penalty" is the same irrespective of the offense. If an officer barely oversteps the line on probable cause and seizes five ounces of heroin from a peddler on the street corner, or an officer without a warrant and without probable cause barges into a home and seizes private papers, the result is automatic—the evidence is barred, the accused is freed, and this is all the "punishment" the officer receives.

Surely the societal values involved in the two incidents are of a totally different magnitude. The error of the officer in dealing with narcotics peddlers should not be overlooked, his misapprehension of the requirement of probable cause should be called to his attention quickly in a way which he will remember, but actual punishment should be relatively minimal. In the instance of an invalid seizure of private papers in the home, the officer should be severely punished for such a gross infraction of Fourth Amendment rights.

The exclusionary rule is applied automatically now when there is no illegal action by investigative officers and hence no possible deterrence to future police misconduct. For example, where government agents have dutifully applied to a judge or magistrate for a search warrant, and executed the warrant in strict conformity with its terms, a warrant which later proves defective will force the judge later to exclude the evidence illegally seized. All that is involved in these instances is a legal error on the part of the judge, magistrate, or perhaps the attorney who drew the papers. It is absurd to say that the court subsequently is "punishing" or attempting to "deter" the judge, magistrate, or attorney who made the legal error by suppressing the evidence and letting the accused go free, but this is what happens now.

If these are valid objectives in seeking a substitute procedure for the exclusionary rule as a method of enforcing Fourth Amendment rights, there seem to be two general approaches which might well be combined in one statute—internal discipline by the law enforcement authorities themselves, and external control by the courts or an independent review board.

INTERNAL DISCIPLINE

Disciplinary action against the offending law enforcement officer could be initiated by the law enforcement organization itself or by the person whose Fourth Amendment rights had been allegedly violated. The police could initiate action either within the regular command structure or by an overall disciplinary board outside the hierarchy of command. Many law enforcement organizations have such disciplinary boards now and they could be made mandatory by statute in all federal law enforcement agencies. Wherever they may be located, the organization would require action to be taken following the seizure of material evidence, if the criminal trial or an independent investigation showed a violation of the Fourth Amendment standards.

The person injured could also initiate action leading to internal discipline of the offending officer by complaint to the agency disciplinary board. Each enforcement agency or department could establish a process to hear and decide the complaint, providing both a penalty for the offending officer (if the violation were proved) and government compensation to the injured party.

This procedure would cover numerous cases in which citizens suffer violations of Fourth Amendment rights, but in which no court action results. The injured party could choose this administrative remedy in lieu of court action, but any award in the administrative proceedings would be taken into account by a court later if a citizen, dissatisfied with the award, instituted further legal action.

The penalty against the officer would be tailored to fit his own culpability; it might be a reprimand, a fine, a delay in promotion, a suspension, or discharge. Factors bearing upon the extent of the penalty would include the extent to which the violation was willful, the manner in which it deviated from approved conduct, the degree to which it invaded the privacy of the injured party, and the extent to which human dignity and societal values were breached.

Providing compensation to the injured party from the government is necessary, for it is simply realistic to make the government liable for the wrongful acts of its agent in order to make the prospect of compensation meaningful. Policemen traditionally are not wealthy and the government has a deep purse. Moreover, higher administrative officials and irate taxpayers may be expected to react adversely to losses resulting from the misconduct of policemen and to do something about their training and exercise of responsibilities.

EXTERNAL CONTROL

When a prosecutor tries a defendant in the wake of a violation of Fourth Amendment rights, the court could conduct a mini-trial of the offending officer after the violation is alleged and proof outlined in the principal criminal case. This mini-trial would be similar to a hearing on a motion to suppress now, but it would be conducted after the main criminal case. The burden would be on the injured party to prove, by preponderance of the evidence, that the officer violated his Fourth Amendment rights. The policeman could submit his case to either the judge or the jury who heard the main criminal case.

By initiating the "trial" of the officer immediately following the criminal case in which he was charged with misconduct, the court could determine the question of his violation speedily and economically. Presumably both the judge and jury have been thoroughly familiarized with the facts of the main case and are able to put the conduct of the officer in perspective.

Such a mini-trial would provide an outside disciplinary force that the injured party could utilize in lieu of internal discipline by the agency. Any previous administrative action taken against the officer would be considered by the judge and jury, if a penalty were to be assessed as a result of the mini-trial. The same factors bearing on the penalty to the officer and compensation to the injured party as discussed under the administrative remedy would be relevant in the mini-trial.

In those instances where police violate Fourth Amendment rights but the prosecutor does not bring charges against the suspect, the wronged party should be able to bring a statutory civil action against the government and the officer. Both would be named as defendants: the officer to defend against any individual penalty, the government to be able to respond adequately in damages to the injured party if such were found. Many instances of Fourth Amendment violation now go unnoticed because no criminal charge is brought and the injured party is not in position to bring a *Bivens*-type suit for the alleged constitutional violation. The burden of proof on the factors in regard to penalty and compensation would be the same as in a mini-trial following the principal criminal case, as discussed above.

The creation of this civil remedy could be accomplished by simple amendment to the present Federal Tort Claims Act. This is the procedure followed in many other countries, among them Canada.

> . . . the remedy in tort has proved reasonably effective; Canadian juries are quick to resent illegal activity on the part of the police and to express that resentment by a proportionate judgment for damages.

Disciplinary punishment and civil penalties directly against the erring officer involved would certainly provide a far more effective deterrent than the Supreme Court has created in the exclusionary rule. The creation of a civil remedy for violations of privacy, whether or not the invasion resulted in a criminal prosecution, would provide a remedy for the innocent victims of Fourth Amendment violations which the exclusionary rule has never pretended to give. And the rationale that the "government should not 'profit' from its own agent's misconduct" would disappear completely if erring officers were punished and injured parties compensated when there was a Fourth Amendment violation. If such a law and procedure were enforced, there would be no remaining objection to the subject of search and seizure still receiving his appropriate punishment for his crime.

CONCLUSION

All of the above was written before I read Professor Kamisar's ["Is the exclusionary rule an 'illogical' or 'unnatural' interpretation of the Fourth Amendment?" 62 Judicature 66.] It is apparent that our respective positions are widely divergent. After pondering his statement, I believe it fair to say that he must attempt to defend his position on one of two grounds, and that on analysis neither is defensible.

First, if Professor Kamisar believes that the Fourth Amendment necessarily mandates the exclusionary rule, then he ought to cite Supreme Court authority for this position. Nowhere in his article does he do so. It is undeniable that at no time in the Court's history has a majority in any case ever so held, and I do not believe that any more than two individual justices in the Court's history have so expressed themselves. In contrast, numerous justices, both favoring and opposing the rule, have stated that the rule itself is *not* mandated by the Fourth Amendment.

Second, if Professor Kamisar's article is intended only to say that under the Constitution we have a choice of methods to enforce the ban against "unreasonable searches and seizures," and that the exclusionary rule is a good choice only because of "the imperative of judicial integrity," then I submit both logic and experience in this country and all other countries refutes this. If the Su-

preme Court or the Congress has a choice of methods under the Constitution, then it simply will not do to rest the choice of exclusionary rule solely on the high principle of "judicial integrity" and to ignore the pragmatic result, the failure to achieve the objective of enforcement and the other pernicious side effects discussed above, which themselves strongly discredit judicial integrity.

If we have a choice, to attempt to justify the continuation of the exclusionary rule on this basis is to be stubbornly blind to 65 years of experience. If we have a choice, to insist on continuing a method of enforcement with as many demonstrated faults as the exclusionary rule is to be blindly stubborn. If we have a choice, let us calmly and carefully consider the available alternatives, draw upon the experience of other nations with systems of justice similar to our own, and by abolishing the rule permit in the laboratories of our 51 jurisdictions the experimentation with various possible alternatives promising far more than the now discredited exclusionary rule.

NO

Yale Kamisar

THE STRUGGLE TO MAKE
THE FOURTH AMENDMENT
MORE THAN "AN EMPTY BLESSING"

In the 65 years since the Supreme Court adopted the exclusionary rule, few critics have attacked it with as much vigor and on as many fronts as did Judge Malcolm Wilkey in his recent *Judicature* article, "The exclusionary rule: why suppress valid evidence?" (November 1978).

According to Judge Wilkey, there is virtually nothing good about the rule and a great deal bad about it. He thinks the rule is partly to blame for "the distressing rate of street crimes." He tells us that it "discourages internal disciplinary action by the police themselves"; actually results in "encouraging highly pernicious police behavior" (e.g., perjury, harassment and corruption); "makes it virtually impossible for any state, not only the federal government, to experiment with any methods of controlling police"; and "undermines the reputation of and destroys the respect for the entire judicial system."

Judge Wilkey claims, too, that the rule "dooms" "every scheme of gun control . . . to be totally ineffective in preventing the habitual use of weapons in street crimes." Until we rid ourselves of this rule, he argues, "the criminal can parade in the street with a great bulge in his pocket or a submachine gun in a blanket under his arm" and "laugh in the face of the officer who might wish to search him for it."

UNTHINKING, EMOTIONAL ATTACHMENT?

Why, then, has the rule survived? "The greatest obstacle to replacing the exclusionary rule with a rational process," Judge Wilkey maintains, is "the powerful, unthinking emotional attachment" to the rule. If you put the issue to a representative group of lawyers and judges, he concedes, "you would doubtless hear some support" for the rule, but only from those "heavily imbued with a mystique of the exclusionary rule as of almost divine origin."

From Yale Kamisar, "The Exclusionary Rule in Historical Perspective: The Struggle to Make the Fourth Amendment More Than 'an Empty Blessing,' " *Judicature* (February 1979). Copyright © 1979 by Yale Kamisar. Reprinted by permission of the author.

It is hard to believe that nothing more substantial than "unthinking emotional attachment" or mystical veneration accounts for support for the rule by Justices Holmes and Brandeis [and,] more recently, by such battlescarred veterans as Roger Traynor, Earl Warren and Tom Clark.

In the beginning, Judge Traynor was not attached to the rule, emotionally or otherwise. Indeed, in 1942 he wrote the opinion of the California Supreme Court reaffirming the admissibility of illegally seized evidence. But by 1955, it became apparent to Traynor that illegally seized evidence "was being offered and admitted as a routine procedure" and "it became impossible to ignore the corollary that illegal searches and seizures were also a routine procedure, subject to no effective deterrent."

[W]ithout fear of criminal punishment or other discipline, law enforcement officers . . . casually regard [illegal searches and seizures] as nothing more than the performance of their ordinary duties for which the City employs and pays them.

In light of these circumstances, Traynor overruled the court's earlier decision.

And consider Earl Warren. During the 24 years he spent in state law enforcement work in California (as deputy district attorney, district attorney and attorney general), California admitted illegally seized evidence. Indeed, Warren was the California Attorney General who successfully urged Judge Traynor and his brethren to reaffirm that rule in 1942. In 1954, during his first year as Chief Justice of the United States, he heard a case involving police misconduct so outrageous as to be "almost incredible if it were not admitted" (the infamous Irvine case), but he resisted the tempta-

tion to impose the exclusionary rule on the states, even in such extreme cases. It was not until 1961 that he joined in the opinion for the Court in Mapp, which imposed the rule on the states.

Chief Justice Warren knew the exclusionary rule's limitations as a tool of judicial control, but at the end of an extraordinary public career—in which he had served more years as a prosecutor than any other person who has ascended to the Supreme Court—Warren observed:

[I]n our system, evidentiary rulings provide the context in which the judicial process of inclusion and exclusion approves some conduct as comporting with constitutional guarantees and disapproves other actions by state agents. A ruling admitting evidence in a criminal trial, we recognize, has the necessary effect of legitimizing the conduct which produced the evidence, while an application of the exclusionary rule withholds the constitutional imprimatur.

The author of the Mapp opinion, Tom Clark, was, of course, U.S. Attorney General for four years before he became a Supreme Court justice and he was assistant attorney general in charge of the criminal division before that. Evidently, nothing in his experience gave Clark reason to believe that the rule had "handcuffed" federal officials or would cripple state law enforcement. And he never changed his views about the need for the exclusionary rule during his 18 years on the Court or the 10 years he spent in the administration of justice following his retirement. Indeed, shortly before his death, he warmly defended Mapp and Weeks.

Moreover, nothing in Justice Clark's career suggests that he endorsed Mapp out of "sentimentality" or in awe of the "divine origins" of the exclusionary rule. More likely, he was impressed with the failure of *Wolf* and *Irvine* to stimulate any meaningful alternative to the exclusionary rule in the more than 20 states that still admitted illegally seized evidence at the time of *Mapp*.

I do not mean to suggest that Judge Wilkey's views on the exclusionary rule are aberrational among lawyers and judges; many members of the bench and bar share his deep distress with the rule. Indeed, when Judge Wilkey asks us to abolish the exclusionary rule now—without waiting for a meaningful alternative to emerge—he but follows the lead of Chief Justice Burger, who recently maintained:

> [T]he continued existence of the rule, as presently implemented, inhibits the development of rational alternatives. . . .
> It can no longer be assumed that other branches of government will act while judges cling to this Draconian, discredited device in its present absolutist form.

Because so many share Judge Wilkey's hostility to the exclusionary rule, it is important to examine and to evaluate Wilkey's arguments at some length. Only then can we determine whether the rule is as irrational and pernicious as he and other critics maintain—and whether we can abolish it before we have developed an alternative.

CRIME AND THE RULE

A year before the California Supreme Court adopted the exclusionary rule on its own—and years before the "revolution" in American criminal procedure began—William H. Parker, the Chief of the Los Angeles Police Department, said:

> [O]ur most accurate crime statistics indicate that crime rates rise and fall on the tides of economic, social, and political cycles with embarrassingly little attention to the most determined efforts of our police.

Almost as soon as the California Supreme Court adopted the exclusionary rule, though, Chief Parker began blaming the rule for the high rate of crime in Los Angeles, calling it "catastrophic as far as efficient law enforcement is concerned," and insisting "that the imposition of the exclusionary rule has rendered the people powerless to adequately protect themselves against the criminal army."

Such criticism of the *Cahan* rule was only a preview of the attack on *Mapp*. Chief Justice Traynor, speaking about the debate following the *Mapp* decision, rightly observed that: "Articulate comment about [*Mapp*] . . . was drowned out in the din about handcuffing the police.

Thus, it is not surprising that Judge Wilkey would claim on his very first page that "[w]e can see [the] huge social cost [of *Weeks* and *Mapp*] most clearly in the distressing rate of street crimes . . . which flourish in no small degree simply because of the exclusionary rule." Nevertheless, it is disappointing to hear a critic repeat this charge, because after 65 years of debate, there was reason to hope that this criticism, at least, would no longer be made. As Professor James Vorenberg pointed out, shortly after he completed his two years of service as Executive Director of the President's Commission on Law Enforcement and Administration of Justice:

> What the Supreme Court does has practically no effect on the amount of crime in this country, and what the

police do has far less effect than is generally realized.

Even Professor Dallin Oaks (now a university president), upon whose work Judge Wilkey relies so heavily, advised a decade ago:

> The whole argument about the exclusionary rule 'handcuffing' the police should be abandoned. If this is a negative effect, then it is an effect of the constitutional rules, not an effect of the exclusionary rule as the means chosen for their enforcement.
>
> Police officials and prosecutors should stop claiming that the exclusionary rule prevents effective law enforcement. In doing so they attribute far greater effect to the exclusionary rule than the evidence warrants, and they are also in the untenable position of urging that the sanction be abolished so that they can continue to violate the [constitutional] rules with impunity.

A WEAK LINK

Over the years, I have written about the impact of *Cahan*, *Mapp* and other decisions on crime rates and police-prosecution efficiency. I will not restate my findings again, especially since Judge Wilkey has presented no statistical support for his assertion. I would, however, like to summarize a few points:

• Long before the exclusionary rule became law in the states—indeed, long before any of the procedural safeguards in the federal Constitution was held applicable to the states—invidious comparisons were made between the rate of crime in our nation and the incidence of crime in others.

Thus, in 1911, the distinguished ex-president of Cornell University, Andrew D. White, pointed out that, although London's population was two million larger than New York's, there were 10 times more murders in New York. And in 1920, Edwin W. Sims, the first head of the Chicago Crime Commission, pointed out that "[d]uring 1919 there were more murders in Chicago (with a population of three million) than in the entire British Isles (with a population of forty million)." This history ought to raise some doubts about the alleged causal link between the high rate of crime in America and the exclusionary rule.

• England and Wales have not experienced anything like the "revolution" in American criminal procedure which began at least as early as the 1961 *Mapp* case. Nevertheless, from 1955–65 (a decade which happened to be subjected to a most intensive study), the number of indictable offenses against the person in England and Wales increased 162 percent. How do opponents of the exclusionary rule explain such increases in countries which did not suffer from the wounds the Warren Court supposedly inflicted upon America?

• In the decade before *Mapp*, Maryland admitted illegally seized evidence in all felony prosecutions; Virginia, in all cases. District of Columbia police, on the other hand, were subject to both the exclusionary rule and the *McNabb-Mallory* rule, a rule which "hampered" no other police department during this period. Nevertheless, during this decade the felony rate per 100,000 population increased much more in the three Virginia and Maryland suburbs of the District (69 percent) than in the District itself (a puny one percent).

• The predictions and descriptions of near-disaster in California law enforcement which greeted the 1955 *Cahan* decision find precious little empirical support. The percentage of narcotics convictions did drop almost 10 points (to 77 percent), but only possession cases were significantly affected. Meanwhile, both the rate of arrests and felony complaints filed for narcotics offenses actually increased! Thus, in 1959–60, 20 percent more persons were convicted of narcotics offenses in California superior courts than in the record conviction percentage years before *Cahan*.

The overall felony conviction rate was 84.5 percent for the three years before *Cahan*, 85.4 percent for the *Cahan* year and 86.4 percent in the three years after *Cahan* (even including the low narcotic percentages). Conviction rates for murder, manslaughter, felony assault, rape, robbery and burglary remained almost the same, though the number of convicted felons rose steadily.

The exclusionary rule, to be sure, does free some "guilty criminals" (as would an effective tort remedy that inhibited the police from making illegal searches and seizures in the first place), but very rarely are they robbers or murderers. Rather they are "offenders caught in the everyday world of police initiated vice and narcotics enforcement. . . ."

> Though critics of the exclusionary rule sometimes sound as though it constitutes the main loophole in the administration of justice, the fact is that it is only a minor escape route in a system that filters out far more offenders through police, prosecutorial, and judicial discretion than it tries, convicts and sentences. . . .
>
> Moreover, the critics' concentration on the formal issue of conviction tends to overlook the very real sanctions that are imposed even on defendants who 'escape' via the suppression of evidence [e.g., among the poor, most suffer at least several days of imprisonment, regardless of the ultimate verdict; many

> lose their jobs as a result and have a hard time finding another]. . . .
>
> When one considers that many convictions in the courts that deal with large numbers of motions to suppress often amount to small fines, suspended sentences, and probation, the distinction between conviction and escape becomes even more blurred.

AN UNDEMONSTRATED CONNECTION

. . . Judge Wilkey hints darkly that there is a "connection" between America's high crime rate and its "unique" exclusionary rule. So far as I am aware, no one has been able to demonstrate such a connection on the basis of the annual *Uniform Crime Reports* or any other statistical data. In Michigan, for example, the rate of violent crime seems to have fluctuated without regard to the life and death of the state's "anti-exclusionary" proviso.

From 1960–64, the robbery rate increased only slightly in the Detroit Metropolitan Statistical Area but it quadrupled from 1964 to 1970 (from 152.5 per 100,000 to 648.5). When the Michigan Supreme Court struck down the state's "anti-exclusionary" proviso in 1970, the robbery rate fell (to 470.3 per 100,000 in 1973), climbed (to 604.2 in 1975), then dropped again (to 454.3 in 1977, the lowest it has been since the 1960's).

From 1960–64, the murder and non-negligent manslaughter rate remained almost the same in the Detroit area, but it rose extraordinarily the next six years (5.0 in 1964 to 14.7 in 1970). In the next four years it continued to climb (but less sharply) to 20.2 in 1974. Then it dropped to 14.1 in 1977, the lowest it has been since the 1960's.

Finally, I must take issue with Judge Wilkey's case of the criminal who "parade[s] in the streets with a great bulge in his pocket or a submachine gun in a blanket under his arm," "laugh[ing] in the face of the officer who might wish to search him for it." If American criminals "know the difficulties of the police in making a valid search," as Judge Wilkey tells us, they know, too, that the exclusionary rule has "virtually no applicability" in "large areas of police activity which do not result in criminal prosecutions" and that confiscation of weapons is one of them. (The criminal might get back his blanket, but not the submachine gun).

Moreover, it is not at all clear that an officer who notices a "great bulge" in a person's pocket or, as in the recent *Mimms* case, a "large bulge" under a person's sports jacket, lacks lawful authority to conduct a limited search for weapons. Indeed, *Mimms* seems to say that a policeman *does* have the authority under such circumstances. Even if I am wrong, however, even if the Fourth Amendment does not permit an officer to make such a limited search for weapons, *abolishing the exclusionary rule wouldn't change that.* If an officer now lacks the lawful authority to conduct a "frisk" under these circumstances, he would still lack the lawful authority to do so if the rule were abolished. This is a basic point, one that I shall focus on in the next section.

A BASIC CONFUSION

In my earlier *Judicature* article, I pointed out how police and prosecutors have treated the exclusionary rule as if it were itself the guaranty against unreasonable search and seizure (which is one good

reason for retaining the rule). At several places Judge Wilkey's article reflects the same confusion.

He complains, for example, that if a search or frisk turns up a deadly weapon, that weapon cannot be used in evidence if the officer lacked the constitutionally required cause for making the search or frisk in the first place. But this is really an attack on the constitutional guaranty itself, not the exclusionary rule. Prohibiting the use of illegally seized evidence may be poor "public relations" because by then we know who the criminal is, but an *after-the-fact* prohibition

> prevents convictions in no greater degree than would effective prior direction to police to search only by legal means . . . [T]he maintenance of existing standards by means of exclusion is not open to attack unless it can be doubted whether the standards themselves are necessary.

If we replace the exclusionary rule with "disciplinary punishment and civil penalties directly against the erring officer involved," as Judge Wilkey proposes, and if these alternatives "would certainly provide a far more effective deterrent than . . . the exclusionary rule," as the judge assures us, the weapon still would not be brought in as evidence in the case he poses because the officer would not *make* the search or frisk if he lacked the requisite cause to do so.

Judge Wilkey points enviously to England, where "the criminals know that the police have a right to search them *on the slightest suspicion,* and they know that if a weapon is found they will be prosecuted" (emphasis added). But what is the relevance of this point in an article discussing the exclusionary rule and its alternatives? Abolishing the rule would not confer a *right* on our police to search "on the slightest suspicion"; it would not affect lawful police practices in any way. Only a change in the substantive law of search and seizure can do that. . . . And replacing the exclusionary rule with a statutory remedy against the government would not bring about an increase in unlawful police activity if the alternative were equally effective—and Judge Wilkey expects it to be "a far more effective deterrent."

I venture to say that Judge Wilkey has confused the *content* of the law of search seizure (which proponents of the exclusionary rule need not, and have not always, defended) with the *exclusionary rule*—which "merely states the consequences of a breach of whatever principles might be adopted to control law enforcement officers." The confusion was pointed out more than 50 years ago by one who had the temerity to reply to the great Wigmore's famous criticism of the rule. Every student of the problem knows Wigmore's views on this subject, but very few are familiar with Connor Hall's reply. It is worth recalling:

> When it is proposed to secure the citizen his constitutional rights by the direct punishment of the violating officer, we must assume that the proposer is honest, and that he would have such consistent prosecution and such heavy punishment of the offending officer as would cause violations to cease and thus put a stop to the seizure of papers and other tangible evidence through unlawful search.
>
> If this, then, is to be the result, no evidence in any appreciable number of cases would be obtained through unlawful searches, and the result would be the same, so far as the conviction of criminals goes, as if the constitutional right was enforced by a return of the evidence.

Then why such anger in celestial breasts? Justice can be rendered inefficient and the criminal classes coddled by the rule laid down in *Weeks* only upon the assumption that the officer will not be directly punished, but that the court will receive the fruits of his lawful acts, will do no more than denounce and threaten him with jail or the penitentiary and, at the same time, with its tongue in its cheek, give him to understand how fearful a thing it is to violate the Constitution. This has been the result previous to the rule adopted by the Supreme Court, and that is what the courts are asked to continue.

. . . If punishment of the officer is effective to prevent unlawful searches, then equally by this is justice rendered inefficient and criminals coddled. It is only by violations that the great god Efficiency can thrive.

WAITING FOR ALTERNATIVES

Judge Wilkey makes plain his agreement with Chief Justice Burger that "the continued existence of [the exclusionary rule] . . . inhibits the development of rational alternatives" and that "incentives for developing new procedures or remedies will remain minimal or nonexistent so long as the exclusionary rule is retained in its present form."

Thus, Judge Wilkey warns that "we will never have any alternative in operation until the rule is abolished. So long as we keep the rule, the police are not going to investigate and discipline their men, and thus sabotage prosecutions by invalidating the admissibility of vital evidence. . . ." He argues that *Mapp* "removed from the states both the incentive and the opportunity to deal with illegal search and seizure by means other than suppression." And he concludes his first article with these words:

> [L]et us . . . by abolishing the rule permit in the laboratories of our 51 jurisdictions the experimentation with the various possible alternatives promising far more than the now discredited exclusionary rule.

In light of our history, these comments (both the Chief Justice's and Judge Wilkey's) are simply baffling. First, the fear of "sabotaging" prosecutions has never inhibited law enforcement administrators from disciplining officers for committing the "many unlawful searches of homes and automobiles of innocent people which turn up nothing incriminating, in which no arrest is made, about which courts do nothing, and about which we never hear."

Second, both defenders of the rule and its critics recognize that

> there are large areas of police activity which do not result in criminal prosecutions [e.g., arrest or confiscation as a punitive sanction (common in gambling and liquor law violations), illegal detentions which do not result in the acquisition of evidence, unnecessary destruction of property]—hence the rule has virtually no applicability and no effect in such situations.

Whatever the reason for the failure to discipline officers for "mistakes" in these "large areas of police activities," it cannot be the existence of the exclusionary rule.

Finally, and most importantly, *for many decades* a majority of the states had no exclusionary rule but *none of them* developed any meaningful alternative. Thirty-five years passed between the time the federal courts adopted the exclusionary rule and the time *Wolf* was decided in 1949, but none of the 31 states which still admitted illegally seized evidence had established an alternative method of controlling the police. Twelve more years passed before *Mapp* imposed the rule on the state courts, but none of the 24 states which still rejected the exclusionary rule had instituted an alternative remedy. This half-century of post-*Weeks* "freedom to experiment" did not produce any meaningful alternative to the exclusionary rule anywhere.

DISPARITY BETWEEN FACT AND THEORY

Of course, few critics of the exclusionary rule have failed to suggest alternative remedies that *might be devised* or that *warranted study*. None of them has become a reality.

In 1922, for example, Dean Wigmore maintained that "the natural way to do justice" would be to enforce the Fourth Amendment directly "by sending for the high-handed, overzealous marshal who had searched without a warrant, imposing a 30-day imprisonment for his contempt of the Constitution, and then proceeding to affirm the sentence of the convicted criminal." Nothing ever came of that proposal. Another critic of the rule suggested that a civil rights office be established, independent of the regular prosecutor, "charged solely with the responsibility of investigating and prosecuting alleged violations of the Constitution by law-enforcement officials." Nothing came of that proposal either.

Judge Wilkey recognizes that "policemen traditionally are not wealthy," but "[t]he government has a deep purse." Thus, as did Chief Justice Burger in his *Bivens* dissent, Judge Wilkey proposes that in lieu of the exclusion of illegally seized evidence there be a statutory remedy against the government itself to afford meaningful compensation and restitution for the victims of police illegality. Two leading commentators, Caleb Foote and Edward Barrett, Jr., made the same suggestion 20 years ago, but none of the many states that admitted illegally seized evidence at the time seemed interested in experimenting along these lines.

Indeed, the need for, and the desirability of, a statutory remedy against the government itself was pointed out at least as long ago as 1936. In a famous article published that year, Jerome Hall noted that the prospects of satisfying a judgment against a police officer were so poor that the tort remedy in the books "collapses at its initial application to fact." Said Hall:

> [W]here there is liability (as in the case of the policeman), the fact of financial irresponsibility is operative and, presumably, conclusive; while, where financial responsibility exists (as in the case of a city), there is no liability.

"This disparity between theory and fact, between an empty shell of relief and substantial compensation," observed Professor Hall—43 years ago—"could not remain unnoticed."

This disparity—no longer unnoticed, but still uncorrected—has troubled even the strongest critics of the rule. Thus, more than 35 years ago, J. A. C. Grant suggested "implement[ing] the law covering actions for trespass, even going so far as to hold the government liable in damages for the torts of its agents." And William Plumb, Jr., accompanied his powerful attack on the rule with a similar suggestion.

MAPP'S TRAUMATIC EFFECTS

At the time of Plumb's article, the admissibility of illegally seized evidence had "once more become a burning question in New York." Delegates to the 1938 constitutional convention had defeated an effort to write the exclusionary rule into the constitution, but only after a long and bitter debate. The battle then moved to the legislature, where bills were pending to exclude illegally obtained, or at least illegally wiretapped, evidence.

Against this background, Plumb offered a whole basketful of alternatives to the rule and he said the state legislature "should make a thorough study of the problem of devising effective direct remedies [such as those he had outlined] to make the constitutional guarantee 'a real, not an empty blessing.' " But nothing happened.

Otherwise why would a New York City Police Commissioner say of *Mapp* some 20 years later:

> I can think of no decision in recent times in the field of law enforcement which had such a dramatic effect as this. . . . I was immediately caught up in the entire problem of reevaluating our procedures which had followed the *Defore* rule, and modifying, amending, and creating new policies and new instructions for the implementation of *Mapp*. The problems were manifold. [Supreme Court decisions such as *Mapp*] create tidal waves and earthquakes which require rebuilding of our institutions sometimes from their very foundations upward. Retraining sessions had to be held from the very top administrators down to each of the thousands of foot patrolmen. . . .

In theory, *Defore*, which rejected the exclusionary rule in New York, had not expanded lawful police powers one iota. Nor, in theory, had *Mapp* reduced these powers. What was an illegal search before *Defore* was still an illegal search. What was an unlawful arrest before *Mapp* was still an unlawful arrest.

The *Defore* rule, of course, was based largely upon the premise that New York did not need to adopt the exclusionary rule because existing remedies were adequate to effectuate the guaranty against illegal search and seizure. Cardozo said that:

> The officer might have been resisted[!], or sued for damages or even prosecuted for oppression. He was subject to removal or other discipline at the hands of his superiors.

Why, then, did *Mapp* have such a "dramatic" and "traumatic" effect? Why did it necessitate "creating new policies"? What were the old policies like? Why did it necessitate retraining sessions from top to bottom? What was the *old* training like? What did the commissioner mean when he said that before *Mapp* his department had "followed the *Defore* rule"?

> On behalf of the New York City Police Department as well as law enforcement in general, I state unequivocally that every effort was directed and is still being directed at compliance with and implementation of *Mapp*. . . .

Isn't it peculiar to talk about police "compliance with" and "implementation of" a *remedy* for a violation of a body of law the police were supposed to be complying with and implementing all along? Why did the police have to make such strenuous efforts to comply with *Mapp* unless they had not been complying with the Fourth Amendment?

> Flowing from the *Mapp* case is the issue of defining probable cause to constitute a lawful arrest and subsequent search and seizure.

Doesn't this issue flow from the Fourth Amendment itself? Isn't that what the Fourth Amendment is all about?

The police reaction to *Mapp* demonstrates the unsoundness of the underlying premise of *Defore*. Otherwise why, at a post-*Mapp* training session on the law of search and seizure, would Leonard Reisman, then the New York Deputy Police Commissioner in charge of legal matters, comment:

> The *Mapp* case was a shock to us. We had to reorganize our thinking, frankly. Before this, nobody bothered to take out search warrants. Although the U.S. Constitution requires warrants in most cases, the U.S. Supreme Court had ruled [until 1961] that evidence obtained without a warrant—illegally if you will—was admissible in state courts. So the feeling was, why bother?

NO INCENTIVE FOR CHANGE

As I have already indicated, critics of the exclusionary rule have often made proposals for effectuating the Fourth Amendment by means other than the exclusionary rule—but almost always as a *quid pro quo* for rejecting or repealing the rule. Who has ever heard of a police-prosecution spokesman urging—or a law enforcement group supporting—an effective "direct remedy" for illegal searches and seizures in a jurisdiction which *admitted* illegally seized evidence? Abandoning the exclusionary rule without waiting for a meaningful alternative (as Judge Wilkey and Chief Justice Burger would have us do) will not furnish an incentive for devising an alternative, but *relieve* whatever pressure there now exists for doing so.

I spoke in my earlier article of the great symbolic value of the exclusionary rule. Abolition of the exclusionary rule, after the long, bitter struggle to attain it, would be even more important as a symbol.

During the 12-year reign of *Wolf*, some state judges

remained mindful of the cogent reasons for the admission of illegally obtained evidence and clung to the fragile hope that the very brazenness of lawless police methods would bring on effective deterrents other than the exclusionary rule.

Their hope proved to be in vain. *Wolf* established the "underlying constitutional doctrine" that "the Federal Constitution, by virtue of the Fourteenth Amendment, prohibits unreasonable searches and seizures by state officers" (though it did not require exclusion of the resulting evidence); *Irvine* warned that if the state "defaulted and there were no demonstrably effective deterrents to unreasonable searches and seizures in lieu of the exclusionary rule, the Supreme Court might yet decide that they had not complied with 'minimal standards' of due process." But neither *Wolf* nor *Irvine* stimulated a single state legislature or a single law enforcement agency to demonstrate that the problem could be handled in other ways.

The disappointing 12 years between *Wolf* and *Mapp* give added weight to Francis Allen's thoughtful commentary on the *Wolf* case at the time it was handed down:

This deference to local authority revealed in the *Wolf* case stands in marked contrast to the position of the court in other cases arising within the last decade involving rights 'basic to a free society.' It seems safe to assert that in no other area of civil liberties litigation is there evidence that the court has construed the obligations of federalism

to require so high a degree of judicial self-abnegation.

. . . [I]n no other area in the civil liberties has the court felt justified in trusting to public protest for protection of basic personal rights. Indeed, since the rights of privacy are usually asserted by those charged with crime and since the demands of efficient law enforcement are so insistent, it would seem that reliance on public opinion in these cases can be less justified than in almost any other. . . .

Now Judge Wilkey asks us to believe that the resurrection of *Wolf* (and evidently the overruling of the 65-year-old *Weeks* case as well) will permit "the laboratories of our 51 jurisdictions" to produce meaningful alternatives to the exclusionary rule. His ideological ally, Chief Justice Burger, is even more optimistic. He asks us to believe that a return to the pre-exclusionary rule days "would inspire a surge of activity toward providing some kind of statutory remedy for persons injured by police mistakes or misconduct."

And to think that Judge Wilkey accuses *defenders* of the exclusionary rule of being "stubbornly blind to 65 years of experience"!

POSTSCRIPT

Should the Exclusionary Rule Be Abolished?

Wilkey is not the only federal judge opposed to the exclusionary rule. The most famous judicial critic is former Supreme Court chief justice Warren E. Burger. Burger's opposition to the rule, however, has not led to an overturning of *Mapp* or *Weeks*, at least not yet. But during the past several decades, there have been a substantial number of cases in which the Court considered the rule and restricted its scope. Thus, while the rule can still be invoked by a defendant at a criminal trial, it cannot be used at a grand jury proceeding (see *United States v. Calandra*, 414 U.S. 338, 1974), in a *habeas corpus* proceeding by a state prisoner (see *Stone v. Powell*, 428 U.S. 465, 1976), when the illegal search is conducted on someone other than the defendant (see *United States v. Payner*, 447 U.S. 727, 1980), or when the illegal search was conducted outside the United States (see *U.S. v. Verdugo-Urguidez*, 110 S. Ct. 1056, 1990). Many cases have involved automobiles, the most recent being *California v. Acevedo*, 111 S. Ct. 1982 (1991).

The Court has approved a good faith exception to the rule in cases where the police officer believed that he was acting lawfully, even though the warrant may have been defective or procured illegally (*Massachusetts v. Sheppard*, 104 S. Ct. 3424, 1984). It has also ruled that search warrants are not required for school officials to search school lockers if there are reasonable grounds for believing the search will reveal evidence of criminal behavior (*New Jersey v. T. L. O., A Juvenile*, 105 S. Ct. 733, 1985). The Burger and Rehnquist courts have generally been lenient in upholding police law enforcement practices and the policy of limiting the defendant's opportunities for invoking the exclusionary rule seems likely to continue.

In part, the resistance to the exclusionary rule is based on a belief that it does not deter illegal police conduct. An interesting debate on the subject, which examines many of the relevant research studies, is found in a series of articles in *Judicature*: B. Canon, "The Exclusionary Rule: Have Critics Proven That It Doesn't Deter Police?" (March 1979), and S. S. Schlesinger, "The Exclusionary Rule: Have Proponents Proven That It Is a Deterrent to Police?" (March 1979). Recent articles include Nelson, "The Paradox of the Exclusionary Rule," *The Public Interest* (Summer 1989); LaFave, "Pinguitudinous Police, Pachydermatous Prey: Whence Fourth Amendment 'Seizures'?" 1991 *University of Illinois Law Review* 729 (1991); C. Slobogin, "The World Without A Fourth Amendment," 39 *UCLA Law Review* 1 (1991); and Note, "Cameras in Teddy Bears: Electronic Visual Surveillance and the Fourth Amendment," 58 *University of Chicago Law Review* 1045 (1991).

ISSUE 14

Should "Battered Wife Syndrome" Be Barred as a Defense in a Murder Case?

YES: Burley B. Mitchell, Jr., from Majority Opinion, *State of North Carolina v. Judy Ann Laws Norman*, Supreme Court of North Carolina (1989)

NO: Harry C. Martin, from Dissenting Opinion, *State of North Carolina v. Judy Ann Laws Norman*, Supreme Court of North Carolina (1989)

ISSUE SUMMARY

YES: Justice Burley B. Mitchell, Jr., is unwilling to recognize "battered wife syndrome" as meeting the standards of immediacy and necessity needed for a self-defense claim in a homicide case.

NO: Justice Harry C. Martin, dissenting in the same case, believes that, given the actions of the husband, the wife's behavior can be viewed in such a way as to meet the standards of self-defense.

The statistics are quite startling. In the United States, one in every five women involved in an intimate relationship with a man is beaten repeatedly by that man. In at least half the cases in which women are battered, children are also battered. Of the children who witness domestic violence, 60 percent of the boys eventually become batterers, and 50 percent of the girls become victims. Battery is the single major cause of injury to women, exceeding even muggings and automobile accidents. Four women, on average, are beaten to death every day in the United States.

As the following readings reveal, the law is having considerable difficulty with this issue. The case involves a woman on trial for killing her husband. Should the trial judge recognize the fact that she was beaten repeatedly, that she suffered from "battered wife syndrome," as constituting a claim of self-defense?

The issue discussed here does not put forward a solution to the problem of spouse abuse. The legal issue is focused quite narrowly on what kind of evidence the trial court may hear and consider. You might reasonably ask whether the legal system's struggle to develop an approach to the condition of "battered wife syndrome" itself suggests failure on the part of the legal system. That such a syndrome exists implies, at least, that the woman has not been protected from repeated battering, and that the legal authorities have failed to intervene effectively.

Spouse abuse is an issue that can be traced back to antiquity. The law in this country has dealt with it for hundreds of years. In the mid-1800s, for example, a North Carolina judge wrote:

the wife must be subject to the husband. Every man must govern his household, and if by reason of an unruly temper, or an unbridled tongue, the wife persistently treats her husband with disrespect, and he submits to it, he not only loses all sense of self-respect, but loses the respect of other members of his family, without which he cannot expect to govern them, and forfeits the respect of his neighbors. Such have been the incidents of the marriage relation from the beginning of the human race. Unto the woman it is said: 'Thy desire shall be to thy husband, and he shall rule over thee': Gen. iii, 16. It follows that the law gives the husband the power to use such a degree of force as is necessary to make the wife behave herself and know her place. (*Joyner v. Joyner*, 59 N.C. 322, 1962)

Interestingly, a little more than a decade later, the same court considered the issue again and reached a different conclusion:

We may assume that the old doctrine that a husband had a right to whip his wife, provided he used a switch no larger than his thumb, is not law in North Carolina. Indeed, the Courts have advanced from that barbarism until they have reached the position that the husband has no right to chastise his wife under any circumstances. (*State v. Oliver*, 70 N.C. 60, 1874)

It was not until 1883 that Maryland became the first state to outlaw wife beating by legislation. As you read the following opinions, ask yourself what might account for the rather ineffective response of governmental institutions to enforcing the law and coming to terms with the problem of spousal abuse.

YES

Burley B. Mitchell, Jr.

MAJORITY OPINION

NORTH CAROLINA v. NORMAN

Opinion by Justice Mitchell:

The defendant was tried at the 16 February 1987 Criminal Session of Superior Court for Rutherford County upon a proper indictment charging her with the first degree murder of her husband. The jury found the defendant guilty of voluntary manslaughter. The defendant appealed from the trial court's judgment sentencing her to six years imprisonment.

The Court of Appeals granted a new trial, citing as error the trial court's refusal to submit a possible verdict of acquittal by reason of perfect self-defense. Notwithstanding the uncontroverted evidence that the defendant shot her husband three times in the back of the head as he lay sleeping in his bed, the Court of Appeals held that the defendant's evidence that she exhibited what has come to be called "the battered wife syndrome" entitled her to have the jury consider whether the homicide was an act of perfect self-defense and, thus, not a legal wrong.

We conclude that the evidence introduced in this case would not support a finding that the defendant killed her husband due to a reasonable fear of imminent death or great bodily harm, as is required before a defendant is entitled to jury instructions concerning either perfect or imperfect self-defense. Therefore, the trial court properly declined to instruct the jury on the law relating to self-defense. Accordingly, we reverse the Court of Appeals.

At trial, the State presented the testimony of Deputy Sheriff R. H. Epley of the Rutherford County Sheriff's Department, who was called to the Norman residence on the night of 12 June 1985. Inside the home, Epley found the defendant's husband, John Thomas Norman, lying on a bed in a rear bedroom with his face toward the wall and his back toward the middle of the room. He was dead, but blood was still coming from wounds to the back of his head. A later autopsy revealed three gunshot wounds to the head, two of

From *State of North Carolina v. Judy Ann Laws Norman*, 324 N.C. 253, 378 S.E.2d 8 (1989). Notes and some case citations omitted.

which caused fatal brain injury. The autopsy also revealed a .12 percent blood alcohol level in the victim's body.

Later that night, the defendant related an account of the events leading to the killing, after Epley had advised her of her constitutional rights and she had waived her right to remain silent. The defendant told Epley that her husband had been beating her all day and had made her lie down on the floor while he slept on the bed. After her husband fell asleep, the defendant carried her grandchild to the defendant's mother's house. The defendant took a pistol from her mother's purse and walked the short distance back to her home. She pointed the pistol at the back of her sleeping husband's head, but it jammed the first time she tried to shoot him. She fixed the gun and then shot her husband in the back of the head as he lay sleeping. After one shot, she felt her husband's chest and determined that he was still breathing and making sounds. She then shot him twice more in the back of the head. The defendant told Epley that she killed her husband because "she took all she was going to take from him so she shot him."

The defendant presented evidence tending to show a long history of physical and mental abuse by her husband due to his alcoholism. At the time of the killing, the thirty-nine-year-old defendant and her husband had been married almost twenty-five years and had several children. The defendant testified that her husband had started drinking and abusing her about five years after they were married. His physical abuse of her consisted of frequent assaults that included slapping, punching and kicking her, striking her with various objects, and throwing glasses, beer bottles and other objects at her. The defendant described other specific incidents of abuse, such as her husband putting her cigarettes out on her, throwing hot coffee on her, breaking glass against her face and crushing food on her face. Although the defendant did not present evidence of ever having received medical treatment for any physical injuries inflicted by her husband, she displayed several scars about her face which she attributed to her husband's assaults.

The defendant's evidence also tended to show other indignities inflicted upon her by her husband. Her evidence tended to show that her husband did not work and forced her to make money by prostitution, and that he made humor of that fact to family and friends. He would beat her if she resisted going out to prostitute herself or if he was unsatisfied with the amounts of money she made. He routinely called the defendant "dog," "bitch" and "whore," and on a few occasions made her eat pet food out of the pets' bowls and bark like a dog. He often made her sleep on the floor. At times, he deprived her of food and refused to let her get food for the family. During those years of abuse, the defendant's husband threatened numerous times to kill her and to maim her in various ways.

The defendant said her husband's abuse occurred only when he was intoxicated, but that he would not give up drinking. She said she and her husband "got along very well when he was sober," and that he was "a good guy" when he was not drunk. She had accompanied her husband to the local mental health center for sporadic counseling sessions for his problem, but he continued to drink.

In the early morning hours on the day before his death, the defendant's husband, who was intoxicated, went to a rest area off I-85 near Kings Mountain where the defendant was engaging in prostitution and assaulted her. While driving home, he was stopped by a patrolman and jailed on a charge of driving while impaired. After the defendant's mother got him out of jail at the defendant's request later that morning, he resumed his drinking and abuse of the defendant.

The defendant's evidence also tended to show that her husband seemed angrier than ever after he was released from jail and that his abuse of the defendant was more frequent. That evening, sheriff's deputies were called to the Norman residence, and the defendant complained that her husband had been beating her all day and she could not take it anymore. The defendant was advised to file a complaint, but she said she was afraid her husband would kill her if she had him arrested. The deputies told her they needed a warrant before they could arrest her husband, and they left the scene.

The deputies were called back less than an hour later after the defendant had taken a bottle of pills. The defendant's husband cursed her and called her names as she was attended by paramedics, and he told them to let her die. A sheriff's deputy finally chased him back into his house as the defendant was put into an ambulance. The defendant's stomach was pumped at the local hospital, and she was sent home with her mother.

While in the hospital, the defendant was visited by a therapist with whom she discussed filing charges against her husband and having him committed for treatment. Before the therapist left, the defendant agreed to go to the mental health center the next day to discuss those possibilities. The therapist testified at trial that the defendant seemed depressed in the hospital, and that she expressed considerable anger toward her husband. He testified that the defendant threatened a number of times that night to kill her husband and that she said she should kill him "because of the things he had done to her."

The next day, the day she shot her husband, the defendant went to the mental health center to talk about charges and possible commitment, and she confronted her husband with that possibility. She testified that she told her husband later that day: "J. T., straighten up. Quit drinking. I'm going to have you committed to help you." She said her husband then told her he would "see them coming" and would cut her throat before they got to him.

The defendant also went to the social services office that day to seek welfare benefits, but her husband followed her there, interrupted her interview and made her go home with him. He continued his abuse of her, threatening to kill and to maim her, slapping her, kicking her, and throwing objects at her. At one point, he took her cigarette and put it out on her, causing a small burn on her upper torso. He would not let her eat or bring food into the house for their children.

That evening, the defendant and her husband went into their bedroom to lie down, and he called her a "dog" and made her lie on the floor when he lay down on the bed. Their daughter brought in her baby to leave with the defendant, and the defendant's husband agreed to let her baby-sit. After the defendant's husband fell asleep, the baby started crying and the defendant took it to her mother's house so it would not wake up her husband. She returned shortly with the pistol and killed her husband.

The defendant testified at trial that she was too afraid of her husband to press charges against him or to leave him. She said that she had temporarily left their home on several previous occasions, but he had always found her, brought her home and beaten her. Asked why she killed her husband, the defendant replied: "Because I was scared of him and I knowed when he woke up, it was going to be the same thing, and I was scared when he took me to the truck stop that night it was going to be worse than he had ever been. I just couldn't take it no more. There ain't no way, even if it means going to prison. It's better than living in that. That's worse hell than anything."

The defendant and other witnesses testified that for years her husband had frequently threatened to kill her and to maim her. When asked if she believed those threats, the defendant replied: "Yes. I believed him he would, he would kill me if he got a chance. If he thought he wouldn't a had to went to jail, he would a done it."

Two expert witnesses in forensic psychology and psychiatry who examined the defendant after the shooting, Dr. William Tyson and Dr. Robert Rollins, testified that the defendant fit the profile of battered wife syndrome. This condition, they testified, is characterized by such abuse and degradation that the battered wife comes to believe she is unable to help herself and cannot expect help from anyone else. She believes that she cannot escape the complete control of her husband and that he is invulnerable to law enforcement and other sources of help.

Dr. Tyson, a psychologist, was asked his opinion as to whether, on 12 June 1985, "it appeared reasonably necessary for Judy Norman to shoot J. T. Norman?" He replied: "I believe that . . . Mrs. Norman believed herself to be doomed . . . to a life of the worst kind of torture and abuse, degradation that she had experienced over the years in a progressive way that it would only get worse, and that death was inevitable. . . ." Dr. Tyson later added: "I think Judy Norman felt that she had no choice, both in the protection of herself and her family, but to engage, exhibit deadly force against Mr. Norman, and that in so doing, she was sacrificing herself, both for herself and for her family."

Dr. Rollins, who was the defendant's attending physician at Dorothea Dix Hospital when she was sent there for evaluation, testified that in his opinion the defendant was a typical abused spouse and that "[s]he saw herself as powerless to deal with the situation, that there was no alternative, no way she could escape it." Dr. Rollins was asked his opinion as to whether "on June 12th, 1985, it appeared reasonably necessary that Judy Norman would take the life of J. T. Norman?" Dr. Rollins replied that in his opinion, "that course of action did appear necessary to Mrs. Norman."

Based on the evidence that the defendant exhibited battered wife syndrome, that she believed she could not escape her husband nor expect help from others, that her husband had threatened her, and that her husband's abuse of her had worsened in the two days preceding his death, the Court of Appeals concluded that a jury reasonably could have found that her killing of her husband was justified as an act of perfect self-defense. The Court of Appeals reasoned that the nature of battered wife syndrome is such that a jury could not be precluded from finding the defendant killed her husband lawfully in perfect self-defense, even though he was asleep when she killed him. We disagree.

The right to kill in self-defense is based on the necessity, real or reasonably apparent, of killing an unlawful aggressor to save oneself from imminent death or great bodily harm at his hands. *State v. Gappins*, 320 N.C. 64, 357 S.E. 2d 654 (1987). Our law has recognized that self-preservation under such circumstances springs from a primal impulse and is an inherent right of natural law. *State v. Holland*, 193 N.C. 713, 718, 138 S.E. 8, 10 (1927).

In North Carolina, a defendant is entitled to have the jury consider acquittal by reason of perfect self-defense when the evidence, viewed in the light most favorable to the defendant, tends to show that at the time of the killing it appeared to the defendant and she believed it to be necessary to kill the decedent to save herself from imminent death or great bodily harm. *State v. Gappins*, 320 N.C. at 71, 357 S.E. 2d at 659. That belief must be reasonable, however, in that the circumstances as they appeared to the defendant would create such a belief in the mind of a person of ordinary firmness. Further, the defendant must not have been the initial aggressor provoking the fatal confrontation. A killing in the proper exercise of the right of perfect self-defense is always completely justified in law and constitutes no legal wrong.

Our law also recognizes an imperfect right of self-defense in certain circumstances, including, for example, when the defendant is the initial aggressor, but without intent to kill or to seriously injure the decedent, and the decedent escalates the confrontation to a point where it reasonably appears to the defendant to

be necessary to kill the decedent to save herself from imminent death or great bodily harm. *State v. Mize*, 316 N.C. 48, 340 S.E. 2d 439 (1986); *State v. Wilson*, 304 N.C. 689, 285 S.E. 2d 804 (1982). Although the culpability of a defendant who kills in the exercise of imperfect self-defense is reduced, such a defendant is not justified in the killing so as to be entitled to acquittal, but is guilty at least of voluntary manslaughter. *State v. Mize*, 316 N.C. at 52, 340 S.E. 2d at 441.

The defendant in the present case was not entitled to a jury instruction on either perfect or imperfect self-defense. The trial court was not required to instruct on either form of self-defense unless evidence was introduced tending to show that at the time of the killing the defendant reasonably believed herself to be confronted by circumstances which necessitated her killing her husband to save herself from imminent death or great bodily harm. No such evidence was introduced in this case, and it would have been error for the trial court to instruct the jury on either perfect or imperfect self-defense.

The jury found the defendant guilty only of voluntary manslaughter in the present case. As we have indicated, an instruction on imperfect self-defense would have entitled the defendant to nothing more, since one who kills in the exercise of imperfect self-defense is guilty at least of voluntary manslaughter. Therefore, even if it is assumed *arguendo* that the defendant was entitled to an instruction on imperfect self-defense—a notion we have specifically rejected—the failure to give such an instruction was harmless in this case. Accordingly, although we recognize that the imminence requirement applies to both types of self-defense for almost identical reasons, we limit our consideration in the remainder of this opinion to the issue of whether the trial court erred in failing to instruct the jury to consider acquittal on the ground that the killing was justified and, thus, lawful as an act of perfect self-defense.

The killing of another human being is the most extreme recourse to our inherent right of self-preservation and can be justified in law only by the utmost real or apparent necessity brought about by the decedent. For that reason, our law of self-defense has required that a defendant claiming that a homicide was justified and, as a result, inherently lawful by reason of perfect self-defense must establish that she reasonably believed at the time of the killing she otherwise would have immediately suffered death or great bodily harm. Only if defendants are required to show that they killed due to a reasonable belief that death or great bodily harm was imminent can the justification for homicide remain clearly and firmly rooted in necessity. The imminence requirement ensures that deadly force will be used only where it is necessary as a last resort in the exercise of the inherent right of self-preservation. It also ensures that before a homicide is justified and, as a result, not a legal wrong, it will be reliably determined that the defendant reasonably believed that absent the use of deadly force, not only would an unlawful attack have occurred, but also that the attack would have caused death or great bodily harm. The law does not sanction the use of deadly force to repel simple assaults.

The term "imminent," as used to describe such perceived threats of death or great bodily harm as will justify a homicide by reason of perfect self-defense, has been defined as "immediate danger, such as must be instantly met, such as

cannot be guarded against by calling for the assistance of others or the protection of the law." Black's Law Dictionary 676 (5th ed. 1979). Our cases have sometimes used the phrase "about to suffer" interchangeably with "imminent" to describe the immediacy of threat that is required to justify killing in self-defense.

The evidence in this case did not tend to show that the defendant reasonably believed that she was confronted by a threat of imminent death or great bodily harm. The evidence tended to show that no harm was "imminent" or about to happen to the defendant when she shot her husband. The uncontroverted evidence was that her husband had been asleep for some time when she walked to her mother's house, returned with the pistol, fixed the pistol after it jammed and then shot her husband three times in the back of the head. The defendant was not faced with an instantaneous choice between killing her husband or being killed or seriously injured. Instead, all of the evidence tended to show that the defendant had ample time and opportunity to resort to other means of preventing further abuse by her husband. There was no action underway by the decedent from which the jury could have found that the defendant had reasonable grounds to believe either that a felonious assault was imminent or that it might result in her death or great bodily injury. Additionally, no such action by the decedent had been underway immediately prior to his falling asleep.

Faced with somewhat similar facts, we have previously held that a defendant who believed himself to be threatened by the decedent was not entitled to a jury instruction on either perfect or imperfect self-defense when it was the defendant who went to the decedent and initiated the final, fatal confrontation. *State v. Mize*, 316 N.C. 48, 340 S.E. 2d 439 (1986). In *Mize*, the decedent Joe McDonald was reported to be looking for the defendant George Mize to get revenge for Mize's alleged rape of McDonald's girl friend, which had exacerbated existing animosity between Mize and McDonald. After hiding from McDonald for most of the day, Mize finally went to McDonald's residence, woke him up and then shot and killed him. Mize claimed that he feared McDonald was going to kill him and that his killing of McDonald was in self-defense. Rejecting Mize's argument that his jury should have been instructed on self-defense, we stated:

> Here, although the victim had pursued defendant during the day approximately eight hours before the killing, defendant Mize was in no imminent danger while McDonald was at home asleep. When Mize went to McDonald's trailer with his shotgun, it was a new confrontation. Therefore, even if Mize believed it was necessary to kill McDonald to avoid his own imminent death, that belief was unreasonable.

The same reasoning applies in the present case.

Additionally, the lack of any belief by the defendant—reasonable or otherwise— that she faced a threat of imminent death or great bodily harm from the drunk and sleeping victim in the present case was illustrated by the defendant and her own expert witnesses when testifying about her subjective assessment of her situation at the time of the killing. The psychologist and psychiatrist replied affirmatively when asked their opinions of whether killing her husband "appeared reasonably necessary" to the defendant at the time of the homicide. That testimony spoke of no imminent threat nor of any

fear by the defendant of death or great bodily harm, imminent or otherwise. Testimony in the form of a conclusion that a killing "appeared reasonably necessary" to a defendant does not tend to show all that must be shown to establish self-defense. More specifically, for a killing to be in self-defense, the perceived necessity must arise from a reasonable fear of imminent death or great bodily harm.

Dr. Tyson additionally testified that the defendant "believed herself to be doomed . . . to a life of the worst kind of torture and abuse, degradation that she had experienced over the years in a progressive way that it would only get worse, and that death was inevitable." Such evidence of the defendant's speculative beliefs concerning her remote and indefinite future, while indicating she had felt generally threatened, did not tend to show that she killed in the belief—reasonable or otherwise— that her husband presented a threat of imminent death or great bodily harm. Under our law of self-defense, a defendant's subjective belief of what might be "inevitable" at some indefinite point in the future does not equate to what she believes to be "imminent." Dr. Tyson's opinion that the defendant believed it was necessary to kill her husband for "the protection of herself and her family" was similarly indefinite and devoid of time frame and did not tend to show a threat or fear of imminent harm.

The defendant testified that, "I knowed when he woke up, it was going to be the same thing, and I was scared when he took me to the truck stop that night it was going to be worse than he had ever been." She also testified, when asked if she believed her husband's threats: "Yes. . . . [H]e would kill me if he got a chance. If he thought he wouldn't a had to went to jail, he would a done it." Testimony about such indefinite fears concerning what her sleeping husband might do at some time in the future did not tend to establish a fear—reasonable or otherwise—of imminent death or great bodily harm at the time of the killing.

We are not persuaded by the reasoning of our Court of Appeals in this case that when there is evidence of battered wife syndrome, neither an actual attack nor threat of attack by the husband at the moment the wife uses deadly force is required to justify the wife's killing of him in perfect self-defense. The Court of Appeals concluded that to impose such requirements would ignore the "learned helplessness," meekness and other realities of battered wife syndrome and would effectively preclude such women from exercising their right of self-defense. 89 N.C. App. 384, 392–393, 366 S.E. 2d 586, 591–592 (1988). See Mather, The Skeleton in the Closet: The Battered Woman Syndrome, Self-Defense, and Expert Testimony, 39 Mercer L. Rev. 545 (1988); Eber, The Battered Wife's Dilemma: To Kill Or To Be Killed, 32 Hastings L.J. 895 (1981). Other jurisdictions which have addressed this question under similar facts are divided in their views, and we can discern no clear majority position on facts closely similar to those of this case.

The reasoning of our Court of Appeals in this case proposes to change the established law of self-defense by giving the term "imminent" a meaning substantially more indefinite and all-encompassing than its present meaning. This would result in a substantial relaxation of the requirement of real or apparent necessity to justify homicide. Such reasoning proposes justifying the taking of human life

not upon the reasonable belief it is necessary to prevent death or great bodily harm—which the imminence requirement ensures—but upon purely subjective speculation that the decedent probably would present a threat to life at a future time and that the defendant would not be able to avoid the predicted threat.

The Court of Appeals suggests that such speculation would have been particularly reliable in the present case because the jury, based on the evidence of the decedent's intensified abuse during the thirty-six hours preceding his death, could have found that the decedent's passive state at the time of his death was "but a momentary hiatus in a continuous reign of terror by the decedent [and] the defendant merely took advantage of her first opportunity to protect herself." 89 N.C. App. at 394, 366 S.E. 2d at 592. Requiring jury instructions on perfect self-defense in such situations, however, would still tend to make opportune homicide lawful as a result of mere subjective predictions of indefinite future assaults and circumstances. Such predictions of future assaults to justify the defendant's use of deadly force in this case would be entirely speculative, because there was no evidence that her husband had ever inflicted any harm upon her that approached life-threatening injury, even during the "reign of terror." It is far from clear in the defendant's poignant evidence that any abuse by the decedent had ever involved the degree of physical threat required to justify the defendant in using deadly force, even when those threats were imminent. The use of deadly force in self-defense to prevent harm other than death or great bodily harm is excessive as a matter of law. *State v. Hunter*, 315 N.C. 371, 338 S.E. 2d 99 (1986).

As we have stated, stretching the law of self-defense to fit the facts of this case would require changing the "imminent death or great bodily harm" requirement to something substantially more indefinite than previously required and would weaken our assurances that justification for the taking of human life remains firmly rooted in real or apparent necessity. That result in principle could not be limited to a few cases decided on evidence as poignant as this. The relaxed requirements for perfect self-defense proposed by our Court of Appeals would tend to categorically legalize the opportune killing of abusive husbands by their wives solely on the basis of the wives' testimony concerning their subjective speculation as to the probability of future felonious assaults by their husbands. Homicidal self-help would then become a lawful solution, and perhaps the easiest and most effective solution, to this problem. See generally Rosen, The Excuse of Self-Defense: Correcting A Historical Accident on Behalf of Battered Women Who Kill, 36 Am. U.L. Rev. 11 (1986) (advocating changing the basis of self-defense acquittals to excuse rather than justification, so that excusing battered women's killing of their husbands under circumstances not fitting within the traditional requirements of self-defense would not be seen as justifying and therefore encouraging such self-help killing); Mitchell, Does Wife Abuse Justify Homicide?, 24 Wayne L. Rev. 1705 (1978) (advocating institutional rather than self-help solutions to wife abuse and citing case studies at the trial level where traditional defenses to homicide appeared stretched to accommodate poignant facts, resulting in justifications of some killings which appeared to be motivated by revenge rather than protection from death or great bodily harm). It has even been suggested that the relaxed requirements of self-defense found in what is often called the "battered woman's defense" could be extended in principle to any type of case in which a defendant testified that he or she subjectively believed that killing was necessary and proportionate to any perceived threat. Rosen, The Excuse of Self-Defense: Correcting A Historical Accident on Behalf of Battered Women Who Kill, 36 Am. U.L. Rev. 11, 44 (1986).

In conclusion, we decline to expand our law of self-defense beyond the limits of immediacy and necessity which have heretofore provided an appropriately narrow but firm basis upon which homicide may be justified and, thus, lawful by reason of perfect self-defense or upon which a defendant's culpability may be reduced by reason of imperfect self-defense. As we have shown, the evidence in this case did not entitle the defendant to jury instructions on either perfect or imperfect self-defense.

For the foregoing reasons, we conclude that the defendant's conviction for voluntary manslaughter and the trial court's judgment sentencing her to a six-year term of imprisonment were without error. Therefore, we must reverse the decision of the Court of Appeals which awarded the defendant a new trial.

Reversed.

NO

Harry C. Martin

DISSENTING OPINION OF
HARRY C. MARTIN

Justice Martin dissenting.

At the outset it is to be noted that the peril of fabricated evidence is not unique to the trials of battered wives who kill. The possibility of invented evidence arises in all cases in which a party is seeking the benefit of self-defense. Moreover, in this case there were a number of witnesses other than defendant who testified as to the actual presence of circumstances support-ing a claim of self-defense. This record contains no reasonable basis to attack the credibility of evidence for the defendant.

Likewise, the difficulty of rebutting defendant's evidence because the only other witness to many of the events is deceased is not unique to this type of case. This situation is also commonplace in cases in which self-defense is raised, although, again, in the case *sub judice* there was more than one surviving witness to such events. In considering the argument that the state is faced with a difficult burden in attempting to rebut evidence of which defendant is the only surviving witness, one must not overlook the law: the burden is always on the state to prove that the killing was intentional beyond a reasonable doubt. "Defendant may always rest ultimately on the weakness of the state's case and the state's failure to carry its burden of proof." *State v. Patterson*, 297 N.C. 247, 256, 254 S.E. 2d 604, 610 (1979).

At the heart of the majority's reasoning is its unsubstantiated concern that to find that the evidence presented by defendant would support an instruc-tion on self-defense would "expand our law of self-defense beyond the limits of immediacy and necessity." Defendant does not seek to expand or relax the requirements of self-defense and thereby "legalize the opportune killing of allegedly abusive husbands by their wives," as the majority overstates. Rather, defendant contends that the evidence as gauged by the existing laws of self-defense is sufficient to require the submission of a self-defense instruction to the jury. The proper issue for this Court is to determine whether the evidence, viewed in the light most favorable to the defendant, was sufficient to require the trial court to instruct on the law of self-defense. I conclude that it was.

From *State of North Carolina v. Judy Ann Laws Norman,* 324 N.C. 253, 378 S.E.2d 8 (1989). Notes and some case citations omitted.

In every jury trial, it is the duty of the court to charge the jury on all substantial features of the case arising on the evidence, whether or not such instructions have been requested. All defenses presented by the defendant's evidence are substantial features of the case, even if that evidence contains discrepancies or is contradicted by evidence from the state. This rule reflects the principle in our jurisprudence that it is the jury, not the judge, that weighs the evidence.

A defendant is entitled to an instruction on self-defense when there is evidence, viewed in the light most favorable to the defendant, that these four elements existed at the time of the killing:

1. it appeared to defendant and he believed it to be necessary to kill the deceased in order to save himself from death or great bodily harm and

2. defendant's belief was reasonable in that the circumstances as they appeared to him at the time were sufficient to create such a belief in the mind of a person of ordinary firmness and

3. defendant was not the aggressor in bringing on the affray, i.e., he did not aggressively and willingly enter into the fight without legal excuse or provocation and

4. defendant did not use excessive force, i.e., did not use more force than was necessary or reasonably appeared to him to be necessary under the circumstances to protect himself from death or great bodily harm.

The first element requires that there be evidence that the defendant believed it was necessary to kill in order to protect herself from serious bodily harm or death; the second requires that the circumstances as defendant perceived them were sufficient to create such a belief in the mind of a person of ordinary firm-

ness. Both elements were supported by evidence at defendant's trial.

Evidence presented by defendant described a twenty-year history of beatings and other dehumanizing and degrading treatment by her husband. In his expert testimony a clinical psychologist concluded that defendant fit "and exceed[ed]" the profile of an abused or battered spouse, analogizing this treatment to the dehumanization process suffered by prisoners of war under the Nazis during the Second World War and the brainwashing techniques of the Korean War. The psychologist described the defendant as a woman incarcerated by abuse, by fear, and by her conviction that her husband was invincible and inescapable:

Mrs. Norman didn't leave because she believed, fully believed that escape was totally impossible. There was no place to go. He, she had left before he had come and gotten her. She had gone to the Department of Social Services. He had come and gotten her. The law, she believed the law could not protect her no one could protect her, and I must admit, looking over the records, that there was nothing done that would contradict that belief. She fully believed that he was invulnerable to the law and to all social agencies that were available that nobody could withstand his power. As a result, there was no such thing as escape.

When asked if he had an opinion whether it appeared reasonably necessary for Judy Norman to shoot her husband, this witness responded:

Yes. . . . I believe that in examining the facts of this case and examining the psychological data, that Mrs. Norman believed herself to be doomed . . . to a life of the worst kind of torture and abuse, degradation that she had experienced over the years in a progressive way that it would only get worse, and that death was inevitable death of herself, which was not such, I don't think was such an issue for her, as she had attempted to commit suicide, and in her continuing conviction of J. T. Norman's power over her, and even failed at that form of escape. I believe she also came to the point of beginning to fear for family members and her children, that were she to commit suicide that the abuse and the treatment that was heaped on her would be transferred onto them.

This testimony describes defendant's perception of circumstances in which she was held hostage to her husband's abuse for two decades and which ultimately compelled her to kill him. This testimony alone is evidence amply indicating the first two elements required for entitlement to an instruction on self-defense.

In addition to the testimony of the clinical psychologist, defendant presented the testimony of witnesses who had actually seen defendant's husband abuse her. These witnesses described circumstances that caused not only defendant to believe escape was impossible, but that also convinced them of its impossibility. Defendant's isolation and helplessness were evident in testimony that her family was intimidated by her husband into acquiescing in his torture of her. Witnesses also described defendant's experience with social service agencies and the law, which had contributed to her sense of futility and abandonment through the inefficacy of their protection and the strength of her husband's wrath when they failed. Where torture appears interminable and escape impossible, the belief that only the death of the oppressor can provide relief is reasonable in the mind of a person of ordinary firm-

ness, let alone in the mind of the defendant, who, like a prisoner of war of some years, has been deprived of her humanity and is held hostage by fear.

In *State v. Mize*, 316 N.C. 48, 53, 340 S.E. 2d 439, 442 (1986), this Court noted that if the defendant was in "no imminent danger" at the time of the killing, then his belief that it was necessary to kill the man who had pursued him eight hours before was unreasonable. The second element of self-defense was therefore not satisfied. In the context of the doctrine of self-defense, the definition of "imminent" must be informed by the defendant's perceptions. It is not bounded merely by measurable time, but by all of the facts and circumstances. Its meaning depends upon the assessment of the facts by one of "ordinary firmness" with regard to whether the defendant's perception of impending death or injury was so pressing as to render reasonable her belief that it was necessary to kill.

Evidence presented in the case *sub judice* revealed no letup of tension or fear, no moment in which the defendant felt released from impending serious harm, even while the decedent slept. This, in fact, is a state of mind common to the battered spouse, and one that dramatically distinguishes Judy Norman's belief in the imminence of serious harm from that asserted by the defendant in *Mize*. Psychologists have observed and commentators have described a "constant state of fear" brought on by the cyclical nature of battering as well as the battered spouse's perception that her abuser is both "omnipotent and unstoppable." See Comment, The Admissibility of Expert Testimony on the Battered Woman Syndrome in Support of a Claim of Self-Defense, 15 Conn. L. Rev. 121, 131 (1982). Constant fear means a perpetual anticipation of the next blow, a perpetual expectation that the next blow will kill. "[T]he battered wife is constantly in a heightened state of terror because she is certain that one day her husband will kill her during the course of a beating. . . . Thus from the perspective of the battered wife, the danger is constantly 'immediate.' " Eber, The Battered Wife's Dilemma: To Kill or To Be Killed, 32 Hastings L.J. 895, 928–29 (1981). For the battered wife, if there is no escape, if there is no window of relief or momentary sense of safety, then the next attack, which could be the fatal one, is imminent. In the context of the doctrine of self-defense, "imminent" is a term the meaning of which must be grasped from the defendant's point of view. Properly stated, the second prong of the question is not whether the threat was in fact imminent, but whether defendant's belief in the impending nature of the threat, given the circumstances as she saw them, was reasonable in the mind of a person of ordinary firmness.

Defendant's intense fear, based on her belief that her husband intended not only to maim or deface her, as he had in the past, but to kill her, was evident in the testimony of witnesses who recounted events of the last three days of the decedent's life. This testimony could have led a juror to conclude that defendant reasonably perceived a threat to her life as "imminent," even while her husband slept. Over these three days, her husband's anger was exhibited in an unprecedented crescendo of violence. The evidence showed defendant's fear and sense of hopelessness similarly intensifying, leading to an unsuccessful attempt to escape through suicide and culminating in her belief that escape would be possible only through her husband's death.

Defendant testified that on 10 June, two days before her husband's death, he had again forced her to go to a rest stop near Kings Mountain to make money by prostitution. Her daughter Phyllis and Phyllis's boyfriend Mark Navarra accompanied her on this occasion because, defendant said, whenever her husband took her there, he would beat her. Phyllis corroborated this account. She testified that her father had arrived some time later and had begun beating her mother, asking how much money she had. Defendant said they all then drove off. Shortly afterwards an officer arrested defendant's husband for driving under the influence. He spent the night in jail and was released the next morning on bond paid by defendant's mother.

Defendant testified that her husband was argumentative and abusive all through the next day, 11 June. Mark Navarra testified that at one point defendant's husband threw a sandwich that defendant had made for him on the floor. She made another; he threw it on the floor, as well, then insisted she prepare one without touching it. Defendant's husband had then taken the third sandwich, which defendant had wrapped in paper towels, and smeared it on her face. Both Navarra and Phyllis testified that they had later watched defendant's husband seize defendant's cigarette and put it out on her neck, the scars from which defendant displayed to the jury.

A police officer testified that he arrived at defendant's home at 8:00 that evening in response to a call reporting a domestic quarrel. Defendant, whose face was bruised, was crying, and she told the officer that her husband had beaten her all day long and that she could not take it any longer. The officer told her that he could do nothing for her unless she took out a warrant on her husband. She responded that if she did, her husband would kill her. The officer left but was soon radioed to return because defendant had taken an overdose of pills. The officer testified that defendant's husband was interfering with ambulance attendants, saying "Let the bitch die." When he refused to respond to the officer's warning that if he continued to hinder the attendants, he would be arrested, the officer was compelled to chase him into the house.

Defendant's mother testified that her son-in-law had reacted to the discovery that her daughter had taken the pills with cursing and obscenities and threats such as, "Now, you're going to pay for taking those pills," and "I'll kill you, your mother and your grandmother." His rage was such that defendant's mother feared he might kill the whole family, and knowing defendant's sister had a gun in her purse, she took the gun and placed it in her own.

Defendant was taken to the hospital, treated, and released at 2:30 a.m. She spent the remainder of the night at her grandmother's house. Defendant testified that the next day, 12 June, she felt dazed all day long. She went in the morning to the county mental health center for guidance on domestic abuse. When she returned home, she tried to talk to her husband, telling him to "straighten up. Quit drinking. . . . I'm going to have you committed to help you." Her husband responded, "If you do, I'll see them coming and before they get here, I'll cut your throat."

Later, her husband made her drive him and his friend to Spartanburg to pick up the friend's paycheck. On the way, the friend testified, defendant's husband "started slapping on her" when she was following a truck too closely, and he periodically poured his beer into a glass, then reached over and poured it on defendant's head. At one point defendant's husband lay down on the front seat with his head on the arm rest, "like he was going to go to sleep," and kicked defendant, who was still driving, in the side of the head.

Mark Navarra testified that in the year and a half he had lived with the Normans, he had never seen defendant's husband madder than he was on 12 June, opining that it was the DUI arrest two days before that had ignited J.T.'s fury. Phyllis testified that her father had beaten her mother "all day long." She testified that this was the third day defendant's husband had forbidden her to eat any food. Phyllis said defendant's family tried to get her to eat, but defendant, fearing a beating, would not. Although Phyllis's grandmother had sent over a bag of groceries that day, defendant's husband had made defendant put them back in the bag and would not let anyone eat them.

Early in the evening of 12 June, defendant's husband told defendant, "Let's go to bed." Phyllis testified that although there were two beds in the room, her father had forbidden defendant from sleeping on either. Instead, he had made her lie down on the concrete floor between the two beds, saying, "Dogs don't lay in the bed. They lay in the floor." Shortly afterward, defendant testified, Phyllis came in and asked her father if defendant could take care of her baby while she went to the store. He assented and eventually went to sleep. Defendant was still on the floor, the baby on the small bed. The baby started to cry and defendant "snuck up and took him out there to [her] mother's [house]." She asked her mother to watch the baby, then asked if her mother had anything for a headache, as her head was "busting." Her mother responded that she had some pain pills in her purse. Defendant went in to get the pills, "and the gun was in there, and I don't know, I just seen the gun, and I took it out, and I went back there and shot him."

From this evidence of the exacerbated nature of the last three days of twenty years of provocation, a juror could conclude that defendant believed that her husband's threats to her life were viable, that serious bodily harm was imminent, and that it was necessary to kill her husband to escape that harm. And from this evidence a juror could find defendant's belief in the necessity to kill her husband not merely reasonable but compelling.

The third element for entitlement to an instruction on self-defense requires that there be evidence that the defendant was not the aggressor in bringing on the affray. If the defendant was the aggressor and killed with murderous intent, that is, the intent to kill or inflict serious bodily harm, then she is not entitled to an instruction on self-defense. *State v. Mize*, 316 N.C. 48, 340 S.E. 2d 439. A hiatus between provocation by the decedent and the killing can mark the initiation of a new confrontation between the defendant and the decedent, such that the defendant's earlier perception of imminent danger no longer appears reasonable and the defendant becomes the aggressor.

For example, in *Mize*, the defendant, who had been told the day before that the decedent was "out to get" him, went to the decedent's trailer with a shotgun, knocked on the front door, and hid under the steps when the decedent opened

the door and asked who was there. Defendant then went to the back door, knocked again, and shot the decedent. When the defendant went with his shotgun to the decedent's trailer, this Court said, it was a new confrontation, and if the defendant still believed that it was necessary to kill the decedent to avoid his own imminent death, that belief was unreasonable.

Where the defendant is a battered wife, there is no analogue to the victim-turned-aggressor, who, as in *Mize*, turns the tables on the decedent in a fresh confrontation. Where the defendant is a battered wife, the affray out of which the killing arises can be a continuing assault. There was evidence before the jury that it had not been defendant but her husband who had initiated "the affray," which the jury could have regarded as lasting twenty years, three days, or any number of hours preceding his death. And there was evidence from which the jury could infer that in defendant's mind the affray reached beyond the moment at which her husband fell asleep. Like the ongoing threats of death or great bodily harm, which she might reasonably have perceived as imminent, her husband continued to be the aggressor and she the victim.

Finally, the fourth element of self-defense poses the question of whether there was any evidence tending to show that the force used by defendant to repel her husband was not excessive, that is, more than reasonably appeared to be necessary under the circumstances. This question is answered in part by abundant testimony describing defendant's immobilization by fear caused by abuse by her husband. Three witnesses, including the decedent's best friend, all recounted incidents in which defendant passively accepted beatings, kicks, commands, or humiliating affronts without striking back. From such evidence that she was paralyzed by her husband's presence, a jury could infer that it reasonably appeared to defendant to be necessary to kill her husband in order ultimately to protect herself from the death he had threatened and from severe bodily injury, a foretaste of which she had already experienced.

In *State v. Wingler*, 184 N.C. 747, 115 S.E. 59 (1922), in which the defendant was found guilty for the murder of his wife, Justice (later Chief Justice) Stacy recognized the pain and oppression under which a woman suffers at the hands of an abusive husband: "The supreme tragedy of life is the immolation of woman. With a heavy hand, nature exacts from her a high tax of blood and tears." at 751, 115 S.E. at 61. By his barbaric conduct over the course of twenty years, J. T. Norman reduced the quality of the defendant's life to such an abysmal state that, given the opportunity to do so, the jury might well have found that she was justified in acting in self-defense for the preservation of her tragic life.

It is to be remembered that defendant does not have the burden of persuasion as to self-defense; the burden remains with the state to prove beyond a reasonable doubt that defendant intentionally killed decedent without excuse or justification. If the evidence in support of self-defense is sufficient to create a reasonable doubt in the mind of a rational juror whether the state has proved an intentional killing without justification or excuse, self-defense must be submitted to the jury. This is such a case.

POSTSCRIPT

Should "Battered Wife Syndrome" Be Barred as a Defense in a Murder Case?

This case presents not only a disagreement by the two judges, but a very graphic and disturbing description of a particular woman's plight over time. The Court focuses on whether a particular psychological condition, "battered wife syndrome," can be raised at trial to prove self-defense. The Court does not see its role as requiring it to get into the issue of what the authorities were doing during the years when the defendant was being battered.

Who is responsible for the lack of attention paid to this issue? One obvious answer is that sexism has colored the attitudes of many of those who are responsible for enforcing the law. It has been written, for example, that the seeds of wife beating lie in the subordination of females to male authority and control. This relationship between women and men has been institutionalized in the structure of the patriarchal family and is supported by economic, political, and religious systems that make such relationships seem natural, morally just, even sacred (Susan Brooks Thistlewaite, "Battered Women of the Bible: From Subjection to Liberation," *Christianity and Crisis*, p. 308 [November 2, 1981]).

The case you just read makes it clear that the law does not enforce itself. The police exercise a great deal of discretion in how to respond to a "domestic disturbance" and in whether or not to make an arrest. District attorneys have some discretion in what charges to file. Judges have discretion in what sentences to hand out. There are, in other words, numerous opportunities for biases and prejudices to creep into the enforcement process and shape it.

There is a long tradition of legal noninvolvement in "family matters." There is also a longstanding tendency among many to view victims as somehow deserving of their beatings and many have difficulty comprehending how it is possible for someone who has been beaten many times to continue to stay with their spouse. You might ask whether or not the following perspective is reflected in the first reading in this issue:

> They [are] both beaten and blamed for not ending their beatings. Told they have the freedom to leave a violent situation, they are blamed for the destruction of their family life. Free to live alone, they cannot expect equal pay for equal work. Encouraged to express their feelings, they are beaten when they express anger. They have the same inalienable right to the pursuit of happiness as men do, but they must make sure that their men's and children's rights are met first. They are blamed for not seeking help, yet when they do, they are advised to go home and stop the inappropriate behavior which causes their mate to hurt them. (Lenore Walker, *The Battered Woman*, p. 15 [1979])

Recommended readings on the issue of family violence include the following: M. Mahoney, "Legal Images of Battered Women: Redefining the Issue of Separation," 90 *Michigan Law Review* 1 (1990); F. McNulty, *The Burning Bed* (Bantam Books, 1980); A. Browne, *When Battered Women Kill* (The Free Press, 1987); G. Walker, *Family Violence and the Women's Movement* (University of Toronto Press, 1990); E. Pleck, *The Making of American Social Policy Against Family Violence from Colonial Times to the Present* (Oxford University Press, 1987); L. Walker, *The Battered Woman* (Harper & Row, 1979); L. Dickstein and C. Nadelson, eds., *Family Violence: Emerging Issues of a National Crisis* (American Psychiatric Press, 1989); and L. Okun, *Woman Abuse: Facts Replacing Myth* (State University of New York Press, 1986).

ISSUE 15

Should a National Gun Control Policy Be Established?

YES: Mark Udulutch, from "The Constitutional Implications of Gun Control and Several Realistic Gun Control Proposals," *American Journal of Criminal Law* (vol. 17, 1989)

NO: James D. Wright, from "Second Thoughts About Gun Control," *The Public Interest* (Spring 1988)

ISSUE SUMMARY

YES: Law clerk Mark Udulutch examines the gun control problem and asserts that gun control is necessary and that effective and enforceable federal regulations are feasible.
NO: Professor of sociology James D. Wright concludes, after examining how guns are used, that banning guns would not be beneficial.

Unlike previous assassinations or attempted assassinations, the attempt on former president Ronald Reagan's life in 1981 did not lead to a widespread debate about gun control. The issue that captured public discussion was the insanity defense raised by his would-be assassin, John Hinckley. Probably because Reagan opposed gun control legislation, Hinckley's act did little to further the cause of gun control on the federal level. In fact, there have been some efforts to weaken federal limitations on interstate purchases of handguns. There have been recent attempts by cities and towns to restrict handguns, but some of these, such as those in San Francisco, have been invalidated by the courts, and their impact is necessarily limited.

The issue of handgun regulation is interesting partly because there is a history of gun control laws, both in this country and abroad, that can be looked to for guidance. Such an examination suggests that there are cultural traditions and attitudes toward violence that need to be considered in evaluating why some gun legislation is effective and some is not.

One of the most frequently mentioned legal justifications for permitting individuals to possess handguns is the Second Amendment to the Constitution. This amendment states, "A well regulated Militia, being necessary to the security of a free State, the right of the people to keep and bear Arms, shall not be infringed." Yet, due to court interpretations of the meaning of these words, the amendment has become almost irrelevant to the issue of gun control. Certainly, one convicted of violating a firearms statute is unlikely to win his or her case by relying on the Second Amendment.

Although many people are familiar with the last half of the Amendment, the crucial words are contained in the first part. The right to bear arms is not absolute. Rather, it is a right related to the need for a state militia. This was the ruling of the Supreme Court in the case of *United States v. Miller*, 307 U.S. 174 (1939), the only case interpreting the Second Amendment as it relates to the federal government. In that case, two men were charged in federal court with transporting an unregistered sawed-off shotgun and violating the National Firearms Act. The defendants claimed that they were protected by the Second Amendment and won in the trial court. The Supreme Court, however, interpreted the rights granted by the Second Amendment differently. Justice James C. McReynolds wrote,

> In the absence of any evidence tending to show that possession or use of a "shotgun having a barrel of less than eighteen inches in length" at this time has some reasonable relationship to the preservation or efficiency of a well regulated militia, we cannot say that the Second Amendment guarantees the right to keep and bear such an instrument. . . .
>
> The Constitution as originally adopted granted to the Congress power—"To provide for calling forth the Militia to execute the Laws of the Union, suppress Insurrections and repel Invasions." . . . With obvious purpose to assure the continuation and render possible the effectiveness of [the Militia] the declaration and guarantee of the Second Amendment were made. It must be interpreted and applied with that end in view.

In the following selections, Mark Udulutch offers some proposals for instituting what he believes is a much-needed national gun control policy, while James D. Wright argues that more gun control legislation would have no beneficial effects.

YES

Mark Udulutch

THE CONSTITUTIONAL IMPLICATIONS OF GUN CONTROL AND SEVERAL REALISTIC GUN CONTROL PROPOSALS

INTRODUCTION

The public is polarized on the issue of gun control. Anti-gun control activists believe that it is each and every American's individual right to bear arms. Various pro-gun control organizations disagree and propose different methods of gun control. For example, there are individuals who would ban all handguns; as well as those who take a less radical stand and who would simply increase the controls on firearms. Moderate gun control groups propose measures such as requiring an individual to successfully complete a firearms safety course before possession of a gun is allowed, or to wait for a mandatory period of time before taking possession of a gun.

Today, there are approximately 20,000 different gun control laws in existence, ranging from those enacted by municipalities and states, to those enacted by the federal government. Individuals opposed to gun control point to this fact, and assert that gun control is a failure. The truth is that, for the most part, these laws are ineffective because they lack scope, breadth and enforcement.[1]

SHOULD THERE BE GUN CONTROL?

In a democratic society, such as the United States, two things need consideration prior to the enactment of legislation for the purpose of solving a social problem. The first concern is whether there is a problem that can, in fact, be controlled through legislation. The second is whether the majority of Americans would support governmental intervention to provide a solution to that problem. Both of these questions must be answered affirmatively or further discussion of gun control legislation would be senseless.

Excerpted from Mark Udulutch, "The Constitutional Implications of Gun Control and Several Realistic Gun Control Proposals," *American Journal of Criminal Law,* vol. 17 (1989), pp. 19–54. Copyright © 1989 by *American Journal of Criminal Law.* Reprinted by permission. Some notes omitted.

Firearms are used to murder nearly 12,000 people annually;[2] another 1,750 persons suffer death by accident; and an estimated 200,000 people are injured. In addition, more than 16,000 people use firearms to take their own lives each year. Although they constitute only a third of all firearms, handguns are used in three-fourths of all firearm murders and one-half of all murders. Even in light of these statistics, the pro-gun advocates continue to herald the "virtues" of gun ownership.

Over the years, both sides of the gun control debate have used statistics in attempts to make their arguments. Statisticians, however, point out that the persuasiveness of a statistic lies in its ability to be factually verified. Here, the pro-gun control forces have had an advantage over the anti-gun control activists. They present the corpses and shattered limbs that result from the misuse of firearms as the evidence needed to successfully state their position. The pro-gun activists, however, argue that firearms actually prevent murders, rapes and burglaries. The problem with this argument is that it lacks credible statistical verification.

Returning to the central question, should additional legislative action be taken to regulate the nearly 70,000,000 handguns and 140,000,000 long guns now in the United States? The answer is yes. Firearms are certainly needed for national defense and law enforcement, but they are not needed by individual citizens to serve as the tools for social violence. Rational, workable federal legislation is the appropriate means to stop the misuse of firearms.

More aggressive gun control laws are needed to reduce the problem. However, legislative measures will work only to the extent they are supported by the majority of the people. While the public has not given its support to every form of increased gun control legislation, it has supported the less intrusive proposals.

Based on the analysis of public opinion polls from 1938 through 1972, one author wrote that "[t]he vast majority of Americans have favored some kind of action for the control of civilian firearms at least as long as modern polling has been in existence."[3] It should be noted that, depending upon how a question is phrased, public opinion polls on gun control generate different responses. For example, one Gallup Poll posed the question, "Would you favor or oppose a law which would require a person to obtain a police permit before he or she could buy a gun?" The first response given was 75% in favor of the law; that response has subsequently fluctuated from 68% to 78% in follow-up polls. In contrast, another poll asked, "Do you think that people like yourself have to be prepared to defend their homes against crime and violence, or can the police take care of that?" Some 52% of the people felt that they needed to be prepared. The difference in these questions was that the first dealt with other persons, while the second was concerned with the person responding directly to the question. . . .

SEVERAL REALISTIC GUN CONTROL PROPOSALS

When more than 30,000 people are killed annually by firearms and another 200,000 are injured, it is clear to most individuals that a serious problem exists.[4] Recognizing the problem is the first step toward a solution. Finding a solution is not easy, nor is it achieved quickly, but this should not obviate gun control.

Given American society and its attraction to firearms, legislation must not be so restrictive that, at its outset, it fails to enlist the cooperation of the American public. At this time, it would be unrealistic to ban all firearms from the private sector. Many pro-gun activists try to attack the pro-control position by arguing that one control will lead to another, and eventually guns will be outlawed all together. Although such a result is conceivable, a complete ban will never be successful unless it is supported by the people. Only public disinterest in firearms would truly result in eliminating them from the social environment.

Neither the approach of a total ban on firearms, as some gun control advocates propose, nor the do-nothing attitude of the anti-gun control activists, are realistic at this time. Yet firearms are a serious problem to the American society. Their destructive misuse cannot be allowed to continue. Some increases in regulations are definitely needed. These regulations will require a realistic compromise between the two extremes in the gun control debate.[5]

When constructing these controls, two goals must remain constant. First, and most importantly, it is necessary to decrease as much as possible the victimization of individuals through the misuse of firearms. Second, it is important to structure legislation in ways that accomplish the intended purposes while not being overly intrusive upon the individual. In essence, a utilitarian approach must be taken toward gun control. The benefits to society must be maximized, while the possible intrusions to individuals must be minimized.

Federal Legislation: The Only Realistic Answer

Even with 20,000 gun control laws already in existence, the serious problems due to firearm misuse continue. Obviously,

the controls that have been designed have not been sufficiently effective. There are three identifiable reasons for this problem: 1) the lack of uniform legislation; 2) the fact that most controls do not go far enough in their attempt to prevent the problems of firearm misuse; and, 3) the controls in place are not effectively enforced.

Sweeping federal legislation would go a long way toward resolving all three of these problems. Such legislation could offer a coherent, orderly means of addressing the gun problem, unlike the present hodgepodge of local, state and federal legislation.

One of the most significant problems resulting from the discrepancy in local, state and federal firearm laws is the transportation of firearms from one state to another. If every state had uniformly strict firearm control laws, interstate transport would not be a major problem. No longer would an individual like John Hinckley be able to purchase a firearm in a state with weak gun control laws, transport his weapon across state lines, and then use it to shoot the President of the United States. However, going to the legislatures of the fifty states to achieve uniformly strict firearm controls is not the most efficient course of action. The failure of even one state to adopt the uniform controls would severely weaken the entire chain of controls. Federal legislation would be far more effective; only one body of lawmakers would have to deal with the increased controls instead of fifty. Furthermore, once established, the controls could not be weakened by the efforts of one state legislature.

The Proposals

Having concluded that federal legislation is the best way to effectively control firearm possession and use, the next question is what kind of legislation? Some intelligently drafted controls are already in place,[6] but they have not proven sufficient. Controls that go further than present federal legislation in preventing the problems of firearm misuse and that are more rigorously enforced are needed.

1. *Licensing and Education*—A nationwide licensing program would be an effective first step. Such a program already exists for sellers, manufacturers and importers of firearms, but it does not extend to private citizens who buy and use the guns. Not every person who wants to own a firearm should be trusted with it.

To obtain a license, a person would have to meet three criteria. First, he or she could not belong to any of the classes of persons denied the privilege of possessing firearms. Section 922 of the Firearms Owners' Protection Act denies felons, fugitives from justice, drug addicts, illegal aliens, individuals dishonorably discharged from the military, individuals who have renounced their United States citizenship, and mental incompetents the privilege of owning guns. It would be wise to add to this list persons under eighteen years of age. A second criteria for obtaining a firearm license would be to pass a firearm safety course. Drivers are required to pass a drivers' training course, so why shouldn't a comparable test be administered to license potential gun owners? A firearm's safety course would reinforce student awareness of the danger involved in firearm use and misuse. A course of this nature could, at a minimum, be expected to decrease the number of accidental killings and injuries occurring from gun misuse.

The third criteria would require an extensive background check on a prospective licensee to make sure he or she did not belong to one of the classes of persons prohibited from owning firearms. This check would be made by the police department where the applicant resided. Additionally, this investigative program would be overseen by the Bureau of Alcohol, Tobacco and Firearms.

The cost of such a licensing program would not be insignificant, and, initially, some federal monies would be needed to organize it. Federal dollars, however, should not be used to keep the system running. Instead of being funded by general tax dollars, the licensing program should be funded by persons wanting to own firearms. These funds would be classified as special federal monies, to be used by the Bureau of Alcohol, Tobacco and Firearms to administer the licensing program and to subsidize local police forces for the costs involved in investigating applicants. Training programs would be conducted by federally regulated private businesses that charge for their services. Once a person acquired a firearm license, he or she would be allowed to possess a firearm within the limits imposed by other firearm controls. If after receiving a license to own a firearm the licensee fell into a disallowed class, the license would be revoked on a permanent basis.

2. *Firearm Registration*—With nearly 210,000,000 firearms already present in the United States, it is foolish to believe that a licensing program by itself will keep firearms out of the hands of people who should not have them. Another step toward keeping firearms from untrustworthy people is to require that all firearms be registered. Federal law already requires that "each manufacturer, importer and maker shall register each firearm that he manufactures, imports, or makes." However, because of the proposed licens-

ing requirements and the uncertainty of who currently owns what firearm, all firearms in the United States must be registered by their current owners. Each licensed firearm owner would pay for the costs involved in registering his or her own firearms.

Registration need not be a bothersome proposition to law abiding citizens. To keep a gun a citizen would only be expected to successfully complete the licensing process. Following the passage of legislation, all persons not licensed within a designated time, and still possessing a gun, would be required to sell the gun to a licensed owner. Failing to comply with this regulation would subject the person to harsh penalties. Suggested penalties include permanently losing the ability to become a licensed owner, a mandatory jail term, and forfeiture of a significant amount of money. The purpose of these penalties would be to make noncompliance with registration laws so risky that people would be forced to comply. Enforcement would take place in conjunction with normal police procedures. If during an investigation a person is found to be an unlicensed gun possessor, he or she would be prosecuted.

Realistically, not every individual now owning a firearm will comply with this firearm control. Some criminals will still have guns; this cannot be denied. However, with every gun removed from the hands of unqualified possessors, it is expected that the misuse of firearms will decrease.

3. *Mandatory Investigation of All Firearm Transferees*—A system whereby transferees are automatically investigated for fitness as a gun owner prior to any actual transfer of the weapon is needed to keep track of firearm ownership. Presently,

section 5812 of the National Firearms Act requires transferors to file applications for the transfer of their firearms with the Secretary of the Treasury. The transferor provides some information about the transferee in the application. In addition, section 922 of the Firearms Owners' Protection Act provides that it is a crime for anyone "to sell or otherwise dispose of any firearm . . . to any person knowing or having reasonable cause to believe that such a person" is a member of one of the groups of people not allowed to possess firearms. Unfortunately, neither of these requirements is sufficient since each fails to provide for actual investigation of the transferee.

Because the only lawful transferee of a firearm is one who possesses a valid firearm's license, the investigation required need not be extensive. The person would already have been investigated prior to obtaining his or her firearm's license. The transferee's history, dating from the time the license was received or from the time a firearm was last transferred to the transferee, is all that must be investigated.

None of the transfer costs would be assumed by the federal or local governments. They would instead be paid by the transferor. Unlike the original licensing investigation where the transferee paid the fee, the transferor would pay for the cost of the transfer investigation. In this way any possibility of violating the transferee's fifth amendment right against self-incrimination would be avoided. The failure of the transferor to comply with the transfer laws would subject him or her to the same penalties applicable to persons who fail to register firearms.

4. *A Waiting Period*—Intricately related to the formalities of a firearm transfer is a mandatory waiting period. Though the

idea of a waiting period is not new it is critical that it be established on the federal level. In 1988 Congress considered the "Brady Amendment," which required a one week waiting period before a transferee could possess a transferred handgun. During this time the police could conduct a thorough background check of the transferee. In the scheme presented here, the transfer investigation would take place during the waiting period.

Unfortunately, the "Brady Amendment" was defeated in Congress. Much of the blame for its defeat must be attributed to the National Rifle Association. The organization produced a mass mailing urging its members to contact their congressmen and to tell them to vote against the bill. The mailing contained substantial factual distortions; for example, that the Brady Amendment would devise "a system where firearm ownership is no longer . . . a guaranteed right but one controlled by a government bureaucrat who has dictatorial powers and you have no right of appeal on his decision." The letter went on to say that Congress could "call the bill whatever they want to, but it sets up a system that will eventually take away all your firearm rights and ban gun ownership in America." In reality the Brady Amendment had no intentions of banning guns, and, as discussed above, there exists no individual constitutional right to bear arms. All that this bill was attempting to do was to add a degree of sanity to the nation's handling of firearms.

A waiting period would not only allow time for the police to verify a prospective transferee's status, but it would also serve as a "cooling off" period. The otherwise reasonable person who, in the heat of the moment, wants to buy a gun to commit a crime will have to wait to get it. The expectation is that such a person will reconsider his or her plans while waiting.

Anti-gun control organizations are quick to point out that the majority of persons going through the legal channels to purchase a firearm are not in need of any "cooling off" period. Furthermore, they say that anyone who wants a gun badly enough can find a way around the law. These arguments are valid in many situations, but not in all. It is doubtful that a waiting period would stop a hardcore criminal in the quest for a gun. However, some individuals with criminal aspirations or designs will be thwarted. The inconvenience to prospective gun owners of waiting one, two or three weeks to obtain a firearm is minor when compared to the significance of the tragedies that could be avoided. A waiting period is needed.

5. *Taxing Measure for Keeping Firearms Out of City Limits*—It seems unlikely that most Americans would accept a ban on all firearms within the limits of their communities. This, together with the fact that most cases of firearm misuse occur in heavily populated areas, produces a serious dilemma. One of the principal reasons for owning a firearm within a city is for self-protection. Some people believe that if they have a firearm they will be able to ward off anyone wishing to do them harm. Although this reasoning is questionable, it has many adherents. The proposed solution is a combination tax burden-tax incentive scheme.

Those persons licensed to own guns and living in a city may still keep their guns at home, but will be subject to a federal tax for doing so. This tax should be progressive to avoid inflicting a disproportionate hardship on those least capable of paying. Even so, the tax would apply to everyone wishing to keep firearms at a private residence within city limits, and it must be relatively high in order to discourage people from exercising this privilege. Furthermore, the tax would double for every firearm over the first one kept at a private residence. All collected taxes would be used for increased law enforcement. Although the federal government would allow licensed individuals to keep their guns in their city residences, there is nothing that would prevent a community from banning firearm possession within its city limits.

Those persons licensed to possess a firearm who do not wish to keep them at their city residence may store their guns under lock and key at a gun club. The adoption of such proposals would no doubt encourage the growth of gun clubs. Guns stored at these clubs would not be subject to the federal taxes imposed on privately housed guns. Only club membership fees would have to be paid. This plan should create a migration of firearms from city residences. Gun clubs could be located either in the country or within city limits. Their main purpose would be to create a centralized secure place where firearms could be kept.

For enforcement purposes, guns would have to be returned nightly to the gun club. Exceptions would be made for hunters wishing to take their guns on hunting trips. To take their guns with them, the hunters would register removal with the club, which, in turn, would report those firearms not returned on time. To ensure that each gun club complies with the law, it would be subject to periodic, unannounced investigations by the Bureau of Alcohol, Tobacco and Firearms or the Internal Revenue

Service. It would be presumed that those licensed gun owners not returning their guns to the gun clubs had opted to keep their guns at home, and would, therefore, be subject to the gun tax.

6. *Banning All Automatic and Military Style Semi-Automatic Weapons*—A semi-automatic weapon is one which requires a separate pull of the trigger for each shot. The weapons differ from automatic weapon[s] which fire more than one shot at the pull of the trigger. When addressing the need for increased controls on semi-automatic weapons, one must make a distinction between the types of semi-automatic weapons. There are two general categories of these weapons: the hunting style semi-automatic weapon and the military style semi-automatic weapon. The military style weapons are those semi-automatic weapons designed as assault weapons. They are designed and marketed with large capacity magazines, which allow them to fire many rounds without reloading. Senator Howard Metzenbaum has introduced legislation into Congress that would ban these weapons. Semi-automatic hunting weapons would remain unaffected by this legislation.

Unaltered, a military style semi-automatic weapon is quite formidable; however, its destructive potential can be increased even further by transforming it into a fully automatic weapon.[7] Such a conversion is generally not a difficult operation for a knowledgeable gunsmith.[8] As of 1985, it was estimated that 125,000 of the then existing 500,000 military style semi-automatic weapons had been converted to fully-automatic weapons. Actual statistics on the number of military style semi-automatic weapons in private hands do not exist because, unless the gun is technically considered an automatic weapon, the buyer need not be licensed. Even if owners of both automatic and military style semi-automatic weapons were licensed, the primary problem would still remain: namely, the possibility that the considerable firepower of these weapons could find its way into the hands of a disturbed individual.

There are numerous examples of semi-automatic and converted semi-automatics used in slayings. One such instance is the January 19, 1989, slaying of five school children in Stockton, California by a distraught gunman. The killer used an unconverted AKM-56S military style semi-automatic weapon. Also, in January of 1989, a member of the Los Angeles Crips Gang was indicted for possession of a converted M-11 with a silencer that had been used to commit murder. In December of 1988, six members of an Algona, Iowa family were killed by a Mini-14 semi-automatic rifle. Yet another incident took place in March of 1988, when nine people were killed in a crack house by an AR-15 semi-automatic rifle. In light of such occurrences, and the comparatively inconsequential benefits to society in allowing private citizens to possess these weapons, it is apparent that greater controls must be placed upon both automatic and military style semi-automatic weapons. These weapons were designed for one primary reason, to kill people quickly and in large numbers.

While Americans do not seem willing to accept a total ban on firearms, they might accept a ban on automatic and military style semi-automatic weapons. There will be some resistance to a ban on automatic and military style semi-automatic weapons, but its enforcement will be relatively easy compared to a ban on all firearms, or a ban just on handguns,

in that there are far fewer of these weapons in the market place.[9] The sale of new automatic weapons, to persons not having specific governmental authorization, was halted May 19, 1986.[10] In addition, all transfers of those weapons, lawfully possessed before that date, are now required to have specific governmental authorization.[11] The result of these measures is that the identity of a significant number of people owning automatic weapons is known. If needed, this information will help apprehend them. As for the military style semi-automatic and the converted military style semi-automatic weapons, no provisions have been made by the federal government to keep track of their whereabouts.

The average owner of a military style semi-automatic weapon, or an automatic weapon, is not a criminal, and substantial compliance with a ban on these weapons could be expected. This would be especially true if the federal government offered to buy these weapons. After a reasonable period of time given to comply, persons still in possession of automatic and military style semi-automatic weapons would be subject to harsh penalties. A ban on military style semi-automatic and automatic weapons is especially needed now, because these weapons have become the weapons of choice for the drug gangs in the United States. Congress made a good start when it required an additional mandatory ten year imprisonment for those individuals involved in a violent or drug trafficking crime in which an automatic weapon was used.[12] Nevertheless, the law, as applied to automatic weapons, is not yet broad enough, and it does not address the problem of military style semi-automatic weapons. The ten year mandatory penalty is sufficiently stern, but it should be extended to all persons in possession of an automatic or a military style semi-automatic weapon after the expiration of a buy back date. The potential for disaster that these weapons present is simply too great to allow them in the hands of the general public.

CONCLUSION

The need for strong, realistic gun control legislation becomes obvious whenever another life is taken or an injury inflicted as the result of the misuse of a firearm. This note has presented a number of proposals for increasing gun control nationwide. To be most effective, these proposals should be adopted together and they should be addressed by the federal government. The time to pass increased firearm controls is now. Too many lives have been lost because of firearm misuse.

NOTES

1. Kleck, *Policy Lessons from Recent Gun Control Research*, 49 LAW & CONTEMP. PROBS. 35, 50 (1986); *see also* TASK FORCE ON FIREARMS, NATIONAL COMMITTEE ON THE CAUSES AND PREVENTION OF VIOLENCE, FIREARMS AND VIOLENCE IN AMERICAN LIFE 87-95 (1969); J. WRIGHT, P. ROSSI & K. DALY, *supra* note 6, at 244. "Political jurisdictions with rather restrictive regulations often abut jurisdictions with barely any controls at all, [thus creating] an invitation to widespread law evasions." *Id.* Some pro-gun control advocates blame the National Rifle Association for the lack of unified legislation. The National Rifle Association is often referred to as the most effective lobby in Washington D.C. Note, *A Shot at Stricter Controls: Strict Liability for Gun Manufacturers*, 15 PAC L.J. 171, 192 (1983) (authored by Rose Safarian).

2. This figure was derived by taking the average number of murders committed with firearms from 1980 through 1987. . . . 11,403 persons on average are murdered by firearms each year. BUREAU OF THE CENSUS, U.S. DEP'T OF COMMERCE, NATIONAL DATA BOOK AND GUIDE TO SOURCES: STATISTICAL ABSTRACT OF THE UNITED STATES 1989, AT 168 (109th ed. 1989) (graph no. 281); BUREAU OF THE CENSUS, U.S. DEP'T OF COMMERCE, NATIONAL

DATA BOOK AND GUIDE TO SOURCES: STATISTICAL ABSTRACT OF THE UNITED STATES 1986, at 171 (106th ed. 1986) (graph no. 290). . . .

Murder is "the 11th leading cause of death and the 6th leading cause of the loss of potential years of life before age 65." Sloan, Kellerman, Reay, Ferris, Koepsell, Rivara, Rice, Gray & LoGerfo, *Handgun Regulations, Crime, Assaults, and Homicide: A Tale of Two Cities*, 319 NEW ENG. J. OF MED. 1256, 1256 (1988) [hereinafter Sloan & Kellerman].

3. Erskine, *The Polls: Gun Control*, 36 PUB. OPINION Q. 455 (1972); *see* Wright, *Public Opinion and Gun Control: A Comparison of Results from Two Recent National Surveys*, 455 ANNALS 24, 31 (1981).

The following are representative examples of gun control polls. First, a 1975 Gallup Poll found that 66% of all Americans living in cities of more than one million people favored a ban on handguns. Drinan, *Gun Control: The Good Outweighs the Evil*, in THE GREAT GUN CONTROL DEBATE 12 (1976) (Second Amendment Foundation Monograph Series). Second, an October 1987 Gallup Poll found that "60 percent [of the adult population surveyed] favored stricter laws on handgun sales," and 42% favored a ban on handgun possession. N.Y. Times, Oct. 25, 1987, § 4, at 5, col. 2. Lastly, a 1981 Gallup Poll showed that nine out of ten people favored a waiting period for the purchase of a handgun. N.Y. Times, Apr. 15, 1987, at A27, col. 3.

4. The mentality of anti-gun control organizations like the National Rifle Association is dangerously self-perpetuated. This is evidenced by a report commissioned by The Remington Arms Company. Columnist Jack Anderson commented in an article based on the Remington Arms Study that the zealous supporters of the National Rifle Association live "in a make-believe world of sacred rights, ancient skills and coonskins . . . like the inhabitants of Hitler's bunker in 1945, they talk only to themselves, reinforcing their own views." UNITED STATES CONFERENCE OF MAYORS, ORGANIZING FOR HANDGUN CONTROL 4 (1977).

5. One author contends that increased controls on firearms may have little effect on the overall rate of robberies and assaults but that the homicide rate at the minimum would be decreased. Cook, *The Effect of Gun Availability on Violent Crime Patterns*, 455 ANNALS 63, 78 (1981). A decrease in the homicide rate alone would be enough to justify increased gun control measures. *See generally 7 Deadly Days*, TIME, July 17, 1989, at 30.

6. *See, e.g.*, 18 U.S.C. § 922(d) (1988) (It is illegal to sell a firearm to a felon, a fugitive from justice, a drug addict, a mental incompetent, an illegal alien, one who has renounced his or her U.S. citizenship, one who was dishonorably dis-

charged from the military); 18 U.S.C. § 922(g) (1988) (It is illegal for a felon, drug addict, fugitive from justice, mental incompetent, illegal alien, one who was dishonorably discharged from the military, or one who has renounced his or her U.S. citizenship to possess or transport a firearm); 18 U.S.C. § 924(c)(1) (1988) (A mandatory sentence is imposed when a firearm is used in a crime of violence or a drug-trafficking crime).

7. Without federal or state authority to possess, make or transfer a machine gun, one violates the law in converting a semi-automatic weapon into a fully-automatic weapon, 27 C.F.R. § 179.105(a), (e) (1988).

8. Church, *The Other Arms Race*, TIME, Feb. 6, 1989, at 20, 22–23. Conversion kits are available today through some gun dealers, and until recently, through many gun magazines. *Machine Gun, supra* note 199, at 48. The buying and selling of conversion kits is of questionable legality since it is illegal for an unlicensed person to possess a fully automatic weapon. 18 U.S.C. § 922(o) (1988).

9. Currently the Bureau of Alcohol, Tobacco and Firearms estimates that there are between two and three million semi-automatic assault weapons in the United States today.

10. 18 U.S.C. § 922(o) (1988).

11. 18 U.S.C. § 922(o)(2)(A) (1988).

12. 18 U.S.C. § 924(c)(1) (1988).

NO

James D. Wright

SECOND THOUGHTS ABOUT GUN CONTROL

Gun control, it has been said, is the acid test of liberalism. All good liberals favor stricter gun controls. After all, doesn't the United States have the most heavily armed population on earth? Are we not the world's most violent people? Surely these facts must be causally connected. The apparently desperate need to "do something" about the vast quantity of firearms and firearms abuse is, to the good liberal, obvious.

At one time, it seemed evident to me, we needed to mount a campaign to resolve the crisis of handgun proliferation. Guns are employed in an enormous number of crimes in this country. In other countries with stricter gun laws, gun crime is rare. Many of the firearms involved in crime are cheap handguns, so-called Saturday Night Specials, for which no legitimate use or need exists. Many families buy these guns because they feel the need to protect themselves; eventually, they end up shooting one another. If there were fewer guns around, there would also be less crime and less violence. Most of the public also believes this, and has supported stricter gun control for as long as pollsters have been asking the question. Yet Congress has refused to act in a meaningful way, owing mainly to the all-powerful "gun lobby" headed by the National Rifle Association. Were the power of this lobby somehow effectively countered by the power of public opinion, stricter gun laws would follow quickly, and we would begin to achieve a safer and more civilized society.

When I first began research on the topic of private firearms, in the mid-1970s, I shared this conventional and widely held view of the issue. Indeed, much of it struck me as self-evidently true. My initial interest in the topic resulted from a life-long fascination with the bizarre: I certainly did not own a gun (I still don't), and neither, as far as I knew, did many of my friends. Still, readily available survey evidence showed that half the families in the United States did own one, and I wondered what unspeakable oddities or even pathologies an analysis of this half of the American population would reveal.

From James D. Wright, "Second Thoughts About Gun Control," *The Public Interest*, no. 91 (Spring 1988), pp. 23–39. Copyright © 1988 by National Affairs, Inc. Reprinted by permission of *The Public Interest* and the author.

My first scholarly paper on the topic, "The Ownership of the Means of Destruction," appeared in 1975. This demographic comparison between gun-owning and non-gun-owning households revealed no shocking information. Gun owners, it turned out, were largely small-town and rural Protestants of higher-than-average income. Fear of crime, interestingly enough, did not seem to be related to gun ownership. The general tone of my piece remained unmistakably "anti-gun," but the findings did not provide much new information to strengthen the "anti-gun" lobby's arguments. At about the same time, I prepared a more polemical version of the paper, which was eventually published in the *Nation*. The General Counsel of the National Rifle Association described the piece as "emotionally supercharged drum-beating masquerading as scholarly analysis." Clearly, I was on the right track; I had managed to offend the right people.

The *Nation* article was abridged and reprinted in the Sunday Chicago *Tribune*, a newspaper read by about two million people, many of whom saw fit to write me after the piece appeared. Almost all the letters I received were provocative; some were very favorable, but most were vitriolic attacks from gun nuts. I was accused of being "incredibly biased," "strange and contradictory," of telling "many outright 100% lies," of being "sophistic" and "intellectually dishonest," of being "unable to grasp truth," and of taking "thousands of words to say *nothing* constructive." I answered every letter I received. In a few cases, a long and profitable correspondence developed. The first wave of correspondence over the *Tribune* piece affirmed my assumption that many gun owners were crazy. Subsequent waves, however, convinced

me that many were indeed thoughtful, intelligent, often remarkably well-read people who were passionately concerned about their "right to keep and bear arms," but were willing, nonetheless, to listen to reason.

Two years later, in 1977, my colleague Peter Rossi and I received a grant from the National Institute of Justice to undertake a comprehensive, critical overview of the research literature on guns, crime, and violence in America. The results of this overview were published in 1981 in a three-volume government report and in 1983 as a commercial monograph, entitled *Under the Gun*. Subsequent to this work, we received another grant to gather original data on gun acquisition, ownership, and use from about 2,000 men doing felony time in ten state prisons all over the United States. We assembled this information in a government report and later in a monograph, *Armed and Considered Dangerous*. The felon survey marked the temporary end of my firearms research program, one that ran roughly from 1974 through 1986, when *Armed and Considered Dangerous* was finally published.

As I have already suggested, at the outset of the research program I had a strong feeling that the pro-gun-control forces had never marshalled their evidence in the most compelling way, that they were being seriously undercut by the more artful polemics of the National Rifle Association and related pro-gun groups. That the best available evidence, critically considered, would eventually prove favorable to the pro-control viewpoint was not in serious doubt—at least not to me, not in the beginning.

In the course of my research, however, I have come to question nearly every element of the conventional wisdom about guns, crime, and violence. Indeed, I am now of the opinion that a compelling case for "stricter gun control" *cannot be made*, at least not on empirical grounds. I have nothing but respect for the various pro-gun-control advocates with whom I have come into contact over the past years. They are, for the most part, sensitive, humane, and intelligent people, and their ultimate aim, to reduce death and violence in our society, is one that every civilized person must share. I have, however, come to be convinced that they are barking up the wrong tree.

WHAT IS "GUN CONTROL"?

Before I describe the intellectual odyssey that led to my change in thinking, it is critical to stress that "gun control" is an exceedingly nebulous concept. To say that one favors gun control, or opposes it, is to speak in ambiguities. In the present-day American political context, "stricter gun control" can mean anything from federal registration of firearms, to mandatory sentences for gun use in crime, to outright bans on the manufacture, sale, or possession of certain types of firearms. One can control the manufacturers of firearms, the wholesalers, the retailers, or the purchasers; one can control the firearms themselves, the ammunition they require, or the uses to which they are put. And one can likewise control their purchase, their carrying, or their mere possession. "Gun control" thus covers a wide range of specific interventions, and it would be useful indeed if the people who say they favor or oppose gun control were explicit about what, exactly, they are for and against.

In doing the research for *Under the Gun*, I learned that there are approximately 20,000 gun laws of various sorts already on the books in the United States. A few of these are federal laws (such as the Gun Control Act of 1968), but most are state and local regulations. It is a misstatement to say, as pro-gun-control advocates sometimes do, that the United States has "no meaningful gun control legislation." The problem is not that laws do not exist but that the regulations in force vary enormously from one place to the next, or, in some cases, that the regulations carried on the books are not or cannot be enforced.

Much of the gun legislation now in force, whether enacted by federal, state, or local statutes, falls into the category of reasonable social precaution, being neither more nor less stringent than measures taken to safeguard against abuses of other potentially life-threatening objects, such as automobiles. It seems reasonable, for example, that people should be required to obtain a permit to carry a concealed weapon, as they are virtually everywhere in the United States. It is likewise reasonable that people not be allowed to own automatic weapons without special permission, and that felons, drug addicts, and other sociopaths be prevented from legally acquiring guns. Both these restrictions are in force everywhere in the United States, because they are elements of federal law. About three-fourths of the American population lives in jurisdictions where the registration of firearms purchases is required. It is thus apparent that many states and localities also find this to be a useful precaution against something. And many jurisdictions also require "waiting periods" or "cooling off" periods between application and actual possession of a new firearms purchase. These too seem reasonable, since there are very few legitimate purposes to which a firearm might be put that would be thwarted if the user had to wait a few days, or even a few weeks, to get the gun.

Thus, when I state that "a compelling case for 'stricter gun control' cannot be made," I do not refer to the sorts of obvious and reasonable precautions discussed above, or to related precautionary measures. I refer, rather, to measures substantially more strict than "reasonable precaution," and more specifically, to measures that would deny or seriously restrict the right of the general population to own a firearm, or that would ban the sale or possession of certain kinds of firearms, such as handguns or even the small, cheap handguns known colloquially as "Saturday Night Specials."

EFFECTS OF GUN LAWS

One wonders, with some 20,000 firearms regulations now on the books, why the clamor continues for even more laws. The answer is obvious: none of the laws so far enacted has significantly reduced the rate of criminal violence. *Under the Gun* reviewed several dozen research studies that had attempted to measure the effects of gun laws in reducing crime; none of them showed any conclusive long-term benefits.

As it happens, both sides of the gun-control debate grant this point; they disagree, though as to why there is no apparent connection between gun-control laws and crime rates. The NRA maintains that gun laws don't work because they can't work. Widely ignored (especially by criminals) and unenforceable, gun-control laws go about the problem in the wrong way. For this reason, the NRA has long supported mandatory and severe sentences for the use of firearms in felonies, contending that we should punish firearms abusers once it is proven that an abuse has occurred, and leave legitimate users alone until they have actually done something illegal with their weapon.

The pro-control forces argue that gun laws don't work because there are too many of them, because they are indifferently enforced, and because the laws vary widely from one jurisdiction to the next. What we need, they would argue, are federal firearms regulations that are strictly enforced all across the nation. They would say that we have never given gun control a fair test, because we lack an aggressive *national* firearms policy.

This example illustrates an important point that I have learned and relearned throughout my career in applied social research: the policy consequences of a scientific finding are seldom obvious. On this particular point, the science is reasonably clear-cut: gun control laws do not reduce crime. But what is the implication? One possible implication is that we should stop trying to control crime by controlling guns. The other possible implication is that we need to get much more serious than we have been thus far about controlling guns, with much stricter, nationally-standardized gun-control policies. There is little or nothing in the scientific literature that would allow one to choose between these possibilities; either could well be correct.

GUNS, CRIMES, AND NUMBERS

What is the annual firearms toll in this country? Our review of the data sources revealed that some components of the toll, especially the annual fatality count, are well known, whereas other components are not. In recent years, the total number of homicides occurring in the United States has been right around 20,000. Of these, approximately 60 percent are committed with firearms. There are somewhat fewer than 30,000 suicides committed in an average recent year, of which about half involve a firearm. Deaths from firearms accidents have represented about 2 percent of the total accidental deaths in the nation for as long as data have been collected, and add about 2,000 deaths per year to the toll. Taken together, then, there are about 30,000 deaths from firearms in an average year; this amounts to some 1–2 percent of all deaths from any cause.

Both camps in the gun control war like to spew out exaggerated rhetoric. In the case of gun deaths, the anti-control forces shout that the total deaths due to firearms in a year are less than the deaths due to automobile accidents (about 50,000)—"but nobody wants to ban cars!" To counter, the pro-control people express the gun toll as a number of deaths per unit of time. The resulting figure is dramatic: on average, someone in the United States dies from a firearm every seventeen or eighteen minutes.

Death is not the whole story, of course. One must also include non-fatal but injurious firearms accidents, crimes other than homicide or suicide committed with guns, unsuccessful suicide attempts involving firearms, and so on. None of these things is known with much precision, and the lack of firm data is an invitation to exuberant formulations on both sides. Still, reasonable compromise values for the various components suggest a total incident count of fewer than a million per year—that is, incidents in which a firearm of some sort was involved in some way in some kind of

violent or criminal incident (intentional or accidental, fatal or not). Pro-gun people have dismissed this estimate as much too high, and anti-gun people have dismissed it as much too low, so I figure it can't be too far off.

When we shift to the guns side of the "guns and crime" equation, the numbers jump by a few orders of magnitude, although here, too, some caution is needed. In the course of the twentieth century, so far as can be told, some 250 million total firearms (excluding military weapons) have been manufactured in or imported into the United States. Published guesses about the number of guns in private hands in this country run upwards to a billion—an absurd and inconceivably large estimate. Most of the published estimates are produced by advocates and thus are not to be trusted, most of all since both sides have vested interests in publishing the largest possible numbers: the pro-gun people, to show the vast number of people whose rights would be infringed by stricter gun controls; the anti-gun people, to show the obvious urgency of the situation.

It is not known for certain how many of the 250 million guns of the twentieth century remain in private hands; 150 million is a sensible guess. Survey evidence dating from at least 1959 routinely shows that about 50 percent of all American households possess at least one firearm, with the average number owned (among those owning at least one) being just over three. Whatever the exact number, it is obvious that there are lots and lots of guns out there—many tens of millions at the very least. . . .

The numbers do speak clearly to at least one point: if we are going to try to "control" guns as a means of controlling crime, then we are going to have to deal with the guns already in private hands; controls over new purchases alone will not suffice. Taking the highest plausible value for the number of gun incidents— 1 million per year—and the lowest plausible value for the number of guns presently owned—say, 100 million—we see rather quickly that the guns now owned exceed the annual incident count by a factor of at least a hundred; in other words, the existing stock is adequate to supply all conceivable nefarious purposes for at least the next century.

These figures can be considered in another way. Suppose we did embark on a program of firearms confiscation, with the ultimate aim of achieving a "no guns" condition. We would have to confiscate at least a hundred guns to get just one gun that, in any typical year, would be involved in any kind of gun incident; several hundred to get just one that would otherwise be involved in a chargeable gun crime; and several thousand to get just one that would otherwise be used to bring about someone's death. Whatever else one might want to say about such a policy, it is not very efficient.

DEMAND CREATES ITS OWN SUPPLY

One of the favorite aphorisms of the pro-gun forces is that "if guns are outlawed, only outlaws will have guns." Sophisticated liberals laugh at this point, but they shouldn't. No matter what laws we enact, they will be obeyed only by the law-abiding—this follows by definition. If we were to outlaw, say, the ownership of handguns, millions of law-abiding handgun owners would no doubt turn theirs in. But why should we expect the average armed robber or street thug to do

likewise? Why should we expect felons to comply with a gun law when they readily violate laws against robbery, assault, and murder?

For the average criminal, a firearm is an income-producing tool with a consequent value that is several times its initial cost. According to data published by Phillip Cook of Duke University, the average "take" in a robbery committed with a firearm is more than $150 (in 1976 dollars) and is three times the take for a robbery committed with any other weapon; the major reason for the difference is that criminals with guns rob more lucrative targets. Right now, one can acquire a handgun in any major American city in a matter of a few hours for roughly $100. Even if the street price of handguns tripled, a robber armed with a handgun could (on the average) recoup his entire capital outlay in the first two or three transactions.

As long as there are *any* handguns around (and even "ban handgun" advocates make an exception for police or military handguns), they will obviously be available to anyone *at some price*. Given Cook's data, the average street thug would come out well ahead even if he spent several hundred—perhaps even a few thousand—on a suitable weapon. At those prices, demand will always create its own supply: just as there will always be cocaine available to anyone willing to pay $200 a gram for it, so too will handguns always be available to anyone willing to pay a thousand dollars to obtain one.

The more militant "ban handgun" advocates urge what is easily recognized as the handgun equivalent of Prohibition. Why would we expect the outcome of "handgun prohibition" to differ from its 1920s predecessor? A black market in guns, run by organized crime, would almost certainly spring up to service the demand. It is, after all, no more difficult to manufacture a serviceable firearm in one's basement than to brew up a batch of home-made gin. Afghani tribesmen, using wood fires and metal-working equipment much inferior to what can be ordered from a Sears catalogue, hand-manufacture rifles that fire the Russian AK-47 cartridge. Do we ascribe less ability to the Mafia or the average do-it-yourselfer?

A recent poll of the U.S. adult population asked people to agree or disagree with this proposition: "Gun control laws affect only law-abiding citizens; criminals will always be able to find guns." Seventy-eight percent agreed. There is no reasonable doubt that the majority, in this case, is right.

CRIMES OF PASSION

Sophisticated advocates on both sides by now grant most of the preceding points. No one still expects "stricter gun control" to solve the problem of hard-core criminal violence, or even make a dent in it. Much of the argument has thus shifted toward violence perpetrated not for economic gain, or for any other good reason, but rather in the "heat of the moment"— the so-called "crimes of passion" that turn injurious or lethal not so much because anyone intended them to, but because, in a moment of rage, a firearm was at hand. Certainly, we could expect incidents of this sort to decline if we could somehow reduce the availability of firearms for the purpose. Or could we?

Crimes of passion certainly occur, but how often? Are "heat of the moment" homicides common or rare? The fact is, nobody knows. The assumption that they are very common, characteristic of the pro-control world view, is derived from the well-known fact that most homicides involve persons known to one another before the event—typically family members, friends, or other acquaintances. But ordinarily, the only people one would ever have any good reason to kill would be people known intimately to oneself. Contrary to the common assumption, prior acquaintance definitely does *not* rule out willful, murderous intent.

The "crime of passion" most often discussed is that of family members killing one another. One pertinent study, conducted in Kansas City, looked into every family homicide that occurred in a single year. In 85 percent of the cases examined, the police had previously (within the prior five years) been called to the family residence to break up a domestic quarrel; in half the cases, the police had been there five or more times. It would therefore be misleading to see these homicides as isolated and unfortunate outbursts occurring among normally placid and loving individuals. They are, rather, the culminating episodes of an extended history of violence and abuse among the parties.

Analysis of the family homicide data reveals an interesting pattern. When women kill men, they often use a gun. When men kill women, they usually do it in some more degrading or brutalizing way—such as strangulation or knifing. The reason for the difference seems obvious: although the world is full of potentially lethal objects, almost all of them are better suited to male than to female use. The gun is the single exception: all else held constant, it is equally deadly in anyone's hands. Firearms equalize the means of physical terror between men and women. In denying the wife of an abusive man the right to have a firearm, we may only be guaranteeing her husband the right to beat her at his pleasure. One argument against "stricter gun control" is thus that a woman should have as much right to kill her husband as a man has to kill his wife.

Some will gasp at this statement; no one, after all, has a "right" to kill anyone. But this, of course, is false: every jurisdiction in the United States recognizes justifiable homicides in at least some extenuating circumstances, and increasingly a persistent and long-standing pattern of physical abuse is acknowledged to be one of them. True, in the best of all possible worlds, we would simply do away with whatever gives rise to murderous rage. This is not, regrettably, the world in which we live. . . .

THE SATURDAY NIGHT SPECIAL

The notorious Saturday Night Special has received a great deal of attention. The term is used loosely: it can refer to a gun of low price, inferior quality, small caliber, short barrel length, or some combination of these. The attention is typically justified on two grounds: first, these guns have no legitimate sport or recreational use, and secondly, they are the firearms preferred by criminals. Thus, the argument goes, we could just ban them altogether; in doing so, we would directly reduce the number of guns available to criminals without restricting anyone's legitimate ownership rights.

The idea that the Saturday Night Special is the criminal's gun of choice turns out to be wrong. Our felon survey showed, overwhelmingly, that serious criminals both prefer to carry and actu-ally do carry relatively large, big-bore, well-made handguns. Indeed, not more than about one in seven of these criminals' handguns would qualify as small and cheap. Most of the felons wanted to be and actually were at least as well armed as their most likely adversaries, the police. There may well be good reason to ban Saturday Night Specials, but the criminal interest in such weapons is not one of them. Most serious felons look on the Saturday Night Special with considerable contempt.

It is too early to tell how these data will be interpreted among "Ban Saturday Night Special" advocates. The most recent wrinkle I have encountered is that they should be banned not because they are preferred or used by criminals, but because, being cheap, they tend to be owned by unknowledgeable, inexperienced, or irresponsible people. One may assume that cheap handguns, like cheap commodities of all sorts, tend to be owned by poor people. The further implication—that poor gun owners are less knowledgeable, experienced, or responsible than more affluent owners—has, however, never been researched; it is also the sort of "elitist" argument that ordinarily arouses liberal indignation.

What about the other side of the argument—that these guns have no legitimate use? It is amazing how easily people who know little about guns render such judgments. When I commenced my own research, it occurred to me that I ought to find out what gun owners themselves had to say on some of these matters. So I picked up the latest issues of about a half-dozen gun magazines. It is remarkable how informative this simple exercise turned out to be.

One magazine that surfaced is called *Handgunning*, which is specifically for devotees of handgun sports. Every issue of the magazine is full of articles on the sporting and recreational uses of handguns of all kinds. I learned, for example, that people actually hunt game with handguns, which never would have occurred to me. In reading a few articles, the reason quickly became obvious: it is more sporting than hunting with shoulder weapons, and it requires much more skill, which makes a successful handgun hunt a much more satisfying accomplishment.

In my journey through this alien turf, I came upon what are called "trail guns" or "pack guns." These are handguns carried outdoors, in the woods or the wilds, for no particular reason except to have a gun available "just in case" one encounters unfriendly fauna, or gets lost and needs small game for food, or is injured and needs to signal for help. The more I read about trail guns, the more it seemed that people who spend a lot of time alone in the wilds, in isolated and out-of-the-way places, are probably being pretty sensible in carrying these weapons.

One discussion went on in some detail about the characteristics to look for in a trail gun. It ought to be small and light, of course, for the same reason that serious backpackers carry nylon rather than canvas tents. "Small and light" implies small caliber (a .22 or .25), a short barrel, and a stainless-steel frame (to afford greater protection from the elements). The article mentioned that some of the finest weapons of this sort were being manufactured in Europe, and at very reasonable prices. And suddenly it dawned on me: the small, low-caliber, short-barreled, imported, not-too-expensive guns the article was describing were what are otherwise known as Saturday

Night Specials. And thus I came to learn that we cannot say that Saturday Night Specials have "no legitimate sport or recreational use."

It would be sophistic to claim that most Saturday Night Specials are purchased for use as trail guns; my point is only that some are. Most small, cheap handguns are probably purchased by persons of modest means to protect themselves against crime. It is arguable whether protection against crime is a "legitimate" or "illegitimate" use; the issues involved are too complex to treat fairly in this article. It is worth stressing, however, that poor, black, central-city residents are by far the most likely potential victims of crime; if self-protection justifies owning a gun, then a ban on small, cheap handguns would effectively deny the means of self-protection to those most evidently in need of it.

There is another argument against banning small, cheap handguns: a ban on Saturday Night Specials would leave heavy-duty handguns available as substitute weapons. It is convenient to suppose that in the absence of small, cheap handguns, most people would just give up and not use guns for whatever they had in mind. But certainly some of them, and perhaps many of them, would move up to bigger and better handguns instead. We would do well to remember that the most commonly owned handgun in America today is a .38 caliber double-action revolver, the so-called Police Special that functions as the service revolver for about 90 percent of American police. If we somehow got rid of all the junk handguns, how many thugs, assailants, and assassins would choose to use this gun, or other guns like it, instead? And what consequences might we then anticipate?

The handgun used by John Hinckley in his attack on President Reagan was a .22 caliber revolver, a Saturday Night Special. Some have supported banning the Saturday Night Special so as to thwart psychopaths in search of weapons. But would a psychopath intent on assassinating a President simply give up in the absence of a cheap handgun? Or would he, in that event, naturally pick up some other gun instead? Suppose he did pick up the most commonly owned handgun available in the United States, the .38 Special. Suppose further that he got off the same six rounds and inflicted the same wounds that he inflicted with the .22. A .38 slug entering Jim Brady's head where the .22 entered would, at the range in question, probably have killed him instantly. The Washington policeman would not have had a severed artery but would have been missing the larger part of his neck. The round deflected from its path to President Reagan's heart might have reached its target. One can readily imagine at least three deaths, including the President's, had Hinkley fired a more powerful weapon.

POSTSCRIPT

Should a National Gun Control Policy Be Established?

The United States has about 20,000 gun control laws, the vast majority of which are state or local ordinances. There is considerable variation, therefore, from place to place. There have been several federal statutes enacted to control firearms. The Federal Firearms Act of 1934 regulated possession of submachine guns, silencers, and several other weapons. In 1938, the National Firearms Act was passed, requiring the licensing of firearms manufacturers and dealers. As a result, all new weapons sold in the United States since 1938 have been registered and can be traced. The most important federal action was taken with the passage of the Gun Control Act of 1968. The Act prohibited the interstate retailing of all firearms. Its purpose was to prevent individuals who cannot legally own a gun from ordering guns by mail under phony names.

There has been renewed attention to the issue of gun control lately, partly as a result of rising drug-related violence and partly because of Robert Purdy's shooting spree at an elementary school in Stockton, California, on January 17, 1989. Five children were killed and 30 injured. Purdy had a semiautomatic assault rifle, with which he sprayed the schoolyard, and a handgun, with which he killed himself. Following this incident, California banned the sale, manufacture, or unregistered possession of a wide variety of semiautomatic weapons. On the federal level, President Bush banned the importation of assault-style weapons. No restrictions were placed on the domestic manufacture of such weapons, which account for about three-quarters of those sold.

Public opinion polls suggest that a majority of the public wants more regulation. Ninety-one percent of adults surveyed in June, 1981, by the Gallup organization said they favored a law requiring a 21-day waiting period before a gun could be purchased, during which time a check would be made to see if the prospective owner had a criminal record. Legislation to require a seven-day waiting period is currently pending before Congress. Many states do not require such background checks. While there is a prohibition against selling guns to minors, convicted felons, fugitives, drug addicts, and several other classes of persons, no prior check is required, and there is no way for dealers to know whether or not customers are legally qualified to own guns. In general, the Gallup poll found 65 percent favored stronger regulations. Yet, by a three to two ratio, those polled rejected an outright ban on the possession of handguns.

The meaning and history of the Second Amendment is discussed in Levinson, "The Embarrassing Second Amendment," 99 *Yale Law Journal* 637

(1989); Brown, "Guns, Cowboys, Philadelphia Mayors, and Civic Republicanism: On S. Levinson's 'The Embarrassing Second Amendment,' " 99 *Yale Law Journal* 661 (1989); Hardy, "Armed Citizens, Citizen Armies: Toward A Jurisprudence of the Second Amendment," 9 *Harvard Journal of Law and Public Policy* 559 (1986); and S. Halbrook, *That Every Man Be Armed* (University of New Mexico Press, 1984). Recent discussions of handgun regulation are contained in F. Zimring and G. Hawkins, *The Citizen's Guide to Gun Control* (Macmillan, 1987); J. Wright and P. Rossi, *Armed and Considered Dangerous* (Aldine De Gruyter, 1986); D. Kates, ed., *Firearms and Violence* (Pacific Institute for Public Policy Research, 1984); and Symposium, "Gun Control," *Law and Contemporary Problems* (vol. 46, 1986).

ISSUE 16

Does Caller ID Invade Privacy?

YES: Janlori Goldman, from Statement Before the Subcommittee on Technology and the Law, Committee on the Judiciary, U.S. Senate (August 1, 1990)

NO: Arthur R. Miller, from Statement Before the Subcommittee on Technology and the Law, Committee on the Judiciary, U.S. Senate (August 1, 1990)

ISSUE SUMMARY

YES: Attorney Janlori Goldman believes that regulation of Caller ID is needed to protect privacy and to prevent misuse of the technology that reveals the telephone number of callers.
NO: Professor Arthur R. Miller evaluates the rights of callers and those being called and concludes that the privacy rights of the latter are deserving of more protection, which Caller ID provides.

> The right to be let alone—the most comprehensive of rights and the right most valued by civilized men.
>
> —Justice Louis Brandeis

The telephone has attained the status of one of life's necessities. There are telephones in approximately 93 percent of the homes in the United States. There are few communications devices as flexible as the telephone or that are used as often. It is used by children as well as adults, it can both send and receive information, it is used for personal as well as business reasons, and it miraculously communicates over any distance almost instantaneously.

The telephone that most of us use differs considerably from the instrument that previous generations used. It may look similar and do all of the things telephones used to do, but it can also do more, and it operates differently. The telephone has become a computerized high-tech instrument. As this has occurred, the telephone has become a smarter and more powerful instrument than it once was. Various new services have been added to the basic capability of one person calling another, among them the controversial Caller ID service.

Caller ID is a service that allows anyone receiving a telephone call to know the telephone number of the caller. The service has a simple and broad appeal, since it promises to reduce the number of harassing or obscene telephone calls by taking away the anonymity of the caller. This benefit, however, comes at some cost, because there are people who have legitimate reasons for not wanting their telephone numbers displayed. Doctors calling patients, teachers calling the parents of students, victims calling hotlines, journalists calling sources, as well as others with unlisted numbers, may not want to have their numbers displayed. Is there some way to satisfy the concerns of these people and still help those who suffer from obscene callers? As one Canadian journalist wrote after Caller ID was instituted there:

> I have four telephones, three of which are listed numbers that ring or send me faxes at all hours of the day or night, seven days a week. My fourth phone—the one that rings in my kitchen and in my bedroom and in the rec room and in several private spaces in my house—is unlisted. Very few people have that number, and my office never gives it out.
>
> I pay B.C. Tel [Bell Canada Telephone] an extra $2.15 a month for that unlisted line, and have done so for at least 15 years—a fair chunk of change, over time.
>
> But now my unlisted line and the extra money I pay for it don't mean phhttt. Anyone I call can see my number in a flash, at which point it's no longer private.
>
> And if you could see some of the people I call in the course of my job (occasionally from home), you'd understand why this is a concern. We're talking Mars-to-Earth, here. I do not want these folks calling me at home after their call displays have let them peek into my private boudoir.

The law has been involved with the telephone since shortly after it was invented and much of this relationship has centered on privacy concerns. Wiretapping has been the subject of many cases and statutes. In general, courts have recognized that wiretapping is a search and that constitutional standards apply before such an invasion of privacy will be allowed. Courts have been more lenient with telephone records, however. In a famous case decided in 1979, *Smith v. Maryland*, 442 U.S. 735, the U.S. Supreme Court ruled that pen registers, which record when a call is being made and the number being called, can be employed without a search warrant.

Caller ID is one of many technology-related privacy questions that will surface as the new information technologies proliferate. Whether it is regulated and how privacy concerns are handled will also have a continuing impact on us.

YES

Janlori Goldman

TESTIMONY OF JANLORI GOLDMAN

New telephone technologies promise to enhance privacy and give individuals greater control over their lives, but also threaten to undermine these very same rights. One such device is Caller ID, or Automatic Number Identification (ANI), which displays the telephone number of an incoming call as the phone is ringing. The introduction of Caller ID has sparked an emotional and divisive debate that affects everyone who uses the telephone. Federal legislation is needed to resolve ambiguities in the scope of ECPA [Electronic Communications Privacy Act] and to establish uniform, national privacy policy in this area. In the absence of federal legislation, phone companies around the country will continue to market Caller ID in a variety of conflicting ways that will only create inconsistency and chaos in the development of public policy in the area of privacy and telecommunications.

PRIVACY AND THE RIGHT TO CONTROL
PERSONAL INFORMATION

New communication technologies are changing the ways we deal with each other. Few social and commercial relationships remain unaffected by the introduction of new technologies such as cellular and cordless phones, electronic mail, bulletin boards, and pagers. Traditional barriers of distance, time, and location are disappearing as our society comes to take these advanced forms of communication for granted. As new technologies become available, a tension is often created between existing societal values and expectations, and the commercial opportunities posed by these advances.

However, people's expectations of privacy should not be measured against what is technically possible. New technologies pose new risks to traditional civil liberties. Today's hearing provides us with the opportunity to examine a technological advance in light of widely shared expectations of privacy to avoid the erosion of essential liberties.

People care deeply about their privacy, and cherish the ability to control personal information. Even if they have done nothing wrong, or have

From U.S. Senate. Committee on the Judiciary. Subcommittee on Technology and the Law. *Caller-ID Technology.* Hearing, August 1, 1990. Washington, DC: Government Printing Office, 1990. (S.Hrg 101-1264.) Some notes omitted.

nothing to hide, most people are offended if they are denied the ability to keep certain personal information confidential. Crucial to one's sense of self is the right to maintain some decision-making power over what information to divulge, to whom, and for what purpose. The uses of new technologies are always threatening to overtake current law, leaving society without a new set of laws and social mores to limit and define the extent to which new devices can be used to know all we can about each other, often without regard to each other's wish to keep information private.

National polls document a growing demand for privacy protection. A *Trends and Forecasts* survey released in May, 1989 found that 7 out of 10 consumers feel that personal privacy is very important to them, with many expressing the fear that their privacy is in jeopardy.

A June, 1990 survey by Louis Harris & Associates, *Consumers in the Information Age,* found a growing public demand for privacy legislation, documenting that an overwhelming majority of people believe that the right to privacy is in jeopardy. The survey also found that 79% of the American public stated that if the Declaration of Independence were rewritten today, they would add privacy to the list of "life, liberty and the pursuit of happiness" as a fundamental right. In an analysis of an earlier survey, Harris concluded:

> Particularly striking is the pervasiveness of support for tough new ground rules governing computers and other information technology. Americans are not willing to endure abuse or misuse of information, and they overwhelmingly support action to do something about it.

. . . The new technology at issue in today's hearing is Caller ID, or Automatic Number Identification (ANI)[1], a small device that can be attached to a telephone which allows people on the receiving end of a call to see the number of an incoming call as the phone is ringing. Traditionally, without Caller ID, people have no way of learning a caller's phone number unless it is voluntarily given. As callers, people assume that the phone number from which they are calling will remain confidential unless they choose to reveal it. Caller ID reverses this status quo. However, a blocking feature planned in a number of jurisdictions provides callers with a mechanism to block the display of their number when they want to maintain confidentiality. Before we can discuss the significant privacy issues posed by this Caller ID, it is important to review the constitutional and statutory foundation for privacy protections.

The Constitutional Right to Privacy

The right to privacy—as imbedded in the U.S. Constitution and numerous federal and state statutes—is the central principle that limits, as well as fosters, the use of new technologies. The right to privacy encompasses fundamental values of liberty and autonomy, including both "the right to be let alone," as Justice Louis Brandeis defined it, and the right to control the dissemination of personal information.

Although the word "privacy" does not appear in the U.S. Constitution, the U.S. Supreme Court has interpreted the Constitution to grant individuals a right of privacy, based on the First Amendment freedom of association and expression, the Fifth Amendment privilege against self-incrimination, the Fourteenth Amendment's guarantee of "ordered liberty," the unenumerated rights guaranteed by the Ninth Amendment, and most principally, in the Fourth Amendment protection of persons, places, papers, and effects against unreasonable searches and seizures.

The scope of the Fourth Amendment once hinged on property-based notions of liberty that linked people's privacy rights to their relationship to certain places. However, in 1967, in *United States v. Katz*, the Supreme Court expanded its interpretation by ruling that the Fourth amendment protects people, not places. In *Katz*, the Court held that warrantless wiretapping is unconstitutional, and created a standard for determining constitutionally protected "zones of privacy" based on whether an individual has a "reasonable expectation of privacy" in the conduct or information disclosed. Central to the *Katz* formulation is whether the individual takes certain measures to preserve his or her privacy.

In practice, the *Katz* "reasonable expectation of privacy" standard has often been used to weaken privacy protections. The objective "expectation" model can only reflect, not prevent, deterioration in societal respect for privacy. Applying *Katz*, the Court in later cases determined that an individual's privacy has not been violated by certain intrusions because society's "expectation of privacy" has been persistently lowered by the circumstances of modern existence. The Court's rulings are not surprising since many people can no longer claim to "reasonably" expect privacy even in the most intimate activities of their lives.

In one of those Fourth Amendment cases, *Smith v. Maryland*, the Court ruled that law enforcement officials do not need a search warrant to install a pen register, a device that records the numbers dialed from a telephone. Applying the *Katz* standard, the Court found that

people have no reasonable expectation of privacy in the numbers that they dial. Congress later rejected this approach.

Congressional Response

In response to the Supreme Court's rigid interpretation of the Constitutional right to information privacy, Congress has enacted legislation that gives people expectations of privacy in certain information held by others, including credit, education, financial, cable and video records.

In the area of communications, following *Katz*, Congress passed the Wiretap Act of 1968, which limits severely the government's ability to intercept and record communications. And, in 1986, Congress passed the Electronic Communications Privacy Act (ECPA) to update the Wiretap Act to cover the interception of new forms of electronic, non-aural communication. In addition, in ECPA Congress rejected the Supreme Court's conclusion in *Smith v. Maryland* that telephone toll records are not entitled to privacy protection.

ECPA provides that "no person may install or use a pen register or trap and trace device[2] without first obtaining a court order" that certifies "that information likely to be obtained is relevant to an ongoing criminal investigation being conducted" by a particular law enforcement agency. This general prohibition does not apply if used by a *provider* of: electronic or wire communication service—

(1) relating to the operation, maintenance, and testing of a wire or electronic communication service or to the protection of the rights or property of such provider, or to the protection of users of that service from abuse of service or unlawful use of service; or

(2) to record the fact that a wire or electronic communication was initiated

or completed in order to protect such provider, another provider furnishing services towards completion of the wire communication, or a user of that service, from fraudulent, unlawful, or abusive use of service; or

(3) where the consent of the user of that service has been obtained.

CALLER ID AND CURRENT LAW

A serious question exists as to whether Caller ID, as a trap and trace device, is legal under current federal law. As drafted, ECPA contemplates the use of trap and trace devices by only two parties—law enforcement, which must first obtain a court order, and telephone service providers, which must meet one of three exceptions. All other uses are prohibited.

Caller ID devices squarely fit the law's definition of a trap and [trace] device as one that "captures" and identifies "the originating number . . . from which a wire or electronic communication was transmitted." ECPA prohibits the use of a trap and trace device without a court order unless one of three exceptions are met. The three exceptions only apply to "providers" of telephone services. Thus, it appears that the use of a trap and trace device by a telephone *subscriber* is prohibited. The Congressional Research Service (CRS) arrived at the same conclusion. In an opinion issued last fall, CRS interpreted the exceptions to the general prohibition to apply only to the use of trap and trace devices by providers of communication services, and not users of the services. The language of ECPA and its legislative history are clear that the intent is to allow providers to use trap and trace devices primarily to verify billing, and to detect illegal activity. In addition, other sections of the law refer explicitly to both providers and customers.

Even if it is determined that "providers" may provide Caller ID to telephone subscribers, none of the three exceptions apply to authorize its general, unrestricted use. The first exception applies to the use of a trap and trace device in the "operation, maintenance, and testing" of the service, or to "protect the rights or property of the provider" or to protect the users of that service from unlawful or abusive use of the service. The legislative history is clear that this first exception was intended to cover only use of a pen register by the phone company.

The second exception authorizes a provider to use a trap and trace device to protect providers and users from fraudulent, unlawful or abusive use of service. Again, the second exception is inapplicable to the everyday use of Caller ID by telephone subscribers. In addressing the first two exceptions, CRS concluded:

> Any suggestion that either of these exceptions authorizes a user's employment of a trap and trace device to identify all incoming calls in order to avoid answering those from sources likely to be obscene or harassing overlooks the fact that permissible use is limited to providers.

The third exception authorizes providers to use trap and trace devices "where the consent of the user of that service has been obtained." At best, the scope of this exception is ambiguous. First, is the user the caller or the receiver of a phone call? Or is it the subscriber? Logically, since it is the caller who takes the active step to initiate a phone call, and it is his or her number that is being revealed, it follows that it is the caller's consent that should be obtained prior to the provider using a trap and trace device.

Even assuming that "the user" is found to be either party to a phone call, in its analysis CRS interprets the third exception to be:

> restricted to consent to use a trap and trace in connection with a particular call where there is only a single user who may consent, as opposed to continuous use of a trap and trace device in connection with a particular line which might over the course of time have many users. . . . The consent exception therefore cannot embody consent of a telephone subscriber to include a continuously operating trap and trace device as a feature of his or her telephone service.

We do know, though, that in 1986 the development of Caller ID technology was in its infancy, and was not considered explicitly by either the Congress or the various groups that supported passage of ECPA. Nevertheless, Congress did intend ECPA's scope to be elastic enough to cover the development of new communications technologies:

> The first principle [upon which ECPA is based] is that legislation which protects electronic communications from interception by either private parties or the Government should be comprehensive, and not limited to particular types or techniques of communication. . . . Any attempt to write a law which tries to protect only those technologies which exist in the marketplace today . . . is destined to be outmoded within a few years.

One of the primary achievements of ECPA was to ensure that communications privacy would not be diminished by the advent of new technologies. In this context, the law's general prohibition on the use of trap and trace devices must be read broadly. Caller ID, as a trap and [trace] device, may not be used unless an explicit statutory exception applies.

No federal court has interpreted ECPA's trap and trace law as applied to Caller ID. However, on May 30, 1990, the Commonwealth Court of Pennsylvania ruled that the use of Caller ID is illegal and unconstitutional under its state law, which is modeled on and virtually identical to the federal law. In its decision, the court relied heavily on the State's trap and trace law to conclude that Caller ID, with or without a blocking mechanism, violates individuals' privacy and due process rights. In addition, last week the Public Service Commission of the District of Columbia determined that Caller ID must be offered with blocking to avoid any question of violating ECPA. The rulings in Pennsylvania and the District of Columbia lend support to our position that Caller ID is prohibited under current law.

POLICY CONSIDERATIONS AND LEGISLATIVE PROPOSALS: THE FUTURE OF CALLER ID

. . . The ACLU believes that while Caller ID holds the prospect of enhancing people's privacy, it also threatens to severely undermine cherished expectations of confidentiality. If not properly restricted, Caller ID will automatically reveal a caller's number, and possibly identity and location. Without a mechanism that allows callers to selectively block the display of their numbers on the receiving end, people will no longer control when and to whom to give their numbers.

The controversy generated over Caller ID is unique in that the competing privacy interests are most often held by the same people—*those who make and receive phone calls.* In fact, when they see themselves as receivers of phone calls, most people are eager for Caller ID. But, as makers of phone calls, most people want the power to block the display of their numbers. The most recent Harris survey—*Consumers in the Information Age*—documented the public's views on Caller ID. Nearly half of the American people (48%) believe Caller ID should be permitted only if blocking is available, and over a quarter (27%) feel Caller ID should be prohibited by law. Significantly, only 23% of those polled say Caller ID should be available without any limitations.

The common thread running through the Caller ID debate is that each party, at different times and for different reasons, has an interest in receiving phone numbers and in limiting dissemination of their numbers. (Admittedly, Caller ID has a limited utility for consumers, since people will not instantly recognize most phone numbers. Most people want to know *who* is calling.)

What is actually at stake here?

Interest in Receiving Numbers

1. Consumers can see the number from which a call is being placed to decide whether or not to answer the phone. The familiarity or unfamiliarity of a number will provide them with more information to make decisions about calls coming into their home.

2. Businesses want to use the technology to gather information about people who call them. Some businesses claim that the devices make it more efficient to automatically bring up files, and allows for the creation and linkage of databases for marketing purposes.

3. Law enforcement officials and emergency service providers want the technology to locate people in danger or people using the phone to make obscene or harassing calls, or to identify other illegal use.

Interest in Limiting Disclosure

1. The automatic display of one's phone number can create life threatening situations, including: calls to or from battered women's shelters; calls made by a woman to a batterer; and calls by social workers, doctors, and others who protect their safety by keeping their phone numbers unlisted. In addition, law enforcement officials in a number of states, including Illinois, Pennsylvania and Florida, are concerned that Caller ID will hamper undercover operations, and may discourage informants from calling police departments.

2. Automatic number identification will be used by businesses, including phone companies, to create and enhance databases of consumer information to be used for marketing purposes.

An individual's dual interest in receiving information and in limiting disclosure are important here. The technology exists to take into account and balance both of these interests by providing blocking as part of the Caller ID service. In fact, blocking actually provides people with more information—that the person calling does not want to reveal their number, identity or location. A call from someone who has blocked may discourage the person on the receiving end from picking up the phone.

Some phone companies claim they want to offer Caller ID without blocking primarily to give women who receive obscene or harassing phone calls the ability to get the number of the person calling them. Clearly, obscene and harassing phone calls are a very serious problem. However, there is another service currently available in many areas, known as Call Trace, that is rarely advertised and much more effective than Caller ID for combatting harassing phone callers. With Call Trace, a person who receives such a call can instantly send a signal to the phone company and the police that records the phone number of the caller and alerts law enforcement officials that the call was just received. Most importantly, *Call Trace is still effective even if the caller blocks.*

It is untenable for a phone company to suggest that Caller ID without blocking will protect women from harassing phone calls, particularly in light of the advice phone company representatives have given for years to women who receive these phone calls—"just hang up and report the call." Caller ID may deter some harassing callers, thereby decreasing the number of complaints received by phone companies each year. And, those who persist in making harassing calls may block the display of their number. But, if people are reluctant to answer blocked calls, the harassing call never happens. In the event that a harassing caller does not block, what do phone company representatives suggest women do with the caller's number? Call back? Threaten the caller? Such a vigilante approach is dangerous. It is irresponsible for a phone company to use Caller ID technology to wash its hands of this serious problem.

There is a lack of hard data on how per-call blocking would actually affect the use of Caller ID. The phone companies that are currently offering the device without blocking failed to test a per-call blocking option. However, the New York Public Utility Commission mandated that the phone company in Rochester offer both per-call and per-line (permanent) blocking in its preliminary trial of Caller ID. Early results from that trial confirm what many have been saying all along. A very small percentage of phone numbers are actually blocked. In addition, U.S. West is also offering Caller ID with blocking in its trials of the service.

A number of reasons exist as to why few calls are blocked. One, people are reluctant to answer blocked calls. Second, blocking requires an affirmative act on the part of the caller. A caller must want to keep his or her number confidential, at least before the phone is answered, and must take steps (punching in a code) to block the display of the number. It is important to recognize that there is a burden associated with requiring people to "do something" to protect their privacy. Most likely, there will be many instances when people who want to safeguard the confidentiality of their phone numbers will forget to block.

THE COMMERCIAL USE OF AUTOMATIC NUMBER IDENTIFICATION (ANI)

The use of Caller ID by businesses to collect phone numbers for commercial purposes poses significant privacy concerns, in particular, that people are increasingly losing control over personal information in exchange for receiving goods and services, often without the individual's knowledge and consent. The commercial use of Caller ID is especially troubling since most businesses can not claim to have a privacy interest in receiving phone numbers before calls are answered. In fact, many businesses welcome calls from consumers, and aren't likely to be reluctant to answer a blocked call. On the other hand, a person's phone number has become a very valuable piece of information.

A phone number is much like a social security number in that it is perceived as a unique identifier. A person's phone number may easily be used as a key to "unlock" databases containing personal information, allowing for a variety of information to be compiled, exchanged, manipulated, and sold for commercial purposes. The commercial use of Caller ID allows businesses to capture phone numbers and match them with names, addresses, buying habits, credit history and other information to build valuable consumer profile databases for marketing.

The phone number itself reveals personal information. For instance, it may be significant that a person placed a call from a particular number. Or, the number may be otherwise unavailable because it is unlisted. Many businesses are becoming more anxious to receive unlisted numbers since between 30–55% of telephone subscribers, depending on the area, currently pay to keep their numbers unlisted.

The phone number as a hot, new commodity has been well documented by the media. As the Christian Science Monitor reported last month: "Bell Atlantic, Bell South and Ameritech plan to efficiently link this transmission system [Caller ID] with every car dealer, insurance salesman and telemarketer. The Bell companies will be selling a database of your home phone number, telephone records, and buying patterns for a massive, automated telephone assault."

A Wall Street Journal article from last fall entitled "Making a Phone Call Might Mean Telling the World About You: Number Identification Service is a Dream for Marketers But a Threat to Privacy," posed the question: "Does a public utility—the phone company—have the right to release phone numbers, particularly unlisted ones, to individuals and institutions willing to pay a fee for the information?"

Telephone companies plan to use ANI technology to profit from the collection and use of people's phone numbers, and other personal information generated by use of the phone. This bundle of information passing through phone company systems on its way somewhere else is known as Telephone Transaction Generated Information (TTGI). TTGI encompasses information generated by phone usage, and transactions relating to the service. One commentator notes the growing demand for TTGI by non-telephone companies that value it for marketing purposes in:

> characterizing, identifying, and locating their constituencies. . . . TTGI may be even more telling than census and other data in defining the characteristics of individuals. . . . [Citing Justice Brennan] "The transactions of an individual give a fairly accurate account of his religion, ideology, opinions and interests."

Against this backdrop, Caller ID should not be authorized unless callers are given the ability to block the transmission of their phone numbers.

NOTES

1. Caller ID is the term used to describe the use of the technology by local subscribers. Automatic Number Identification (ANI) is the service provided to commercial subscribers of 800 and 900 services.

2. A trap and trace device is defined as a "device which captures the originating electronic or other impulses which identify the originating number of an instrument or device from which a wire or electronic communication was transmitted." 18 U.S.C. 3127 (4).

NO

Arthur R. Miller

STATEMENT OF ARTHUR R. MILLER

In modern society, information and surveillance technology are advancing so quickly that we must be ever mindful of the possible impact these technological developments have on an individual's right to privacy. In some contexts, there are multiple, conflicting claims of privacy, and to determine where the greater privacy interest lies, it is important to analyze the interests carefully and make an informed judgment, rather than simply seeking to protect the interests of the parties who are the most vocal in advocating their position.

The advent of telecommunications technology such as Caller ID brings into conflict the privacy right of the telephone caller and the privacy right of the person being called. The telephone caller is concerned about disclosure of what he or she believes to be private information (his telephone number), while the person being called is concerned about an intrusion upon his or her right to be left alone. After evaluating and weighing these concerns in the context of Caller ID, I believe that the right of the person being called must be afforded greater weight.

Let me explain the reasons for this conclusion. The United States Supreme Court has ruled that telephone customers do not have a legitimate expectation of privacy with respect to their numbers. Additionally, I believe that the caller who does not want his or her number revealed is not asking for privacy, but rather anonymity at the very time he or she is seeking to intrude on the solitude of another. Society traditionally has rejected affording individuals that degree of anonymity.

The right against disclosure of private information, which the telephone caller is concerned about, is preserved, most frequently, in statutory law. For instance, the Fair Credit Reporting Act and Bank Secrecy Act govern the revelation of personal financial information. Because credit agencies and banks are required to compile sensitive personal information on individuals, either for their own security or by government mandate, the information must be protected from unfettered public dissemination. The revolution in computer and telecommunications technology, particularly in the area of data processing, has spurred the need for protection against the disclosure of private information.

From U.S. Senate. Committee on the Judiciary. Subcommittee on Technology and the Law. *Caller-ID Technology.* Hearing, August 1, 1990. Washington, DC: Government Printing Office, 1990. (S.Hrg 101-1264.)

The need for this protection essentially, however, is stronger when an individual is coerced into revealing the information. Hence, in filing tax returns or responding to the census, for example, an individual has a reasonable expectation of privacy. The question that relates to Caller ID is this: what reasonable expectation of privacy does the telephone caller have? On balance, I believe the caller's claim is rather weak.

First, the element of coercion in revealing information, evident in the tax return and census examples cited above, is not present in the telephone context. Persons not wishing to reveal personal information such as their own telephone numbers have the option of using an operator to place the call, or another private line, or a pay telephone, or not to make the call. In other words, unlike in the tax return or census questionnaire analogy, the telephone caller has the means available to accomplish the intended activity (calling another person) without revealing the telephone number. Caller ID may circumscribe, but it does not destroy, a caller's privacy. Because the right of privacy has developed in response to the increasing demands by government and other societal institutions on individuals to reveal personal information, it should not be expanded into providing protection for more consensual activities.

Unlike revealing information to file a tax return, a telephone call is a consensual activity. In *Smith v. Maryland*, 442 U.S. 735 (1979), the United States Supreme Court ruled that customers do not have a legitimate expectation of privacy with respect to their telephone numbers. The Court noted that: "All telephone users realize that they must 'convey' phone numbers to the telephone company, since it is through telephone company switching equipment that their calls are completed. All subscribers realize, moreover, that the phone company has facilities for making permanent records of the numbers they dial." *Id.* at 742. The Court also pointed out that the "switching equipment that process[es] [telephone] numbers is merely the modern counterpart of the operator, who, in an early day, personally completed calls for the subscriber." *Id.* at 744. Indeed, Caller ID represents a true return to the origins of the telephone network, when the operator connected and announced all calls. With the advent of automation, the use of live operators to connect and announce calls became increasingly inefficient. Caller ID simply restores accountability to the telephone calling process.

As already indicated, I believe that anonymity—not privacy—is what is being sought by a telephone caller who objects to having the telephone number revealed by Caller ID. The question then is whether a person has a right to hide behind a veil of anonymity in making a telephone call over the public telephone network. Although I strongly favor the individual's right to be let alone to enjoy autonomy and some anonymity, I recognize that it is not an absolute. Society, for example, requires that automobiles have license plates to travel on a public road. This modest deprivation of anonymity is designed to promote accountability. Those who insist on anonymity in placing telephone calls are, in essence, saying they do not want to be accountable on the communications network, which is quite analogous to driving without a license plate.

Having determined that the person being called has the superior privacy right, I also must conclude that the effectiveness of Caller ID should not be blunted, let alone be debilitated, by permitting the telephone caller to block the transmission of his or her telephone number to the person being called. To reiterate the key point—society requires accountability. For most individuals, society generally is unwilling to allow the anonymity implicitly sought by those who object to having their telephone numbers revealed through Caller ID. Nonetheless, society also recognizes that other legitimate interests conflict with Caller ID, such as the need to keep a battered women's shelter anonymous. Similarly, the need to protect the identity, and consequently the telephone number, of an undercover law enforcement officer is another legitimate interest that has been recognized. In these cases the telephone companies have worked with the affected groups to offer solutions that still provide accountability through a telephone number (e.g., calls through an operator, or "two-line" calling), rather than providing blocking. Again, the point is accountability for *everyone* using a public "passageway"—even the police must have license plates on their cruisers.

The position of the caller should be contrasted with that of the person being called. The latter is passive, typically in a zone where there is an expectation of privacy—the home or a private office—and is the person whose privacy is being intruded upon. In my judgment, even though we welcome receiving most calls, it is the recipient who deserves the greater protection. Caller ID is, simply stated, the modern technological solution to the individual's quest for protection from intrusion and the right to be left alone.

Caller ID is the functional equivalent of looking out the window or through a "peep hole" in the front door to see who is ringing the bell. A person who uses Caller ID service, in essence, is making a statement to the world: I do not want my privacy breached, unless I so choose. Caller ID protects the right of the individual to be free from intrusion. If the public does not want this protection, Caller ID will not be a popular service, and it will not be continued. Early results from most of the test markets indicate that the public wants this protection from obtrusive invasion, and Caller ID has proven very popular. Caller ID seems fairly narrowly tailored to protect the right of individuals to be free from unwanted intrusions. It is something we can offer our citizens against the threats to our privacy. We should make certain it is effective.

One final point should be mentioned. The debate has been cast in terms of calling parties versus called parties. Yet in the real world, the same group does both, given the fact that we both make and receive calls. By balancing the relative rights in favor of the called party, you actually protect *both* interests. After all, the people who object to having their number revealed are not concerned that others have their number, but rather that others might call them back. Protecting the rights of *called* parties, through Caller ID, takes care of that concern.

POSTSCRIPT

Does Caller ID Invade Privacy?

The Caller ID controversy is important in and of itself and also because it is the forerunner of many cases that will arise in which privacy concerns will need to be balanced against economic concerns. We live in an "information society." In such a society information is a valued commodity. People want information for many different reasons, and they are often willing to pay for it. In addition, new electronic information technologies make it much easier to store, obtain, and process information once it is received.

The telephone is able to extend ourselves, or at least our voices, through distances that would have been unimaginable to our ancestors. This has personal consequences, in that the telephone helps us maintain relationships. It also has economic consequences, in that the telephone is an important tool for many businesses.

Telephone lines are used for much more than sending the human voice from one place to another. What relates to the telephone also relates to sending data information over telephone lines, to communication between computer and computer and between human and computer. As this postscript is being written during the summer of 1992, Congress is considering legislation to regulate the use of Caller ID. The Telephone Privacy Act would allow callers opportunities to block the display of their telephone number. Whether or not this act passes and in what form will provide some indication of how Congress may deal with future privacy-technology issues that will arise as telephone lines are employed for novel purposes.

Some readings about Caller ID and about technology and privacy are as follows: S. P. Oates, "Caller ID: Privacy Protector or Privacy Invader?" 1992 *University of Illinois Law Review* 219 (1992); G. C. Smith, "We've Got Your Number! (Is It Constitutional To Give It Out?): Caller Identification Technology and the Right to Informational Privacy," 37 *UCLA Law Review* 145 (1989); Electronic Communications Privacy Act, 18 U.S.C. §§ 3121–3127 (1988); *Barasch v. Pennsylvania*, 576 A.2d 79 (1990); *Southern Bell v. Hamm*, 409 S.E.2d 775 (1991); D. Brenner, "Telephone Company Entry Into Video Services: A First Amendment Analysis," 67 *Notre Dame Law Review* 97 (1991); K. Hafner and J. Markoff, *Cyberpunk: Outlaws and Hackers on the Computer Frontier* (Simon & Schuster, 1991); and E. Katsh, *The Electronic Media and the Transformation of Law* (Oxford University Press, 1989).

ISSUE 17

Should the Insanity Defense Be Abolished?

YES: Jonathan Rowe, from "Why Liberals Should Hate the Insanity Defense," *The Washington Monthly* (May 1984)

NO: Richard Bonnie, from Statement Before the Committee on the Judiciary, U.S. Senate (August 2, 1982)

ISSUE SUMMARY

YES: Editor Jonathan Rowe examines the insanity defense as it is now administered and finds that it is most likely to be used by white middle- or upper-class defendants and that its application is unfair and leads to unjust results.

NO: Professor of law Richard Bonnie argues that the abolition of the insanity defense would be immoral and would leave no alternative for those who are not responsible for their actions.

The verdict in the 1982 trial of John Hinckley, accused of shooting former president Ronald Reagan, brought the insanity defense out of the pages of legal journals and onto the front pages of newspapers and popular magazines. What had been a subject of considerable scholarly and judicial debate during the previous 20 years became a newsworthy topic as well. That an attempted assassination of a political figure has led to calls for abolishing the insanity defense is somewhat ironic, since the modern standard for the insanity defense originated in a similar incident about 150 years ago.

In 1843, Daniel McNaughtan, suffering from delusions of persecution, fired a shot at a man he believed was British prime minister Robert Peel. Actually, the victim was the prime minister's secretary and the bullet killed him. Englishmen were outraged, since three other attempted assassinations of political officials had recently taken place, and Queen Victoria was prompted to send her husband, Prince Albert, to the trial as an observer. When McNaughtan was found not guilty by reason of insanity, Victoria sent a letter to the House of Lords, complaining that McNaughtan and the other assassins were "perfectly conscious and aware of what they did." The Lords summoned 15 judges who, after considering the matter, pronounced the McNaughtan rule (commonly referred to as the M'Naghten rule) as the most appropriate formulation of the insanity defense. This test requires that a jury must find that the defendant, when the act was committed, did not know the nature and quality of his act or that he could not tell right from wrong.

One of the problems with the insanity defense is in defining insanity. If one argues in favor of the defense, one should be able to define insanity with reasonable precision and in a way that can be applied consistently. The great difficulty in providing a definition is the basic argument against the insanity defense. The insanity defense issue has caused great controversy between lawyers and psychiatrists over the meaning of insanity and mental illness and over the ability of psychiatrists reliably to diagnose the problems of defendants.

A frequent objection to the M'Naghten rule was that there were persons who could distinguish between good and evil but still could not control their behavior. One response to this critique was the "irresistible impulse" test. Using this standard, a defendant would be relieved of responsibility for his or her actions even if he or she could distinguish right from wrong but, because of mental disease, could not avoid the action in question. A somewhat broader and more flexible version of the combined M'Naghten-irresistible impulse test was recommended by the American Law Institute in 1962. Under this formulation, people are not responsible for criminal conduct if they lack *substantial capacity* to appreciate the criminality of their conduct or to conform their conduct to the requirements of the law.

The most noteworthy and radical experiment with the reformulation of the insanity defense occurred in *Durham v. United States*, 214 F.2d 862 (1954). The District of Columbia Court of Appeals ruled that an accused was not criminally responsible if his act was the product of mental disease or defect. The effect of this rule was to increase the amount of expert psychiatric testimony presented in court about whether or not mental disease was present and whether or not the act was a product of the disease. While welcomed by many since it allowed for a more complete psychiatric picture to be presented to the jury, the rule proved to be too vague and led to too much power being given to psychiatric experts. As a result, in *United States v. Brawner*, 471 F.2d 969 (1972), the Durham experiment was abandoned.

Examination of the insanity defense opens up some extremely important issues of law. For example, what are the purposes of punishment? What assumptions does the law make about human nature, free will, and personal responsibility? What should be the role of the jury and what authority should be given medical and psychiatric experts in evaluating deviant behavior? How should we deal with the often competing goals of rehabilitation, retribution, and deterrence? These are among the questions raised in the following arguments presented by Jonathan Rowe and Richard Bonnie on the need for reforming or abolishing the insanity defense.

YES
Jonathan Rowe

WHY LIBERALS SHOULD HATE THE INSANITY DEFENSE

"It's the fallacy of your legal system," said Gary Trapnell, a bank robber who not long afterwards would hijack a TWA 707 flying from Los Angeles to New York. "Either the man falls under this antiquated psychiatric scheme of things, or he doesn't." Trapnell was talking about the insanity defense, which he had used with great acumen to avoid jail for his innumerable crimes over the years. "I have no right to be on the streets," he added.

The insanity defense has been much in the news of late. We read cases such as that of the Michigan ex-convict who pleaded insanity after seven killings, won an acquittal, but returned to the streets two months later when he was declared sane. In a month, he was charged with murdering his wife. Or take the 23-year-old Connecticut man who left the state hospital three months after an insanity acquittal for stabbing a man. The acquittee's mother pleaded to have him recommitted, but to no avail. Shortly thereafter, he repeatedly stabbed a man whose home he was burglarizing. Once again he was declared not guilty by reason of insanity.

It sounds like the warmup for a right-wing tirade against the coddlers of criminals. But the much publicized trials of John Hinckley and others have cast the issue in a somewhat different light. In a strange way, by jumbling liberal and conservative loyalties, these have made debate on the subject not only necessary, but possible as well. Take the "Twinkie Defense," which enabled former San Francisco City Supervisor Dan White to get off with a light eight-year sentence after shooting, with obvious deliberation, San Francisco Mayor George Moscone and his city administrator, Harvey Milk. As Milk was both liberal and openly homosexual, thousands who probably never before identified with the cause of law and order were outraged that this brutal act of (at least symbolic) homophobia should go lightly punished. John Hinckley, for his part, was the son of a wealthy upper-middle-class family, and not the sort of fellow who evoked sympathies usually reserved for the downtrodden. His trial prompted even *The Nation*, which rarely

From Jonathan Rowe, "Why Liberals Should Hate the Insanity Defense," *The Washington Monthly*, vol. 16, no. 4 (May 1984). Copyright © 1984 by The Washington Monthly Company, 1611 Connecticut Avenue, NW, Washington, DC 20009; (202) 462–0128. Reprinted by permission of *The Washington Monthly*.

concedes the cops an inch, to suggest some mild reforms in the insanity defense.

In the wake of the Hinckley trial, a number of reforms have been suggested. *The Nation,* along with many others, advocates that we put the burden of proof upon the defendant. (In the Hinckley case, the prosecutors actually had to prove him sane, which is no mean feat.) Others have called for a tighter legal definition of insanity itself. Such changes might be helpful, but they amount to fiddling. The only way to resolve the injustices of the insanity defense is to do away with it entirely. This may sound cruel, but it is not. Nor is it a proposal to "lock 'em up and throw away the key." To the contrary, the injustices of this defense go much deeper than a few criminals getting off the hook. They go close to the core of our current practices regarding punishment and correction. Getting rid of the insanity defense would help to make us confront the need for humane reform in the way we sentence and confine those who break the law.

SUCH A DEAL

The insanity defense looms a good deal larger in our minds than it does in actual life. Somewhere between 1,000 and 2,000 criminals make use of it each year, or about 1 percent to 2 percent of felonies that go to trial (over 90 percent in many jurisdictions are plea-bargained before trial). The issue is important not because it arises frequently, but because it tends to arise in the most serious crimes: think of Son of Sam, for example, or the Hillside Strangler. Such people tend to be dangerous, and their trials attract so much publicity that they put our entire

system of justice to a test. What single event of the last two years affected your view of the criminal justice system more than the Hinckley trial did?

It is hard to read about such trials without getting the impression that something is fundamentally wrong. Take the case of Robert H. Torsney, the New York City policeman who shot a 15-year-old black youth in the head from two feet away in November of 1978. In an article in the *Journal of Legal Medicine,* Abraham Halpern, director of psychiatry at the United Hospital, Port Chester, New York, tells the case in salient detail.

At first, Torsney's lawyer resisted any suggestion of psychological observation or treatment for his client. Such treatment for an officer who was only acting in the line of duty was "worse than putting him in the electric chair," the attorney said. As public indignation rose, however, and acquittal became more and more unlikely, the attorney decided that Torsney might have deep-seated psychological problems after all. At a hearing on Torsney's insanity defense, his paid psychiatrist explained the policeman's errant account of the incident, which was contradicted by other witnesses as an "involuntary retrospective falsification." Not a lie, mind you. The psychiatrist went on to explain that Torsney shot the kid because of an "organic psychomotor seizure" arising from a "mental defect."

The jury found Torsney not guilty by reason of insanity. After a year, however, the staff at the mental hospital recommended that he be released because they could find nothing wrong with him. When the lower court balked—such hasty releases are unseemly if nothing else—Torsney's attorney indignantly filed an appeal. "It can't be seriously argued," he wrote, "that the record in this case establishes that Mr. Torsney is either seriously mentally ill or presently dangerous. At most he may be said to have a personality flaw, which certainly does not distinguish him from the rest of society."

What really distinguished Torsney, it seemed, was that he had shot somebody and deserved to be punished. That such simple observations can become so obscured is largely the result of the wholesale invasion of psychiatry into the courtroom that has been underway since the 1950s. Back then, the stars of psychiatry and psychoactive drugs were shining bright. To many, we were on the threshold of a new age, in which psychiatrists could measure such things as responsibility and mental disease down to minute calibrations and effect cures with the precision of engineers. If only we could let these new wizards into the courtroom, to bring their expertise to bear upon the processes of justice.

The main opening came in 1954, when federal appeals Judge David Bazelon, of the Washington, D.C., District Court, declared the so-called "Durham Rule." Under the old "M'Naghten Rule," a criminal could be judged insane only if he or she didn't know right from wrong. This crimped the psychiatrists somewhat, since they tend to shrug their shoulders on questions of values. In the *Durham* case Judge Bazelon set them free, declaring that henceforth in the District of Columbia an accused was not criminally responsible "if his unlawful act was the product of mental disease or defect." Bazelon received a special award from the American Psychiatric Association, but not everyone was that enthused. The American Law Institute (ALI) produced a sort of compromise,

declaring that a person wouldn't be responsible for a misdeed if he couldn't appreciate the wrongfulness of it or if he "lacked a substantial capacity . . . to conform his conduct to the requirements of the law." Though somewhat stiffer on paper, this ALI rule didn't vary from the Durham Rule in practice all that much. Adopted by a majority of the states, its various permutations have given the psychiatrists virtual free rein in the courtroom ever since.

The Hinckley trial demonstrated what the heavenly city of courtroom psychiatry has become. Three teams of psychiatrists— 11 in all—picked over Hinckley's mind for hours in an exercise that 200 years from now will no doubt seem much the way that the heated debates over the medieval heresies seem to us today. The resulting trial dragged on for 52 excruciating days. One defense psychiatrist, Thomas C. Goldman, told the jury with a straight face that Hinckley saw actress Jody Foster as an "idealized mother who is all-giving and endowed with magical power," while President Reagan was an "all evil prohibitive figure who hates him, seeks to destroy him, and deny access to the idealized mother figure." No wonder he tried to shoot the man.

Or take the comments of Richard Delman, a psychiatrist who testified for the defense in the Dan White trial. As Lee Coleman, also a psychiatrist, tells it in his new book, *The Reign of Error*, Delman concluded on the basis of inkblot and other tests that it was White's deep concern for others that led him to sneak into San Francisco City Hall through a window rather than walk in through the front door. "He didn't want to embarrass the officer who was operating the metal detector [and would have discovered his gun]," Delman said.

On at least one occasion this kind of analysis has been more than even the defendant could take. Coleman cites the case of Inez Garcia, who was raped by two men in Soledad, California; afterwards, she went home, got a rifle, and shot one of her attackers. At her trial she sat listening to defense psychiatrist Jane Olden go on and on about her "reactive formations" and her self-image as a "saint-like idealized virgin." "If you trigger her negative feelings, which would be provoked by such an act as rape," Olden explained, "being a hysterical person who was striving always to express this sensuality and aggression, then you could indeed throw her into a state where she is emotionally relating to her own conflict."

Garcia stood up and yelled at the judge, "I killed the motherfucker because I was raped and I'd kill him again."

If you smell a fish in such psychologizing, it is with good reason. There is a cadre of so-called "forensic psychiatrists," who show up in these insanity trials again and again, plying their offensive or defensive specialties. Dr. Alan Stone of Harvard, former head of the American Psychiatric Association, describes the kind of trial that results as a "three-ring circus, in which lawyers are the ringmasters and the psychiatric witnesses are the clowns, and if they are carefully trained, then they will be trained clowns." Another Harvard psychiatrist, David Baer, was a defense witness in the Hinckley trial but does not regularly participate in these affairs, and he revealed some of the details to a reporter from *Harper's*. He spent, he said, at least 20 to 25 hours rehearsing his testimony with the lawyers, who admonished him, among other things, not to "weaken your answers with all the quali-

fications you think you ought to make." They said, "Oh, don't mention the exploding bullets. My God, that's so damaging to the case," he recalls. Baer, who was paid $35,000 for his efforts, added that he was "determined never to tell a lie."

That may be. But what happens to most psychiatrists who resist the "training" of the defense lawyers? "If a man doesn't testify the right way, he is not rehired," said one defense attorney in a study published in the *Rutgers Law Journal*. (Section 6 of the "Principles of Medical Ethics" of the American Psychiatric Association, by the way, reads: "A physician should not dispose of his services under terms or conditions which tend to interfere with or impair the free and complete exercise of his medical judgment.")

DID YOU HEAR VOICES?

The theory behind our "adversary" system is that when you pit one group of experts like these against another the truth will somehow emerge. When the hired-gun psychiatrists do their act, however, the result is not information, but confusion. "None of them had the same conclusion," complained Nathalia Brown, a shop mechanic at the local electric utility and a Hinckley juror. "All of them said he had this illness, that illness, so how are we to know what illness he has? I felt on the brink of insanity myself going through this, you know."

This, of course, is precisely what defense lawyers seek. As far back as 1945, Julian Carroll, the New York attorney who handled poet Ezra Pound's famous insanity defense against treason charges, wrote a friend that insanity trials are a "farce" in which the "learned medicos for each side squarely contradict each other and completely befuddle the jury." What was true then is even more true today, and all it took was confusion and nagging doubts in the minds of the jurors to gain Hinckley's acquittal.

In the nation's prisons, fooling the shrinks is getting to be a science. Inkblot tests offer fertile ground for displays of psychosis, and inmates who have successfully pleaded insanity have instructed their cohorts on what to see— sexual acts, genitalia, and the like. Ken Bianchi, the Hillside Strangler, studied books on psychology and hypnosis before convincing a number of psychiatrists he had a dual personality, and only an especially alert one found him out. An experiment at Stanford University suggested that conning these psychiatrists may not be all that hard. Eight subjects, all without any record of mental illness, feigned hearing voices and thereby gained admission to 12 different mental hospitals. They did not falsify any details of their lives other than that they heard voices. Eleven of the 12 were diagnosed as "schizophrenic" while the 12th was diagnosed "manic depressive."

"I probably know more about psychiatry . . . than your average resident psychiatrist," boasted Gary Trapnell, who had some justification for his claim. "I can bullshit the hell out of one in ten minutes."

It's not that psychiatry has nothing to tell us, nor that many of its practitioners are not dedicated to helping others. The problem is the way this specialty is used in insanity trials: the endeavor itself is in many ways absurd. These psychiatrists are interviewing criminals who know that if they come off seeming a little bananas, they might get off the hook. The notion that something resembling

scientific data will always result from such subjective encounters is, well, a little bananas itself. On top of that, the courtroom psychiatrists are not purporting to inform us of a defendant's *present* mental state, though even that can be elusive enough. They are claiming to divine the defendant's mental state when he committed the crime, which probably was months before. "I can't even tell you what *I* was thinking about a week ago, or a year ago, let alone what someone else was thinking," says criminal psychologist Stanton Samenow, author of *Inside the Criminal Mind*, whose eight years working at St. Elizabeths hospital in Washington made him deeply skeptical of traditional attempts to understand and catalogue criminals according to Freudian concepts: Indeed, how would you begin to *prove* an assertion such as the one that John Hinckley tried to shoot Reagan because he saw the president as an "all evil prohibitive figure"? This is not evidence. It is vaporizing. Coleman testifies at criminal trials with delightful iconoclasm that psychiatrists such as himself have no more ability than anyone else to inform the jury as to what was going on in a criminal's mind at any given time.

POOR RELATIONS

But one should not conclude that the only thing wrong with the insanity defense is that it lets the felons free on the basis of recondite psychiatric excuses. The injustice goes much deeper. Some psychiatrists, for example, lend their courtroom aura and mantle of expertise to the prosecution. Jim Grigson, the so-called "Hanging Shrink" of Texas, will tell a jury after a 90-minute interview with a defendant that this individual "has complete disregard for another human being's life" and that "no treatment, no medicine, nothing is going to change this behavior." Psychiatric opinionizing can cut both ways.

There's the further problem that psychiatrists, the gatekeepers of this defense, have their greatest rapport with the problems of those closest to their own social status. A few years ago, Dr. Daniel Irving, a psychiatrist in Washington, demonstrated this attitude in an article Blain Harden wrote for *The Washington Post*. "I hate to say this," Irving confided, "but I don't like to work with poor people. . . . They are talking about stuff that doesn't interest me particularly. They are the kind of people who don't interest me." Over 95 percent of all psychiatric patients are white, and James Collins, a black psychiatrist who is chairman of the Howard University Medical School Department of Psychiatry, told Harden that "[the] biggest problem is that many psychiatrists cannot relate to poor people."

In fact, the insanity defense itself can be weighted heavily towards those who are well-off. This is not just because a Hinckley family can muster upwards of a million dollars to mount a prodigious legal and psychiatric defense. On a subtler level, someone from a "nice" upper-middle-class background who commits a heinous crime is more readily seen as off his rocker than is someone from a poorer background in which crime is closer to the norm (or is at least perceived to be). During the Hinckley trial the jury witnessed his family sitting behind him, the "perfect couple," as one observer said later. "Hinckley's father was sitting there with a pondering look on his face; his mother was wearing red, white, and blue outfits; and his sister was a former cheer-leader and homecoming queen. Real Americans." Surely there must be something wrong with a young man who could enjoy such advantages and still go out and shoot a president. It was the sort of tableau that a black felon from, say, East St. Louis, might have some trouble assembling.

Such, considerations may help explain why Henry Steadman of the New York State Department of Mental Hygiene found that while whites account for only 31 percent of the prison population in his state, they were a full 65 percent of those found not guilty by reason of insanity. "Racial discrimination favoring whites in successful insanity defenses is strongly suggested by these figures," writes Abraham Halpern.

This in turn points to something even more fundamentally unjust about the insanity defense: the way it draws arbitrary and culture-bound distinctions between defendants with different kinds of life burdens and afflictions. A John Hinckley may well harbor anger against his parents and anguish at his unrequited love for actress Jody Foster. Such problems can be very real for those who go through them. But they are no *more* real, no *more* inclined to affect behavior, than are the problems of a teenager of lesser means, who may be ugly, or kept back in school two or three times, or whose parents may not love him and who may have been "passed around" among relatives and older siblings for as long as he can remember, or who may find doors closed to him because he is not blond and blue-eyed the way Hinckley is. If a Hinckley merits our compassion, then surely those with hard life circumstances do also. Under the insanity defense, we absolve Hinckley totally of responsibility, while we label his hypothetical counterpart a bad person and send him to jail.

So arbitrary is the line that the insanity defense invites us to draw that all sorts of prejudices and vagaries can enter, of which racial and class bias are just two. "The actual psychological state of the defendant may be a rather minor factor" in the decision even to use the insanity defense, writes C. R. Jeffrey in his book, *Criminal Responsibility and Mental Disease.* Rather, this decision is based on such factors as "the economic position of the defendant, the nature of the criminal charges, the medical facilities in the community," and the like.

BIG DIFFERENCE

This is not to say that you won't find any poor people or non-Caucasians in the maximum-security hospitals in which insanity acquittees are kept. You will, but it's important to understand how they got there. It probably wasn't through the kind of circus trial that John Hinckley could afford. Very likely, it was a plea bargain, in which a prosecutor decided it was better to put a dangerous person away, even if just for a short time, than to devote scarce resources to a trial that he or she might lose. One study, published in the *Rutgers Law Review,* found at least two jurisdictions in which the prosecutors actually raised the insanity defense more frequently than the defense attorney did. "Clearly the prosecutor saw the [insanity] defense as a means to lock defendants up without having their guilt proved beyond a reasonable doubt," the study concludes.

Given such realities, it should not be surprising that there is often not much difference between those who end up in maximum security mental hospitals and

those who end up in their penal counterparts. "Lots of people could have ended up in either one or the other," says E. Fuller Torrey, a psychiatrist at St. Elizabeths mental hospital in Washington. Samenow goes further. On the basis of his own experience studying insanity acquittees at St. Elizabeths, he declares flatly that "neither [his colleague Dr. Samuel] Yochelson nor I found that any of the men we evaluated were insane unless one took tremendous liberties with that word."

That may be a bit of an exaggeration. But the similarities between criminals we call "insane," and those we call simply "criminals," cannot be dismissed. Take recidivism. There is evidence that criminals released from mental hospitals tend to repeat their crimes with about the same frequency as their counterparts released from prison. This point is crucial because the purpose of a criminal justice system is not just to punish offenders; it is to protect the rest of us from dangerous people as well. Through the insanity defense, we go to lengths that are often ridiculous to make a distinction that in many cases is without a difference.

Sometimes the experts are the last to see what needs to be done. Listen to Lawrence Coffey, one of the Hinckley jurors who was unhappy with the verdict for which he himself voted. "I think it [the law] should be changed," he told a Senate hearing, "in some way where the defendant gets mental help enough that where he's not harmful to himself and society, and then be punished for what he has done wrong." Maryland Copelin, also one of the jurors, agreed. "I think they [defendants] should get the help they need and also punishment for the act they did." In other words, Hinckley needed treatment, but he deserved punishment, too. Who could argue with that? Well, the law, for one. It said that Hinckley was either guilty or not guilty by reason of insanity. "We could not do any better than what we did," Copelin said, "on account of your forms," which gave the jury only these two options.

In short, the insanity defense cuts the deck the wrong way. I makes no provision for the vast middle ground in which offenders have problems but should bear responsibility too. Instead of persisting in making this artificial distinction between "normal" criminals (whatever that means) and "insane" ones, we should ask first a very simple question: did the individual commit the crime? That established in a trial, we should then, in a sentencing phase, take all relevant factors into account in deciding what combination of punishment and treatment is appropriate. "Either you did it or you didn't do it," says Samenow, who supports the abolition of the insanity defense. "I think we should try the criminal first, and then worry about treatment." In other words, don't expect the jury to make Talmudic distinctions on which even the experts cannot agree. Get the psychiatrists out of the courtroom, where they cause confusion, and put them into the sentencing and treatment process, where they may be able to help.

In this sentencing phase, which would take on a new importance, Hinckley's infatuation with Jody Foster, and Dan White's overindulgence in junk food, would be given due regard. So too would the incapacity of one who was totally deranged. The crucial difference from current practice is that the examination would be done by court-appointed psychiatrists (or other professionals) instead of by hired guns proffered by either side. Since psychiatrists are as human as the rest of us, this system would not be perfect. It would, however, be better than what we have today.

In almost all cases, some punishment would be in order. You don't have to believe that retribution is the whole purpose of the law to acknowledge that something very basic in us requires that when someone causes serious harm to someone else, he should pay. This approach would eliminate perhaps the most dangerous absurdity of the present insanity defense. When a criminal wins acquittal on this ground, the criminal justice system has no more claim on him. The only way he can be kept in confinement is if he is declared insane and committed to a mental institution through a totally separate procedure. (Some states require an automatic confinement for one or two months, ostensibly to "observe" the acquittee.) No Problem, you say. They've just been declared insane. The problem is, *that* insanity was at the time of the crime, which may have been a year or more before. By the time of the commitment hearing, the old problem may have miraculously cleared up. The commitment authorities are then faced with two bad options. Either they tell the truth and let a dangerous person out or they fill a bed in a crowded mental hospital with someone who will be there not for treatment, but only to be kept off the streets. Eliminating the insanity defense would eliminate such charades.

Once punishment is completed, the question of danger to society would come to the fore. First offenders committing nonviolent crimes generally pose little such threat, and in most cases could be safely paroled. At the other extreme, violent repeat offenders would be locked up for a very long time. While reform is always possible, the sad fact is that most repeat offenders will keep on repeating until they reach a "burn-out" period sometime after they reach age 40. Since the recidivism rates cut across the categories we call "normal" and "insane" criminality, the insanity defense simply doesn't help us deal with reality in this regard.

Hot-blooded crimes, such as the Dan White shooting, should be seen for what they are. Such people generally don't pose a great threat because the circumstances of their crime are not likely to happen again. It costs between $10,000 and $20,000 a year to keep a prisoner in jail, and that money would be better spent on those for whom it's really needed. In other words, White's eight-year sentence was not necessarily wrong. The wrong was in the psychiatric speculation through which that result was justified. We can achieve justice in such cases through simpler and more honest means.

WHAT A TIME

But isn't the insanity defense necessary to protect the infirm? "People who are mentally ill deserve treatment," says Flora Rheta Schreiber, whose book *The Shoemaker* details the sad story of a troubled murderer. "They don't deserve to be locked up in prison."

Fair enough. The trouble is, virtually all criminals have mental problems. The difference between a bank robber and yourself is not in your shirt size or the shape of your hands. Is there any such thing as a "sane" rape or a "sane" axe murder? If anyone did such deeds with calm and rational deliberation, would that individual not be the most insane—and dangerous—of all? Samenow, more-over, says that for the vast majority of criminals, the kind of treatment that might be effective is pretty much the same. The secret scandal of the insanity defense is the way it justifies our atrocious penal system by purporting to show kindness for one group that is selected arbitrarily in the first place. We deny treatment to the many under the pretext of providing it for a few.

And a pretext it often is. Talk to someone who has visited a maximum-security hospital for the criminally insane. To be sure, there are good ones here and there. But in his book *Beating the Rap*, Henry Steadman describes a reality that is probably more common than not. Such hospitals in his state are "prisonlike," he writes, with "locked wards, security officers, and barbed wire fences. . . . There is a substantial level of patient-patient assault; homosexuality, both consenting and nonconsenting, is common, and guards are sometimes unnecessarily brutal . . . *It is simply doing time in a different setting.*" (Emphasis added.) Barbara Weiner, who heads a special outpatient program for insanity acquittees in Chicago—one of the few programs of its kind in the country—told a Senate hearing that "few states have specialized programs for treating mentally ill offenders." (Those of means, of course, can often arrange a transfer to private facilities at which conditions are more genteel.)

So averse are American psychiatrists to helping people in life's lower stations that over half the staffs of this country's public mental hospitals are graduates of foreign medical schools, where standards may not be awfully high. In 11 states, including Illinois and Ohio, the figure is over 70 percent. Just try to imagine a psychiatrist from, say, India, trying to understand a felon from the South Bronx. Torrey cites a psychiatrist who left the Illinois state hospital system telling of a colleague in charge of prescribing drugs who did not know that .8 and .80 were the same number.

Much of the problem is that most of us prefer to keep a comfortable arm's length from such realities. The people who run our criminal justice system are no exception. After observing a year's worth of mental incompetency hearings in New York, Steadman observed that "of about 35 judges, 12 attorneys, six district attorneys, and 12 psychiatrists, not one had ever seen or been inside either of the two facilities to which incompetent defen-

dants are committed." A former public defender in Washington, D.C., who had pleaded before the Supreme Court the case of an insanity-acquittee who was trying to get out of St. Elizabeths, told me he had never met the individual for whose release he was pleading.

Getting rid of the insanity defense would help to break the spell and make us confront the deficiencies in our correctional systems. No longer could we congratulate ourselves that we are being humane and just when we are being neither. If eliminating the defense would help get a few dangerous felons off the street, so much the better. But a great deal more is at stake.

NO
Richard Bonnie

THE NEED FOR THE INSANITY DEFENSE

The effect of most of the proposals now before you would be to abolish the insanity defense as it has existed for centuries in Anglo-American criminal law. I urge you to reject these sweeping proposals. The insanity defense should be retained, in modified form, because some defendants afflicted by severe mental disorder cannot justly be blamed for their criminal conduct and do not, therefore, deserve to be punished. The defense, in short, is essential to the moral integrity of the criminal law.

I realize that the figure of John Hinckley looms before us today. Doubts about the moral accuracy of the jurors' verdict in this sad case have now been turned on the insanity defense itself. I do not want to second guess the verdict in the Hinckley case, but I do urge you to keep the case in proper perspective.

The highly visible insanity claim, pitting the experts in courtroom battle, is the aberrational case. The plea is raised in no more than 2% of felony cases and the defense is rarely successful when the question is contested in a jury trial. Most psychiatric dispositions in the criminal process are arranged without fanfare, without disagreement among the experts, and without dissent by the prosecution. In short, the exhaustive media coverage of cases like Hinckley's gives the public a distorted picture of the relative insignificance of the insanity defense in the day-to-day administration of justice.

In another way, however, the public debate about the aberrant case is highly to be desired because the trial of insanity claims keeps the community in touch with the moral premises of the criminal law. The legitimacy of the institution of punishment rests on the moral belief that we are all capable of rational choice and therefore deserve to be punished if we choose to do wrong. By acknowledging the exception, we reaffirm the rule. I have no doubt that the Hinckley trial and verdict have exposed the fundamental moral postulates of the criminal law to vigorous debate in every living room in the Nation. Thus, in a sense, whether John Hinckley was or was not legally insane may be less important than the fact that the question was asked at all.

These are the reasons I do not favor abolition of the insanity defense. However, I do not discount or dismiss the possibility that the defense

From U.S. Senate. Committee on the Judiciary. *Insanity Defense.* Hearing, August 2, 1982. Washington, DC: Government Printing Office, 1982. (Y4.J89/2:J-97-126.)

occasionally may be successfully invoked in questionable cases. There is, in fact, some evidence that insanity acquittals have increased in recent years. However, I am persuaded that the possibility of moral mistakes in the administration of the insanity defense can be adequately reduced by narrowing the defense and by placing the burden of proof on the defendant.

THE OPTIONS

You have basically three options before you.

The Existing (Model Penal Code) Law
One option is to leave the law as it now stands, by judicial ruling, in all of the federal courts (and, parenthetically, as it now stands in a majority of the states). Apart from technical variations, this means the test proposed by the American Law Institute in its Model Penal Code. Under this approach, a person whose perceptual capacities were sufficiently intact that he had the criminal "intent" required in the definition of the offense can nonetheless be found "not guilty by reason of insanity" if, by virtue of mental disease or defect, he lacked substantial capacity *either* to understand or appreciate the legal or moral significance of his actions, *or* to conform his conduct to the requirements of law. In other words, a person may be excused if his thinking was severely disordered— this is the so-called volitional prong of the defense.

Revival of M'Naghten
The second option is to retain the insanity defense as an independent exculpatory doctrine—independent, that is, of mens rea—but to restrict its scope by eliminating the volitional prong. This is the approach that I favor, for reasons I will outline below. Basically, this option is to restore the *M'Naghten* test—although I do not think you should be bound by the language used by the House of Lords in 1843—as the sole basis for exculpation or ground of insanity. Although this is now distinctly the minority position in this country—it is used in less than one third of the states—it is still the law in England.

Abolition: The Mens Rea Approach
The third option is the one I have characterized as abolition of the defense. Technically, this characterization is accurate because the essential substantive effect of the so-called "mens rea" approach (or "elements" approach) would be to eliminate any criterion of exculpation, based on mental disease, which is independent of the elements of particular crimes. To put it another way, the bills taking this approach would eliminate any separate exculpatory doctrine based on proof of mental disease; instead mentally ill (or retarded) defendants would be treated just like everyone else. A normal person cannot escape liability by proving that he did not know or appreciate the fact that his conduct was wrong, and—under the mens rea approach—neither could a psychotic person.

THE CASE AGAINST THE MENS REA APPROACH

Most of the bills now before you would adopt the mens rea option, the approach recently enacted in Montana and Idaho. As I have already noted, this change, abolishing the insanity defense, would constitute an abrupt and unfortunate departure from the Anglo-American legal tradition.

If the insanity defense were abolished, the law would not take adequate account of the incapacitating effects of severe mental illness. Some mentally ill defendants may be said to have "intended" to do what they did—that is, their technical guilt can be established—but they nonetheless may have been so severely disturbed that they were unable to appreciate the significance of their actions. These cases do not frequently arise, but when they do, a criminal conviction—signifying the societal judgment that the defendant *deserves* punishment—would offend the basic moral intuitions of the community. Judges and juries would then be forced either to return a verdict which they regard as morally obtuse or to acquit the defendant in defiance of the law. They should be spared such moral embarrassment.

Let me illustrate this point with a real case evaluated at our Institute's Forensic Clinic in 1975. Ms. Joy Baker, a thirty-one-year-old woman, admitted killing her aunt. She had no previous history of mental illness, although her mother was mentally ill and had spent all of Ms. Baker's early years in mental hospitals. Ms. Baker was raised by her grandparents and her aunt in a rural area of the state. After high school graduation Ms. Baker married and had two children. The marriage ended in divorce six years later and Ms. Baker remarried. This second marriage was stressful from the outset. Mr. Baker was a heavy drinker and abusive to his wife. He also was extremely jealous and repeatedly accused his wife of seeing other men.

The night before the shooting Mr. Baker took his wife on a ride in his truck. He kept a gun on the seat between them and stopped repeatedly. At each place he told listeners that his wife was an adultress. He insisted his wife throw her wedding ring from the car, which she did because she was afraid of her husband's anger. The Bakers didn't return home until three in the morning. At that time Ms. Baker woke her children and fed them, then stayed up while her husband slept because she was afraid "something terrible would happen."

During this time and for the three days prior to the day of the shooting Ms. Baker had become increasingly agitated and fearful. Her condition rapidly deteriorated and she began to lose contact with reality. She felt that her dogs were going to attack her and she also believed her children and the neighbors had been possessed by the devil.

On the morning of the shooting, Ms. Baker asked her husband not to leave and told him that something horrible was about to happen. When he left anyway she locked the doors. She ran frantically around the house holding the gun. She made her children sit on the sofa and read the Twenty-Third Psalm over and over. She was both afraid of what they might do and of what she might do but felt that reading the Bible would protect them. Shortly afterwards, Ms. Baker's aunt made an unexpected visit. Ms. Baker told her to go away but the aunt persisted and went to the back door. Ms. Baker was afraid of the dog which was out on the back porch and repeatedly urged her aunt to leave. At this time the aunt seemed to Ms. Baker to be sneering at her.

When her aunt suddenly reached through the screening to unlock the door Ms. Baker said, "I had my aunt over there and this black dog over here, and both of them were bothering me. . . . And then I had that black dog in front of me and she turned around and I was trying to kick the dog and my aunt was coming in the door and I just—took my hands I just went like this—right through the screen. . . . I shot her."

Ms. Baker's aunt fell backward into the mud behind the porch. Although she was bleeding profusely from her chest, she did not die immediately. "Why, Joy?" she asked. "Because you're the devil, and you came to hurt me," Joy answered. Her aunt said, "Honey, no, I came to help you." At this point, Ms. Baker said, she saw that her aunt was hurting and became very confused. Then, according to her statement, "I took the gun and shot her again just to relieve the pain she was having because she said she was hurt." Her aunt died after the second shot.

All the psychiatrists who examined Ms. Baker concluded that she was acutely psychotic and out of touch with reality at the time she shot her aunt. The police who arrested her and others in the small rural community concluded that she must have been crazy because there was no other explanation for her conduct. After Ms. Baker was stabilized on anti-psychotic medication, she was permitted to leave the state to live with relatives in a neighboring state. Eventually the case against her was dismissed by the court, with the consent of the prosecution, after a preliminary hearing at which the examining psychiatrists testified. She was never indicted or brought to trial.

It seems clear, even to a layman, that Ms. Baker was so delusional and regressed at the time of the shooting that she did not understand or appreciate the wrongfulness of her conduct. It would be morally obtuse to condemn and punish her. Yet, Ms. Baker had the state of mind required for some form of criminal homi-

cide. If there were no insanity defense, she could be acquitted only in defiance of the law.

Let me explain. The "states of mind" which are required for homicide and other criminal offenses refer to various aspects of conscious awareness. They do not have any qualitative dimension. There is good reason for this, of course. The exclusive focus on conscious perceptions and beliefs enhances predictability, precision and equality in the penal law. If the law tried to take into account degrees of psychological aberration in the definition of offenses, the result would be a debilitating individualization of the standards of criminal liability.

At the time of the first shot, it could be argued that Ms. Baker lacked the "state of mind" required for murder because she did not intend to shoot a "human being" but rather intended to shoot a person whom she believed to be possessed by the devil. At common law, this claim would probably be characterized as a mistake of fact. Since the mistake was, by definition, an unreasonable one—i.e., one that only a crazy person would make—she would most likely be guilty of some form of homicide (at least manslaughter) if ordinary mens rea principles were applied. Even under the modern criminal codes, . . . , she would be guilty of negligent homicide since an ordinary person in her situation would have been aware of the risk that her aunt was a human being. And she possibly could be found guilty of manslaughter since she was probably aware of the risk that her aunt was a human being even though she was so regressed that she disregarded the risk.

It might also be argued that Ms. Baker's first shot would have been justified if her delusional beliefs had been true since she would have been defending herself against imminent annihilation at the hands of the devil. Again, however, the application of ordinary common-law principles of justification . . . would indicate that she was unreasonably mistaken as to the existence of justificatory facts (the necessity for killing to protect oneself) and her defense would fail, although the grade of the offense would probably be reduced to manslaughter on the basis of her "imperfect" justification.

At the time of the second shot, Ms. Baker was in somewhat better contact with reality. At a very superficial level she "knew" that she was shooting her aunt and did so for the non-delusional purpose of relieving her aunt's pain. But euthanasia is no justification for homicide. Thus, if we look only at her legally relevant "state of mind" at the time of the second shot, and we do not take into account her highly regressed and disorganized emotional condition, she is technically guilty of murder.

I believe that Joy Baker's case convincingly demonstrates why, in theoretical terms, the mens rea approach does not take sufficient account of the morally significant aberrations of mental functioning associated with severe mental disorder. I readily concede, however, that these technical points may make little practical difference in the courtroom. If the expert testimony in Joy Baker's case and others like it were admitted to disprove the existence of mens rea, juries may behave as many observers believe they do now—they may ignore the technical aspects of the law and decide, very bluntly, whether the defendant was too crazy to be convicted. However, I do not believe that rational criminal law reform is served by designing rules of law in the expectation that they will be ignored or nullified when they appear unjust in individual cases.

IMPROVING THE QUALITY OF EXPERT TESTIMONY

I have tried to show that perpetuation of the insanity defense is essential to the moral integrity of the criminal law. Yet an abstract commitment to the moral relevance of claims of psychological aberration may have to bend to the need for reliability in the administration of the law.

I fully recognize that the litigation of insanity claims is occasionally imperfect. The defense is sometimes difficult to administer reliably and fairly. In particular, I recognize that we cannot calibrate the severity of a person's mental disability, and it is sometimes hard to know whether the disability was profound enough to establish irresponsibility. Nor can we be confident that every fabricated claim will be recognized. Yet these concerns are not unlike those presented by traditional defenses such as mistake, duress and other excuses which no one is seeking to abolish. Indeed, problems in sorting valid from invalid defensive claims are best seen as part of the price of a humane and just penal law. Thus, to the extent that the abolitionists would eradicate the insanity defense in response to imperfections in its administration, I would reply that a decent respect for the moral integrity of the criminal law sometimes requires us to ask questions that can be answered only by approximation. Rather than abolishing the defense we should focus our attention on ways in which its administration can be improved.

Some of the abolitionist sentiment among lawyers seems to be responsive to doubts about the competence—and, unfortunately, the ethics—of expert witnesses. The cry for abolition is also raised by psychiatrists and psychologists who believe that the law forces experts to "take sides" and to offer opinions on issues outside their sphere of expertise. These are all legitimate concerns and I have no doubt that the current controversy about the insanity defense accurately reflects a rising level of mutual professional irritation about its administration. However, the correct solution is not to abolish the insanity defense but rather to clarify the roles and obligations of expert witnesses in the criminal process. Some assistance in this effort can be expected from the American Bar Association's Criminal Justice-Mental Health Standards now being drafted by interdisciplinary panels of experts in the field.

A properly trained expert can help the judge or jury to understand aberrations of the human mind. However, training in psychiatry or psychology does not, by itself, qualify a person to be an expert witness in criminal cases. Specialized training in forensic evaluation is necessary, and a major aim of such special training must be to assure that the expert is sensitive to the limits of his or her knowledge.

THE CASE FOR
TIGHTENING THE DEFENSE

I do not favor abolition of the "cognitive" prong of the insanity defense. However, I do agree with those critics who believe the risks of fabrication and "moral mistakes" in administering the defense are greatest when the experts and the jury are asked to speculate whether the defendant had the capacity to "control" himself or whether he could have "resisted" the criminal impulse.

Few would dispute the moral predicate for the control test—that a person who "cannot help" doing what he did is not blameworthy. Unfortunately, however, there is no scientific basis for measuring a person's capacity for self-control or for calibrating the impairment of such capacity. There is, in short, no objective basis for distinguishing between offenders who were undeterrable. and those who were merely undeterred, between the impulse that was irresistible and the impulse not resisted, or between substantial impairment of capacity and some lesser impairment. Whatever the precise terms of the volitional test, the question is unanswerable—or can be answered only by "moral guesses." To ask it at all, in my opinion, invites fabricated claims, undermines equal administration of the penal law, and compromises its deterrent effect. . . .

The sole test of legal insanity should be whether the defendant, as a result of mental disease, lacked "substantial capacity to appreciate the wrongfulness of his conduct." This language, drawn from the Model Penal Code, uses clinically meaningful terms to ask the same question posed by the House of Lords in *M'Naghten* 150 years ago. During the past ten years, I have not seen a single case at our Clinic involving a claim of irresponsibility that I personally thought was morally compelling which would not be comprehended by this formulation. Thus, I am convinced that this test is fully compatible with the ethical premises of the penal law, and that results reached by judges and juries in particular cases ordinarily would be congruent with the community's moral sense.

In sum, then, I believe that the insanity defense, as I have defined it, should be narrowed, not abandoned, and that the burden of persuasion may properly be shifted to the defendant. Like the mens rea proposal, this approach adequately responds to public concern about possible misuse of the insanity defense. Unlike the mens rea proposal, however, I believe this approach is compatible with the basic doctrines and principles of Anglo-American penal law.

POSTSCRIPT

Should the Insanity Defense Be Abolished?

The furor over the Hinckley case led to some changes in the federal insanity defense standard. As part of a major anticrime bill passed in 1984, Congress has required the defendant to have the burden of proving that he or she was insane. In the Hinckley trial, the prosecution was required to prove beyond a reasonable doubt that Hinckley was sane. The defendant in such a case must now persuade a jury that, as a result of a severe mental disease or defect, he or she was unable to appreciate the nature and wrongfulness of the act.

In addition to raising questions about the diagnosis of mental illness, the insanity defense also requires consideration of treatment, of sentencing, and of institutionalization. Those advocating its retention argue not only that blameless people should not be punished, but also that such individuals need care and treatment for their problems. The fact that many mental institutions have failed to provide adequate treatment or are, by their nature, inappropriate places for some individuals who need help but not institutionalization, has been recognized recently in various lawsuits. As a result, the number of people in institutions has been declining. The ineffectiveness of prisons and mental institutions in reducing recidivism or promoting treatment should be considered in the debate over the insanity defense, since even those who wish to abolish the defense are willing to take the mental state of the defendant into account at the time of sentencing. There is, in addition, a possible relationship between the increase in the number of defendants invoking the insanity defense and the deinstitutionalization trend. The reason for this is that the insanity defense becomes more appealing as the expectation of a long stay in a mental institution decreases.

Recommended readings on the insanity defense include Smith and Meyer, *Law, Behavior, and Mental Health* (New York University Press, 1987); Eisner, "Returning the Not Guilty By Reason of Insanity to the Community: A New Scale to Determine Readiness," 17 *The Bulletin of the American Academy of Psychiatry and the Law* 401 (1989); Klofas and Yandrasits, " 'Guilty But Mentally Ill' and the Jury Trial: A Case Study," 24 *Criminal Law Bulletin* 424 (1988); Symposium, "The Insanity Defense," *The Annals* (January 1985); Goldstein, *The Insanity Defense* (Yale University Press, 1967); Fingarette, *The Meaning of Criminal Insanity* (University of California Press, 1972); and Szasz, *Law, Liberty and Psychiatry* (Macmillan, 1963). Moran, *Knowing Right from Wrong: The Insanity Defense of Daniel McNaughtan* (Free Press, 1981), provides an interesting look at McNaughtan's trial and at the central figure in the history of the insanity defense. Other books about particular cases include Kaplan and Waltz, *The Trial of Jack Ruby* (Macmillan, 1965); Gaylin, *The Killing of Bonnie Garland* (Simon & Schuster, 1982); and Caplan, *The Insanity Defense and the Trial of John W. Hinckley, Jr.* (David Godine, 1983).

CONTRIBUTORS
TO THIS VOLUME

EDITOR

M. ETHAN KATSH, a graduate of Yale Law School, is a professor of legal studies at the University of Massachusetts–Amherst. He has served as the chairman of the legal studies department at the University of Massachusetts and as the president of the American Legal Studies Association. His articles have appeared in scholarly journals as well as such popular publications as the *Wall Street Journal, TV Guide,* and *Saturday Review.* He is the coauthor of *Before the Law* (Houghton Mifflin) and the author of *The Electronic Media and the Transformation of the Law* (Oxford University Press, 1989). Professor Katsh has also produced simulation games on plea bargaining and mediation, and he is a codesigner of *Rock 'n Roll LEXIS,* multimedia software that teaches electronic legal research.

STAFF

Marguerite L. Egan   Program Manager
Brenda S. Filley   Production Manager
Whit Vye   Designer
Libra Ann Cusack   Typesetting Supervisor
Juliana Arbo   Typesetter
David Brackley   Copy Editor
David Dean   Administrative Assistant
Diane Barker   Editorial Assistant

AUTHORS

MELVIN P. ANTELL is the presiding justice of the Superior Court of New Jersey, Appellate Division, Part A.

SARAH EVANS BARKER is a judge in the Indiana District Court (south district). She is on the board of directors of the New Hope of Indiana and a member of the Indianapolis Bar Association.

RICHARD BONNIE is the John S. Battle Professor of Law at the University of Virginia School of Law and the director of the university's Institute of Law, Psychiatry, and Public Policy. He has written extensively on the legal aspects of mental disability and behavioral health, and he was recently elected to the National Academy of Sciences Institute of Medicine.

WILLIAM J. BRENNAN, JR., is a former associate justice of the U.S. Supreme Court. He served on the Supreme Court from 1956 to 1990, when he retired at the age of 84.

ANDREA DWORKIN, a coauthor of the Indianapolis legislation that defines *pornography* as a violation of women's civil rights, is an American nonfiction writer, essayist, novelist, and short story writer. She is best known for her controversial nonfiction works that examine the status of women in modern society, including *Letters from a War Zone: Writings 1976–1989* (E. P. Dutton, 1989).

JANLORI GOLDMAN is the director of the American Civil Liberty Union's Project on Privacy and Technology. She has testified before Congress and has appeared on panels that have investigated numerous privacy issues, including the Federal Privacy Act.

JACK GREENBERG is a professor of law at Columbia University and the author of *Judicial Process and Social Change: Constitutional Litigation, Cases and Materials* (West, 1977).

PETER HUBER, a lawyer and a writer, is a legal counsel to the law firm of Mayer, Brown, and Platt in Chicago, Illinois. He has clerked for Judge Ruth Bader Ginsburg on the U.S. Court of Appeals for the District of Columbia Circuit and for Associate Justice Sandra Day O'Connor on the U.S. Supreme Court. His publications include *The Liability Maze* (Brookings Institution, 1991).

KENNETH JOST is a legal affairs journalist in Washington, D.C., and an adjunct professor at Georgetown University Law Center. He is a former chief legislative assistant to then-representative Albert Gore.

YALE KAMISAR is a lawyer and a professor of law at the University of Michigan Law School. He is the author of *Police Interrogation and Confessions: Essays in Law and Policy* (University of Michigan Press, 1980).

ANTHONY KENNEDY is an associate justice of the U.S. Supreme Court. He worked for law firms in San Francisco and Sacramento, California before being nominated by former president Ford to the U.S. Court of Appeals for the Ninth Circuit in 1975. He served in that capacity until his nomination to the Supreme Court by former president Reagan in 1988.

KENNETH KIPNIS is a professor of philosophy at the University of Hawaii at Manoa. He is the editor of several volumes on legal, social, and political philosophy, and the author of *Legal Ethics* (Prentice Hall, 1986).

THURGOOD MARSHALL was an associate justice of the U.S. Supreme Court for 24 years. Nominated by former president Johnson, he holds the distinction as being the first African American appointed to the Supreme Court, where he served from 1967 to 1991.

HARRY C. MARTIN is an associate justice of the Supreme Court of North Carolina. He has served in a judicial capacity in North Carolina for 30 years, first as a judge in its superior court and its court of appeals before being appointed to its supreme court in 1982.

ARTHUR R. MILLER is the Bruce Bromley Professor of Law at Harvard Law School, where he has been teaching since 1971. He is widely known for his work in the field of the right of privacy, a subject on which he has written, testified, debated, and helped formulate legislation. He has appeared weekly on ABC's *Good Morning America* as the program's legal editor since July 1980.

BURLEY B. MITCHELL, JR., is an associate justice of the Supreme Court of North Carolina. He has served as an assistant attorney general for North Carolina, a district attorney for Raleigh, and a judge in the North Carolina Court of Appeals.

JOHN B. MITCHELL is a clinical professor of law at the University of Puget Sound School of Law in Tacoma, Washington. He has authored or coauthored numerous articles on lawyers' ethics, and he is a coauthor, with Marilyn J. Berger and Ronald H. Clark, of *Trial Advocacy: Planning, Analysis, and Strategy* (Little, Brown, 1989).

SANDRA DAY O'CONNOR is an associate justice of the U.S. Supreme Court. She worked in various legal capacities both in the United States and in Germany until she was appointed to the Arizona state senate in 1969. She served as a state senator for four years and served in the Arizona judiciary for six years before she was nominated to the Supreme Court by former president Reagan in 1981.

WILLIAM H. REHNQUIST became the 16th chief justice of the U.S. Supreme Court in 1986. He engaged in a general practice of law with a primary emphasis on civil litigation for 16 years before being appointed assistant attorney general, Office of Legal Counsel, by former president Nixon in 1969. He was nominated by Nixon to the Supreme Court in 1972.

JONATHAN ROWE is a contributing editor of *The Washington Monthly.*

ANTONIN SCALIA is an associate justice of the U.S. Supreme Court. He taught law at the University of Virginia, the American Enterprise Institute, Georgetown University, and the University of Chicago before being nominated to the U.S. Court of Appeals by former president Reagan in 1982. He served in that capacity until his nomination by Reagan to the Supreme Court in 1986.

NICK SCHWEITZER is an assistant district attorney for Rock County, Wisconsin. He has been a member of the Wisconsin Bar Association since 1985.

JOHN PAUL STEVENS is an associate justice of the U.S. Supreme Court. He worked for law firms in Chicago, Illinois, for 20 years before being nominated by former president Nixon to the U.S. Court of Appeals in 1970. He served in that capacity until his nomination to the Supreme Court by former president Ford in 1975.

POTTER STEWART (1915–1985) was an associate justice of the U.S. Supreme Court for 23 years, from his nomination by former president Eisenhower in 1958 to his retirement at the age of 66 in 1981.

HARRY I. SUBIN is a professor of law in the School of Law at New York University. He is the author of *Criminal Justice in Metropolitan Court* (Da Capo Press, 1973).

HEWITT P. TOMLIN, JR., is the presiding judge in the Tennessee Court of Appeals, Western Section.

MARK UDULUTCH is a law clerk to Judge William Moser of the Wisconsin Court of Appeals.

ERNEST van den HAAG is a distinguished scholar at the Heritage Foundation, a public policy research and education institute whose programs are intended to apply a conservative philosophy to current policy questions, and a contributing editor for *National Review* magazine. He has contributed more than 200 articles to magazines and sociology journals in the United States, England, France, and Italy, and he is the coauthor, with John P. Conrad, of *The Death Penalty: A Debate* (Plenum, 1983).

MALCOLM RICHARD WILKEY, a former judge in the U.S. Court of Appeals for the District of Columbia Circuit, was recently appointed by Attorney General William P. Barr as special counsel in the House of Representative's bank scandal investigations. He is also a fellow of the American Bar Foundation and a member of the American Bar Association.

JAMES D. WRIGHT is the Charles and Leo Favrot Professor of Human Relations in the Department of Sociology at Tulane University. He is the author of 12 books, including 2 about the homeless, and 140 journal articles, book chapters, essays, and reviews.

INDEX

Stewart, Potter, on affirmative action,
195–198
Subin, Harry I: on criminal lawyer's right to
present false case, 26–39; reaction to
views of, 40–50
*Superintendent of Belchertown State School
v. Saikewicz,* 204, 205
Supreme Court, 57, 58; *see also,* individual
court cases
*Swann v. Charlotte-Mecklenburg Board of
Education,* 192

Tennessee v. Garner, 83
Terminiello v. Chicago, 98
Texas v. Johnson, 110, 111
Thirteenth Amendment, 187
Thompson v. Oklahoma, 217
*Thornburgh v. American College of
Obstetricians & Gynecologists,* 147, 152,
157
Tomkins v. Public Serv. Elec. & Gas Co., 180
Tomlin, Hewitt P., Jr., argument of, against
homosexual parents being given child
custody, 226–234
tort claims, 271, 274, 284
truth, controversy over criminal lawyer's right
to present false case and, 26–50
Twin City Bank v. Nebeker, 207

Udulutch, Mark, on gun control, 310–319
Union Pacific R. Co. v. Botsford, 203, 216
United Jewish Organization v. Carey, 192
United States v. Cruikshank, 188
United States v. Katz, 336
United States v. Martinez-Fuerte, 82, 85, 90,
91
United States v. Montgomery, 265
United States v. Montoyo de Hernandez, 82
United States v. Ramsey, 82
United States v. Reese, 188
United States v. Robel, 86
United States v. Wade, 27
United States v. Wiley, 55
United States v. Willy Robinson, 265

van den Haag, Ernest, argument of, in favor
of capital punishment, 255–260
vegetative state, controversy over right to die
and, 202–221
victimless crimes, 71
violence, pornography and, 174, 177
Viscusi, W. Kip, 14, 15, 16, 19–20
Vitek v. Jones, 208
volitional prong, of insanity defense, 359, 363

waiting period, mandatory, for gun purchases,
310, 314–316, 322
Walz v. Tax Comm'n of New York City, 129
Ward v. Rock Against Racism, 100
Washington v. Harper, 208, 215

Webster v. Reproductive Health Services,
149, 152, 153
Weeks v. United States, 264, 267, 271, 277,
283, 286
West Virginia Board of Education v. Barnette,
131–132
White, Dan, 348, 355, 356
wife beating, controversy over "battered wife
syndrome" as defense and, 290–305
Wilkey, Malcolm Richard: on exclusionary
rule, 264–275, 276; reaction to views of,
278, 280, 281, 282, 283, 284, 285, 286,
288, 290
Witherspoon v. Illinois, 249
women, in pornography, 162–181
Woodby v. INS, 209
Woodson v. North Carolina, 249, 252
Wright, James D., on gun control, 320–329

Yick Wo v. Hopkins, 196
Young v. American Mini Theatres, Inc., 107,
110, 111, 166, 169
Youngberg v. Romeo, 208, 217

Zablocki v. Redhail, 215